Political Campaign Communication

Inside and Out

Larry Powell
The University of Alabama at Birmingham

Joseph Cowart

Boston   New York   San Francisco
Mexico City   Montreal   Toronto   London   Madrid   Munich   Paris
Hong Kong   Singapore   Tokyo   Cape Town   Sydney

Editor in Chief: Karen Hanson
Executive Editor: Karon Bowers
Editorial Assistant: Jennifer Trebby
Marketing Manager: Mandee Eckersley
Editorial Production Administrator: Anna Socrates
Editorial-Production Service: Lauren Green Shafer
Composition and Prepress Buyer: Linda Cox
Manufacturing Buyer: JoAnne Sweeney
Cover Administrator: Kristina Mose-Libon
Electronic Composition: Omegatype Typography, Inc.

For related titles and support materials, visit our online catalog at www.ablongman.com.

Between the time web site information is gathered and published, it is not unusual for some sites to have closed. Also, the transcription of URLs can result in unintended typographical errors. The publisher would appreciate notification where these errors occur so that they may be corrected in subsequent editions.

Library of Congress Cataloging-in-Publication Data

Powell, Larry, 1948–
       Political campaign communication : inside and out / Larry Powell, Joseph Cowart.
          p. cm.
       Includes bibliographical references and index.
       ISBN 0-205-31843-6
       1. Campaign management—United States.   2. Political campaigns—United States.   3.
       Communication in politics—United States.   I. Cowart, Joseph, 1944– II. Title.

    JK2281 .P684 2002
    324.7'0973—dc21

                                                                                2002071109

Printed in the United States of America
10 9 8 7 6 5 4 3 2 1   06 05 04 03 02

CONTENTS

PREFACE

Both of the authors of *Political Campaign Communication: Inside and Out* grew up in political environments, among families who assumed that political involvement was both a right and a responsibility of American citizens. The importance of politics was drilled into each of us well before we reached high school.

At the age of eight, Joseph Cowart worked a precinct handing out literature for Wallace "Wah-Wah" Jones, a candidate for sheriff in Fayette County, Kentucky. By the time he was sixteen, Cowart was a precinct captain despite the fact he was not yet old enough to vote. By the age of twenty, he was a veteran political organizer and eventually became a full-time political consultant.

Larry Powell, by comparison, was a relatively late bloomer. His first campaign activity came at the age of thirteen, distributing literature during his father's run for a state legislature position. As a junior in high school, he ran for student body president and won decisively. His actual tenure in office, though, was less successful—teaching him that he was more successful at understanding the campaign process than at governing.

For Cowart, politics was the family business. They made no money from this activity, but it was, as his mother said, "Our contribution to make our community a better place to live." She instilled a respect of, and duty to, democracy. Her lessons remain with him even after years of representing veteran politicians, managing multimillion dollar campaigns, editing television spots late into the night, and shmoozing at length by telephone with reporters. His resulting philosophy of campaign leadership is simple. Don't make the candidate something he or she is not. Never lie. Always tell the objective truth and never "settle" for the technical truth. Don't ever mistake the candidate's accomplishments for your own accomplishments.

As a campaign professional, Cowart's contribution to these ideals has been to keep them foremost in his mind and in his planning while applying the latest technology, tactics, and strategy to the political landscape. His goal has remained the completion of campaigns in which candidates have had the opportunity to express their ideas to an audience receptive enough to elect them to public office.

In Larry Powell's family, his father was the political acitivist. Harold Powell was a news junkie decades before CNN or any of the other news networks went on the air. Evenings at home began with watching *NBC Nightly News,* the only network broadcast available in the Powell's rural home. Sunday mornings meant rising early enough to watch *Meet the Press* before heading to church. This all seemed normal at the time; Larry Powell didn't learn until he studied the Nielsen ratings at Auburn University that fewer than 3 percent of U.S. households tune into the show.

Both of us realize that others may not share our desire to understand the intricacies and controversies of our chosen field of study. We do hope, however, that students will share our trust in the democratic process, and that this book will help you to better understand that process. We believe that by looking at campaigns from both an inside and outside perspective, each reader can become a more critical observer of the process.

Our "inside and out" approach to learning about political communication is similar to that of participant-observation research. We hope to provide analytical information useful to the outside observer, along with a campaign perspective that will contribute to an understanding of strategic decision making.

One of us is a professional outsider, a member of the academic community who studies campaigns as an observer. The other is a professional insider, a campaign consultant whose career is that of a campaign participant. In this text, each chapter approaches its topic from both perspectives, although the seesaw of which view gets more attention will vary by topic. Interviews and campaign case studies further illuminate the insider persective.

Organizationally, the book is divided into three sections. The first part provides an overview of political communication issues. Chapter 1, an introduction, identifies some of the distinctive elements of political campaign communication. Chapter 2 looks at academic research related to the development of political attitudes. This topic is often omitted from campaign-related books, but we feel it is important for understanding the different perspectives that voters bring to any political campaign. Campaign professionals who overlook the socialization process are dooming themselves to defeat, and outside observers who do not consider it will typically over-simplify the causes of any particular electoral victory or defeat. Chapter 3 provides both an overview of campaign strategies as well as the book's first in-depth look at the inside of campaigns. This information provides the reader with some understanding of the processes involved in developing a campaign strategy and of the factors that can influence that strategy. Chapter 4 looks at the images of political candidates, an area that has drawn a great deal of attention from both the academic and consulting communities. It is also one in which the two communities seem to be converging toward a common approach of defining and understanding how electorates develop, maintain, and constantly re-evaluate their image of a candidate. Chapter 5 examines media theory, with a heavy focus on the academic perspectives regarding the media and their influence on campaigns. Academic research on this topic has been extensive, and many of its resulting conclusions have filtered into campaigns.

The second part of the book provides more insight into the insider view by looking at the campaign team. Chapter 6 starts by looking at the team itself—the campaign organization. This chapter identifies and describes some of the roles and functions that an effective campaign organization must perform. Chapter 7 focuses more closely on campaign communication in the mass media. This chapter is the "inside" complement to Chapter 5, which looked at media from the "outside" perspective. The focus here is on the mechanics of developing, distributing, and assessing the effects of campaign media. Chapter 8 examines an often overlooked aspect of campaign communication: direct voter contact. There was a time when this was the major form of campaigning for many candidates—a time when winning an election meant seeing as many people as possible, shaking hands, kissing babies, and connecting with more voters than the opposition did. The rise of television diminished this role somewhat, but it has never disappeared. Further, as cable networks fragment modern television audiences, new forms of direct voter contact are expanding. Chapter 9 discusses the role of political speeches in campaigns. Our focus will be on distinguishing political speeches from other forms of speechmaking. An understanding of those differences helps the reader to understand how the construction and delivery of any one political message is related to the campaign process. The last chapter in this section looks at political polling, one of the mathematical components of any political campaign. We hope to demystify this process by explaining how a political poll is developed, implemented, analyzed, and used in a campaign.

The third and final part of this book looks at five specific campaign concerns. Chapter 10 addresses press coverage and media relations, a topic that has practical implications for campaigns and creates serious philosophical issues for the academic community. The focus is on understanding the symbiotic relationship between the press and a campaign. We hope such an understanding will provide insight as to why some issues are covered and others dismissed, and why some candidates are treated as legitimate contenders by the press while others receive little coverage. Chapter 12 looks at the role of political money in campaigns. One of the biggest differences between the academic and consulting views of campaigns may revolve around the role of campaign finances. Our goal here is both to help the reader understand the rules of the game as they apply to campaign finances and to focus on the rhetorical impact that money can have on campaigns. Chapter 13 focuses on the role of interpersonal influence; this topic has received a great deal of research from the academic community. As a result, communications scholars have gathered a great deal of insight into the way that voters converse with each other on political topics. A related topic, interpersonal communication among political elites, has received less attention. We take a look at the factors involved here, including lobbying and legislative cue-giving. Chapter 14 discusses critical events analysis—a topic of equal interest to both the academic and consulting communities. Many times, the public's response to any political candidate is based upon the events associated with that candidate: An intern disappears from her Washington, D.C., apartment and a California congressman loses reelection; terrorists fly planes into the World Trade Center and the Pentagon, and campaigns alter their schedules, cancel fund-raising events, and increase their use of patriotic appeals in campaign messages. Finally, we end with Chapter 15 and a consideration of ethical questions in political communication. We don't propose to offer too many answers, but we do hope the reader will give ethical concerns more thought.

To fully consider these ethical issues, the readers should also realize that the two authors come from different ideological backgrounds. Joe Cowart's family roots are those of lifelong liberals. He has continued their tradition by working entirely for Democratic efforts and their allies (labor unions, for example). Larry Powell comes from a conservative political family. He grew up in an Alabama environment in which conservative Democrats became the first generation of Republicans in the south.

Our ideological differences have never been a problem. Neither of us believes that either party has a monopoly on the truth. We are both skeptical of any person—regardless of his or her political orientation—who argues otherwise.

We both believe in the value of the two-party system, but we both also believe this system was more effective when the disagreements between the parties were about issues rather than personalities. Perhaps this book will make a small contribution toward redirecting the focus toward issues.

If so, we will consider ourselves successful.

Acknowledgments

Larry Powell wishes to acknowledge the contributions that several others made toward the completion of this book. His wife Clarine gets first nod, for her love, patience, and tolerance during his writing of this book. His father, Harold Powell, planted the seeds for this work decades ago when he instilled an appreciation of politics. Political pollster James T. Kitchens has been a colleague, friend, and coworker since their days together at the University of Florida; many of the ideas in this book are the result of conversations with him. Senator Richard and Dr. Annette Shelby gave a young assistant professor his first chance to work in a real campaign. Editor Karon Bowers and coauthor Joseph Cowart deserve special thanks for always working to improve the final version. And thanks to Dr. Mark Hickson for encouraging its completion.

Joseph Cowart acknowledges his wife, Marthena, for her understanding, encouragement, suggestions, and love over the nearly four years of this undertaking. Deep appreciation also goes to U.S. Senator Zell Miller for giving him a beginning in the business and an early appreciation of the intellectual underpinnings of campaigns aimed at governance and to Larry Powell, a coauthor of infinite patience who built and maintained the structure and substance of this work.

We would also like to thank the reviewers of this text for their valuable comments and suggestions: Vanessa Beasley, Texas A&M University; Hal Fulmer, Georgia Southern University; John Gastil, University of Washington; Steven Livingston, George Washington University; James McDaniel, Northern Illinois University; John Murphy, University of Georgia; Robert Sahr, Oregon State University; and Robert Terrill, Indiana University.

Larry Powell
Joseph Cowart

PART ONE

An Overview of Political Communication Issues

Forgive those of us in academia for our insistence on organization, but there is a reason for our obsessiveness. Organized information is easier to learn and easier to teach. With that in mind, *Political Campaign Communication: Inside and Out* is organized into three major sections.

The first part is an overview of political communication issues. Chapter 1 begins at a basic level—defining the concept. As elementary as that seems, it is a crucial beginning point. Discussion of all subsequent issues will depend on a common understanding of "political communication." Agreement on something as simple as a definition is not always easy. In fact, a key aspect of this chapter will be understanding how political communication is defined differently by the academic and consulting communities. Further looks at the topic will reveal that definitions of the topic vary dramatically, even within the academic community. Sometimes "political communication" is defined so broadly that it can encompass almost any form of interaction between groups or individuals. Sometimes it is defined so narrowly that it fits within only one area of study. We will define it so that its primary focus is on communication related to political campaigns. That does not mean we will look only at campaign communications, since many of the messages offered by politicians and candidates during non-election periods are also campaign related.

Chapter 2 focuses on political socialization—how people form, develop, and maintain their political attitudes. Some books that focus on campaign communication omit this topic. After all, the socialization process begins at an early age, before most people are even old enough to vote. As such, some might argue, it has little direct relationship to any specific election campaign. We disagree. This topic is approached early because the formation of partisan attitudes influences most subsequent elements of the campaign process. People who are lifelong Democrats or Republicans are often resistant to persuasive efforts from the other side. Understanding why they are so resistant is important to understanding political campaign communication.

Chapter 3 looks at campaign strategies. After completing a list of readings on campaign strategies, a graduate student approached one of the authors and described herself as "naive." "I always assumed that candidates simply put themselves on the ballot, presented their ideas to the public, and the public selected the one they preferred," she said. Hardly. Most successful campaigns are organized around well-defined campaign strategies that provide guidelines for the selection of campaign messages, the timing of campaign activities, and the choice of tactics employed. Strategies are generally campaign specific—a new one is devised for each particular campaign. But some general strategic models have been developed, and they are presented in this chapter. Furthermore, the techniques used to develop such strategies are described in more detail.

Chapter 4 looks at the images of political candidates. This chapter offers both an academic and a consulting view of the topic. In the past, some academic studies of candidate images have focused on breaking the concept down into its component parts. A number of different approaches have been suggested for that, and several of these are discussed. Other academic viewpoints assume that the candidate's image is a holistic concept that can be hard to dissect. The consulting community generally agrees with this approach. As a part of the campaign's persuasive efforts, consultants try to identify what factors contribute to an overall positive or negative opinion of a candidate or politician. Pragmatically, the goal is to identify those elements that can enhance the image of your candidate or detract from the image of the opposition. Despite these two divergent goals, though, both fields have a great deal in common on this topic.

Chapter 5 provides an overview of media theory as it relates to political communication. This chapter is heavily oriented toward the academic view of political communication, so much so that some campaign-based books leave this subject out. Some academic books on political communication will focus entirely on this topic. We believe this chapter is essential to a broad understanding of campaign communication. Modern media theories such as Agenda Setting, Uses-Gratifications, and the Limited Effects model have direct campaign implications. Consultants often make use of the ideas developed by the theories, even if those same consultants can't name the specific theory behind their tactics. We believe an understanding of these concepts will make the reader a more informed and objective observer of the political campaign process. That is, after all, the major purpose of this book.

1 Political Communication: An Introduction

The 2000 U.S. presidential election was one of the closest and most controversial in the history of the nation. The prize of the presidency depended on which candidate would win Florida, something that was far from clear on election night and remained in dispute for weeks afterward. The television networks, using exit poll data, first put Florida into Al Gore's win column. Later, they withdrew that prediction and subsequently called George W. Bush the winner. Before the night was over, though, they had to concede that they might be wrong again.

For weeks afterward, both sides argued their cases before state and federal courts, with both the candidates and their supporters feeling the ups and downs of court decisions. Eventually, a decision by the U.S. Supreme Court sealed the victory for the Bush team.

George W. Bush moved from candidate to officeholder. Al Gore, once the Democratic nominee for president, became just another citizen. But both men would continue to be political communicators—people who address and communicate with others within the political arena. Both men—one an officeholder and the other a private citizen—would continue to be players in that area of inquiry known as political communication.

The term "political communication" evokes images of candidates and campaigns, debates and issues, propaganda and persuasion. As a subject, it is both simple and complex. It is simple because it focuses on such a narrow and specific topic. It is complex because it incorporates so many diverse disciplines and addresses a mass audience. Consultants and other political practitioners often come from diverse educational backgrounds and yet work together in a specialized environment. Scholars who study the topic find themselves following tangential lines of research that lead through the fields of mass communication, political science, law, advertising, marketing, and rhetoric.

In a democracy, political campaigns are at the center of this collection of processes (see Figure 1.1). They are the beginning and ending points for political communication. Ideas flow into a campaign and flow out as messages. As the messages are presented within the campaign context, some are accepted or rejected by the voters, who make their decision known by the candidates they support. As messages become refined, they are transformed from time to time as legislative proposals. Those proposals are offered by elected officials who consider their actions in the context of and as a rationalization of both their past campaign and their next campaign. Meanwhile, an ongoing community often exists in the background—a community composed of newspaper editors, special interests, public interests, lobbyists, and others. As the campaign debate continues, their input results in the emergence of other proposals for legislative action.

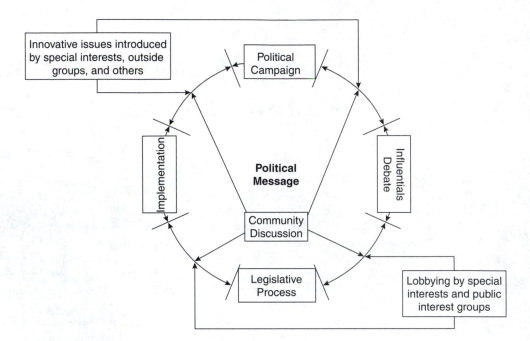

FIGURE 1.1   The Flow of Campaign Messages

As the proposal passes through the legislative process, it becomes a factor in the next campaign. If it becomes law, it proceeds to an implementation phase where special interests and public interests and others attempt to reshape it within legislative parameters. The proposal then returns to the political campaign as an accomplishment, something a candidate can tout as an achievement that merits reelection. If it fails in the legislative process, and if interest remains, it becomes fodder for a new campaign message, something the candidate can use as a message regarding a problem that still needs to be addressed. And the process begins anew.

Tying down this concept merely emphasizes its complexity. One colleague tried to explain it to a student by saying that political communication was a combination of persuasion and organizational communication. His explanation was correct but insufficient. Without understanding the path it follows—into, through, and after political campaigns—comprehending political communication will be difficult, if not impossible.

To offer useful insights and an understanding of this complex system, our discussion will include (1) the U.S. political system, (2) the actors within that system—particularly the consultants, and (3) those communication processes that focus primarily on the campaign and legislative processes. A number of valuable political communication studies have been done on systems outside the United States; we will refer to these when their results have some relevancy to the American political system. We will focus heavily on the roles of the actors within the system, particularly the role of political consultants. We believe that a better understanding of these roles and the communication behaviors associated with them will provide a better understanding of the political campaign process.

Most of the discussion will focus on the political campaign process. Campaign activities often offer valuable insights into effective political communication. Hart (2000) argues that campaigns are essential to the function of a democracy; they inform us about issues, sensitize us to the concerns of others, and increase our awareness of the political world. Campaigns are the focal point for most political communication activities. Campaigns are the source of much of our information about political issues. Campaigns are obviously the route by which many politicians attain public office. Once elected, they become part of a perpetual, even permanent, campaign in which they must constantly work toward reelection (Blumenthal, 1980). If they choose not to run again, the campaign communication continues anyway as both parties maneuver to enhance the chances for their chosen candidates. Because of this, legislatures (both state and federal) have become increasingly concerned over the ballot-box implications of their decisions. For that reason, we will also look at political communication at the legislative level, particularly as it applies to political campaigns. Both political parties maintain year-round strategy-planning teams whose purpose is to evaluate and respond to current events in terms of their long-term electoral implications. Even at the local level, zoning and other decisions are often influenced by electoral implications (Staley, 2001).

Our major goals will be twofold. First, we hope to broaden the reader's perspective on the role of political consultants. These campaign professionals sometimes appear to have split personalities; sometimes they are viewed as kingmakers by the press and the public and sometimes they are maligned as unethical campaign practitioners. We will examine their role by analyzing what they do in campaigns and by providing insights from the consultants themselves. We invite the reader into that discussion by examining their role at various levels within a campaign.

Second, we hope to shed light on the relationship between the consultants and the academic community that studies political campaigns. In the past there was often an arms-length relationship between the two. That boundary seems to be shrinking as more university professors serve as independent campaign consultants, while an increasing number of consultants serve as university lecturers. If that gap is closed even more, we believe that both groups can benefit. The consulting community could benefit from the constant expansion of ideas among the academic community for communicating with the public. The academic community's ability to objectively observe campaigns could benefit if they have a better understanding of the role of campaign consultants. Neither will reach full productivity until they understand each other.

Academic Observers vs. Professional Practitioners

Political communication is both an area of academic study and a professional activity. The differences between the two communities are enough that they do not even use the term "political communication" in the same way. Academicians speak of political *communication,* in the singular. Consultants are more likely to use the phrase political communication*s,* adding an *s* to speak of the concept in the plural. The plural form is rarely used in the academic community, and the different forms of expression reflect one of the philosophical differences between the academic and the consulting communities. Academicians view political "communication" (singular form) as a collective noun describing a single academic discipline; when more specificity is needed, it is used (still in its singular form) to represent a holistic process, an abstraction that captures all the variables and factors related to the discipline. For consultants, political "communications" (plural form) refers to the messages used by candidates and their campaign to communicate with the voting public. Any particular political communication (singular form) is a singular noun referring to a specific message. Thus, when the academic and consulting communities sit down to discuss the topic, they frequently do so with different semantic meanings attached to the term. Unless both are aware of those differences, they may find themselves talking about different things.

Philosophically, academicians are more likely to approach the topic from an outside perspective with the intent of describing the process so it can be understood better and making suggestions to improve the process. Political professionals (candidates and consultants) are more likely to approach the topic from an internal and personal perspective with the intent to (1) improve their ability to communicate with their target audience, (2) increase their chances of promoting their political agenda, (3) make a profit, and (4) improve their reputations for future marketing purposes.

Media consultant Raymond Strother (1999) believes most academicians have a negative view of consultants, one that "is taken from movies and stories attributed to a group of bottom-feeders . . ." (p. xiii). Some members of the academic community have also criticized political consultants for dysfunctions in the campaign process. Consultants say they advise their clients in a way that assists them in ducking and weaving through a process complicated by legally mandated financial restrictions, governmental regulation of advertising, survey research, message development, the creation of TV ads, radio ads, print ads, telephone banks, direct mail, and collateral print pieces. As such, consultants often take an amoral perspective on their campaigns. As Lippmann (1965, p. 241) noted, ". . . the power of the expert depends upon separating himself from those who make decisions, upon not caring . . . what decision is made."

An outgrowth of academic study is the development of recommendations on how to improve the electoral process. Such recommendations usually bring little reaction from political consultants. Instead, they are more interested in using the existing rules of the game to their client's advantage. They coach the tactics of political counterpunching, using their skills to recognize when such tactics are necessary.

The Outside View of Academics

The field of political communication attracts academic interest from a number of areas. Speech communication professionals often study the process in terms of public speaking, campaign strategies, and media usage. Journalism classes will examine campaigns and issues in terms of news coverage. Political scientists are interested in how the campaign process can influence and affect government institutions. Psychologists study the attitudinal factors related to voting decisions. Sociologists examine the broader implications of political trends on society. Regardless of the academic discipline, academicians tend to approach the topic as skeptical, outside observers. Lippmann (1965, p. 49) once argued that campaigns often ". . . substitute misleading fictions for workable ideas." Similarly, Edelman (1964) was skeptical of politicians and their ability to lead public opinion in a new direction. He argued, instead, that much public opinion formation is a strategic process in which opinion leaders try to persuade the public to think about issues along particular lines, to activate existing values, prejudices, and ideas.

Some academicians are also skeptical about the role of the media in the political process. After reviewing media coverage of the 1968 presidential campaign, Graber (1971) concluded, "The public received an image of the ideal president based primarily on personal qualities, with little information provided on [a] candidate's political philosophy or executive ability." Two separate studies on the 1980 and 1984 presidential elections found that most news coverage of the elections was about competition and controversy rather than issues (Patterson, 1980; Patterson & Davis, 1985). Robinson and Sheehan (1983) reported that a majority of the news coverage in 1980 failed to contain even one issue-related sentence.

Some academicians are also skeptical about the ability of a relatively uninformed public to make rational decisions. Typical of this view is that advocated by Nimmo (1974), who argued for the need of the public to become "politically self-competent persons" who are capable of better and more rational decisions. Nimmo's goal is representative of the "rational man" concept in classic democratic theory, a tendency to view ideal voting behavior as being motivated by an issue orientation.

And, as noted earlier, academicians are sometimes skeptical about the role of political consultants in the electoral process. Typical of this view is Nimmo's (1970, p. 197) assertion that the consultants' ". . . orientation toward business and technology threatens the very bases of the new politics." Furthermore, he added, when ". . . a candidate uses opinion surveys and image advertising to give the appearance of being the leader of a popular movement, he is captive not only of the movement but of the technicians as well. He becomes a manufactured, contrived 'personality.' . . ."

Such attitudes are understandable. The academic community is, after all, an arbiter and guardian of democratic values and principles. Academicians are, in a way, the caretakers of the tools of democracy, protecting us from unrestrained pragmatism on the part of the consultants. Academicians serves as watchful critics who provide checks and balances on professional politicians by instructing the media how and when to put the brakes on consultants. In that sense, the academic community plays a role in holding campaign communication accountable for what is said and done. One goal of this book, indeed, is to increase the number of such "watchdogs" by enhancing the critical skills of the average citizen in making an informed voting decision.

The Inside View of Political Professionals

Today's campaigns are run by professional consultants who provide services related to media, polling, and other forms of communication. The average voter often has only a cursory understanding of how they do their job; more often, as Medvic (2000) noted, their activities ". . . are shrouded in mystery" (p. 91). Johnson (2000) divided what they do into three broad categories: strategists, who develop campaign messages; specialists, who provide essential services such as fund-raising, opposition research, and speech writing; and vendors, who supply campaign products and services. Major campaigns will use all three types, with varying degrees of success.

Despite the modern emphasis on consultants, their role is nothing new. Nimmo (1970, p. 36) argued that the consulting industry is a direct descendant of the public relations profession that matured in the 1920s as the nation became increasingly influenced by mass media. In 1933, Clem Whitaker and Leone Baxter used basic consulting principles to help defeat a referendum question in California, and their success sparked the formation of their consulting firm, Campaign, Inc. (Friedenberg, 1997). During the mid-1940s, Murray Chotiner was a consultant to a number of Republican senatorial and congressional campaigns; one candidate under his tutelage was a neophyte California congressional candidate named Richard Nixon. During the 1950s, Stephen Shadegg started providing consulting services to Barry Goldwater. By then, the industry was visible enough to attract the attention of academic investigators (Bernays, 1947; Pitchell, 1958). The dean of the modern consulting industry, Matt Reese, first opened his office in Washington, D.C. in the early 1960s. By the early 1980s, the growth in the use of campaign consultants prompted Sabato (1981, p. 3) to write, "There is no more significant change in the conduct of campaigns than the consultant's recent rise to prominence, if not preeminence, during the election season."

When experts discuss the controversial growth of the consulting industry, one aspect that is often overlooked is what role the consultants replaced—that of the political bosses (Perlmutter, 1999, p. 1). Before the advent of national media, many elections were often decided by a handful of individuals who made their decisions in backroom deals. While remnants of that system still exist in isolated areas, much of it has faded away. As Herrnson (2000) noted, "Campaign professionals have replaced local party organizations as the intermediaries between candidates and voters" (p. 88). The increasing role of the media, and of consultants, has essentially killed that system because the use of the mass media provides a way for candidates to communicate with the voters directly while bypassing the political bosses.

Consultants bring a blend of experience and expertise to the political arena—expertise in the fields of communication technology, strategy development, and experience in the campaign process. Their presence in a campaign can affect an election, but not necessarily decide it. As Herrnson (2000) noted, "Campaign professionals cannot eliminate the advantages of incumbency, nor can they turn an incompetent politician into one of presidential timber . . ." (p. 88).

They do, however, bring an expertise to a campaign that can make a difference in many elections. They may lack, though, an academic background for their professional expertise. As Franzen (1999) wrote, "Although several universities now have programs in campaign strategy and management, most consultants have no academic training in the profession, and many would scoff at the notion that it could be learned in school" (p. 295). Perhaps because of that attitude, the academic community has sometimes targeted the role of consultants in campaigns. Bloom (1973), for example, argued that political consultants are a bane on the process, creating a "crisis in democracy." Consultants themselves paint a more pleasant picture. Allyn (1999) argued that consultants serve a positive role, simplifying complex issues so that they can be comprehended by average voters. Today's consultants, he argued, "make democracy . . . work on an everyman level, a valuable leveling service to the system" (p. 306).

Regardless of whichever impression is the more accurate, consultants are a part of the reality of modern politics. Major political campaigns are dominated by political professionals, and that may include both the candidate and the consultant. Their task is to identify a message and find a means of communicating that message to the people who have decisional power (the voters). Thus, for political professionals, the goal of any specific campaign is a pragmatic one of finding the best combination of tactics and strategies that will provide the best chance of winning over the most voters to their side.

Any one campaign is only part of the overall picture. Apart from any specific campaign, political consultants also run businesses (Johnson, 2000). They have ongoing expenses that include personnel, office space, travel expenses, and general office overhead. This overhead requires sufficient revenues to maintain operations. So, while they take a pragmatic approach to aiding a candidate, they also take a pragmatic approach to the day-to-day activities of running their business. Idealism is nice, they might agree, but it doesn't pay the bills. As Denton and Woodward (1985, p. 52) noted, "Today's professional politicians are politicians only insofar as they earn their living working for political candidates and campaigns. They are professionals in the sense that they possess unique skills and knowledge relevant to human motivation and mass communication technology. They are experts and specialists first, and political in the traditional use of the word second."

Professional consultants are sometimes skeptical toward academic approaches to campaigns. Most would not attempt to develop their own theory of political communication; even if they did, they would likely abandon it by the next election as new situations dictated new strategic moves. Moreover, most consultants maintain that it is impossible to adequately understand the political environment unless issues suggested by funding, moving public opinion targets, and variations in campaign communication skills are considered.

One element that the consultants and academicians have in common is an emphasis on their professional reputations. While an academic reputation adds to a professor's credibility, a consulting reputation is valued primarily because it can add to the consultant's bank account. As Perlmutter and Wu (1999, p. 332) noted, consultants "are only as reputable as their last election performance. . . ." Thus, from a consultant's view, winning an election is a positive goal, because it demonstrates success at working with a particular client. Even more important, victories enhance the consultant's reputation and serve as a marketing tool for future sales efforts. Upset wins, in which a long-shot candidate beats a heavily favored opponent, are particularly important. They become reference points that can anchor a consultant's entire marketing effort for the next election cycle.

Areas of Research Related to Political Campaign Communication

Political campaign communication is related to a number of other disciplines, and yet is also distinctly different from each.

Persuasion

As Mutz, Sniderman, and Brody (1996, p. 1) noted, "Politics, at its core, is about persuasion." The persuasive elements of political communication are one feature that attracts students in fields such as marketing and public relations. Political communication, though, is a very specific form of persuasion. Its persuasive intent differs from those who do professional marketing and commercial advertising in very distinct forms. In politics, the idea, issue, or candidate is sold to a self-qualifying public on election day, using modified mainstream principles.

Organizational Communication

Political campaigns are often the product of an organization that uses paid personnel, volunteers, and subcontractors to achieve its goal. Indeed, many techniques learned from

Interview with James T. Kitchens

The Conflict Between Academics and Consultants

James T. ("Jim") Kitchens is one of the few people who have viewed political communication as both an academician and as a consultant. Before becoming a full-time political pollster, Kitchens served as an assistant professor of communication at Texas Christian University; some of the research he conducted during his academic tenure is cited elsewhere in this book. His consulting credentials include work for a number of statewide and congressional candidates, including former Speaker of the U.S. House of Representatives Jim Wright (Dem.-Texas), Congressional leader Martin Frost (Dem.-Texas), Alabama Governor Fob James, Kentucky Attorney General Ben Chandler, and dozens of congressional candidates.

Q: How would you describe the general view that consultants have of academics?

A: I think most consultants believe academicians are out of touch with the reality of political campaigns. Academicians work in such a theoretical environment that they often have no idea of how campaigns function.

Q: Why do you think that?

A: Because of the way they write about campaigns. There's two things that you notice. First, there's an incredible focus in the academic community on presidential campaigns, using conclusions from those to generalize to political campaigning in general. But presidential campaigns are so unique, so different from everything else, and academicians seem to often overlook that. Second, academicians often don't recognize the pragmatic reality behind many campaigns. They write about what each campaign should be doing, in an ideal world, without considering the fact that most campaigns have to make their decisions with limited resources and a finite amount of money. Most campaigns are always struggling for money, and they make decisions that are cost efficient, not ideal.

Q: What's the other side, how do academicians view consultants?

A: Probably as charlatans, people who will sell any idea to anybody and who really don't believe in anything. They think of consultants as people who will work for other people, whether they believe in them or not. If academicians decide to work in a campaign, they prefer to think they would only work for somebody they believe in.

Q: Where does that image of consultants as charlatans come from?

A: They see that kind of consultant on television. They see the kind of consultant who talks about how they manipulate people, or how they trick the voters into supporting their candidate. There are a limited number of consultants like that, but the exposure they get creates an image for all political consultants. I also think there's a general lack of communication between the consulting community and the academic community. I know the AAPC [American Association of Political Consultants] is working on a program to create more joint communication between the two communities, but not a lot has been done yet.

Q: But consultants do have a basic ethical code. For one thing, most work only for one political party.

A: I think that's more of a pragmatic business move than an ethical code. Candidates don't trust consultants who work for both parties. Most consultants get into the business through one party or the other, and they stick to that party for their careers. Dick Morris is the only person I know of who has been able to work for both Democrats and Republicans over a long period of time.

Q: There seems to be a basic difference in goals. Academicians aim for a democratic process in which the truth will prevail. They sometimes believe consultants are only interested in winning, not the truth.

A: The truth doesn't always emerge at all. Both sides of a political campaign will argue their case, but their positions on any issues have gotten so extreme. Messages become extreme because extreme messages are effective. That's what the electorate wants and responds to. In some ways, you could say the electorate gets the type of political campaign that it wants and deserves.

Q: Where do the consultants fit in this search for the truth?

A: Consultants are not on a search for the truth. Consultants are effects oriented. Consultants are paid to win. We're like football coaches—if we don't win, we don't work. That means that the candidate is the moral conscience of the campaign. Ultimately, it is up to the candidate to say they do or do not want to use some particular technique or some particular argument.

Q: Does that mean that positions on issues are irrelevant?

A: The consultant is not on a search for the truth about any particular issue. I'm not in the business of government; I'm in the business of politics.

Q: What's the difference?

A: Government is concerned with policy, and a policy needs time to emerge. Most public policies cannot be judged on a short-term basis, and that includes the few months' duration of a campaign. It takes time to see how policies work. In politics, the voters look for general answers; government looks for specific details. The battle of a campaign is a battle of ideas and messages about where we want to go. Government is the process of working out the details of that. You can't do that in thirty-second TV ads. You can't do it in a thirty-minute program or a nationally televised debate either, because not enough people watch either of those. You have to do campaigns with general messages about where we want to go. The specifics is the job of government.

Q: What do consultants see as the major benefit of the academic community?

A: I don't know that other consultants think a lot about academics. I do, because I come from that background, but most don't even think about academics. They should, because I've seen how valuable it can be. A lot of our strategic recommendations are based on theories of communication. We take the theory and apply it to a specific situation. And some academic research is very valuable. Most consultants don't know that, though, because they never read an academic journal. That's the way that political mythologies develop. "You never mention your opponent's name." That's a political mythology. There's no theory behind that. There are plenty of instances in which you had better mention your opponent's name. Another one you often get is, "That approach doesn't work here." That's just not true. We know that the principles of communication theory are general principles that work regardless of the area of the nation where that particular campaign is held. The "that-doesn't-work" mentality usually means that the last person who used it lost the election, but they could have lost it for a dozen other reasons. The technique may still be effective there, if there's a theoretical justification for using it.

(continued)

Interview with James T. Kitchens   Continued

Q: What can the academic community learn from consultants?

A: First, they can learn some pragmatic things about the way campaigns work and how decisions are made with limited resources. Second, they can learn more about the persuasive process if they'd look down the ballot. A lot of the early studies were done on presidential campaigns, and that's not the place to be looking for media effects.

Q: What do you see as the major weakness of consultants, as viewed from an academic perspective?

A: The biggest problem is that there is no licensing procedure within the profession. Anybody who wants to do so can call themselves a political consultant. There is no requirement that they have the academic or educational credentials to do so. That creates a situation in which we have a relatively naive consumer group—candidates—who have no means of evaluating consultants. All they have to go on is whether the consultant has worked for winners, even if the consultant had little impact on those winning campaigns. It's hard to imagine that we've turned over our democratic process to a group of people who don't have to prove they know what they're doing, but that's what happened. The candidates, at least, need some criteria for evaluating consultants. I'd like to see some minimum educational requirements established, but I don't think we'll ever see it.

Source: Reprinted by permission of James T. Kitchens.

organizational communication can make a campaign organization more productive. Still, a campaign is not a typical organization. Frequently, the campaign organization more closely resembles Berne's (1963) definition of a "crowd" (a differentiated but unstructured collection of people) rather than a "group" or an "organization." While a small group of individuals form the core of the campaign organization, effective implementation of the campaign often relies upon loosely formed coalitions of supporters and volunteers who may be unknown to the candidates themselves.

Another difference between political communication and organizational communication is what's known as the "famous-versus-rich" question: If you had your choice, would you rather be famous or rich? In a business organization, the answer is "rich"; the goal of most business organizations is to make a profit. In political campaign communication, the answer is "famous"; politicians have to be well known to be successful. That difference shows up in a number of subtle ways, including speeches. Politicians make speeches to enhance their credibility, while businessmen make speeches to increase the profit margin for their organization. Peggy Noonan, a speechwriter who has worked in both fields, described the difference as, "Politicians want to look good so they can get things done. CEOs want to get things done so they can look good" (p. 133).

Advertising

Students from the field of advertising are often attracted to political communication. After all, modern politics is an exercise in advertising. Politicians communicate their ideas to the voters by way of the mass media while using a variety of advertising techniques. Yet, people whose training is limited to advertising are often ineffective as political consultants. There is an intensity to a political campaign that is totally different from that of most campaigns for a commercial product. Success is based on a much higher standard: the politician must get a majority of the target audience, not just a significant market share. Also, most advertising campaigns are designed for ongoing sales; few advertisers are used to handling the concept of a one-day, one-time sale (election day).

Marketing

When students from the field of marketing look at political communication, they see an area in which they can provide insight; at the same time they can learn something new about their profession. As with many related fields, political communication encompasses some elements taken from the field of marketing, but makes adjustments for what is still an unusual marketing situation. One element that political communication experts have learned from the marketing profession is the concept of demographic targeting. Candidates don't try to persuade all of the voters to support them, just a majority. This can often be done by identifying subgroups of voters who can be united to form that necessary majority. Still, such demographic targeting is usually ineffective by itself, producing the "I-should-have-won" postelection response. Furthermore, the targets of political communication and marketing tend to differ dramatically. A successful political coalition, for example, might include support from both older voters and low-income voters, two groups that are seldom targeted by commercial marketing firms (Harwood, 1998; Jamieson, 1984).

Group Communication

Students of group communication find a number of interesting factors that may attract them to political communication. Political interest groups are a key component of the political communication process. Campaign activities and decisions are typically made as a result of group discussions and group decision making. Special interest groups form to advocate special issues or to serve as a focal point for ideological views. Social movements develop around groups as the public and the press look to them as representatives of ideas. Activated group members may lobby politicians on behalf of their causes. Coalitions are formed as the campaign group solicits support from a number of other groups, encouraging them to focus their efforts on a common goal.

Religious groups, in particular, have been active in the political arena. Separation of church and state may be a key element of the constitution, but there is no clause that mandates a separation of church and politics. The two elements are often linked in today's political arena. The most obvious linkage is an ideological one. The Religious Right has become an active participant in state and local politics, using the political arena to advocate its positions on issues of morals and values. But the ties go back much further. Martin Luther King, Jr. launched his civil rights protests from the pulpit of the Dexter Street Baptist Church in Montgomery, Alabama. The church provided King with (1) a platform to articulate his ideas, (2) a ready-made organization to implement them, and (3) moral justification for his actions (Selby, 2001). King's success in the public arena can also be traced back to his religious background, particularly his training as a speaker. Political candidates often seek from voters the same type of passionate devotion to a cause that a preacher seeks from his parishioners.

Political Science

Political scientists have an obvious interest in political communication, particularly as it relates to political campaigns. The campaign process can influence and affect government institutions in dramatic ways by influencing leadership decisions and legislative actions. Still, the two concepts are not synonymous. The field of political science is primarily interested in government; political communication is studied in terms of how it affects that broader concept. For students of political communication, government is the secondary concept; it is studied in terms of its relationship to the communication process. That relationship has grown closer over the years. As a result, a number of incumbent activities and decisions—factors that were once the domain of government—are now being increasingly evaluated in terms of their campaign implications (Blumenthal, 1980).

The Distinctive Nature of Political Communication

Whether a campaign is for a public office or for a referendum, the candidate or the issue require a specialized form of marketing. Such marketing is characterized by outcome planning for a maximum positive result for the particular day that voters go to the polls. As a result, despite its relationship to several other forms of communication, political communication retains a very distinctive flavor. As Jamieson and Campbell (1997) noted, a political campaign is more short-lived and intense than a campaign for a commercial product. Denton and Woodward (1985, pp. 8–12) identified five general characteristics of political communication: (1) short-term goals, (2) communication based on objectives, (3) importance of the mass media, (4) short-term orientation, and (5) the importance of considering audiences.

Perhaps the most distinctive feature of the campaign process is the one-day sale idea. Most election campaigns are based on audience response during a relatively short span of time (often just a single day). Even with the development of mail-in elections and the growth of early and absentee voting in many states, the time span in which the "sale" must be made is relatively short compared to the continuous sales of many consumer products. While public opinion polls may show who is ahead at any interval leading up to the election, the ultimate decision is based only on the total responses received by one specified date. The entire campaign process is targeted toward maximizing responses on election day.

That day can be critical. In 1968, Democratic candidate Hubert Humphrey staged a major comeback late in the presidential campaign, nearly finishing in a dead heat with Republican Richard Nixon. Some pundits believe Humphrey might have won the election if it had been held three or four days later. Such might-have-beens make for interesting speculation, but are ultimately irrelevant to the process. What is important is who is ahead on election day, not three days before or after.

Commercial advertisers have to take an entirely different perspective. If they're selling soap, they want to sell it every day—not just once every four years. Their persuasive campaigns have to be oriented toward that approach. Furthermore, they have to be concerned with point-of-sale displays, packaging, ongoing promotions, and even factors such as seasonal impact. Soap can be easily purchased, picked up at any number of stores that stock it on their shelves. Not so for the political candidate. Voting requires a level of effort and participation that commercial products seldom encounter. A voter has to go to one specific polling place to cast a vote. Making that trip is nearly always an interruption to the individual's normal routine. Voting is not an easy activity, particularly when compared to the ease with which commercial products can be purchased. For a vote to count, the voter must cast a ballot in a specific manner, one that is consistent with state and local laws. In the 2000 presidential election, for example, some 20,000 votes in Florida—most of which were probably intended for Al Gore—were disqualified because they had been double-punched for two presidential candidates (Gore and Independent Pat Buchanan).

Despite the added difficulty of the process, political professionals are judged by a stronger standard than commercial advertisers. As Jamieson and Campbell (1997) noted, commercial advertisers can often be quite content with a relatively small share of the market. If a product consistently garners 20 percent of the market, for example, it can be highly successful and profitable. A political candidate who only gets 20 percent of the vote, however, has typically lost by a landslide. Typically, success is measured by the ability to get at least 50 percent-plus-one of the vote. Granted, there are some exceptions to that trend. The winner of some primaries is based on a simple plurality of the votes, rather than a majority. Some states are using extended absentee voting periods and others are opening voting to a several-week or longer period. But even in those instances, the size of the market that must be captured and the limited time available to advance ideas is daunting by consumer-based standards. Political consultants also have a harder job when it comes to image development. As Jamieson (1984) noted, the politician brings a documentable past to the political arena. All campaign messages have to either use those elements of the candidate's record or to be ready to defend them.

One factor is common to both domains. Like most other forms of communication, political communication assumes that the audience can function as an agent for change. Still, political communication has its own distinctive spin to this concept. Sometimes, change can occur very quickly with little impetus from individual participants. The vote of a single person can contribute to the majority decision that ousts one set of leaders and replaces them with another. That gives the political communication process distinct advantages over other systems, some of which lead to the deaths of the ousted leaders.

Finally, the financial aspects of political communication make it distinctly different from many other forms of communication. While most of the attention on a campaign focuses on the campaign itself, another campaign is being run behind the scenes. At the same time candidates *spend* money to communicate with the voters, they must simultaneously *raise* money to fund the process. This dual spend-raise role is not unique to campaigns; many charities operate on a similar basis. It is a process that makes it distinctively different from most other forms of commercial advertising.

Defining Political Communication

Given the diverse fields that affect political communication, it should not be surprising that academicians often disagree about its most basic concept: how to define it. Conceptualizations vary widely, from scholars who discuss international politics to those who equate it with power plays within an organization. Who has not heard the complaint, for example, that an unqualified employee got a company promotion only because they knew how to "play politics" within the organization (Kennedy, 1980)? While that approach goes beyond the scope of this book, it does serve to emphasize the broad range of definitions that academicians, professionals, and voters have regarding the concept.

Others view the concept of political communication as being inherently unethical. Corcoran (1979, p. xv), for example, argues that politicians typically use communication ". . . not to convey information, but to conceal or distort it . . . , (bearing) no relationship to the organization, coherency and clarification of information and ideas." Many others might agree with George Orwell's (1949, p. 363) assessment that ". . . political speech and writing are largely the defense of the indefensible." But such approaches are not really definitions so much as judgments about the process. In essence, as Denton and Woodward (1985) noted, such descriptions leave political communication "deficient by definition" (p. 13). More can be learned about the process by approaching political communication from an objective viewpoint rather than a judgmental one.

Others have more benign views of political communication. Hart (2001) views political campaign communication as a three-way conversation among political elites, the press, and the public. The exchange of information in that conversation becomes a source of information about issues, the views of other people, and the processes that contribute to political outcomes. Denton and Woodward define political communication as "public discussion about the allocation of resources . . . , official authority . . . , and official sanctions . . ." (p. 15). This approach emphasizes three major factors related to politics—money, power, and sanctions; but even this approach has its limitations. Specifically, the focus on "public discussion" overlooks the role of lobbying, a critical factor in many legislative efforts.

Perloff (1998, p. 8) corrects that problem by defining political communication as "the process by which a nation's leadership, media, and citizenry exchange and confer meaning upon messages that relate to the conduct of public policy." These authors like Perloff's broader view of the field, which is similar to our own. For the purposes of this book, political communication will be defined as *the study of the communication processes that contribute to the exchange of ideas in the democratic political process.* This definition reflects both the simplicity of the concept and the broadness of its application. An important facet of this definition is that it is not merely limited to political campaigns. Legal hearings, FCC regulations, and a variety of forms of popular culture could fall within the realm of that definition. Unfortunately, all of the various manifestations of political communication cannot be adequately encompassed within a single book. This book will narrow that view somewhat by focusing primarily on political communication in its most observable form: the political campaign.

Still, even though this book is campaign oriented, it is important to remember that political campaign communication today is a constant, ongoing activity that extends well beyond those few months immediately preceding an election. Most major politicians have consultants available at all times, and the consultation process is involved in all facets of the communication process (including lobbying). Furthermore, most professionally run campaigns work within an eighteen-month time frame; planning starts in the middle of the year before the next November election; a benchmark poll is conducted fourteen months beforehand; and the consulting activities increase after that as the election draws nearer. For a congressional incumbent, that means that the "nonelection" time is limited to only about the first six to eight months out of every twenty-four. Ignoring that fact would be to not recognize the consultant's view of the process.

Political communication is a form of strategic communication, whether it be a discussion between two individuals in the halls of Congress, a television commercial broadcast over the airwaves during a campaign, or an employee jockeying for a raise from her company. That element of strategic communication is critical and represents a common factor on which the academician and the consultant agree. Overlooking that element will lead to mistakes, causing the consultant to lose a campaign and preventing the academician from furthering his understanding of the process.

We shall focus on the inner workings of both sides to improve the general understanding of their work product, goals, and objectives (how voters think, how to develop a strategy based on that understanding, and considerations regarding the impact of the media). We will start with political socialization, since the formation of partisan attitudes influences most subsequent elements of the campaign process. From there, we shall work through the strategic considerations and the campaign elements, followed by postelection considerations, and finish with a chapter on campaign ethics. Arguably, the discussion of ethics should come first, since it should be—ideally—a value system that guides decisions at each step of the process. We considered this option, but put it last anyway, reasoning that the discussion would be more fruitful if the participants had a more thorough understanding of the process first than if they entered that discussion as neophytes. Ethical discussions about campaign communications are most valuable when they are founded on solid information. This is another of the few issues on which both the academic and consulting communities agree.

We hope this book will provide insights to both perspectives, and thereby make that discussion more useful to both sides of the debate.

Summary

Political communication is defined as the study of the communication process that contributes to the exchange of ideas in the democratic process. This concept is often viewed differently by the academic and consulting communities. Academicians view political "communication" as a collective noun that describes an academic discipline. For consultants, political "communications" refers to the messages used by candidates and their campaigns to communicate with the voting public. Philosophically, academicians are more likely to approach the topic from the perspective of an outside observer, while consultants view the process as inside participants.

Some scholars define "political communication" so broadly that it encompasses almost any form of interaction between groups and individuals. Others define it so narrowly that it fits within only one area of study. This book defines it in terms of campaign communications, an approach that encompasses those messages offered by politicians and candidates during nonelection periods that are also campaign related.

Political communication includes several distinctive elements: (1) short-term goals, (2) communication based on objectives, (3) a reliance on the mass media, (4) a short-term orientation, and (5) an importance placed on audiences. Its more distinctive characteristic is its frequent reliance upon the one-day sale idea—the stated objective is based on an audience response in a relatively short span of time.

Campaigns are the process by which politicians attain public office. Once elected, they become part of a perpetual campaign in which they must constantly work toward reelection. Thus the process of political communication is often a continuous one in which political messages become part of the legislative process, and vice versa.

QUESTIONS FOR DISCUSSION

1. What is the role of consultants in campaigns? Do they contribute to or inhibit the democratic process?

2. What is the role of the academic community? How could that role(s) contribute to or inhibit the democratic process?

3. When asked if positions on issues were irrelevant in campaigns, pollster Jim Kitchens said, "The consultant is not on a search for the truth about any particular issue. I'm not in the business of government; I'm in the business of politics." What, in your opinion, did he mean about the differences between the "business of government" and the "business of politics"?

CHAPTER 2

Political Socialization:
The Development
of Political Attitudes

Lamar County, Alabama, looked like fertile ground for Republicans during the 2000 elections. The rural area in west Alabama fit the stereotype of a conservative, Bible-Belt area that might be receptive to the Republican messages of tax cuts and family values. Polling data indicated the attitudes and values of most of the county's voters were in line with those of the Republican party. When the election was over, though, the Alabama Republican party viewed the results with mixed emotions. Their presidential candidate, George W. Bush, had done well there, as had several statewide candidates, but participation in the local Republican primaries was disappointingly low. Why? One local resident had a simple explanation: "We may be conservative," he said, "but we've always been Democrats."

Such attitudes illustrate the importance of understanding political socialization in modern campaigns. Political socialization plays an essential, if sometimes overlooked, role in the development of political attitudes. Academicians sometimes disregard political socialization as a campaign variable because it has little direct impact on any single election, or those factors that do have an impact occurred years before the event under study. The lifestyles and socialization patterns of baby boomers, for example, may have directly influenced voting behavior during the 1990s. Still, such analyses are more likely to be made on a post-mortem basis, rather than studied in advance of any particular election campaign.

Consultants take a different perspective, although their initial response is similar to that of the academic community. Generally, consultants will disregard the theoretical aspects of political socialization, viewing it as an abstraction that has little impact on any particular campaign in which they are engaged. Still, they pay close attention to the impact of socialization on voting behavior. A distinguishing feature of political consulting is the need to target specific audiences so as to create a distinctive strategy and to deliver a persuasive message. No campaign can expect to win a hundred percent of the vote. Attempting to do so is one of the most common mistakes made by campaign amateurs. Instead, the goal of the campaign is to gain enough votes to win the election or force a runoff.

To do that, the campaign typically divides the electorate into three categories: (1) support for the candidate, (2) support for the opposition, and (3) swing voters. The crucial element of this division is the identification of the opposition's support—voters who are unlikely to support your candidate regardless of what happens during the campaign. Those subgroups are eliminated from campaign targeting, thus reducing the cost of voter communication. Almost equally important is your candidate's own core support, voters who will stick with the candidate regardless of campaign events.

In most cases, core support for or against a candidate is based on partisan allegiances. Party identification is more stable than any other political attitude (Abramson & Ostrom, 1991; Green & Palmquist, 1994). What makes it such a stable anchor of political preferences? The answers are found in the years of political socialization leading up to any particular campaign. Some voters grow up as Democrats and remain Democrats for most of their lives. Others are steadfast Republicans who rarely shift to the Democratic side. In both cases, the individuals are exhibiting behavior based on lifelong partisan attitudes, and those attitudes have an impact on the campaign process.

Those hard-core attitudes and values serve as the bedrock for establishing legislative districts and as the starting point for developing a campaign strategy. Understanding the fault lines between audiences means understanding how voters arrive at their decisions in the context of a political campaign. For the consultant, the question becomes: What is it that makes the voter a Republican or Democrat or Reform or Libertarian and/or conservative and/or liberal, and so forth? For the academic community, the question posed by those who research the process of political socialization is: How do voters develop their political attitudes?

The attempts at answering both questions fall within that realm of academic study known as "political socialization." Political socialization is defined as "the study of the developmental processes by which children and adolescents acquire political cognition, attitudes, and behaviors." Still, the implications of the research are hardly limited to childhood. Quite the contrary, Cook and Scioli (1972) reported that political orientations acquired in childhood have important influences on adult behavior. In other words, the political attitudes developed by children strongly influence which candidates they will support when they become adults.

Since major studies of the socialization process require in-depth analysis over a period of years, many of the current research conclusions are rather tentative in nature and have come from a number of theoretical approaches. Scholars who work in this area frequently debate the relative validity of the different approaches to political socialization. Such a debate is beyond the scope of this book, but it is important to realize that there is more than one perspective. The goal of the academic community is to resolve the discrepancies in those various perspectives while working toward a unified theoretical approach. Consultants are more likely to either ignore the theories, focusing on the common societal impact that they attempt to describe, or to look for insights within each one that might be useful to them.

Atkin (1975) identified three distinctive conceptual frameworks used by political socialization researchers: (1) Systems Theory, (2) a Structural-Functional Approach, and (3) Individual Analysis. The systems theory approach views the political system as one that operates under a continuous process of demands (output) and support (input). In this view, the continuous political socialization of incoming members of the society becomes a major means of support. The Structural-Functional Approach assumes that conformity is a key element in maintaining the cultural system, resulting in the inculcation of youth with a desire to fulfill role expectations concerning normative political behavior. Individual Analysis focuses on those agents or factors that have an influence on the political socialization process.

Despite the variety of approaches, some conclusions have been drawn. Generally, it is believed that most political attitudes develop through a two-step process that begins during the elementary school years (or earlier). At this time, children typically develop abstract emotional attachments and identification with political figures and institutions. This is then supplemented with specific knowledge gained during adolescence (Greenstein, 1968).

Major Socialization Agents

Those who study socialization from the perspective of the individual as the primary unit of analysis have generally sought to identify those agents that are most likely to influence a child's political orientations. Those agents generally viewed as having the strongest influence are the family, the news media, and political parties.

Family

The standard conclusion of most research is that the family is the single most important influence in the development of a child's political orientations, particularly for pre-school children. Research consistently shows a relationship between the political values of parents and their children (Glass, Bengston, & Dunham, 1986). One reason is simply time; before a child reaches school age, they are usually in the company of their parents more than any other source of influence. After the age of six, other factors come into play, including the school system, mass media, and peers. But the family impact remains important. Like most academic inquiries, though, this topic has generated its share of controversy and alternative explanations.

The Simple Transmission Model.   The most basic model for parental influence can be described as the simple transmission model, which is to say, parents pass along their political orientations to their children (Jennings & Niemi, 1968). Thus children who grow up in Republican homes are likely to vote Republican when they become adults. Conversely, children who grow up in Democratic households are likely to be loyal Democrats when they reach adulthood. While this model has some appeal, based purely on its simplicity, critics of the approach argue that it is overrated. While it may have some validity, it is not always fully supported by the data. There is indeed a positive relationship between the parents' political orientations and those of their children, but the strength of the relationship is often unimpressive. Thus, children tend to have similar, but not identical, political values as their parents.

Alternative Explanations.   At least two alternative explanations have been offered to explain this phenomenon. One approach argues that the relationship is a by-product of common experiences. Connell (1972), for example, argues that political attitude formation is shaped by common experiences, not the processes within the family. In essence, this approach argues that older and younger generations may develop their political orientations at the same time, in a parallel developmental process, rather than in a serial form, which is passed from parents to children. Similarly, Sigel (1970) argued that shared social status may account for much parent-child correspondence. Political orientations often correlate closely with social status, with high-income groups generally adopting Republican positions, while low-income voters are often strong Democrats.

Media

According to Becker, McCombs, and McLeod (1975), the media serve an information-giving function to adolescents and younger children, although the permanency of these effects are not certain. The media's impact on children appears to be stronger than it is on adults. Some studies, for example, have found that adults sometimes demonstrate high resistance to media influence, but those studies have not been able to replicate similar results for children. Quite the contrary, children often believe and are influenced by what they see on television and in other media. Furthermore, children have considerable exposure to politically relevant information, especially among older age groups. That exposure is typically in place during the elementary school years, when they begin watching news programs with their parents. After that, exposure increases with age, with political interest often nurtured through exposure to both broadcast, print, and online media.

That exposure does not necessarily translate into political attitudes, but it does have an impact on political knowledge. Chaffee, Ward, and Tipton (1970) reported that the mass media are the single most important source of political knowledge for children. Generally, children consider newspapers to be their best source for information, but they rarely seek it out. Instead, television serves as the heaviest source for most of their political information, particularly for highly "visible" aspects of politics such as the presidency. For example, during 1998 and early 1999, even young children were aware of the possible impeachment of President Clinton, a by-product of their heavy TV viewing habits.

Generally, young people recognize this impact themselves. They perceive that the media have an important influence on their opinions about political issues. Furthermore, the media also have an effect on the public's attitudes toward political institutions. Television entertainment content, in particular, may affect orientations toward such elements of the political system as police and trust in the justice system. The impact of television is even stronger for low-income families. Children from low-income homes, particularly boys, are more reliant on television for their knowledge and less dependent on their parents than are middle-income children.

Still, despite all the evidence for media influence, there is no clear evidence that mass media affect overt political activity. They affect political knowledge, and can have an impact on opinions about specific political issues. But there is no clear indication that the media either increase or decrease voter turnout among young people, or that they directly affect their political party affiliations. The media's impact is often affective in nature, rather than as a stimulus for behavior.

Political Parties

Political parties play dual roles in the political socialization process, sometimes serving as a causal factor influencing the socialization process and often displaying the effects that result from years of socialization. The result is a cyclical process in which new members to the political process identify with one of the parties and then contribute to the socialization process of younger citizens. Modern scholars, however, may continue to debate the nature of that reciprocal process. To what extent do parties contribute to political socialization, and to what extent are they merely a reflection of past socialization trends?

For years, most scholars would have argued that the parties were a major socialization agent, noting that party identification played a powerful role in perceptions and judgments about candidates and issues (Campbell, Converse, Miller, & Stokes, 1960). The Democrat party, for example, dominated elections in the southern United States for decades (Key, 1949). Furthermore, while other parts of the nation lacked the single-party

Reprinted with special permission of King Features Syndicate.

focus that dominated much of the South, that didn't decrease the impact of partisanship nationwide. In general, during the late 1940s and early 1950s, significant numbers of the nation's voters exhibited strong partisan identifications (Key, 1952). Sometime afterward, though, signs of weaker party identifications started appearing. Some observers point to the 1964 presidential election as a key indicator, one in which many white southern Democrats voted heavily for Republican Barry Goldwater (Miller & Shanks, 1996, p. 153). Four years later in the 1968 Nixon-Humphrey election, a definite anti-party trend was apparent among many voters (Jennings & Markus, 1984). By 1976, those same anti-party voters had contributed to a growing decline in party identification (Miller & Shanks, 1982).

The 1990s saw changes in partisan allegiances among American voters, although descriptions and explanations for those changes have varied. An eight-year study (1992–1999) of 13,651 adults by the Scripps Howard Foundation and Ohio University found that the fastest-growing political groups in America are "other" and people who said they were undecided. Fewer than one third of those voters identified themselves as strong partisans for either political party, while 58 percent said they were politically independent. During the time frame of the study, Democrats dropped to their lowest level in 1994 and 1995, when only 14 percent described themselves as strong Democrats; those dates corresponded to the time that Republicans took control of both the U.S. Senate and House of Representatives. Republicans hit their lowest level in 1998 during efforts to impeach President Clinton when only 10 percent identified themselves as strong Republicans. Arterton (2000) attributes the decline in partisan influence to technology and modern campaign practices. One of the major benefits of party organizations, he argued, was to provide a link between candidates and voters, but, he adds, "Modern politics have eviscerated these networks, replacing them with polling and mass communication. In the process, the individual voter has become a cipher, a statistical construct rather than a living, breathing person" (p. 22).

Although partisanship decreased during the 1990s, there was no corresponding drop in ideological independence. Ninety-three percent could identify themselves as either liberal, conservative, or middle of the road, compared to 92 percent in 1992. Others, however, have argued that partisan identification has actually increased, particularly if a longer period of time is examined. Abramowitz and Saunders (1998), using data from the

1976–1994 American National Election Studies, concluded that the 1994 and 1996 elections reflected an increased polarization of partisan identification. They pointed to the Reagan and post-Reagan years as the source of the increased polarization, noting that during that time "clearer differences between the parties' ideological positions made it easier for voters to choose party identification based on their policy preferences" (p. 634).

Some scholars point to 1976 as a watershed year in partisan participation. In that year, both parties (particularly the Democrats) instituted a number of reform rules that changed the state laws regarding delegate selection to the parties' national conventions. As Trent and Friedenberg (2000) noted, ". . . the change in rules and the proliferation of primaries have weakened political parties, the traditional vehicle for building coalitions and forging consensus" (p. 6). But other factors may also be involved. Fiorina (1981) argued that party identification can be influenced by retrospective evaluations of party performance. Subsequent research has indicated that policy preference can be a key factor (Franklin, 1992), particularly when a party takes a strong partisan position that is not supported by the voter. Miller and Shanks (1996) conducted an in-depth study of partisan attitudes over four presidential elections and concluded that long-term party identification was the single strongest predictor of voting choice.

Political parties play a major role in modern campaigns, providing fund-raising, organizational, and rhetorical support to their candidates and the issues they support. Still, such roles are largely dependent upon the parties' ability to attract large numbers of members. Those members provide the party with volunteers who work on campaigns, provide financial assistance, and ensure a core voting bloc from which to expand an electoral base. The question remains, though, as to what extent partisan identification is a result of partisan activities, and how much results from the influence of media or families or from simple partisan shifts that occur over time.

Other Socialization Agents

The family, media, and political parties are generally considered the three biggest influences on a child's political orientations, but two other factors—peers and the educational system—are also known to have an influence.

Peers

Beginning in the early teenage years, one's peers tend to gain more influence on a child's social maturation. Peer pressure becomes more intense, and children become increasingly sensitive to what their friends think of them. Becoming "one of the crowd" is a high-priority goal, one that defines social success for many teens. Surprisingly, though, this stage has relatively little effect on the child's political socialization. There is little indication that friends or peers have a major impact on political development during middle school or high school. The socialization impact of friends and peers during the high school years seems to be more geared to social activities than political orientations. There is some evidence, however, that friends play a significant role in the political attitudes of college students. When that occurs, those orientations can produce long-term effects that influence an individual's political behavior for years.

Schools

Of the major socialization agents, research has generally indicated that education has the least impact on political attitudes. Still, schools do play a significant role in teaching concepts, beliefs, and attitudes about the operation of the political system, particularly for younger children. The schools also impart detailed information about political processes. Teachers are particularly important as sources of information about some of the less visible aspects of government. Typically, for example, children learn more about the Supreme Court, and concepts such as the separation of powers, from school than they do from the media.

Still, the impact of the educational system is largely limited to information. Attempts to use the schools for propaganda purposes (teaching anti-communism courses, for example) have generally been unsuccessful, and social studies or civics classes at the secondary level has little effect. Not surprisingly, then, the educational systems typically have little identifiable impact on the attitudes and values that young people take into the political arena when they become voters. Although explanations for this effect vary, one factor appears to be constant. The impact of the educational system itself is overridden by the effect of the schools as a site of social interaction. Specifically, interaction with peers at school (particularly at college) can have an impact on attitudes that exceeds the impact of the educational system itself. Thus the school, at least, serves as a socialization agent by providing a location in which peers can influence one another.

Political Socialization Styles

Sigel (1970), in an analysis of parental influence on political socialization, argued that the content of parental communication may be less important than the manner in which their political values are transmitted. What may be more important is whether parents encourage their children to engage in self-expression and political controversy. Subsequent research in this area has identified two general approaches to politics, a socio-orientation and a concept orientation. Socio-orientation is a people-based perspective that stresses the importance of maintaining harmonious personal relations, avoiding controversy, and repressing personal feelings. Concept orientation is an ideological or issue perspective that stresses the importance for the child of expressing his or her own ideas, using conversation to discuss controversy, and challenging positions taken by parents and others. Parents can stress either, neither, or both of these styles, resulting in four categories of behavior that can be labeled political socialization styles. Table 2.1 illustrates these categories.

Families that stress neither a concept nor a socio-orientation are called laissez-faire. In these families, children are not prohibited from challenging their parents' views, but neither are they encouraged to do so. Children in such families are given few directions on the use of interpersonal communications. Laissez-faire families have children who spend little time on homework and earn moderate grades in school. They spend little time in political activity, and are moderately knowledgeable about politics. They watch moderate amounts of violence on television.

Families that stress social relations are protective. The children are encouraged to get along with others, taught not to be confrontive or to express dissent, and are given little chance to encounter discrepant information. These children are taught to use interpersonal communication to maintain peace. Protective children spend little time with school work at

Interview with Jack Williams

Religion and Political Attitudes in the South

Jefferson County, Alabama, tax collector Jack Williams is a graduate of Southeastern Bible College. In the religious community, he has served on the pastoral staff of several churches. In the political arena, Williams was Operations Director for the Southern Republican Exchange and was the founding director of the Alabama House Republican Caucus. He has managed numerous local races across Alabama and was also instrumental in persuading former Alabama Governor Fob James (who previously served as a Democrat) to become a Republican. Williams later served as campaign manager for James's successful 1994 guber-natorial campaign. James's election in 1994 made him the first governor to serve Alabama as both a Democrat and a Republican. Williams was appointed by James to serve as Jeffer-son County tax collector in 1995. He was elected to a full six-year term in 1996.

Q: Why does a person become a Republican or a Democrat?

A: There are several reasons. One is the family. If politics are part of the family discussion, children tend to echo the same political sentiments of their parents. That tends to holds true throughout their life, unless a separation develops in their educational level or socioeconomic level.

Q: Give me an example.

A: Most studies recognize that Republicans tend to go further academically, and you'll find more Republicans in higher socioeconomic groups. Voters that identify themselves as Democrats are found in greater numbers in lower socioeconomic groups. Those trends generally hold unless there are other factors involved, such as religion.

Q: How does religion influence political orientations?

A: Religion plays an ever-increasing role in an individual's party affiliation. Voters view some major issues as having religious overtones. In the Sixties, the civil rights move-ment became a rallying point in the Black churches. The church and the community ral-lied around the cause of justice and the opportunity for equal rights. The church, particularly the Black church, became strongly identified with the civil rights move-ment. Or, maybe it would be more accurate to say that the civil rights movement became associated with the Black church. It happened in the 1980s around issues that were beneficial to Republicans, issues such as prayer in schools and abortion. You started seeing white, suburbanite, evangelical voters actively identifying with the Republican party based on religious-based issues. You also saw many blue-collar work-ers who started to identify with the Republican party, simply on the basis of social issues. These were people who had a good standard of living, one that came from their association with their unions. But they disregarded the political positions of the union because they felt that social and religious issues were of greater significance than pock-etbook issues.

Q: You seem to be saying that religion becomes an important factor whenever a political issue is viewed as a moral issue?

A: That's part of it, but people don't automatically rally around issues. In the 1960s, a young, charismatic John Kennedy emerged as president of the United States and as leader of the Democratic party. His charisma, coupled with the overriding social issues of the civil rights movement, really struck a chord with the electorate. It gave hope to the Black community, that they could have a voice. Some of that activity was going on before Kennedy came on the scene. Obviously, the Montgomery boycott occurred years before Kennedy was in the White House. But he captured their frustration and the desire to be equal, to have equal opportunities. In the late 1970s and early 1980s, a charismatic Ronald Reagan took what was actually a Richard Nixon strategy in 1968—going after the formerly Democratic Solid South. Reagan went after the "Silent Majority" and was able to express the dreams and visions of hard-working, middle-class folks, and their vision of the American Dream. In turn, it solidified a bloc of voters who had never identified themselves as Republicans before. In the 1980s, those voters were called Reagan Democrats; for the most part, those voters have been called Republicans in the 1990s.

Q: But a charismatic leader doesn't have to change partisan orientations. Those voters could just split their tickets to vote for that person; they don't have to change their party.

A: That's what they do originally. But as middle-class, blue-collar workers begin to involve themselves in the process, they begin to feel more comfortable with the other party. It's not like a religious, born-again conversion; it's more like a courtship. This is where religion comes into play. The principles that they learn from church provides them with a vision of how society should operate. As they identified with a charismatic leader who expressed their hopes for the future, they also found a political establishment that was responsive to their participation and their vision.

Q: So the Republican party had a positive message which attracted these voters?

A: Part of it was the willingness of the Republican party to embrace that message, and part of it was a rejection of, and in some instances a downright hostility toward, the Democratic party and its positions on some of those principles. I think abortion would be one example; so would the activist homosexual agenda; and prayer in schools was another. From a national perspective, the Democrats were perceived as being intolerant of anyone who did not toe the party line on those issues. It forced some people out of the Democratic party. Now what the Republican party has to avoid is becoming intolerant of people who don't hold to its tenets. You can't succeed long-term if you take in fifty people, and run forty people out.

Q: You seem to be saying that one reason people change parties is because their old party no longer respects their views.

A: Yes. As Democrats changed to the Republican party in droves over the last twelve years, the standard statement was, "I didn't leave the Democratic party, the Democratic party left me." In all honesty, most of the candidates who were party switchers were following the electorate. Not too many of them were climbing out on a limb, and saying, "If I switch parties, I think I can win." They saw voting trends in their area, and they knew it would simply be easier to win in the Republican primary.

Q: I guess you could say that, in the 1960s, the Democratic party had the moral high ground. In the 1980s, the Republican party had the moral high ground. How would you describe the 1990s?

A: Interestingly enough, I've read that some Democratic consultants are claiming that they're going to get God on their side for the new millennium. Democrats recognize the

(continued)

Interview with Jack Williams   Continued

issue of religion. Al Gore talks about his faith. Bill Clinton even embraced that after the impeachment proceedings, quoting the Bible in some of his speeches. I think that what might happen is that you'll see both parties start pandering in such a manner that it could backfire and have no significance. It could take religion off the front burner and make it a secondary issue.

Source: Reprinted by permission of Jack Williams.

home and earn low grades in high school. They spend little time in extracurricular political activities and have a moderate amount of political knowledge. Children in protective homes generally watch high amounts of violence on television.

Pluralistic families are those that emphasize concept-oriented communication. The children are taught that ideas are important and they are encouraged to form opinions and discuss them openly. Children from pluralistic homes have been found to be more knowledgeable about public affairs, earn better grades in school, are more active in school and politics, and want to be more like their parents. They watch very little violence on television.

Consensual families place an emphasis on both socio-orientation and concept orientation. The children are told to both maintain social harmony through communication and introduce diverse points of view into conversations. Thus, consensual children are taught to keep the peace while expressing strong opinions. Consensual children have little political knowledge, spend lots of time on homework but get only moderate grades, and are only moderately active in political matters. They generally watch high amounts of violence on television.

Wheeless and Schrodt (2001) expanded the assumptions behind concept orientation by examining the impact of partisan socialization on information processing. They argued that those voters who had developed rigid views about politics would be both apprehensive about listening to information that was not supportive of their views and more inflexible in responding to that information. Their early research on the subject has supported that concept. Generally, conservatives are more apprehensive about listening to new information than moderates or liberals, and they are more likely to be inflexible when listening to such information. Still, while the differences are statistically significant, they are not always big.

TABLE 2.1   **Types of Political Orientations**

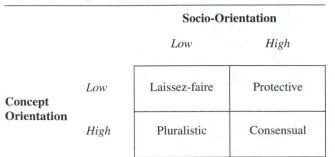

		Socio-Orientation	
		Low	*High*
Concept Orientation	*Low*	Laissez-faire	Protective
	High	Pluralistic	Consensual

It appears that several other socialization factors (as yet unidentified) also affect how political partisans respond to and process political information.

The Invisible Youth Vote

Despite the amount of study devoted to both politics and political socialization, one general conclusion is that the United States, as a whole, as been rather ineffective at instilling its political values into its youth. In the early 1980s, researchers noticed a gradual downward trend in U.S. voter participation (Abramson & Aldrich, 1982), a trend that continued into the 1990s (Teixeira, 1992). In 1997, the Swedish-based International Institute for Democracy and Electoral Assistance reported that voter participation rates in the United States were the lowest of any advanced democracy and lower than most fledgling democracies (Patterson, 1999), with the United States ranking number 139 out of 163 countries. The 1996 presidential election was the first national contest in modern times in which a majority of adults of eligible voting age stayed home. In the 1998 election, only 36 percent of the voters went to the polls.

Some scholars point to a general rise in political apathy as the cause. DeLuca (1995) attributes the rise in apathy to two factors: alienation created by systemic problems in which elites control the process, and individuals who give up their personal responsibility for participating in government. Dionne (1991) blames modern campaign techniques, arguing that "Election campaigns generate less excitement than ever and are dominated by television commercials, direct mail, polling, and other approaches that treat individual voters . . . as mere collections of impulses to be stroked and soothed" (p. 10). Delli Carpini and Keeter (1996) attribute it to a decline in political knowledge, noting that "Compared to what people ought to know . . . , the public is ignorant about much of the details of government and politics . . ." (p. 17).

Much of the low turnout can be attributed to a general decline in voting by younger voters. Generally, American youth have been neither knowledgeable nor interested in politics. In 1979, a Gallup Poll survey of 1,012 teenagers found that teens overwhelmingly failed a five-question quiz about American government. Only six out of ten could name the vice president of the United States. Most (52 percent) could not answer two questions correctly, and only three percent correctly answered all five. Such numbers reflected a growing trend of political ignorance that was of concern to scholars (Bennett, 1988). Gallup also found a correlation between several demographic variables and knowledge scores. Those teens from white-collar families and those whose parents had attended college tended to do well, while those from blue-collar families and whose parents did not attend college did not do well. Those findings added support to the theory that political socialization is influenced by shared social status of younger and older voters.

Later data are even more discouraging. An analysis of the 1998 election indicated that more younger voters are dropping out of the democratic process. That study, which examined the youth vote from 1972 to 1998, showed a continuous drop in turnout among eighteen-to-twenty-four-year-old voters (Patterson, 1999). In the 1972 presidential election, when Richard Nixon defeated George McGovern, almost 50 percent of voters aged eighteen to twenty-four went to the polls. In 1996, when Bill Clinton faced Robert Dole, the number had dropped to 36 percent. In the November 1998 off-year elections, the number dropped to 20 percent—an all-time low.

The latest study added further support to the social status theory (Didion, 2001). There was a double-digit gap in voter turnout between college-educated (41 percent) and non-college educated youth (25 percent). The study also added another variable to the socialization process—religion. Young people who attend religious services every week were more likely to vote in 1998 (43 percent) than those who never attended (25 percent).

Why such low political involvement? Some researchers argue that placing blame on a single cause is impractical (Cassell & Luskin, 1988). Still, many do blame the parents, since most young people (nearly 80 percent) live in homes where politics is rarely mentioned. Others blame the schools for not preparing young people to vote. At the very least, research indicates that the schools can play a vital role in confirming the importance of exercising one's vote (Miller & Shanks, 1996, p. 52). Didion (2001) attributes this low rate of participation to citizens who feel left out of the process, noting that nonvoters have less education, less money, and a lesser feeling of having a stake in the political process than do voters.

Others, however, argue that such pessimistic assessments of the socialization process are unnecessarily negative. Popkin (1991, p. 42), for example, argued that voters do not need a lot of detailed information to make valid voting decisions. "There is much that voters *do* know about government, and many ways in which they manage to consider issues without high levels of information." All that is needed, he argued, is that the voters know something about the state of the economy or proposed legislative measures that could affect them or their values.

Miller and Shanks (1996, pp. 509–511) also questioned the assumptions behind those who bemoaned a decline in voting turnout, arguing that most of the so-called decline was a by-product of lifestyle changes that reflected a normal cyclical process. When nonvoters are eliminated, they argued, ". . . the eventual social and psychological foundations of that participation appear to have been very much the same for each generation" (p. 510). The limitation of their analysis, however, is that it is limited to turnout during presidential elections—those elections that produce the highest voter turnout. They do not address the decline in participation by young voters in other elections.

The Social Cost of Voting

While a teenager, one of the authors volunteered in a voter turnout program aimed at getting rural voters to the polls. After driving to one man's house to provide him with transportation to the polling place, he was surprised when the elderly farmer politely refused the ride, saying, "There's not that much difference between any of them." Later in the day, the real explanation for the elderly gent's response was given by someone who knew him well. He couldn't read, something most of his neighbors did not know. For him, voting would have required assistance that he was too proud to accept.

That story is but one example of the social cost of voting. Many active politicians often overlook the fact that the social cost of voting can create a barrier for some who would otherwise participate in the political process. Such citizens get a "free ride" from the governmental process—accepting government services from elected leaders while not participating in the selection of those leaders (Olson, 1971). Voting requires making time to register, visiting a bureaucratic office, filling out forms, and possibly taking off time from work. While active voters take such factors casually, accepting them as part of the system, newcomers will have a different perspective. Sometimes, those who are new to the process feel uncomfortable in engaging in any of these activities and often fear ridicule if their lack of knowledge of the process were revealed. Add to that a social environment in which those around them do not vote, and there will be little social incentive to behave otherwise (Straits, 1990). Tyson (1999, p. 131) refers to this phenomenon as "intimidation factors associated with voting," noting that "infrequent voters often lack not only a rationale for voting but also knowledge of the process itself. . . ." Faced with both a lack of knowledge and uncertainty about the process, becoming part of that process can be psychologically intimidating. For these voters, tuning out is easier than tuning in.

The social cost of voting can be countered. During the 1960s, massive voter registration drives in the South added thousands of new African American voters to the voter rolls. The desire for recognition of their civil rights was stronger than their inhibitions about the process, and the organizers of the drives recognized the need to educate new voters about the process. Still, it can be difficult to do. Efforts to expand the voter pool must recognize and deal with the uncertainties and fears that inhibit participation.

Partisan Orientations and the Political Consultant

For the political consultant, the pragmatic impact of political socialization is that of partisanship. Generally, the consultants accept the conclusion reached by Miller and Shanks (1996): "As a long-term stable predisposition, party identification is not only a point of departure for electoral analysis; it is the most important of several predispositions that provide continuity across electoral epochs" (p. 512). Most voters, including those who describe themselves as Independents, exhibit a strong degree of loyalty to one or another political party (Keith, et al., 1988). That loyalty can often be described with demographic data, as some demographic groups (low-income voters, for example) tend to lean toward Democratic candidates, while others (high-income groups, for example) tend to be more Republican in their political orientation.

Consultants make assumptions about voters based on such demographic factors and use those assumptions to aid the development of campaign strategies and message targeting. For example, Republicans frequently target upper-income, suburban voters as critical elements in their campaign strategy and Democrats often target older voters, a group often assumed to be sympathetic to issues promoted by the Democratic party.

In general, consultants tend to view such demographic targets as relatively immutable groups, a view that is consistent with findings from socialization research. Political orientations that have been developed through a lifetime of experiences are often difficult to change. Rather than attempting to change them, consultants more frequently recommend working within those constraints according to the maxim of "Work your strengths." Instead of attempting to "cross the fault line," those demographic groups perceived as being in the opposition's corner are simply eliminated from the campaign's target list.

Most such decisions are based on financial concerns. A political campaign with a relatively small budget is unlikely to make major inroads toward changing long-held beliefs. In such cases political consultants use this information to exclude certain groups from their campaign plans. Miller and Shanks (1996, p. 511) identified three major venues for change in party identification: racial, regional, and religious. Most consultants would agree with those categories for targeting purposes, but they would also add other social factors, such as income, to their possible target list. Republicans generally do not target black voters, low-income voters, or voters who live in strong "Democratic" regions; Democrats similarly do not target religious evangelicals, upper-income white voters, or voters who live in districts with a history of supporting Republican candidates.

Still, changes in political orientations do occur. As Miller and Shanks (1996) noted, "Partisan identifications are demonstrably not immune to change after their initial values have been shaped by childhood and early adult experience" (p. 495). After all, the 1960s reflected a time in which young people who joined the political process tended to have liberal views, a political outlook that was more consistent with that of the Democratic party. By the 1980s, the electorate as a whole had become more conservative, with young voters demonstrating more affinity for the Republican party.

What triggers such changes? One explanation is that it is a natural cyclical process, one that tends to occur over about twenty years of development. That approach would predict that the current conservative trend, one that corresponded with the election of Ronald Reagan as president, is approaching an end. Sometime within the next ten years, this approach would argue, the pendulum is likely to swing in the other direction and the U.S. electorate will become more liberal.

Another factor that influences such shifts is the presence of a charismatic leader, particularly at the presidential level. Voters sometimes, in fact, define their partisan leanings in terms of their presidential vote choice (Markus & Converse, 1979). Democratic strengths during the 1960s corresponded with the election of John F. Kennedy, a highly charismatic speaker, as U.S. president. Similarly, Republican swings during the 1980s were associated with the election of a popular and persuasive Republican president, Ronald Reagan (Abramowitz & Saunders, 1998). But the impact of presidential preferences is not limited to popular presidents. As Miller and Shanks (1996) noted, retrospective evaluations of presidential performance often has an impact on partisan preferences: "Most explanations of presidential elections involve some component in which voters may cast their ballots against the incumbent party if they disapprove of the way the president is handling his job" (p. 500).

A charismatic leader rarely accounts for all of the partisan shift, however. Instead, it may only increase ticket-splitting behavior, particularly at first, in that the popular leader is a person who generates personal support. Still, support for the leader may not be translated into partisan shifts for other candidates. Such across-the-board shifts are more likely to be influenced by either dramatic issues or some watershed event. Miller and Shanks (1996, p. 497) described this effect as "the electoral consequences of controversies"; the controversy surrounding a watershed event helps individual citizens define their views of appropriate goals and priorities for government. Thus, while John F. Kennedy may have been a symbol of the Democratic party, a full shift to Democratic partisanship might not have occurred had not other issues (such as the Vietnam War) also affected political attitudes. Similarly, the civil rights movement of the 1960s played a crucial role in defining party allegiance for a number of people (Carmines & Stimson, 1989), particularly new African American voters who were getting their first chance to participate in the electoral process. And while Ronald Reagan may have been personally popular, the popularity of the Republican party as a whole was not increased until conservative economic policies became popular.

Interestingly, issues or controversies that may have the most impact on altering partisan predispositions may have little impact on any one specific election, while issues that have a dramatic impact on an election may have little or no impact on partisan shifts (Page & Brody, 1972; Page & Jones, 1979). Instead, many times such shifts are based on contemporary, short-term forces that can quickly change (Miller & Shanks, 1996, p. 207). For example, voters' perceptions of the economy was the issue that had the greatest impact on Bill Clinton's 1992 presidential win, but that issue had little impact on partisan identification among the voters; conversely, that same year, the abortion issue sharply divided individual voters along partisan lines, with some individuals shifting their partisan identification because of it. Still, abortion had little impact on the outcome of the election (Miller & Shanks, 1996, p. 504).

Political orientations can shift over time (Beck & Jennings, 1991), even among political elites. Ronald Reagan began his political career as a liberal Democrat, but was elected president as a conservative Republican. Alabama Republican Senator Richard Shelby began his career as a liberal Democrat in the Alabama state legislature. Former Texas Senator Phil Gramm—known as one of the most conservative members in Congress—also began his political career as a Democrat. As the lifestyles of voters change, so too can their political orientations. Some liberal Democrats who devote their lives to education may become Republicans once they become part of the free-market economy. Some conservative Republicans may become Democrats if their lifestyles shift out of the marketplace and into other areas of life.

Voters of all ages are constantly acquiring new information, leading to a resulting adjustment of their political orientations (Delli Carpini, 1989). Partisan loyalties may shift, with the advantage of any one party changing slightly, from election to election. But such changes tend to be made gradually, in small increments. As Miller and Shanks (1996, p. 495) wrote, ". . . partisan identifications respond very slowly to voters' impression of current party leaders, their policies, and their success or failure in handling government." Also, campaign communications can alter some assumptions about political orientations. For example, for years the South was viewed as an area that was off-limits to most Republican candidates. The "Solid South" was a Democratic stronghold that Republicans dare not challenge for fear of wasting time and money. That view changed, however, when Ronald Reagan appealed to blue-collar and rural voters in the South with a message about conservative values that was targeted to them (Dallek, 1999; Dallek, 2000; Greffenius, 2001). The "Reagan Democrats" allowed the Republican party to make major gains in the Southern states.

Such an effect might indicate that political orientations are more malleable than many researchers have expected. At the very least, the decade-long decline in partisan allegiances means that consultants have a larger target audience of potential party switchers than existed during the 1980s. If a candidate can target a message that appeals to a particular group of voters, then they might be receptive to those ideas regardless of its partisan source. If so, then the future of political communication might find considerably more flexibility among those voters than in the past. That possibility could be intriguing for both the academic and consulting communities.

Summary

Political socialization, which is how people develop their political orientations, is an important topic for both academics and consultants. For the academic community, studies of political socialization help to explain shifts in political behavior while identifying those agents (media, family, party, peers, friends, schools) that can affect political attitudes. Such information is critical for understanding the modern political process, but the information gleaned from such studies go far beyond politics and reaches into a broad realm of socialization into modern culture. How we develop our political attitudes is closely tied to how we develop our self-concept and how we learn the roles that guide our lives in modern society.

For consultants, an understanding of how people develop core partisan attitudes helps to influence their basic decisions on targeting and messages. The concept is expressed in a basic consulting tenet: "Work your strengths, not your weaknesses." Naive candidates often forget that maxim and try to appeal to everybody in the constituency. The very nature of political socialization, though, is that such efforts are doomed to failure. Any attempt to appeal to all the voters faces the continuous resistance from voters who have spent a lifetime developing attitudes and values that are in direct opposition to some things that the candidate will be advocating. As a result, more experienced consultants merely write off some voters and concentrate on communicating with those who will be more likely to be receptive to their message. A combination of polling data, demographic data, and past voting data will be used to assess and identify those voters, but the ultimate concept will be a simple one. A lifetime of developing political attitudes will make some voters more receptive to your message, while others will be less receptive. Understanding that concept can be crucial to the chances of campaign success.

QUESTIONS FOR DISCUSSION

1. A woman legislator favors a "woman's right to choose" and is opposing a measure that would require a twenty-four-hour waiting period and counseling before receiving an abortion. To whom should she target her position statement? What are the benefits of such targeting? Should she attempt to convince her opponents that they are wrong? Are there any groups she should exclude from her efforts? What socialization factors would be relevant to her decision.

2. The largest newspaper in the state is attacking a candidate for state senate for his pro-gun views. What socialization factors might influence his constituency's views on this topic? How would those factors influence his response to the newspaper?

3. Your parents oppose construction of a new mall on the edge of your neighborhood. You enjoy hanging out at the mall. What socialization factors might explain the differences in your attitudes? What issue or issues will likely be the biggest source of disagreement on this topic? Why?

4. Examine the sources of your own political beliefs. To what extent were you influenced by your parents? By the media? By your friends? By your education? By political parties? Which of these had an influence on your political ideology? Which had an influence on your level of interest (or lack of interest) in politics?

5. The study of political socialization assumes that political orientations obtained in childhood affect adult behavior. To what extent, though, should political socialization be viewed as a lifelong process through which adults also acquire new information and adjust their political orientations?

CHAPTER

3 Campaign Strategies

How important is a campaign strategy? That depends on the experience of the candidates and the type of office they seek. Political amateurs often qualify to run for an office based purely on the hope that they might win or that they can out-hustle the other candidate. Although such campaigns succeed frequently enough to give new candidates hope, particularly at the local level of politics, most are doomed to failure (Thomas, 1999). Furthermore, while a local candidate might have a chance of winning without a plan, one running for federal office will not. For major campaigns, a candidate who enters a political campaign in the twenty-first century without a comprehensive strategy is doomed to failure. A campaign strategy is the controlling authority for the campaign budget, dictating targeting, staffing, fund-raising, scheduling, and nearly every other function of the campaign. It identifies the target groups, thus dictating budget allocations for TV and radio ads, direct mail, and phone banks. It provides a guide for both the on-site staff and consultants who are needed to carry out the campaign plan. These factors, in turn, provide an indication of the cost of the campaign, which leads to the fund-raising targets necessary to be successful.

The modern professional political practitioners began to emerge in 1930s California during the Merriam-Sinclair gubernatorial campaign. America found an increasing use for professional political consultants (Mitchell, 1992) after World War II. One such example came in 1946 when a group of California Republicans, the Committee of 100, pooled their resources to defeat an incumbent Democrat they abhorred (Costello, 1960). After raising funds, the group hired Murray Chotiner, a veteran politico already known for his ability to guide winning Republican campaigns, on a part-time basis to guide their campaign.

Their first obstacle was fundamental—they had no candidate. Democratic representative Jerry Voorhis, the hated incumbent, was believed to be far too strong for conventional Republicans to risk the race. The group undertook a very unconventional recruiting method: they placed an "announcement" in the newspapers of the congressional district. Applications were invited from "any young man, resident of the district, preferably a veteran, with a fair education, no political strings or obligations, and possessed of a few ideas for [the] betterment of the country at large" (Costello, 1960).

The result yielded wide-ranging historical and political consequences. A young naval officer who was finishing his World War II military duty found out about the announcement and responded. The young seaman's name? Richard Nixon. The committee had one main question for him. Was he a Republican? "I guess I am. I voted for Dewey," Nixon reportedly said. The resulting campaign against Voorhis became the beginning of a political career for

Nixon that included terms in the U.S. House of Representatives, the U.S. Senate, the vice presidency, and the presidency.

The Voorhis-Nixon campaign, however, was also remarkable for another of its features—the use of a "hired gun" consultant to run a congressional campaign using a pretested campaign strategy. The strategy developed by Chotiner for that campaign pulled together tactics he had previously developed, tried, and refined in a number of other electoral campaigns. Chotiner advised Nixon to attack Voorhis as a Communist sympathizer. In a time when attacks were often ignored by incumbents, Nixon triumphed. Voorhis, by ignoring the attacks, betrayed his lack of understanding that an attack by a well-funded opponent can be extremely effective.

After the Nixon victory, campaigns learned to take a holistic view of the campaign process. This approach led to the development of a comprehensive campaign model instead of a focus on individual campaign messages. Any specific message is useful only to the extent that it contributes to the overall campaign strategy, as expressed in the strategic model. Thus, for consultants, strategic models—including demographics, voter history, public opinion, the means of communication, potential funding, and others—serve a decisional function: decisions are made in terms of whether an action will contribute to the overall campaign strategy. For academicians, strategic models can serve as a descriptive framework that can be used to analyze a campaign, providing a better understanding of why a campaign was or was not successful.

Strategy Analysis

Before developing a campaign strategy, consultants first evaluate the factors that are likely to affect the outcome of the campaign. The specific process for making this evaluation varies, and several different approaches have been developed for this purpose.

SWOT Analysis

SWOT is an acronym for "Strengths, Weaknesses, Opportunities, and Threats." As the name implies, SWOT analysis forces the campaign to evaluate itself by these four categories.

Strengths are defined as assets of the candidate and the campaign. This includes positive attributes of the candidate, any major voting blocs committed to the candidate, and financial resources. Factors that contribute to the credibility of the candidate, either with the news media or with the voting public, would be listed and discussed in this category. This includes the candidate's record, the ability to attract eminent supporters, and the ability to raise funds, to mention a few.

Weaknesses are the flip side of the coin and include negative aspects of the candidate's record, the inability to attract eminent supporters, and the inability to raise funds. Pollsters Bill Hamilton and Dave Beattie refer to these elements as "sponsor roadblocks." "Whether a first-time candidate or a long-term public servant, every candidate has voted for, said, implied, or done something that will upset some group," they note (Hamilton & Beattie, 1999, p. 99).

Opportunities are factors outside the campaign that could provide a positive benefit to the candidate. These might include the state of the economy, partisan trends that favor the candidate, the general mood of the electorate, or the presence of a major campaign issue on

Interview with Skip Webb

Campaign Strategy and the "Truth Process"

Skip Webb is the president of Campaign Systems, in Columbia, South Carolina. He has been a political telemarketing consultant and a general consultant for almost thirty years.

Q: When you sit down with a new campaign to develop a strategy, what tasks do you undertake?

A: We sit down with the candidate, his or her family, his or her associates, advisers, and staff. We try to find if there are skeletons in the closet, either political or personal. We don't want to get down the road in a campaign and find something we've got to deal with or something that will undercut our effective campaign message. This all falls into what we call a "truth process." It involves interviewing everyone and finding out everything. It also involves finding out what the candidate really believes about the issues. Capital punishment, choice, et cetera. This is the process of building an inventory, and it includes finding out what the candidate holds most dear. I ask the question, "What great issue would you defend with your freedom? What would you go to jail to defend?" All of this is fodder for the development of a benchmark poll.

Q: What is the most important thing to find out in this process?

A: To find out what his "core" is. If the politician doesn't have a core, in the end, he is going to be successfully attacked because he has no roots in the ground. He'll be seen as willing to attach himself to anything, just to be successful.

Q: How important is strategy to the campaign?

A: I think of strategy as defining the campaign message and that's why you've got to have this thorough understanding of the candidate.

Q: Does a time come in a campaign when the strategy needs to be adjusted?

A: Yes, new issues can emerge. In [19]'72 I ran the Tribbitt campaign in Delaware. He had been minority leader and Speaker of the House, and we started in 1970. Russell Peterson was the incumbent Republican. He was a guy on the white horse—he looked perfect. He was a classic, well-liked governor. Our strategy was to undercut him on finances. We suggested he was going to lose control of the budget and that would create real problems for the state. After predicting a $5 million surplus, it turned out that the state had a four-million-dollar deficit. From that point on, we could capitalize on any little thing that came along. We stayed on that message for two years, and we won.

Source: Reprinted by permission of Skip Webb.

which the candidate has a potentially popular record. The analysis of opportunities requires both the art and craft of political practitioners. The goal is to develop a list of possible events that can be used for your candidate's benefit.

Threats are external factors that could adversely affect the campaign. These may include negative moods among the electorate, partisan trends that negatively affect the candidate, and campaign issues that work against the candidate. It also includes institutional and cultural barriers to the candidate's success. The goal for this part of the analysis is to anticipate problems and to limit their negative impact on the campaign.

All four factors of SWOT provide the candidate and his or her consultants with an all-encompassing view of the campaign. While not all events will be anticipated, many can be. As a result, such an analysis can be useful in preparing an overall campaign strategy.

Who'll Say What

Another approach to strategy analysis, and one that can be used in conjunction with SWOT, is to divide anticipated campaign rhetoric into a four-box matrix defined by two categories: "What our candidate will say" vs. "What their candidate will say," and "What will be said about our candidate" vs. "What will be said about their candidate." The result is a four-box matrix, as shown in Figure 3.1.

The result is a chart of anticipated campaign messages, both by your side and by that of the opposition. This chart can then be used for polling purposes (to test the strengths and weaknesses of all messages) and for planning campaign strategies.

CAT Analysis

CAT analysis (Powell & Kitchens, 1986) focuses on identifying the contingencies, assumptions, and tactics of a campaign. Contingencies are those threshold conditions that must be present for the candidate to have a chance to win and for a campaign strategy to be effective. Thus, contingencies are "if-type" statements, such as, "If Condition X is present, then Strategy Y can be effective."

Assumptions are those elements in a campaign that serve as the premises for campaign communications, or the rationales behind campaign decisions. Assumptions, in effect, are predictive statements about the reactions of political communication elements. For example, predictions about how an opponent might respond to a campaign message would fall into this category. So would predictions about a change in the voters' perception of a candidate during a campaign.

FIGURE 3.1   "Who'll Say What" Matrix

	What Will Be Said About . . .	
	Our Candidate	*Their Candidate*
What Our Candidate Will Say	. . . About himself	. . . About the other candidate
What Their Candidate Will Say	. . . About our candidate	. . . About themselves

Interview with Mike Mann

Developing a Compaign Strategy

Mike Mann is the head of Southern Strategies, a consulting firm that provides strategic advice to campaigns for candidates and referendum issues. Much of his work is done as coordinated campaigns for political parties or interest groups. His clients have included the Florida Democratic party, the Louisiana Democratic party, Major League Baseball, the National Football League, the Nature Conservancy, and the National Rifle Association.

Q: How do you go about developing a campaign strategy?

A: The first thing I like to do is a SWOT analysis, a look at the strength, weaknesses, opportunities, and threats of the campaign. You bring most of the inner circle of the campaign together and take a day to go over the strength, weaknesses, opportunities, and threats facing the campaign. That lets everybody have a chance to contribute. Ideally, you don't bring in family members. They're not as candid or as objective as you need to be for this analysis. But you go through everything, with everybody contributing their ideas.

Q: Is it always a clear-cut, easy decision about where things go?

A: No. Some things will fall into more than one category. Money is often one of those. Suppose you have a big contributor who has made a major contribution to the campaign. The fact that you have the money is a strength. But if [the contributor] is a member of an unpopular interest group, that could be a weakness. Your opponent could attack you for being too closely tied to that group.

Q: After you've compiled your list, what's next?

A: You prioritize your strengths and weaknesses. You have to prioritize, because you probably won't be able to deal with everything. In fact, you're never able to deal with everything on your list. Eighty percent of your effort will go to 20 percent of your list.

Q: What's the role of the general consultant in this process?

A: You usually end up with what you need. Usually, the consultant has thought about most of these issues in advance. As you go through the discussion, you already know what many of the conclusions will be. But the discussion process allows everybody to put their stamp on the final strategy. It's all done in a controlled environment, and everybody feels good about their input. All the players have a chance to contribute.

Q: Is this strategy session something that's not really necessary?

A: No, you need it. It gives everybody, including people who could cause you problems later on, a chance to put their scent on it. And you really need their input. I'm often working out of my home state, sometimes in areas where I've never worked before. You need the local wisdom and insight that those people can provide. Now you can't let that local wisdom dictate the strategy, but it needs to be taken into consideration. You have to figure out how much of it is really important to the campaign and what is merely conventional wisdom with no real meaning.

Q: After the strategy session, what's next?

(continued)

Interview with Mike Mann   Continued

A: Next you develop a working document. All other things spring from that. You hire the consultants, based upon the candidate and the type of campaign. You begin fund-raising, identify your opposition, and explore their record.

Q: Where does polling fit into the plan?

A: All campaigns have to be research driven, so you've usually done a poll whenever you go into the meeting. If not, you do one soon afterwards. If you do it afterwards, the poll is merely used to tweak, or adjust, the campaign plan. You use it to adjust the message, not the campaign. Most of the campaign plan will not address the message, or theme, of the campaign itself. The "plan" is a mechanism for dealing with the strengths and weaknesses of the campaign. Some you can't change, and there's no reason to deal with [it]. But others you can, and the campaign plan gives you a mechanism for doing that. The campaign message is only one part of the plan. If the poll says you need to adjust your message, you can do that without changing the rest of your plan.

Q: It sounds like there's two parallel tracks operating at the same time.

A: It doesn't just happen in a one-two-three order. Some things happen simultaneously, and some things have to be done regardless of what the poll says. You don't have to wait for the poll to start fund-raising. You've got to put together an infrastructure for the campaign, and design it in such a manner that it's expandable. The basic nuts-and-bolts of the campaign can be put into place. But your plan gives some reason to what you're doing. It allows you to assign responsibilities to people in a rational way.

Q: How do you develop your communication strategy?

A: With a poll. Without a poll, I have no way to communicate. I have no message, don't know my target audience, and don't know the universe of voters in the electorate. The poll allows you the mechanism for developing your messages and your campaign theme.

Q: At what point would you consider making adjustments in your strategy?

A: Again, that's research driven. You never change your strategy unless your research tells you it's not working or is not working as well as it should. It should only be changed if there is a significant event that affects your bottom line. If your poll numbers are going down, then you're doing something wrong. If your numbers are flat, you may not be doing something right or as well as you should. But you never make decisions to change that strategy without research, even if your gut tells you to do so. Now you may tweak the strategy without data. Working with the pollster and the media consultant, you may figure out ways to say your message a little better. But that's not getting off the basic strategy, that's just improving it.

Source: Reprinted by permission of Michael Mann.

Tactics are the specific maneuvers in a campaign that take advantage of the contingent conditions and/or operationally define the assumptions of the campaign. Frequently, in major campaigns, tactics are the implementation efforts suggested by the campaign consultants. Implementation is often based on polling data, which tests the contingent conditions and assumptions of the campaign. This process allows for conclusions about the rhetorical circumstances of a campaign, the campaigners' perceptions of themselves, and the candidates' perceptions of the voters. The results of CAT analysis provide a schematic description of the elements needed for successful communication in a particular political situation and can be useful in determining why particular political communication attempts are successful.

Different strategies require different tactics. For example, Trent and Friedenberg (2000) categorize campaign styles into incumbent styles and challenger styles and identify specific activities that are associated with each style.

Tactics associated with incumbent campaigning include (p. 82):

1. Creating pseudoevents to attract and control media attention.
2. Making appointments to state and federal jobs, state and national party committees.
3. Creating governmental task forces to investigate issues of public concern.
4. Appropriating federal funds and/or grants.
5. Consulting or negotiating with world leaders.
6. Manipulating the economy or other important domestic issues.
7. Endorsements by party and other important leaders.
8. Emphasizing accomplishments.
9. Creating and maintaining an "above-the-fray" posture.
10. Depending on surrogates for the campaign trail.
11. Interpreting and intensifying a foreign policy problem so that it becomes an international crisis.

Most of these tactics can be subdivided into a few basic tactics. In most cases, they revolve around the incumbent's use of his or her office to influence media attention upon them as individuals, influence the issue agenda of the press and the public, articulate and discuss those factors that have been a benefit to the voters, and increase support among elite opinion leaders.

Some of these tactics are available to nonincumbents, particularly those running for an open seat. Emphasizing accomplishments, such as lauding the amount of federal money brought home to a district, is a common tactic for incumbents, challengers, and open-seat candidates alike. Nearly all candidates for major offices also rely on surrogate campaigners, with family members or friends making appearances on their behalf. Such a tactic is essential given the time constraints on an individual candidate.

Tactics associated with challenger campaigns include (p. 94):

1. Attacking the record of opponents.
2. Taking the offensive position on issues.
3. Calling for a change.
4. Emphasizing optimism for the future.
5. Speaking to traditional values instead of calling for value changes.
6. Appearing to represent the philosophical center of the political party.
7. Delegating personal or harsh attacks in an effort to control demagogic rhetoric.

Trent and Friedenberg generally treat this list as strategy options. Consultants, though, are more likely to regard them as tactical options, that is, as specific moves that may be employed as part of a broader strategic plan. As we will see later, one common strategy for challenging an incumbent—The In Man–Out Man strategy—often uses two of these tactics ("Attacking the record of the opponent" and "delegating harsh attacks") plus one not mentioned by Trent and Friedenberg ("inoculation").

Situational Analysis

Agranoff (1976) discussed the effect of situations on campaign strategies and argued that campaigns can and should be planned, organized, and executed on the basis of a systematic strategy. As a guideline for situational analysis, Agranoff offered the following "Checklist for Strategic Assessment":

1. *Campaign resources.* All campaigns must confront the problems of how to most effectively deploy scarce resources. There is only so much time, so much money, and so much candidate energy that can be expended before election day.
2. *Campaign setting.* All campaigns operate within the confines of a given campaign setting, and that setting includes several factors that are relatively immutable (the campaign will not change) and several factors that are mutable (the campaign can change). The campaign should identify which factors can be changed, and direct their efforts at controlling them.
3. *Strategic assessment.* A crucial element in the overall strategic assessment is to meet three functions of campaigns: conversion (persuading voters to support a candidate), reinforcement (solidifying the commitment of supporters), and activation (getting out the vote). The campaign must draw strategic inferences from its possibilities, knowing that reinforcement and activation are much more likely than conversion.
4. *Planning.* The planning of campaign strategy depends on information and research. The campaign must know as much as possible about the constituency, the candidate, the opposition, and other crucial factors in the race. Campaign information includes both scientific data and political experience and judgment.
5. *Systematic strategy.* All of the above considerations must be integrated into a single, comprehensive, overall strategy. Once the elements of the strategy have been set, the remainder of the campaign should simply unfold according to the dictates of the master plan. The small, day-to-day decisions should be guided by the larger strategic plan.

Jackson (1977) noted that Agranoff sets up an "ideal type" for campaign management, but recognizes that even the best-managed campaigns will fall short of the ideal. He also views the campaign as an ongoing process that does not end with the election. This has evoked criticism, particularly as it applies to the U.S. Congress. Mayhew (1974) argues that congressional effectiveness is limited because the members of Congress are "single-minded seekers of re-election," a mind-set that results in a lack of concern for the programmatic impact of the legislative process. In its extreme form, Mayhew argues that every behavior—every speech, every press release, every roll call vote, every pork-barrel project—is undertaken primarily for the purpose of influencing voters with only an incidental concern for effective public policy or programs. Among the more serious consequences of this behavior are delays in legislation, the shaping of political deals, and efforts to develop symbolic but unproductive legislative acts and resolutions.

Still, for better or worse, it is clear that the political process does continue after elections if for no other reason than a public servant's actions in office become campaign fodder for the next election, as suggested by every analytical model discussed in this chapter. Also, it is the very nature of democracy for the electorate to vote out of office those who do not represent them adequately.

Two Strategic Models

The In Man–Out Man Strategy

The In Man–Out Man strategy (Kitchens & Stiteler, 1979; Powell, 1974), initially developed by Murray Chotiner, is designed for use against an incumbent. The campaign is based on the development of bipolar images for the incumbent (In Man) and the challenger (Out Man). From a CAT analysis perspective, the In Man–Out Man strategy is limited by one contingent condition: It only works when there are only two major contenders, the incumbent and the challenger. It is an ineffective strategy in multicandidate primaries or in general elections that have a serious third-party candidate. Its basic technique of developing bipolar images is effective only when the voters have an either/or choice; a multicandidate race allows a voter to vote against the incumbent without voting for the challenger using the strategy. Former Alabama lieutenant governor Bill Baxley got his start in politics by using the strategy to defeat an incumbent attorney general, an upset victory that was the impetus for a long political career. "People ask me when I knew that I had it won," he has said. "I knew that we had it won on the last day of qualifying when I was the only one to qualify against him, because I knew that we would then be able to implement our strategy."

One major assumption of the In Man–Out Man strategy is the role of negative voting. The primary emphasis of the strategy is to get the electorate to vote *against* the incumbent. As Chotiner said in describing the strategy, ". . . if you do not deflate the opposition candidate before your own candidate gets started, the odds are that you are going to be doomed to defeat." Thus the negative campaign against the incumbent is crucial to demonstrating differences between the challenger and the incumbent.

A second assumption of the In Man–Out Man strategy is the need for the challenger to be perceived as a viable alternative. Research has consistently demonstrated the presence of a proincumbent inertia among the electorate, particularly during good economic times. Thus a negative campaign against an incumbent is usually not, by itself, enough to defeat an incumbent. In the absence of a positive alternative, the probability increases that the voters will either support the incumbent or simply not vote at all. In either scenario, the challenger is likely to lose the election.

A third element of the strategy is the need to inoculate voters from counterattacks on the challenger. If an incumbent discovers that support is diminishing because of attacks from the challenger, the incumbent is likely to counterattack in an effort to stop the challenger's momentum. Inoculation would arrest the challenger's growing support.

The two reported analyses (Kitchens & Stiteler, 1979; Powell, 1974) of the In Man–Out Man strategy have both implemented the strategy in a three-stage developmental pattern, although the specifics of some stages varied slightly. In both studies, the first stage is

Interview with Robin Rorapaugh

A Numerical Approach to Campaign Strategy

> *Robin Rorapaugh was chief of staff for U.S. Representative Peter Deutch (Dem-Fla. Twentieth Congressional District). She has managed many political campaigns, including the 2000 campaign for Florida gubernatorial candidate Buddy MacKay.*

Q: When you undertake a political campaign, what do you do to determine a strategy for victory?

A: First, I try to figure out how many votes it is going to take to win. You can have a perfect campaign, a beautiful candidate, and whatnot, but if you haven't figured out what you need to win, you might fall short. Second, we determine a message that works well with the candidate. Numerous times you'll see candidates jump on the hot issue of the day, but it's not an issue they feel strongly about and you can tell it by their delivery. So, it becomes really important to talk to the client to determine why they are running for this office, what they hope to achieve, and where they are on the issues of the day. Then match that against polling data and figure out where they collide and where they work. Third, try to figure out where to get the money to do the communications to get to the vote total to win the election.

Q: How do you determine what the needed vote total will be?

A: You take voting history from previous elections that cover the same district and you basically bring an average of how many votes have been cast on those elections. You figure out where 50 percent plus one is, and then I usually add 5 percent. Particularly in a state like Florida, we have had low voter turnout in primaries for several cycles in a row, but a very hot turnout may bring it back to where it was in [19]'90 or '92. Also, how much growth has happened in voter registration? How much of that registration is motor voter and how much is actual registration? Sometimes, you will see a special interest group come in, like the Christian Coalition, and do massive voter registration. That is going to affect the Democrats' percentages in a general election. It takes a little snooping around to see who is doing what, and then just a little math to calculate what you need.

Q: Once you have determined how many votes you need, how do you decide how to communicate with them as part of your strategy?

A: You have to find out how voters are receiving their information. Traditionally, if you are running a statewide race, or a large multicounty race, television may be the best way to communicate with voters. But if you are running for a city council race, television is probably a waste of your money and door knocking and direct mail may make more sense. For example, in a Hispanic community they may receive their political information in a little different way than the Anglo community or the African American community. You have to know how people in these communities decide who they are going to vote for. In the smaller races, a lot of it has to do with the opinion leaders and their neighbors. It depends on the size of the race and which is the best way to communicate dollar for dollar and dollar for vote. And you can determine that through polling and previous voter history. In polling, there's a standard question, "Where do you receive your political news?"

Q: How do you determine, strategically, what message to deliver?

A: I favor comparing what the candidate feels strongly about and what the district feels strongly about and see where there is a crossing. Sometimes you will have a candidate who, no matter how popular HMO reform and the patient's bill of rights are, the candidate just doesn't agree. So, you can't have him out there campaigning on it although some people do try that.

Q: In the course of the campaign, do you have to review the strategy?

A: Absolutely. At some point in the campaign, the people have gotten it, they know where your candidate is on an issue, they may be wanting to hear something new and your issue may not be a cogent issue anymore. You should update your polling and focus groups every eight weeks so you can swab out your time line and everything else if it is needed. This is particularly important in the last ninety days because this is where you are going to spend the greatest portion of your campaign dollars.

Q: Is it important to have a formal strategy in written form?

A: A lot of it depends on the candidate. I think it should be formalized. It should be an integral part of the campaign plan with its attendant "to do lists," time lines, and budgets. I do it more formally than most.

Q: Who participates in the process of developing a strategy?

A: Ideally, you want the spouse, the consultants, the pollster, the best friend, the lawyer, and political friends of the campaign. The more involved they are in developing the strategy, the more vested they are in the campaign.

Q: Is there anything about strategy development that is widely misunderstood?

A: I think a lot of people confuse strategy with tactics. Strategy is what is the message that is going to get you to 50 percent plus one. Tactics are your best ways to communicate it . . . how you spend money to get it out. Tactics might change every week. Strategy is something that is affected by the whims of the voters but not overwhelmingly. You'd never ditch a strategy after only a month because it hasn't gotten you all you wanted.

Source: Reprinted by permission of Robin Rorapaugh.

---

an attack stage, but the source of the attack differed. One campaign (Powell, 1974) used attack messages delivered directly by the candidate, while the other (Kitchens & Stiteler, 1979) engaged the incumbent with third-party attacks, reducing the probability (or effectiveness) of a "mud-slinging" charge directed toward the challenger.

The second stage, positive image building, revolves around efforts to get the public to vote for the challenger (Assumption 2). Powell reported an implementation of this stage based on Social Judgment theory, that the campaign assumed that the voters lacked strong commitments to the incumbent. The positive messages for the challenger were designed to attract hard-to-reach voters. Kitchens and Stiteler reported using a media event (a 100-mile walk) to build the positive image.

The third stage, inoculation, was consistent in both reports. Both studies reported the use of McGuire's "threat-motivation" form of inoculation (McGuire & Papageorgis, 1961).

The challenger's supporters were alerted to the potential use of counter-persuasion tech-niques by the incumbent, identifying the possible source and type of the messages, and a reason for the attack. The latter served as a counterattitudinal response, which was designed to limit the effectiveness of the counterattack. In 1992, Eugene Reese, a young lawyer, ran for the Montgomery, Alabama, circuit court judgeship and combined all three elements into a single campaign motto: "The Best Judge Money Can't Buy!"

Assumed Incumbency Strategy

The Assumed Incumbency strategy (Powell & Shelby, 1981) recognizes the value of incumbency in some political campaigns. Incumbency provides automatic legitimacy, increases fund-raising potential, and usually results in the incumbent being considered the front-runner, or likely winner, early in a campaign (Trent & Friedenberg, 2000, pp. 79–82). The Assumed Incumbency strategy seeks to gain those same advantages by generating the perception that Candidate A is the natural choice to replace Incumbent B. The Assumed Incumbency strategy can be effective if three conditions are met: (1) the incumbent is not running for reelection, (2) the incumbent was popular, and (3) some link or argument can be established that Candidate A is the natural choice.

If those conditions are met, then the strategy assumes that direct confrontation between the candidate and the opposition should not occur, since such confrontation would bestow legitimacy on the opponent. Thus, the Assumed Incumbency model works from a candidate-to-issue confrontation, rather than a candidate-to-candidate perspective. The strategy also assumes that past voting behavior for the actual incumbent can serve as a base for establishing vote expectations (and targeting goals) for the assumed incumbent. And finally, the strategy dictates which media should be employed at what times to achieve these effects. Since the strategy progresses through the stages of legitimacy, identification, and reinforcement (discussed in the following paragraphs), the media associated with these pri-mary functions should be used at each stage of the strategy. Press coverage is the primary medium used during the legitimacy stage, because of the status-conferral ability of the press to bestow legitimacy on a candidate (Lazarsfeld & Morton, 1960). Billboards and signs are the primary medium for the identification stage because of their ability to increase name recognition. Finally, broadcast media were used in the reinforcement stage because of the need to communicate a message that needed reinforcement.

As a set of tactics, the Assumed Incumbency strategy is implemented through a three-stage developmental process—legitimacy, identification, and reinforcement. The legiti-macy stage is initially directed to opinion leaders, including the press. This select audience is presumed to already have some acquaintanceship with the candidate and is in a position to disseminate whatever message it receives. If a sufficient level of name recognition does not yet exist, preliminary identification work may be necessary, since voters are unlikely to bestow legitimacy on an unknown candidate. The goal of the legitimacy stage is to gener-ate expectations of the candidate as the front-runner, or likely winner. This goal is achieved with a rhetorical stance that identifies the candidate as the heir apparent or the natural choice for the position. This stage is comparable to Trent's (1978) "surfacing" stage in pres-idential politics, and its intent is to establish the candidate's qualifications for the office with the press. Legitimacy is a threshold that any campaign must reach before it has a chance of being successful. Jimmy Carter, for example, after winning the 1976 presidential election, mentioned several problems that he had had to overcome—being from the South, not being from Washington, a lack of campaign funds, and a weak campaign organization. Still, despite this list of problems, Carter noted that "The biggest problem I had . . . was substantiality of campaign efforts in the minds of the people. Nobody thought I should be taken seriously" (quoted in Schram, 1976, p. 7).

The successful completion of the legitimacy stage will provide an impetus for the second stage—identification. A by-product of status conferral from the press is increased public visibility and wider name recognition for the candidate. The candidate becomes a political celebrity and name recognition increases. Tactics shift to handle the change in goals; press coverage shifts from a focus on establishing legitimacy to one of maintaining one's name before the public. Press releases used during this phase typically announce activities that keep the candidate's name in the media (for example, serving as a guest speaker, receiving political honors, or working on current legislation or political problems). Those political media used primarily to increase name exposure, such as billboards, bumper stickers, signs, and posters, are introduced during this phase.

Increased name recognition leads to the third stage—reinforcement. If the initial stages of legitimacy and identification are successful, then a set of expectations about the candidate are generated. In the reinforcement stage, the campaign must reaffirm the candidate's legitimacy by meeting those expectations. The premise of legitimacy implies that a candidate is competent to hold a position and understands the problems to be faced. The rhetorical stance in this stage, then, is characterized by competency coupled with empathy.

These three stages—legitimacy, identification, and reinforcement—serve as rhetorical guidelines as well as the messages themselves. The value of the messages associated with these stages is supported by Fenno's (1978) analysis of elements essential to building positive voter response—qualification, identification, and empathy. In the Assumed Incumbency model, legitimacy is the initial goal that provides the impetus for communicating these concepts. In 1991, Richard Ieyoub was a candidate for attorney general of Louisiana running in a crowded field to replace a retiring, well-known, and well-liked incumbent. He adopted the motto, "The Only Prosecutor in the Race," and progressed through all three phases.

Three Traditional Models

While new strategic models seemingly arise with each new election, three traditional models for campaign strategies have been around for years: (1) the Easy Decision strategy developed by Stephen Shadegg, (2) the Ticket-Splitting strategy developed by DeVries and Tarrance, and (3) Joseph Napolitan's Least Objectionable Candidate. These three models are important because each makes different assumptions about subgroups of the electorate, particularly in terms of what types of voters make up the critical "swing groups" who decide elections and how those voters are reached with campaign messages.

The Easy Decision

Stephen Shadegg (1972) advocated a multipurpose campaign strategy aimed at making the voting decision an easy one. According to Shadegg, the voting public consists of three

Case Study: The Shelby Campaign

The Assumed Incumbency strategy was developed and implemented for Richard Shelby's 1978 campaign for Congress. Shelby, now a Republican U.S. senator from Alabama, was a Democrat at the time and defeated two other candidates in the Democratic primary to win the post.

The strategy was developed after polling data indicated that incumbent Congressman Walter Flowers, who was vacating the seat to run for the Senate, was the most popular politician in the district. As Flowers's former law partner, Shelby had a direct link to the incumbent that could be used to establish credibility with both the voters and financial contributors. A campaign slogan ("Keep strong leadership") was developed that would serve as an indirect allusion to voter perception that Flowers had done a good job.

The first stage of the active campaign process ("legitimacy") involved individual meetings with press representatives and opinion leaders, a program that successfully generated press coverage and the perception of Shelby as the front-runner in the campaign. That was followed by an identification campaign in which billboards, signs, and bumper stickers were used to expand Shelby's name recognition to a larger voter population. Finally, a round of reinforcement messages touted Shelby's position on a range of issues, including print ads on the need for a balanced federal budget ("Today let's save half a billion dollars") and a television ad touting his experience in the state senate.

Shelby led the first election with 49 percent of the vote, and won the runoff with nearly 60 percent.

Source: Powell, L., & Shelby, A. (1981). A strategy of assumed incumbency: A case study. *Southern Speech Communication Journal, 46,* pp. 105–23.

distinct subgroups—the "committed," the "undecideds," and the "indifferents." The committed voters are those "strongly prejudiced toward one party or another," and few campaign messages are targeted toward them. Undecided voters, he argues, are "frequently those who are truly best informed. They recognize that sometimes only slight shades of gray separate two candidates . . . (and) they frequently find it difficult to make a decision." The crucial swing voters, he argues, are the indifferents, "those who don't vote at all, or vote only in response to an emotional appeal or as the result of some carefully planned campaign technique [that] makes it easy for them to reach a decision." Their votes are based more on emotion than reason, he added. "Political decisions are made by the indifferents," he wrote, "that segment of the body politic [that] really couldn't care less."

To reach these voters, Shadegg recommends strategies that sharpen the differences between candidates. "These differences may have no real bearing upon the candidate's competence. But if they can be displayed in such a fashion as to be easily recognizable, the indifferents will show their gratitude for this assistance by voting." Shadegg admits that such decisional factors may have little direct reference to the issues of the campaign. "Political campaigns generate and fatten on a certain type of hysteria . . . ," he wrote. "In contests where it is sometimes difficult to find a truly major difference between competing candidates, the voter is almost forced to rest his decision upon some relatively unimportant difference."

Ticket-Splitting

DeVries and Tarrance (1972) take an entirely different perspective, arguing that the crucial swing vote in elections are ticket splitters, those voters who vote for both Democratic and Republican candidates in the same election cycle. Furthermore, their perception of this swing vote differs from that of Shadegg's indifferent voter. DeVries and Tarrance describe the ticket splitter as "slightly younger, somewhat more educated, somewhat more white collar, and more suburban than the typical middle-class voter." In addition, the ticket splitter tends to consume more media output about politics and is more politically active than the straight Democrat (but less so than straight Republicans). As described by DeVries and Tarrance, the ticket splitter is not a one-issue voter and cannot be easily reached by highly emotional approaches. Instead, this swing voter is viewed as a complex voter, knowledgeable about campaign issues, and oriented toward problem solving by candidates instead of by political parties.

The implementation of the ticket-splitting strategy reflects the importance placed on these assumptions about the profile of the ticket-splitting voter. Media buys are based on the probability of ticket-splitting behavior (based on voting analysis from past elections). For example, the ticket-splitting broadcast media strategy may focus heavily on newscasts and sporting events, since ticket splitters watch more of those kinds of shows than the average voter. Campaign messages are designed to reflect the issue-oriented, problem-solving emphasis preferred by the ticket splitter. The focus is on providing the voter with information. DeVries and Tarrance even suggest a format for the ideal ad aimed at a ticket splitter: "Present the problem, demonstrate an understanding and ability to handle that problem, and end with a soft-sell editorial."

Ticket-splitting behavior can be easily identified by using both polling and analyses of past voting behavior. As a result, ticket-splitting analysis has become a standard procedure in many campaigns. Still, questions have been raised about the accuracy of DeVries and Tarrance's profile of this voter, such as, Were the data that formed the basis of their conclusion campaign specific or could it be expanded to other campaigns? Initially, DeVries and Tarrance assumed the profile was highly accurate for most campaigns. That supposition seemed to be supported when they ran subsequent campaigns that identified similar profiles for these swing voters.

Doubt was raised in the mid-1970s, however, when Mississippi Republican Gil Carmichael ran a U.S. Senate campaign. Although Carmichael lost to Democratic incumbent James Eastland, Carmichael was successful in getting a significant number of ticket-splitting votes from Mississippi's rural areas—an outcome that went against the traditional profile (Powell & Flick, 1982). Further doubts were cast on the traditional profile when Ronald Reagan ran for president, getting significant support from rural Democrats in the South. More recently, an examination of ticket-splitting behavior in Florida (Kitchens & Powell, 1994) added more data to the doubts, concluding that ticket-splitting was a by-product of campaign communication rather than a trait representative of any particular type of voter. That conclusion assumes that the profile of the so-called typical ticket splitter is likely to change with every election, depending on which groups are targeted for campaign communication.

These instances have been sufficient to cast doubt on the ticket-splitting strategy, particularly among academicians. Still, while the academic community has largely given up on this approach, it still has a major impact on campaigns. Both parties regularly conduct studies on the phenomenon, particularly at the state level. In some places (Florida, for example), the studies have broadened the base of knowledge on ticket splitting down to the precinct, carrier route, and voting box level. Thus, ticket-splitting is one of those rare academic areas in which the consultants have more detailed information than do most academicians. Unfortunately for the academic community, though, this information is closely guarded and used for strategic purposes.

The Least Objectionable Candidate

Shadegg, DeVries, and Tarrance are all Republicans, and their campaign strategies reflected their Republican heritage of looking for an edge that will increase the chances for their candidates. Although there are differences in the campaigns, both assume the need for defining a distinct image for their candidate, one that makes their candidate appear to be the best choice for the voters. Democratic consultant Joseph Napolitan (1972) offered a different approach, arguing that voters do not support their ideal "best" candidate, but merely choose the one who is "the least objectionable." Candidates win, he believes, not because they appeal to the most voters, but because they offend the fewest.

Adherents to this strategy believe that elections are decided by moderates, a group of voters who are neither extremely conservative nor extremely liberal. Any candidate who is identified too strongly on either side of the ideological perspective is likely to lose. Operationally, this leads to campaigns that use generalized messages, overladen with equivocations. Messages are created that can be interpreted by the voter in a manner consistent with the voter's own position. It can also lead to bland campaigns in which the candidate is accused of not taking a firm position on issues. But, if the candidate has still offended only a few, Napolitan would argue that they are in a position to win the election.

Positional Strategies

One approach to strategy development relies on positional rhetoric to distinguish the candidate from the opposition. While each can have its own distinctive elements, most of these approaches are variations of Shadegg's Easy Decision model. In each case, the purpose of the positional strategy is to define a position that will make it easy for the voters to make a decision that favors the candidate. The variations of this approach are too numerous for all of them to be included, but three variations can serve as examples: the "Only Alternative," "Role Definition," and Triangulation strategies.

The Only Alternative, or the "Anybody But Them" approach, attempts to position the candidate as the only viable alternative to an unpopular opponent. When there are only two candidates in the campaign, this approach usually becomes a negative campaign, which is similar to the In Man–Out Man approach. What typically makes it different is the absence of any comparative messages. The messages focus instead on negative factors related to the opponent, with little or no positive messages about the candidate provided. Strategically, that can be a risky gamble; a lack of positive information about candidates can keep voters away from the polls, rather than attract them toward the only alternative.

Another scenario for this approach occurs during the primary nomination process. Although several candidates may officially be on the ballot, one candidate will sometimes campaign on the basis of being the only "viable alternative" for defeating the nominee of the other party. In this instance, the focus of the campaign messages is on the legitimacy or credibility factors of the campaign, rather than the issues. The argument becomes, "Vote for me, because I can defeat the other guy," rather than "Vote for me because I represent your issues."

The Role Definition strategy attempts to gain an advantage with the voters by defining the candidate as an "ideal candidate" (Nimmo & Savage, 1976) for the office being sought. For example, if polling data reveal that the voters' ideal candidate is one who is a problem solver, then the role-definition strategy would try to develop an image of the candidate as either the "only" problem solver among the contenders, or at least the "best" problem solver in the race. The specific nature of the ideal role can vary with each campaign or position, but the overall goal remains the same—the candidate whose image comes closest to the ideal has the best chance of winning the election. The 1990 campaign for attorney general of Alabama is the prototype for the Role Definition strategy. In that campaign, three different candidates were running for the position, but only one of them had experience as a prosecutor. That candidate ran a campaign based on "the-only-one-who-has-prosecuted-criminals" argument and won the election.

When the candidate of a political party finds that winning a political campaign—or even advancing significantly—will be extremely difficult for social, cultural, or even more abstract reasons, he or she may resort to a strategy of triangulation. This approach creates a distraction, which can reduce the number of votes cast for an opponent. Typically, these votes may be deflected to a third candidate or be dissuaded from being cast at all. Perhaps a burning issue may be raised that engenders support from groups that change their customary voting habits. In the days before campaign finance disclosure, straw candidates were recruited by some major candidates to siphon votes away from their opposition. Although this probably happened less than charged, there is no doubting its effectiveness. The emergence of effective third-party candidates (especially H. Ross Perot) replicates the straw candidate effect in recent years.

The strategy can be used, however, without the presence of a third candidate, if an issue or message can be identified that separates the candidate from traditional ties and allows them to siphon votes from demographic targets that were previously hard to reach. In 1985, for example, Virginia State Senator Douglas Wilder was running against Marshall Coleman for the governorship. As a liberal African American in a state with less than 20 percent of the electorate also African American, Wilder had little chance of winning without attracting the support of white voters who typically held moderate or conservative views. Wilder handled the problem by challenging Coleman on the issue of abortion and making it the focus of his campaign. Most of Wilder's television advertising budget was expended on the topic. Republican women voters, particularly in populous northern Virginia, deserted Coleman in sufficient numbers to secure Wilder his victory.

Most famously, following recommendations from political consultant Dick Morris, triangulation became a major buzzword for the presidential campaigns of Bill Clinton. In 1992, Clinton attempted to demonstrate his independence from Jesse Jackson. Before a meeting with Jackson, Clinton criticized a rap singer, Sister Souljah, for being an irresponsible leader of African American youth. White voters took this as a signal that Clinton would be his own man, not beholden to any group, unlike their sense of his Democratic opponents, and helped him beat Jackson and his other rivals for the nomination.

Summary

The study of campaign strategy often seems to have a dual personality, with academicians looking at it objectively and practitioners searching for strategic advantages. Even within the campaign, such dual viewpoints will occur. Hershey (1974) noted that candidates and their campaign managers often view the campaign differently. Part of those different perceptions is due to the differences in role specification, and part from the greater amount of ego involvement demonstrated by the candidate. Still, that dual personality often makes it harder to pin down the specifics of a campaign strategy.

From inside the campaign, the development of a campaign strategy is a precampaign activity. Candidates, their staff, and their consultants develop the campaign plan in advance, using it as a road map for organizing and executing campaign tactics. For academicians, analysis of campaign strategies are more often postelection activities. Unless the particular academic researcher was personally involved in a campaign, they may lack the information necessary to view the strategy as a precampaign activity. And, even if they did have such information, most scholars would wait until after the election to report their conclusions about the strategy. Either way, the dual nature of campaign strategies persist. For consultants, strategies are early campaign decisions. For academicians, strategies are postcampaign analyses.

Furthermore, communication scholars have only recently begun to examine the persuasive implications of some political campaign strategies. Campaign consultants, meanwhile, use specific, if less formalized, strategies to guide their own activities. Although not always developed to a theoretical level, strategies function both as comprehensive plans and decisional models for campaigns. By suggesting an overall framework for a campaign, political communication strategies provide a means of plotting campaign development. As decisional models, they offer a basis for adaptive decision making in responding to events as they occur during a campaign.

Discussing all possible strategies is a task that goes beyond the scope of this book, but those discussed here provide a foundation of basic models. In real life, consultants develop their own hybrid strategy for each campaign, but most of those hybrids are combinations of those mentioned in this chapter. Thus, there are thousands of possible strategies, although most are only minor variations of the archetypes presented here. Most start with some form of strategic analysis, such as the "Who'll Say What" or SWOT analysis, which serves as a framework for helping the consultant develop the strategy. Understanding those approaches and how they are used by consultants can also serve to help academicians analyze campaign strategies.

QUESTIONS FOR DISCUSSION

1. Consider a recent local election in your area. What was the campaign strategy of the winner? Of the loser? Was one candidate slated to win regardless of strategy, or did the strategic moves of the campaign make the difference between winning and losing?

2. What is the difference between strategy and tactics. What is the first step in developing either?

3. Why is it advantageous for a political campaign to have a strategy?

4. A U.S. senator who is finishing his first term is the target of a grand jury investigation, but has already raised enough money to run a viable campaign. Design a strategy for this candidate to follow. What would be a good strategy for the opponent to follow?

5. Some strategists and communicators consider ticket splitters to be the key group in finding support among persuadable voters. Why? What strategic notion might appeal to a ticket splitter?

6. What is the relationship between the elements of strategy and the various stages of communications?

4 The Image of the Political Candidate

In the presidential election of 1948, President Harry Truman was the leader of a splintered Democratic party and faced primary opposition from both a progressive candidate (Henry Wallace) and the "Dixiecrats," represented by Strom Thurmond. After bargaining to retain the party's nomination, he then faced strong Republican opposition from Thomas E. Dewey. Most observers—and most polls at the time—were confident that Dewey would easily defeat the besieged Truman.

Rather than combat that image, Truman took advantage of it. He openly ran as the underdog, telling audiences, "My name's Harry Truman, I work for the government, and I'm trying to keep my job." The approach redefined his image in terms of humility, toughness, and identification with the common person. Dewey, meanwhile, was increasingly seen as slick and urban, "the little man on the top of the wedding cake," as Alice Roosevelt Longworth described him (Combs, 1980, p. 151). Facing those sharp contrasts in images, the voters sided with Truman in an upset victory, one that helped illustrate the impact that candidate images can have on electoral results (Klapp, 1964).

A candidate's image is often the focus of the campaign message as it is amplified for television ads, phone banks, and direct mail. But some observers criticize consultant-based campaigns for focusing on images and relegating issues to the electoral woodshed. The consequence, their argument goes, is that voter decisions are inevitably based on shallow and emotional impressions rather than a rational understanding of candidates and their positions on issues. Consultants often maintain that image-based campaigns appeal to real voter concerns. Moreover, many consultants say that without meeting such image thresholds, voters will not give weight to issue-oriented discussions, since issues and images are often interlinked. Additionally, many consultants believe that unless a candidate can establish a strong personality in a campaign context, voters will not believe that he or she has the tools needed to perform as a political leader in a pluralistic democracy.

The very nature of the controversy has led to extensive academic investigations into the nature of political images. One classic work, by Nimmo and Savage (1976), examined and summarized much of that research up to the mid-1970s. Their work, in turn, spurred other academicians to investigate the concept further. The resulting data are sometimes confusing, given that individual researchers have approached the field with their own code-specific terminology. Understanding that research requires a synthesization of results by looking at studies that have identified similar concepts, although perhaps using different terminology. Most research studies on political images can be divided into one of four general research questions:

1. What is the nature of candidate images?
2. How are such images developed?
3. What influence does the campaign have on the candidates' images? and
4. What influence does the candidate's image have on electoral decisions?

The Nature of Candidate Images

Nimmo and Savage (1976) defined an image as "a human construct imposed on an array of perceived attributes projected by an object, event, or person" (p. 8). This definition views candidate images as multifaceted phenomena with several key dimensions and identifiable modes of orientation. That description implies that the very nature of political images is a complex psychological element that could potentially be described in any number of ways, depending on the viewpoint of the observer. Not surprisingly, that is what has happened in the academic community, as different researchers have described the nature of images in different ways.

Some scholars view the political candidate as an orator whose utterances can be analyzed with theories that go back to the work of Aristotle. From that perspective, the key components of an image are the trustworthiness of the candidates, their authoritativeness on the issues of the day, and the extent to which their rhetoric indicates good intentions toward the audience. That approach was easily adaptable to public debate within the early days of American democracy. Subsequently, several researchers have attempted to describe the nature of public images in an era of mass communication. McCroskey, Jensen, and Todd (1972) recommended a five-factor breakdown for images of public figures: character, competence, sociability, composure, and extroversion. The first two—character and competence—conformed to two of Aristotle's original factors (trustworthiness and authoritativeness), but the other three assume that images conveyed by way of mass media can be multifaceted.

Another approach that considers the interplay between the mass media and images is the concept of the television personality (Lang & Lang, 1968). This approach identifies the political image as a three-factor design composed of television performance, political role, and personal image. A similar perspective is the view that the candidate as a political actor is concerned with two basic dimensions, a political role and a stylistic role (Graber, 1972). Campbell (1966) preferred to eliminate the stylistic role and discuss the image as a composite of four characteristics: background and experience, leadership ability, personal qualifications, and policy stands.

The American Institute for Political Communication, or AIPC (1970), offered a five-dimensional approach: leadership ability, political philosophy, speaking ability, intelligence, and honesty. Its unique contribution to the image is perhaps the third dimension, a recognition that communication skills play an important role in image formation. The nature of television has amplified the importance of one's speaking ability because of the intimate and instant nature of communications in today's world.

The approach used most often by consultants was offered decades ago by Trenaman and McQuail (1961). They viewed the political image as composed of three major components: leadership strength; judgment as a person (having enough humility and integrity); and disposition toward voters (having empathy). This appears to be the approach that comes closest to the consultants on images. Although the terminology used is slightly different, most consultants view the ideal candidate as a strong leader who will lead the voters, a person of integrity who will be honest with the voters, and an empathic person who understands the voters. In fact, it is hard to imagine a successful candidate who did not exemplify these attributes. In particular, academic research on presidential candidates has focused heavily on leadership (Barber, 1964) and character (Barber, 1972), with the ethical controversies of the Clinton administration focusing attention on both elements.

Furthermore, this three-dimensional approach has been somewhat supported by academic research. Researchers into ideal images have identified a hierarchical image type of the ideal public official as political hero (Trenaman & McQuail, 1961, pp. 163–164). The ideal political hero was identified as being first, a strong leader; second, a person of integrity; and third, an empathic person who was perceived as understanding the voters. The only discrepancy from the consultants' three-dimensional approach was that this research also identified a fourth dimension that sometimes came into play—the candidate as hard worker. Most political consultants agree with this fourth dimension; they find it hard to imagine voters choosing a candidate who projected an image of being something other than "hard working."

This approach is also consistent with some traditional approaches to rhetorical theory. Garver (1994), in his examination of Aristotle's rhetorical theories, noted the importance of a speaker integrating logic and character. He emphasized the applications of Aristotle's classic work to modern situations in which an effective speaker understands the importance of both practical reason and virtue in presenting a case to the public. While the terminology may be different, the concept is similar. Modern politicians should be honest with the voters and work to implement reasonable ideas as public policy. The public wants, Garver might argue, a person of character who does the job well.

An alternative view of ideal images suggests that a voter's perception of an ideal candidate will differ in accord with the partisanship and other predispositions of individual voters. Miller and Shanks (1996, p. 501) argued that ". . . the very large bivariate relationships between personal evaluations and vote choice can be traced primarily to the impact on both variables of partisan identification and other predispositions and performances, rather than to the impact on the vote of the candidates' personal qualities per se." Elsewhere they note, this approach does not necessarily "minimize the evidence of consequences of a campaign so much as it recasts the role of the campaign. The selling of a president may still be possible, but the creation of an appealing image would seem to be necessarily based on relatively enduring pre-existing predispositions" (p. 506).

The ideal candidate for one voter may not be the same for another. Research on this matter has identified four distinct and different ideal types (Nimmo & Savage, 1976, p. 68). These four ideal types—the decision maker, the empathic leader, the moral exemplar, and the partisan advocate—are frequently identified in terms of a particular emphasis on one of the four characteristics identified earlier. The decision maker focuses on the candidate's leadership skills and decision-making activities. The empathic leader understands the voters, putting the public ahead of partisan politics. The moral exemplar is a leader of integrity and conviction, a person of reason who articulates his or her convictions. The only ideal type that does not fit the three-dimensional ideal image is that of the partisan advocate. The ideal partisan advocate is honest, but not necessarily empathic; furthermore, such types often reject the idealism of the moral exemplar, particularly if the candidate's ideals are extreme.

The Development of Candidate Images

Questions about the nature of candidate images inevitably lead to additional questions about how voters develop these images? That question has inspired a number of studies into the psychology of image formation, which, in turn, has led to a multitude of possible theories. In fact, nearly any psychological theory related to attitude development or impression formation can be applied to image.

Attribution theory (Heider, 1958; Kelley, 1967; Shaver, 1983) would ascribe image formation to the attributions that voters attach to candidates whom they support and oppose. In such instances, factors such as partisanship and ideology become dimensional antecedents that influence those attributions. Thus conservatives are likely to attribute conservative ideologies to the candidates of their choice, while labeling the opposition as liberal. Perceptual Balance theory argues that images are developed as voters process information about candidates and their position on issues in relationship to the individual voter's own position on such issues. Again, partisanship and ideology are factors used in the psychological synthesis to attain an image that is perceptually balanced for the individual. This leads to voters perceiving in candidates what is favorable to themselves while distorting or ignoring that which is unfavorable. Similarly, advocates of dissonance theory argue that images are a form of psychological rationalization, a process that helps the voter justify a behavioral decision to vote for or against a particular candidate.

Image formation can also be applied to Social Judgment theory. In this approach, the various issue positions and ideological views taken by a candidate are evaluated by the voter in terms of whether those stances were acceptable or unacceptable to the voter. A perception that the candidate's position was similar to that of the voter would trigger a process of assimilation, with the voter forming a positive perceptual image of the candidate. In that case, the voter's image of the candidate would likely include distortions of the candidate's actual position on issues, perceiving the candidate's views to be more similar to their own than they actually are. Conversely, if a candidate's ideological position was at odds with those of the voter, then that candidate would be viewed as unacceptable and an image formed viewed the candidate as more extreme and further away from the ideal of that particular voter.

But regardless of which theory is advocated, some elements remain consistent, including the interrelationship of information about the candidates and the voters' interpretations of those data. As Nimmo and Savage (1976) noted, ". . . a candidate's image is as much a function of what people project to him as of his efforts to project to them" (p. 10). Thus candidates' images consist of how they are perceived by voters, based on both the subjective knowledge possessed by voters and the messages projected by the candidate. The voters use information and perceptions about the candidate to form affective (positive-negative) evaluations that may affect their electoral behavior. Cognition, evaluation, and behavioral manifestations are the factors that outline the essential elements of the image process.

Cognition

Nimmo and Savage (1976) noted that all images have a cognitive element that reflects those portions of a candidate's image that are treated as facts by the voter. These elements are the ones that voters regard as true or false. For example, former president George H. W. Bush is a Republican who fought in World War II as a fighter pilot, served as head of the CIA, and was vice president under Ronald Reagan. Such facts are what a typical voter could know about Bush, but what any given voter knows may vary significantly from what another voter knows. Some voters might remember that he was vice president, for example, but not remember his association with the CIA. Other voters might know other facts about Bush that are even more extensive than what the first group knows (for example, knowing that he played baseball at Yale). All such cognitions—whether accurate or inaccurate—would contribute to a person's total image of George H. W. Bush.

Evaluations

Based on the information (both accurate and inaccurate) that the voter has about a candidate, the voters are then in a position to form an evaluative, positive-or-negative, opinion about that candidate. Describing that process depends upon which of the earlier-mentioned psychological theories you follow, but some elements seem to be common to all theories. The voters apply what they know, understand, and believe about candidates to form inferences about the candidates' ideological, partisan, and moral values. Those perceptions are then compared to a voter's own beliefs. To the extent that a state of homophily (McCroskey, Richmond, & Daly, 1975), or similarity exists, then the voter is likely to form a positive opinion of that candidate. To the extent that there is a difference between the perceived values of the candidate and those of the voter, then a state of hetereophily (nonsimilarity) exists, and the voter is likely to form a negative opinion. This evaluative dimension is the easiest for pollsters to gauge during a campaign, with polls that ascertain favorability ratings or some other form of positive or negative responses that measure both the direction and strength of the voters' affective evaluations of the candidate.

Behavioral Manifestations

The ultimate goal of a political campaign is to have an image with the voters that will result in at least one positive behavioral manifestation (voting). In some cases, a voter's behavioral manifestation may be stronger than an affective image; voters may choose a candidate they do not know or have any opinion about, for a variety of reasons (party orientation, positive response to the person's name, a "favorite son" connection, a common ethnic background, and so forth). Still, in most major campaigns, voting behavior is a result of evaluative images, with the voter more likely to cast a vote for that candidate for whom they have the highest positive rating, or the least negative rating.

Voting, though, is not the only behavioral manifestation associated with a candidate's image. The images of some candidates can trigger a variety of behaviors, ranging from volunteer work on behalf of the campaign or a candidate's cause to an attempt to assassinate the candidate. Some candidates (perhaps with the assistance of their political consultants) seem to be more adept at image manipulation than others, motivating their impassioned followers to donate time, effort, and money to the cause. Others are content to convey milder images to attract a mass following of voters.

What is not fully known, however, is the extent to which behavioral manifestations are a result of candidate image development, and how much is a by-product of the personality of the candidate's followers. During the 1992 presidential election, for example,

Reform candidate H. Ross Perot spurred millions of voters to volunteer for his campaign, distribute literature on his behalf, and actively campaign across the nation. The question remains, however, as to how many of these people were actually inspired just by Perot's rhetoric. Did they engage in such activity because they were swayed by Perot's arguments, or did Perot's image attract a personality type that was more likely to engage in political activity? An example might be drawn by comparing political supporters to audiences at musical concerts. The crowd at a rock concert behaves in a manner that is different from an audience at an opera. But, are the differences in audience behavior a result of the kind of music being played, or does the different kind of music attract a different kind of audience member. The answer is likely to be some combination of both factors, but the nature of that interrelationship needs further analysis.

Image Influences on Election Decisions

Research has consistently reported that candidates' images play a crucial role in voting behavior. Voters respond to candidates on the basis of the images they have of them. Voters are more likely to vote for a candidate for whom they have a positive image, than one for whom they have a negative image. In essence, voters prefer to vote for somebody they like, and that "liking" dimension is heavily influenced by the image they hold of that candidate. It's not always an easy decision, though. Sometimes dissonance exists because the voter has a positive image of all of the candidates, or a negative image of them all; in those cases, relative evaluations come into play, with the voter generally opting for the most positive or least negative option.

Attempting to influence voting decisions without affecting a candidate's image is relatively futile. If a positive image component can be established with a majority of the voters, then vote intention is likely to follow; if not, it can be enhanced by a variety of get-out-the-vote efforts. But such voter turnout programs are doomed to failure if a positive image dimension has not been established.

Consultants assume that the campaign can have an impact on a candidate's image. Furthermore, the academic community tends to agree with this conclusion. Granted, some academicians believe the mass media do not directly contribute to changes in voting intentions. Most of them, however, do not attempt to extend that argument to the images of those candidates. Regardless of its ultimate impact on behavior, the mass media affect what people know about candidates, how they perceive candidates, and how they feel about them. For example, McClure and Patterson (1974) found that televised network news had little impact, but exposure to political advertising had a direct impact on voters' beliefs about the candidates.

The impact of a negative opinion is particularly important, for two reasons. First, a negative feeling toward the candidate of the voter's preferred party can override the impact of partisanship among moderate partisans. Second, negative images tend to be more precisely defined by the voters than are positive ones. Powell (1977) found that most voters could identify only one or two positive dimensions (usually a holistic "good guy" label) about candidates they supported, but they could provide multiple reasons for the candidate they voted against. Clearly, this may be the intended outcome for a campaign that projects a negative image about its opponent both directly and indirectly. A campaign may brag, for example, that its candidate is "The best judge money can't buy."

Interview with Mike McClister

Image in a Narrative Format

Mike McClister, a Democratic media consultant, was professionally involved in some 200 political campaigns, including the presidential campaigns of Lyndon Johnson, Robert Kennedy, Hubert Humphrey, and Jimmy Carter. His other clients included senators Max Baucus, Jim Sasser, and Richard Stone; governors Jim Blanchard, Booth Gardner, and Fob James; U.S. representatives James McClure Clarke, Norman Sisisky, and Gladys Spellman; and the Democratic National Committee. Before establishing his own media firm, McClister was executive vice president of Matt Reese and Associates, one of the nation's first political consulting firms. In 1992, McClister retired from politics to write novels.

Q: What do you consider when thinking about the image of a candidate?

A: I don't like the term "image." That's something that commercial ad agencies talk about, not political agencies. To me, it conveys an idea of something that's contrived as opposed to real. "Image building" is a commercial concept. In politics, you can't just create an image, because you can't get away from who the candidate already is. Instead, you take the candidate, find out who and what he is, or she is, and that's what you use. No candidate enters the campaign with a blank slate. They've got a background—a record and some type of experience—and you've got to work with that background. Even if the candidate is a businessperson with no political experience, he's got a background that has to be acknowledged and used.

Q: How do you use it?

A: That gets to the difference between "telling" and "showing." If you *tell* voters things, they usually don't accept them, or they'll be reluctant. *Show* them things, maybe they will. An "image building" ad tries to *tell* the voters that a candidate has a specific image. If they want the candidate viewed as a leader, they tell the voters that the candidate is a leader. If they want the voters to think the candidate is tough on crime, they tell them he's tough on crime. I don't think that works as well as showing people that the candidate is a leader, or showing that the candidate is tough on crime.

Q: How do you do that?

A: I use stories. I'm a storyteller, that's really what I am, I sit down and talk with the candidate, and I look for the most interesting stories I can find, regardless of what so-called image might be desired. The image has to be the reality, or a reasonable inference from reality, and you get that from specific stories. I remember once that I spent hours with Gladys Spellman in Maryland, trying to get some stories from her. I never did get anything I could use, but finally somebody on the staff said, "We ought to tell you about the midnight phone call." They told me about a time during the Sixties when a group of radical students took over a university administration building late one night. The university negotiated with them, trying to get them to leave, but the only thing that the two sides could agree on was that they would listen to Gladys as an arbitrator. They called her at midnight, and she went to the university and resolved the problem. That incident never even made the newspaper; it happened late at night and was resolved before the next day. But it said something about what type of leader she was. I created an ad called "The Midnight Phone Call." I still remember the opening line: "Sometimes Gladys

Spellman's phone rings in the middle of the night." That was *showing* people she was a leader, not just telling them.

Q: When you think of the three basic areas of an image as defined by some academicians—integrity, leadership, and empathy—which do you consider to be the most important one?

A: They all are. If I was forced to choose one, it would probably be leadership. But I don't even think that way. I just try to tell a story about a candidate, with the story telling something about what the candidate is like and who he is or she is. And I don't try to figure out if that message is about integrity, leadership, or empathy. If it's done right, it's all three. You can't separate them. Separating them is something academics will do so they can talk about it in class, but that's just an abstraction. People in academics need to go downtown and spend a little time in a campaign headquarters. We're not dealing with abstractions; we're dealing with real people and real voters. When I make a political ad, I don't think of it as addressing an abstraction. I don't take it that way, and I don't think the voters do either.

Q: How do the voters take it?

A: They take it at face value. They see an ad, and they respond to what it says and what it conveys. It becomes part of the information that they use in making their voting decision. It is assimilated into their world in a manner that makes sense to them. But they bring their own predispositions against advertising generally and political advertising specifically; so in political media, we've got two strikes against us when we step up to the plate.

Q: How does the concept of image fit into that?

A: Image is truth with its best foot forward. The candidate is what he is. You have to start with what's real; you can put it in the best possible light, but it has to be real; it has to be the truth. If it's not, either the press or the opponent will point it out, and that kills you. The idea of creating an image just doesn't work. In 1986, for example, when I was working for Charlie Graddick in Alabama, we had one ad in which Charlie held up his young daughter, giving her a kiss at the end. The campaign people loved that ad; once we put it on, they wanted us to keep it on. But the polling data showed that it didn't work, and we took it off the air. It didn't work because it was "image building," not storytelling. It didn't say anything about the candidate that was believable or of concern to the voters. But most of the people in the campaign wanted us to keep it on the air. The conventional wisdom of the campaign said it was the perfect ad, but conventional wisdom is nearly always wrong. It was that time, too.

Q: What do you mean, "conventional wisdom is nearly always wrong"?

A: One problem that a consultant has to cope with in a campaign is conventional wisdom. The candidates or their supporters want to do things the way they've seen other people do it. And they're overly sensitive to everything because they know the candidate personally. And they think they can judge the effectiveness of a TV spot because they're "in" politics. So you get what I call a "headquarters mentality" that is often completely isolated from the voters' mentality or the voters' reality—and this can occur despite the best efforts of the pollster. I try to stay away from headquarters because it is a corrupting influence on my job. I'd rather hang out with voters.

Source: Reprinted by permission of Mike McClister.

Finally, the nature of the impact that the campaign has on an image may depend on the type of media employed and/or the nature of the candidate's personal qualities. After the 1952 election, some analysts suggested that television improved Dwight Eisenhower's image, but did little for his opponent, Adlai Stevenson; conversely, Stevenson seemed to benefit by radio coverage of the campaign. Others have made similar arguments about the 1960 Kennedy-Nixon debates, where Kennedy was perceived as having done better among television audiences, while Nixon was perceived as the winner by radio audiences. For that reason, consultants may alter image-related messages on the basis of the nature of the campaign, the candidate, and the opponent.

Campaign Influences on Images

The impact of candidate images on campaigns is widely accepted and sometimes hotly debated. Sometimes overlooked, however, is the opposite phenomenon—the impact of the campaign on the candidates' images. The possibility, even probability, that the campaign can have such an influence justifies the existence of political consultants. Consultants work within the campaign environment, working with verbal and visual messages, in an attempt to enhance the image of their candidate. At the same time, the opposition's campaign is engaged in similar activity on behalf of its candidate.

Many of the campaign factors that contribute to the candidate's image, however, are outside the control of both the candidates and their consultants. A candidate has little control over the campaign messages of the opponent, much of which could be negative information that could adversely affect an image. An opponent's campaign, however, can be forced to expend scarce resources to preserve its own image, thereby limiting its ability to project that image. Also, neither the candidate nor the consultants can, in the end, affect news coverage of the campaign. While all consultants seek favorable coverage of their candidate, the ultimate decisions regarding coverage of both issues and candidates belong to the press itself (Ryan & Wentworth, 1999, p. 80). Those decisions about who, what, and how the press will cover the campaign will ultimately affect the candidates' images (O'Sullivan & Gieger, 1995).

In addition to the news media, the nature of the campaign activates a number of other factors that affect a candidate's image. Topping this list is the partisanship factor. Images are strongly related to the partisanship of the voters, but partisanship by itself does not account for all aspects of a candidate's image. Still, political parties and their candidates exhibit an interrelationship and mutual influence that affect the images of both the candidates and their parties. At the beginning of a general election campaign, that mutual influence appears to affect candidates more than the parties. Partisans more positively evaluate candidates after they become their party's nominee (Raven & Gallo, 1965). When contenders are nominated—particularly in presidential campaigns—and thus become the party's representative, partisanship has a strong influence on voters' images of the candidates. The partisan impact on images not only influences the image of the candidate, but also those of the political parties. As the campaign progresses, the events surrounding the campaign can transfer elements of the candidate's image back to the party. Therefore, if a presidential candidate is viewed as the "champion of the middle class," that image is more likely to be associated with other members of the same party by the time the campaign is over, even if those other candidates are running for positions that are not related to the federal government.

The ultimate impact of the campaign on images may be demonstrated by the very act of winning or losing the election itself, particularly winners who move into positions of authority or losers hoping to live to campaign for another office in the future. Nimmo and Savage referred to these phenomena as "Congratulations Effects" and "Condolences Effects." Key (1961, pp. 478–479) noted that those candidates who support the loser often accept defeat graciously (congratulations) or console themselves with the conclusion that the outcome will probably have little impact on history (condolence). Either way, the images of both the winner and the loser are likely to be altered by the outcome. Two significant effects have been identified: The image of winning candidates is positively enhanced by the victory, and perceptions of different image traits are altered for both the winning and losing candidates.

First, some who voted for losers shift to the winner, reporting that they voted for the winner when they actually did not (Key, 1961). Even if such a dramatic shift does not occur, there is a general tendency for voters to develop more favorable feelings toward the winner (Paul, 1956) as both supporters and opponents accept the victory and react to the winner as a public official instead of as a candidate. The images of the two candidates—the winner and the loser—often become more similar after the election, with both being perceived more favorably (Stricker, 1964). Raven and Gallo (1965) found that phenomenon occurring regardless of whether partisans were rating their own candidate or that of the opposing political party.

Second, perceptions of different image traits are altered. The winner's perception as a person of influence immediately increases, while the loser's decreases. The loss can potentially benefit the loser's image, though, if voters view him or her more positively; the loss reduces the loser's views as a political threat, which decreases the polarization of the political environment. Furthermore, sympathy for the loser can shift the public's focus to stylistic elements of the loser's image. The result could be that the loser becomes less of a political threat but more likable. Thus, while Bob Dole lacked enough popular support to win the 1996 presidential election, his image was still enhanced so much after his loss that he became a popular television spokesman for a commercial product (Visa Check Card), a soft drink (Pepsi), and a medical issue (erectile dysfunction).

In the final analysis, the prime objective of political campaigns is to win. Furthermore, there are campaigns where image is the desirable vehicle to ride to victory. In 1974, former Georgia governor Lester Maddox was being challenged by State House majority leader George Busbee in a three-week runoff election for governor. Maddox was then lieutenant governor and presiding officer of the state senate, but enjoyed attention achieved through stunts like riding the streets around the Capitol on his bicycle—backward! He enjoyed a certain notoriety as a segregationist, if not as an all-out racist, for preventing African Americans from entering his restaurant during the 1950s and 60s.

Busbee was personally pleasant but not completely comfortable with the rigors of public discourse. An attorney, his political experience was primarily twenty-plus years as a backroom operative. The news media felt a responsibility to provide "socially acceptable" coverage. A serious discussion of issues was generally considered to be an invitation to Maddox to raise race as an issue in an effort to motivate a greater turnout among more conservative voters, who were regarded to be less likely to vote in the nonpresidential year. Busbee chose to mount a campaign around the motto, "A Work Horse, Not a Show Horse."

Interview with Rich Niemand

Image as Branding

Rich Niemand is vice president and creative director for BatesNiemand, Inc., a Washington, D.C.–based consulting firm that specializes in direct mail and strategic consulting. They have worked on a number of political campaigns, with a strong emphasis in providing direct mail services. The firm's political clients have run the gamut from U.S. Senate, Congressional, and gubernatorial candidates to state caucus, municipal, grassroots, and initiative campaigns. BatesNiemand has won three first-place awards from the American Association of Political Consultants for excellence in public affairs communications and four citations for excellence in commercial advertising.

Q: How would you describe political advertising today, as it relates to candidates and their images?

A: People have depended too much on television and the bottom has fallen out of the advertising persuasion. The political business is dominated by TV consultants, and these consultants are not going to give up the budgets on these campaigns for other forms of persuasion. So the candidates are never going to get the type of advertising penetration that they need to get.

Q: How does that compare with commercial advertising?

A: If you look at commercial advertising just before the [19]'92 recession, what happened was that media rates were really climbing, making media very expensive. People were spending a helluva lot of money on media, and they were getting less and less for it. They were paying more for gross rating points, but sales were starting to taper off. Part of that could have been competition, but the other part of it was a fragmented audience. There's so much information and media out there, and so many outlets in terms of cable, that it's very hard to reach people just through the broadcast media anymore.

Q: How do you handle that?

A: What the ad industry did back then was to adopt a vertical integration approach based on how many times a person is touched by advertising, and they really racheted it up. Some ad agencies bought direct mail firms and promotion firms. When they could, they picked up some cheap PR and branding firms, too, so they could provide an integrated approach to an advertising campaign.

Q: Give me an example.

A: Take a product like Taco Bell, which has a great campaign with a dog. But the dog is rolled out into coupon promos through direct mail and game promos through promotion. No matter where you go, you're faced with Taco Bell and the whole theme of what they're doing. You're getting a number of different impressions of that product through a number of different media.

Q: How does that relate to political communication?

A: In politics, it looks on the surface to be more efficient to buy TV. But they're only buying TV and nothing else. People are getting a thirty-second commercial that may or may not be reaching them, because of the way audiences are fragmented and because people zap commercials and channel surf. People are not getting enough information and impressions on different levels to actually feel a sense of loyalty toward the candidate or to feel good about voting for them. What we know about advertising is that, in general, the best recommendation you can get in advertising is a recommendation from a friend. What's happened in politics is that recommendations from friends and more intimate contacts have fallen off. You no longer have campaigns that have field workers. You no longer have campaigns that have a lot of door-to-door campaigning. And you no longer have high-information material going to people, such as a piece of direct mail that can talk about an issue in a little more depth than a thirty-second commercial to get a swing voter. Because of that, the candidates have really suffered, especially in districts that are growing really fast with new people moving in.

Q: Today, voters seem to have strong images only of the president and maybe governors. When you get beyond that, there seems to be a great deal of volatility among the voters' attitudes toward candidates. A lot of people seem to be willing to shift. You seem to be saying that candidates are not using enough different media to reach the voters.

A: Part of the problem is that communication with the voters is sporadic. Let's say somebody raises a million dollars to run for Congress and spends it in a month on TV. That November, when the election is over, he turns around and walks away from a million dollars worth of persuasion and goes away for a year. My commercial clients would go absolutely crazy if I suggested they do that, because you've got to be able to continue your contact with people. Now the congressmen claim they do it through franked mail, but franked mail doesn't do much for you. Or they claim they get it in the press. Well, the press doesn't shape your image. The press only reports on what you're doing. The free media that candidates put out doesn't penetrate in a market glutted by information, and the people who read press reports tend not to be swing voters. There's an ongoing problem of trying to build loyalty when (a) candidates don't touch people anymore, and (b) people think government has nothing to do with them, and in some ways they're right.

Q: Would you say that, for a lot of incumbents, the most they have before they start their commercials is name identification and a weak positive or negative rating?

A: Yes. The incumbents have name identification and soft support. We do a lot of down-ballot stuff, and a state senator could be in office for two or three terms and still have very low name recognition and weak support. Now when you go in and run the persuasion program, tell people everything they've done, those candidates usually win. And the incumbents still have a leg up on challengers, at least during a strong economy. But it's very difficult for them to break through.

Q: How does that translate into what you do as a professional?

A: We do a lot of party caucus work. We've actually been talking to them about trying to brand either candidates or brand the caucus, so that there's this identifiable team that people are working with, and they're part of the team, and this team stands for these particular items.

Q: Isn't that heavily influenced by highly visible campaigns. The images of the parties, as a whole, tend to follow what happens at the national level, doesn't it?

A: Unfortunately, they do. On the other hand, some of the things can vary. For example, we did work for the Democratic caucus in North Carolina. Governor Hunt was extremely popular there. If a governor can build a strong context in a state, he can drive the

(continued)

Interview with Rich Niemand   Continued

context. But absent a strong governor, you're right. It is national politics, and you're really at the whim of what goes on up there.

Q: You seem to be saying that the images of individual candidates are partly outside of their control and partly a by-product of frequency of communication. What about the content? Is there any particular element of the image that is critical? It used to be integrity.

A: I'm not sure it isn't still. I think that what they're looking for now is integrity, but the integrity that they're looking for is somebody who actually believes in something, somebody who will stand up for something, and somebody who will be pragmatic. They're looking for pragmatic solutions, little product solutions that will help their lives, make things easier to do.

Q: A couple of decades back, Walter DeVries used to argue that what the swing voter was looking for was a problem solver.

A: Yes. I believe that voters are consumers, and that political people make the mistake of thinking that voters are political people. They're not—not swing voters, at least. We don't spend money on the people who are committed on either side. We don't change their minds, and you can't do much to suppress their vote. So we're just talking to swing voters. And, yes, they just want little solutions. And whoever gives them the solution they want, they'll go with.

Q: You're talking about this in very strong advertising terms, and you seem to be equating branding and imaging. But there are some differences between political and consumer advertising.

A: Yes, but at least for swing voters, the differences are narrowing. Of course you have a shorter period of time in which you have to make a decision, but I really believe that people are buying products through politics, at least where we are right now. These are not huge ideological things. If you look, even at presidential races, what's being offered are little giveaways couched in lifestyle attitudes. I really believe that if you talk to a swing voter, they have almost no ideology.

Source: Reprinted by permission of Richard Niemand.

Consequently, the news media challenged Maddox to prove he was a serious governmental manager, but issues in the traditional sense were never raised. Quickly, the race became a contest of who knew more about the "controls" of government, and Busbee was elected.

The Role of Gender

Hillary Rodham Clinton's election as New York's senator drew a great deal of media attention during the 2000 election, but Ms. Clinton's campaign was but one of many in which women sought elective office. Even though such political bastions as the U.S. Senate are still dominated by males, an increasing number of women have been entering the political arena over the past three decades. Before 1970, few women held major public office at either the state or city level (Mandel, 1981). By 1999, women held more than 20 percent of state legislative offices and were governors of three states. Long gone are the days when Lurleen Wallace campaigned for the governor's seat in Alabama as a surrogate for her husband George, who was prohibited by law from seeking an additional term. Today's women candidates campaign on their own merits and on their own issues.

Still, because of gender stereotypes, women have a number of image problems to overcome that a comparable male candidate might not face (Kahn, 1993, 1994; Norris, 1996; Robertson, 2001). They are often viewed as less competent and unable to handle the tough negotiations associated with politics (Eagly, Makhijani, & Klonsky, 1992). They are expected to be less assertive and aggressive in their speaking styles, a demeanor more appropriate for traditional female stereotypes (Haas, 1979; Newcombe & Arnkoff, 1976). In the past, if they tried to assume a leadership position traditionally held by a man, or use leadership behaviors typically associated with men, women candidates got negative reactions from the voters (Eagly, Makhijani, & Klonsky, 1992).

To overcome such problems, successful women candidates must typically use highly explicit messages, giving precise statements about their position on issues—a demand voters don't generally make of male candidates (Bernstein, 2000). Male candidates may campaign on platitudes about the need for improving education ("We must return the concept of learning to our schools"). On a similar issue, Bernstein argued that women candidates must be more specific in their campaign messages ("We've got to lower the number of students in each classroom, while increasing teacher salaries by ten percent"). Except for the explicitness requirement, most women candidates have adapted to the modern political arena and have adopted many of the same techniques and tactics that have been used by male candidates in the past (Bystrom & Miller, 1999). Female candidates run just as many negative ads as men (Dabelko & Hernson, 1997), but audience expectations on these ads may be different from those of male candidates (Swain, 2001). Typically, women candidates attack their opponents' position on issues (Benze & Declercq, 1985; Kahn, 1993) rather than on personal matters.

Part of the problem may be the male dominance that is still maintained in many other areas of politics. In television entertainment programming, the role of women has expanded dramatically. TV shows such as *The West Wing* showcase independent women who are heavily involved in and sometimes at the center of political issues. Police dramas such as *Police Woman* and *Cagney and Lacy* have depicted women as crime fighters on a par with male detectives. A range of action-adventure serials (*Xena: Warrior Princess, Relic Hunter, Sheena*) have portrayed women as heroes of epic legends.

Such attitudes, however, have not yet fully made their way into the political arena. The identified trend of women adopting the same techniques as male candidates may be merely an artifact of a gender difference because male consultants continue to outnumber female consultants. Men also make up the majority of news anchors and reporters (Paletz, 2002, p. 137) and far outnumber women as makers and sources of political news (Holland, 1987). Often when women do appear in news stories, they are presented as passive respondents to public events rather than as participants in those events (Rakow & Kranich, 1991).

Despite these problems, though, women continue to make progress in the political arena. The image problems faced by women candidates have been worked through a transitional stage that has resulted in increased numbers of women seeking and winning public office. More changes are likely to occur in the future, as both the academic and consulting communities learn more about the impact of elections on the images of women candidates.

Summary

In some respects the juxtaposition of "image versus issues" is a false one. The political commercials that evoke strong reactions from academicians (flag waving, shallow, and so forth), are often criticized equally by consultants for their lack of a specific message. Consultants believe any communications opportunity that does not "move" votes is an opportunity lost, and messages that focus on images often lack the specifics that consultants are seeking.

Academicians must sometimes define such a dichotomy, one that separates issues and images, in order to evaluate images in their research. Such a dichotomy, though, often does not exist in the consultant's world. Images are conveyed through issues, and issues are discussed in terms of the candidate's image. The complex nature of political images will continue to evoke in-depth research on the part of academicians. Meanwhile, consultants continue to simplify the process, at least during the duration of the campaign itself. Working with a limited number of image dimensions—leadership, integrity, and empathy—they continue to work with those cognitive elements that can affect the evaluative dimension of a candidate's image. This work, ultimately, can lead to the voting behavior they seek.

Despite the complexity, some factors have emerged. The image of a political candidate is often a multifaceted impression that includes information about the candidate, personal evaluations of the candidate, and attitudes that affect voting behavior related to the candidate. Voters often seek an ideal candidate, with all candidates falling short of their expectations. Still, they are more likely to vote for the candidate whose image is closest to that ideal.

The complexity of the subject, though, means that the function is never really complete. Candidate images can and will be altered by the campaign itself, and on those events that might precede the next election. Even death will not necessarily end the process; after all, academicians continue to discuss the images of such past political figures as Andrew Jackson, Abraham Lincoln, Franklin Roosevelt, and John F. Kennedy. The candidate may die, but the image lives on.

QUESTIONS FOR DISCUSSION

1. Former Vice President Al Gore can describe himself as a Vietnam veteran, a journalist, a homebuilder, a former congressman, and a U.S. senator. How would such associations assist his campaign? What are the advantages of presenting this sort of resume to voters? What negative associations would his opponent attempt to draw from the same experiences?

2. Can a candidate who is overweight, untidy, and whose voice breaks win a modern television election? How is it possible? How could the campaign harness television to deal with these "problems"?

3. Some observers believe that reliance on "image" detracts from the discussion of "issues." Others maintain that image is a brief way to summarize the candidate's presentation of "issues." Which approach do you accept? Can a discussion of issues alter a candidate's image?

CHAPTER

5

Media Theory and Political Communication

During the 1957 gubernatorial campaign in New Jersey, Democrat Robert Meyner faced Republican Malcolm Forbes in a campaign in which only one television station reached most of the residents in the state (Schram, 1976). Airtime on Channel 13 was a valuable commodity sought by both candidates, particularly the then-popular block programming format in which thirty-minute or hour-long blocks of time were purchased so the candidates could address the voters directly. To make one last appeal to the electorate, Democrat Meyner purchased such an hour-long block from 10:00 to 11:00 P.M. on the night before the election. When Republican Forbes learned of the purchase, he countered by buying the following hour—11:00 P.M. to midnight—so he could get in the last word before voters went to the polls.

True to form, Meyner's program came on the air at 10:00 P.M. But after only fifty-five minutes of speaking, Meyner signed off with a thanks to the voter. That was followed by the playing of the "Star Spangled Banner," and the remainder of Meyner's five minutes was spent showing the station's test pattern. Most viewers, assuming the station had gone off the air for the night, turned off their sets and never heard Forbes's rebuttal. The angry Forbes cried foul, but there was little he could do; the voters never knew of the complaint until after the election. Meyner's program had its maximum media impact, while Forbes was unable to communicate with the voters.

The incident was an early example of the power and prestige that candidates place on the media's ability to communicate with voters. The struggle to prevail in a contest of ideas requires presenting those ideas to targeted publics in a persuasive manner. In modern political terms this means competing candidates must present themselves through advertising, direct mail, telephone banks, printed material, and other techniques. To be successful, the means of communicating must deliver a believable message. Historically, that means of communication has been some form of mass media. Consequently, media scholars have devoted much research to developing and testing media theories. Different scholars have proposed differing frameworks for understanding the cultural and attitudinal impacts of the media. Over time, the focus of these studies have often shifted perspectives, ranging from manipulative approaches to propaganda to audience-based research on media use. The theme that pervades all, though, is that an understanding of media and its impact is important to an understanding of the contemporary climate of political campaigns.

During most of the twentieth century, the academic community often monitored the impact of mass media. Some of its members sometimes expressed surprise and concern at the ability of mass communication to influence the mass public—surprised by the occasional magnitude of media impact and concerned about the potential for its misuse. Other members have scoffed at such issues, sometimes viewing the mass media as an environmental element that has little impact on the lives of people. A third group of members have sought to isolate potential effects in an effort to isolate and identify what impact the media have and what they cannot do.

The result of such studies has led to the development of several theories regarding media impact. The early studies were naively simple by modern standards, alternately viewing media impact as either an uncontrollable monster or a toy soldier with no weapon. Over time, though, more sophisticated theories developed. The consultants, meanwhile, were picking up lessons from each new approach and applying them to the campaign environment.

The growth of modern media theory can be traced to the 1930s when U.S. academicians watched in astonishment as Adolf Hitler rose to power in Germany, a power attained and maintained through the dictator's effective use of propaganda and persuasion. Through his public speeches and public relations campaigns, Hitler developed a solid base of national support for his radical ideas. Observers from other nations looked on with both fear and curiosity, trying to identify and study the persuasive techniques that seemed to be so effective for the German dictator. The result was some of the first serious investigations into the impact of mass media.

The Bullet Theory (Hypodermic Model)

One of the first observations made about Hitler's persuasion efforts were their almost infallible effectiveness. Apparently, if Hitler presented a well-constructed and well-delivered message to the German populace, it was almost invariably effective with most of the populace. This conclusion led observers to make assumptions that came to be considered the first classic model of mass media effects, a theory alternately referred to as either the "bullet" theory or "hypodermic" model (Bineham, 1988). Both terms were based on the same concept, which was that the media had direct and discernible persuasive effects (Hovland, Lumsdaine, & Sheffield, 1949; Werrett, 1933). Audiences were viewed as passive, almost gullible, recipients of the message, particularly if that message was delivered in an effective manner. Thus, mass persuasion was assumed to be effective, if properly used. Research was designed to identify those elements of motivational and persuasion research that increased the effectiveness of the message.

Propaganda Techniques

Much of the early research in this area focused on the propagandists' tricks of rhetoric in explaining the effects of the message. The results were the identification and investigation of several propaganda techniques, including name calling, stacking the deck, and bandwagon effects (a complete list is provided in the box on page 71). Academicians typically decry such propaganda techniques as an unethical form of persuasion that does not encourage a full debate of ideas. Brydon and Scott (1994), for example, describe propaganda techniques as "devices that bypass reasoning altogether in an attempt to persuade the listener at any cost" (p. 417). One exception is Jacques Ellul (1962/1965), who argued that propaganda is an inevitable and desirable tool for stabilizing culture in a modern society. Ellul views propaganda as the dissemination of cultural mores, rather than a deliberate lie. From a pragmatic point of view, most political campaigns generally adopt Ellul's thesis, even if the candidates or consultants involved have never heard of him. Jowett and O'Donnell (1986) describe propaganda as "a form of communication that is different from persuasion because it attempts to achieve a response that furthers the desired intent of the propagandist" (p. 13). That pretty well sums up the candidate's goal in a political campaign, and propaganda prospers as a result.

Propaganda Techniques

The following techniques were those identified by the Institute for Propaganda Analysis in the 1930s.

Name Calling.   A labeling technique used when a person, group, or issue is characterized by a negative term. The propagandist's intent is to evoke a negative emotional reaction. Thus, a proposal might be labeled "liberal," "ultraconservative," or "radical" to describe it in a negative way.

Glittering Generality.   A phrase that sounds good but has no inherent meaning. Many have been used so often that they have become clichés, particularly in the political sense, including such statements as "We must do what's right," "A better tomorrow," and "Representing the people."

Transfer.   A technique in which candidates link themselves with an idea or object that has a positive connotation, or in which they link their opponent to an object that has a negative connotation. A candidate who wants to be perceived as strong on national defense, for example, might be depicted with military hardware.

Testimonials.   The endorsement of a candidate by someone else. Usually, the person offering the endorsement has high credibility, and the intent of the testimonial is to transfer some of the endorser's credibility to the candidate. When a testimonial comes from a relatively unknown person, it is usually intended to create a referent transfer with the group that the endorser represents. Thus, an endorsement from an elderly woman might be used to appeal to elderly voters.

Plain Folks.   An attempt to convey that the candidate is just like the people who vote for him. This sometimes emerges as a "good ole boy" argument.

Stacking the Deck.   The presentation of a one-sided argument that ignores the arguments of the opposition. This approach is frequently used in political literature and advertisements with the intent to imply that the opposition has no legitimate argument.

The Bandwagon Effect.   A manifestation of the "Everybody is doing it" argument. This is frequently seen in political campaigns, often with the "Polls show I'm ahead" argument or the use of multiple endorsements in an attempt to increase credibility ("Every newspaper in the district has endorsed me").

Sources: Ellul, J. (1965). *Propaganda.* Trans. by K. Kellen & J. Lerner. New York: Knopf.

Jowett, G. S., & O'Donnell, V. (1986). *Propaganda and Persuasion.* Beverly Hills, CA: Sage.

Still, as the early studies progressed, the researchers gradually came to the conclusion that mass propaganda was not always effective, particularly with all audiences. At that point, the research tended to branch into subunits as researchers tried to identify which "bullets" were most effective with which "targets" (audiences). Generally, though, the early research had trouble duplicating Hitler's broad persuasive impact, particularly on political issues. Much of Hitler's success was due to his ability to so totally control the media that his message was the only one heard by the German people. In fact, his attempts at similar propaganda techniques to audiences in other countries were generally ineffective (Jowett & O'Donnell, 1986, pp. 137–142). Hitler's propaganda, it turned out, worked only when the population was hearing one side of an issue. In the presence of alternative messages, the effectiveness of many of these propaganda techniques is diminished. In addition, Villa and Rodgers (1999) concluded that the success of the most extreme element of Hitler's rhetoric, the Nazis' "Final Solution" campaign, was not totally due to Hitler's propaganda. Many of the ideas of the Nazi party existed before Hitler came to power, they noted; the Nazi ideology intensified those "views through the use of propaganda, but did not create them" (p. 24).

The Limited Effects Model

While the bullet theory dominated studies of the mass media for a few years, some researchers eventually started to note problems with the model, particularly in the United States. American voters, it turned out, were not nearly as malleable as the German population appeared to be. In fact, they sometimes appeared highly resistant to persuasion, particularly through the mass media. The first serious blows to the bullet theory grew out of studies at Columbia University and the University of Michigan. The first of these was the 1940 Erie County study conducted by Lazarsfeld, Berelson, and Gaudet (1948). This longitudinal study followed voters from May 1940 until the general election in November of that year. The results showed that nearly half of the November voters already knew five to six months before how they would vote. Another 25 percent had decided during the parties' national conventions, when the final nominees were chosen. Only 25 percent actually made their voting decision during the campaign. Of these, only 8 percent actually changed their voting intention, once a decision had been made.

Furthermore, the study concluded that the issues of the campaign were relatively unimportant to the voting decision. Rather than monitoring the media for information to help them make a decision, voters used such information to support vote decisions that were based on social predispositions. In essence, most voters would have made the same vote decision without the media. They merely used the media to seek reinforcement of that decision, not new information.

The results of that study were essentially replicated by Berelson, Lazarsfeld, and McPhee (1954) in a similar study in Elmira, New York, during the 1948 campaign. This time, 67 percent of the voters had made their decision by June. Fifteen percent more decided in August, and another 11 percent soon afterward. Only 10 percent made their voting decision during the actual campaign span of the final month.

The results were again interpreted as showing that the media had only limited effects on voters' decisions, with most votes cast on the basis of social predispositions. Subsequent research by Campbell and Kahn (1952) and Campbell, Gurin, and Miller (1954) identified the influence of party affiliation as one such predisposition, but the basic premises of the limited effects model had been established.

This approach was summarized by Klapper (1960) as the "Rule of Minimal Effects." Under this approach, audience processing of media information was considered to be highly selective, conditioned by partisan predispositions, and subordinate to interpersonal influence, (the two-step flow, which is discussed later). In essence, this approach assumed that political campaigns could make only minor dents on attitudes and were more likely to reinforce an existing cognitive state. Instead, the model assumed that the public generally responds to the media in a selective manner. The overall effect, for most people, is that the media only succeed in reinforcing existing public opinion, instead of contributing to changes to the public opinion development process. Mass persuasion becomes subordinate to interpersonal influence.

Two theoretical explanations were developed as a result of this study: the selectivity hypothesis and the two-step flow. The selectivity hypothesis grew out of the argument that voters selectively used the media to support vote conclusions that were based on their predispositions; in other words, they were seeking reinforcement rather than information. As a result, four separate levels of selectivity were postulated: selective exposure, selective reception, selective perception, and selective retention.

Selective exposure refers to the idea that people tend to choose from the communication experiences available to them, selecting those messages that are more likely to support their existing beliefs and attitudes. In political campaigns, this is frequently exhibited in partisan exposure to campaign messages, which suggests that Republicans will tend to expose themselves to messages from Republicans, and Democrats are more likely to seek out messages about Democrats (Klapper, 1960, p. 20). Although the growth of thirty-second television ads may have watered down this effect somewhat, the concept still has some validity in today's campaign environment.

Selective attention refers to the assumption that audiences are more likely to pay attention to those messages that support their existing beliefs and attitudes. Information theorists note that the eye can process about five million bits of data per second, but the brain is capable of processing only about five-hundred bits during the same time. Given that disparity, only a portion of the available data is actually processed by an individual into any long-term memory bank (Egeth, 1967). In that situation, the selectivity hypothesis argues that the respondent is more likely to process information that is supportive of their current lifestyle, including their current political attitudes.

But what if the voter is both exposed to the message of the opposition, and pays attention to it. That message can still be distorted through the process of selective perception. A person's past experiences, attitudes, and expectations will influence their view of that message. Finally, even if the message is perceived in a manner similar to what was intended, there is no guarantee that it will be remembered for any extended period of time. The principle of selective retention states that a person more accurately remembers messages that are favorable to one's self-image than messages that are unfavorable (Levine & Murphy, 1943). The overall impact of the selection process, therefore, is to limit the impact of any message that reaches voters through the media.

The Two-Step Flow hypothesized that media effects were mediated by the presence of opinion leaders. In this approach, the media had little direct effect because the ultimate interpretation of information reached the public only after it had passed through interpersonal channels. In essence, local opinion leaders interpreted the media in light of the social predispositions of their community, with the result that the media reinforced attitudes instead of having changed them. This hypothesis will be discussed more thoroughly in the chapter on opinion leadership.

Criticisms

Over the years, scholars have identified a number of theoretical problems with the limited effects model. The most obvious of these is that the so-called limited effects are not all that limited. In the classical studies on the topics, the limited effects were typically measured in numbers that ranged from 10 percent to 25 percent. While such percentages may be small in comparison to the entire population, they are more than enough to make a dramatic impact on an election. Presidential elections are rarely decided by more than 20 percentage points; thus a swing by 10 to 20 percent of the voters would be enough to change the outcome of an election.

Second, the classic studies in the limited effects model were all conducted before the widespread use of television as a mass medium, but the conclusions were subsequently generalized to the television's effects. While many of the effects do hold for television, the swing vote is still sufficiently large to have a major impact on elections.

Third, the classic studies focused only on presidential elections, elections that are highly visible and highly partisan. The size of the undecided vote is frequently larger in less visible races, creating a situation in which the impact of the media increases.

Fourth, the nature of the campaigns that were studied for the limited effects model also cast doubts about their conclusions. The 1940 election revolved around the reelection of Franklin Roosevelt, a highly popular president generally credited by the voters with helping them to recover from the Great Depression of the 1930s. It should not be surprising that so many voters knew, in advance of the election, that they planned to vote for him in November, even though it was a tradition-breaking run for a third term.

And, finally, while academicians were reporting the limited effects in Elmira, New York, President Harry Truman was using the 1948 presidential campaign to pull off one of the major upsets in U.S. presidential history. Despite almost universal expectations that Republican Thomas Dewey would win that election, Truman won with an energetic whistle-stop campaign that was reported nationwide by the media. The effects of the media may have been limited, but they were enough for Truman to win.

Campaign Implications

Despite the limitations of the limited effects model, the research did provide insight into voting behavior that has proven to be beneficial to campaign professionals. The first lesson was the importance of attitudinal reinforcement. In terms of campaigns, that lesson was simple: Work your base first. It's easier to motivate your own supporters to vote than to persuade someone who is against you to change his or her mind; in other words, to alter the voting intentions of an opponent's supporter.

Another assumption of the limited effects model was that mass persuasion was subordinate to interpersonal influence. From a campaign perspective, the importance of this view was the influence of opinion leadership and interpersonal communication. It empha-sized the need to identify and persuade opinion leaders. Some campaigns, including George McGovern's 1972 primary campaigns, placed a major emphasis on interpersonal commu-nication programs (Devlin, 1973).

Agenda Setting

The limited effects model dominated mass media theory up until the early 1960s. Eventu-ally, though, researchers became intrigued by the obvious disparity between the theory and the eagerness of politicians and mass marketers to use the media to advance their ideas and sell their products. Furthermore, even if the impact of the media was small, it could still be a significant factor in a campaign. Sometimes only small differences separate winners from losers (Jeffries, 1986, p. 259). At this point, McCombs and Shaw (1972) suggested that media theory should look at a different variable. Instead of persuasion, they suggested, the major role of the mass media was issue definition. In other words, "The mass media may not be successful in telling us what to think, but they are stunningly successful in telling us what to think about." Indeed, the media can play a critical role in defining what is and what is not a public issue. A decade before McCombs and Shaw outlined the basics of agenda setting, Cohen (1963) argued that the media could play a critical role in focusing public attention on an issue. As Tuchman (1982, p. 184) wrote, "News does not mirror society. It helps to constitute it as a shared social phenomenon, for in the process of describing an event, news defines and shapes the event." Roberts (1992) goes further, suggesting that agenda setting might be a two-step process in which acceptance of the media's issue prior-ities can ultimately affect voter behavior. In other words, by influencing what we think about, the media may also be influencing what actions we take.

Part of the impact is due to the pure omnipresence of the media. Woodward (1997) reported that the average adult American spends almost 1,500 hours a year watching televi-sion, and information on television becomes topics for public discussion. Not all of that exposure is on news and public issues, but that makes little difference. Even entertainment programs can have an impact on public perceptions (Gerbner, et al., 1990). The result is public issues as mediated reality—events and people are known only through the media.

Generally, the public opinion process (as it relates to any specific issue) begins when the media focus on an issue. Once the media define an issue, it becomes part of the public opinion agenda. Typically, three distinct stages of public response occur. First, the media raise awareness of the issue. Second, diffusion of information about the issue occurs, as the media and political elites disseminate their views. And third, discussion of the issue, by the public, proceeds. At that point, a cyclical process between the public and the media may be established, that is, as the public discussion increases, the media feed new information about it to the public.

Agenda setting asserts that audiences take note of the saliences of the news media and incorporate a similar set of weights into their personal agenda, which means the media's priorities become the voters' priorities. Lippman (1922) first asserted the idea in his classic book, *Public Opinion*. McCombs and Shaw (1972) tested the hypothesis during the 1968 election, finding a correlation between issues emphasized by the news and what voters regarded as key issues of the campaign. That conclusion was supported by an interpretation of some data from Berelson, Lazarsfeld, and McPhee's study of the 1948 election, which indicated that voters with minimal interpersonal contact were more in line with news coverage of the campaign. Support for the hypothesis has subsequently been relatively strong, with most research indicating that when the public sees news stories about a particular problem on television, they tend to regard the issue as more important and report having stronger feelings about it (Iyengar & Kinder, 1987).

Agenda-Setting Models

Researchers continue to refine the agenda-setting model. Typically, three different models have been investigated: the awareness model, the priorities model, and the salience model (McCombs, 1976; Shaw & McCombs, 1980).

The Awareness Model.   The awareness model of agenda setting is based on the assumption that awareness of an issue depends on media coverage of that issue. It essentially measures whether voters are aware of or ignorant of the issue itself. The awareness model suffers from the unique theoretical fault of being too accurate to have much theoretical importance. If an issue is not covered by the media, most people are not aware of it, making the two terms almost theoretically synonymous.

As a result, most research in this area has turned to the gatekeeping function of the media. Media sources employ gatekeepers, who select the stories to be included in the broadcast or in the newspaper. Larson (1995) argues that gatekeepers hold significant power in determining what the public thinks about, and their gatekeeping decisions have "ripple effects." Larson cited sexual abuse as an example of the agenda-setting function. In the mid-1980s, one gatekeeper featured a story about a child care center in California where evidence of sexual abuse had surfaced. After the initial report, other stories appeared in other cities; newsweeklies and family magazines carried stories about sexual abuse in day care centers.

Gatekeepers function with two kinds of inherent bias: ideological, where stories are chosen to fit in with a certain philosophical viewpoint; and structural, where stories are chosen because they fit the media's format. While ideological bias has received the most criticism, structural bias is predominant. Larson notes that stories that are dramatic and can be squeezed into a twenty- to thirty-second news bite are likely to be considered. Other factors considered are the presence of photographs, "official voices," and issues that affect the local community.

An aspect of gatekeeping that has received more focus recently is that of news priming. News priming refers to the ability of the media to set expectations for viewers (Kenski, 1996). For example, if the news media predict that an election will be close, and then someone wins by a sizable margin, a person in favor of the winning candidate will be more satisfied than if the media had predicted a clear victory. One example of the influence of news priming is the behavior of presidential candidates and their campaigns before televised debates. A candidate's predebate rhetoric is a delicate balancing act that has to simultaneously demonstrate confidence in his or her skills without creating expectations that are too high to be met by his or her actual performance.

The Priorities Model.   The basic assumption behind the priorities model is that media audiences will adopt the same agenda, in the same rank order, as do the media. In simple terms, this approach hypothesizes that media audiences will judge as important what the media judge as important. This, of course, is the most radical approach and does not take into consideration individual differences. Still, despite the extreme nature of the hypothesis, it tends to have the best fit for many situations.

The Salience Model.   The salience model is an intermediate explanation that falls somewhere in between the basic explanation of the awareness model and the extreme fit of the priorities model. The salience model assumes that heavy media emphasis on a topic can move it into the top rank of what is important to the audience. However, it predicts that this movement will occur for only a few issues that are constantly being emphasized in the media. Furthermore, the audience discriminates only in terms of high and low importance. Thus, the exact priorities of the media are not reproduced.

Research Considerations

Agenda setting, as an independent variable, has been operationalized in two ways: the total amount of coverage devoted to an issue (column inches or number of minutes) and by the priority of coverage an issue is given (front page or lead story). Benton (1976) broke agenda setting into three different categories. The first level involved merely the identification of broad issues. At the second level, voters were able to identify subissues, specific problems, causes, and proposed solutions. At the third level, they could identify specific information about subissues, including pro and con arguments. Generally, this line of research has indicated that newspapers have more influence than television does at agenda setting at the upper two levels.

Generally, two different approaches have been used to measure agenda-setting effects. The intrapersonal approach measures those issues that an individual personally considers to be important; in other words, what they think about. The interpersonal approach measures those issues that are most frequently discussed with others; in other words, what they talk about. Generally, the salience model has the best fit on the intrapersonal approach, while the priorities model does well under the interpersonal approach.

Contingent Conditions.   McCombs (1992) noted that, after the first set of tests of the agenda-setting hypothesis, research quickly turned to exploring those contingent conditions that contributed to the phenomenon (McCombs & Weaver, 1973). McCombs (1976) identified four such conditions:

> *High exposure to the mass media.* The media's issue agenda has little effect on those who do not expose themselves to the media.
>
> *A need for orientation.* Agenda setting is more likely to occur among those voters who have an inherent curiosity about their surrounding environment. The media satisfy that curiosity (Weaver, 1980).
>
> *Frequency of interpersonal discussion.* This line of research has tried to expand the two-step flow hypothesis to agenda setting and has done so with mixed results. Frequently, the conflicting results of this research are often a by-product of different definitions of agenda setting, such as the intrapersonal vs. interpersonal approaches.

Wanta and Wu (1992) reported that interpersonal communication enhanced agenda-setting effects for issues that receive extensive media coverage, but inhibited the effects for little-publicized issues by providing salience cues that conflict with media messages. They also found that frequency of discussions is the strongest predictor of issue salience.

Weaver, Zhu, and Willnat (1992) found that interpersonal communication served a bridging function by influencing and linking personal and social perceptions on the salience of drug abuse. Neither personal experience nor exposure to newspaper coverage was significantly correlated with these perceptions. In effect, the media's agenda on drug abuse had been passed along through interpersonal communication to audiences who were not exposed to it by the media.

Low Motivation

Agenda-setting effects appear to be most pronounced on voters who are not highly involved in the election. Highly involved individuals develop a comparative framework for evaluating political information. When news events and information are reported in the media, they can compare that information with their earlier beliefs, attitudes, and values. Voters who are not highly involved frequently lack such frameworks or prior information to make such evaluations. Consequently, they are more susceptible to media influence.

Newspapers vs. Television.   Some studies have sought to identify possible variations in agenda setting between newspapers and television, often with no difference identified. Where distinct differences were found, newspapers were generally more influential, particularly at providing upper-level, in-depth information. Subsequent analysis has reported that newspapers shape the agenda initially, but television dominates during the latter stages of the campaign. At other times, it appears that newspapers influence the agenda of television news coverage. In many cases in the past, major news stories were first reported by newspapers, and television outlets soon followed. More people, though, actually followed such stories on television than in the newspaper. The Watergate scandal involving President Richard Nixon followed such a pattern, with the story being first developed by a newspaper (the *Washington Post*) and then disseminated to the public by television network news. In 1998–1999, during the Clinton-Lewinsky controversy, the Internet frequently served such an agenda-setting function. News stories related to the issue were frequently first mentioned on the Internet before reaching wider dissemination through newspapers and television.

The Internet is just one factor that has altered the agenda-setting function of the press. Today, newspapers are rarely the first to break a major national story. If fact, newspaper agendas are more frequently influenced by media coverage from cable news networks such as CNN, Headline News, MSNBC, and Fox News. These twenty-four-hour news channels are often the first to cover a national story, with newspapers following with printed coverage of the same issue on the following day.

Campaign Implications.   The agenda-setting function of the press was reflected in a number of significant campaign techniques. First, it recognized the value of news coverage as an important campaign factor. This is sometimes described in terms of the "30–30 Rule":

Thirty seconds on the nightly news has more impact than thirty minutes of paid advertisement. The basis of the rule is an assumption by the campaigns that the news media are seen by the voters as a relatively unbiased source of information (as compared to the candidates themselves). Voter responses to any campaign ad can be tempered by cynicism; after all, the candidates are unlikely to say anything bad about themselves or good about their opponent. Thus, campaigns are elated when their candidate receives news coverage from the media, and particularly if that coverage focuses on the major theme or issue of the candidate's campaign. The result of that mentality has been an increased attempt on the part of the campaigns to influence favorable news coverage through press releases, free video segments, and staged events. News priming also comes into play, as campaigns work to develop scenarios that will put their candidate's performance in the best possible light.

The second major impact on campaigns was through the selection of campaign issues. Agenda setting emphasized the need for campaigns to devote much of their efforts to issues that the audience considered important. Campaign polling techniques put more emphasis on questions that could help define that agenda, with strategies being developed that in turn reflected the audience's priorities. When the campaign heats up, particularly during the last two weeks, those issue decisions become critical. Typically, the candidate who is able to control the agenda of the media is the candidate who will most likely win the election.

A candidate often has little or no control over the media's agenda, and that could adversely affect the campaign. In 1980, for example, Jimmy Carter ran for reelection as president while the nation was embroiled in the Iranian hostage crisis (Conover & Sigelman, 1982). In 1979, Iranian activists attacked and captured the U.S. embassy in Iran, holding its employees hostage. Those U.S. citizens were still being held hostage during the 1980 presidential campaign, and the one-year anniversary of the event fell on the same day as the election in 1980. News coverage of the crisis represented an issue that was detrimental to the campaign and likely contributed to Carter's defeat.

Furthermore, despite the media's strength at setting agendas, its capacity to do so is limited. Zhu (1992) argued that this limitation makes agenda setting a zero-sum game in which any issue that garners more attention from the media does so only at the expense of other issues, which lose attention or are dropped completely by the public's attention meter. In essence, only a small number of issues can maintain public interest at the same time, meaning that increased coverage of any one issue will result in decreased coverage of others. Hertog, Finnegan, and Kahn (1994) found little support for that notion and argued that the displacement effect is not as powerful as once assumed. While that notion has been disputed, particularly on medical-related issues (Hertog, Finnegan, & Kahn, 1994), candidates and consultants generally work under such an assumption. Getting a new issue some attention can be difficult.

Research on agenda setting has been so consistent that the focus on the topic has shifted to looking at the topic from new viewpoints (McCombs, 1992), including the exploration of candidate images and political interest as alternative agendas, and studying agenda setting as a dependent variable instead of as an independent variable ("Who sets the news agenda?"). Both of these areas of study have direct implications for campaigns, particularly in terms of candidate images and agenda sources. The indirect impact of agenda setting on candidate images has been an assumption made by most consultants for years, providing part of the impetus for concerted public relations programs. Also, campaigns have similarly worked on tacit programs to identify those who have the most impact on the news agenda of the press, and targeting those individuals with specific information about their candidate and issues.

Interview with Adam Goodman

The Impact of Media in Political Campaigns

Adam Goodman is a member of Donner Public Affairs, a public relations and political consulting firm based in Tampa, Florida, which works with Republican candidates. Goodman has provided media consulting for a number of Republican candidates for statewide and local offices across the nation.

Q: What impact does the mass media have on campaigns?

A: The paid media can have a lot of impact, particularly in terms of establishing themes, messages, ideas, and day-to-day control of the agenda. Sometimes it dominates the campaign, influencing what issues are discussed and what themes and ideas are influencing the voters. Other times, the free media dominates. And sometimes the paid media merely complements what the voter is getting from the free media.

Q: What do you mean by establishing themes and messages?

A: Even in this age of personality politics, winners and losers are more often defined by their themes than by their images. TV evens the playing field. You can take a candidate who is not charismatic and not a great speaker, and give them a chance if you've got a good theme. TV is the great communicator, and it can be used to create an image for a candidate. But the one thing it cannot do is to create a great idea. And great ideas are the difference between winning and losing. If you've got a candidate with a great idea, you can communicate that to the voters.

Q: In the academic community, there are some people who argue that the media doesn't have much impact on elections. What do you think? How much does the paid media influence the outcome of campaigns?

A: It depends upon the campaign. In some instances, TV ads are responsible for a candidate winning the election; in others, for losing it. In some instances, your paid media moves your polling numbers, but it's hard to say if that's what had the ultimate impact in the election. The voters get their news about the campaign from a number of sources, including TV news, radio, and newspapers. Some campaigns receive a lot of news coverage, and your commercials become just one of several sources of information for the voters, while most of their information comes from paid media. Other times, the news media may not cover a campaign hardly at all. When that happens, your paid media increases in importance.

Q: Will the role of media change in the future?

A: The role of media will increase, but the equation is growing more complicated. Two changes have already occurred that have changed it. The first is the emergence of the Fourth Rail: independent expenditures. It used to be that we'd have a campaign; the two candidates would decide on their messages; they'd go at it for the duration of the campaign; and the media would cover the campaign as a third party. Now, we have the entrance of independent expenditures, where anybody who wants to can get involved in the campaign. They've already been involved, and their participation in campaigns will become more in vogue.

Q: What's the other change?

A: The definition of media is already changing. New media will no longer be an after-thought to campaigns, and successful campaigns will be those who are most creative at using the Internet to drive the campaign from start to finish. Those who understand the new media will be the champions of the field.

Q: How will the Internet and other new media be used?

A: Direct voter contact. Campaigns will become more interactive, as the candidate and the campaign communicate more directly with individual voters. People who understand how to use that will be the winners of tomorrow.

Q: Where does TV production fit into that scenario?

A: With the new media, you can communicate with both print and video messages. We're already doing video streaming, where we create a video advertisement that can be e-mailed to targeted groups across a district. We can send it directly to the target audi-ence. That is one of the most dramatic changes that has happened in the field. It's com-parable to the impact on campaigns that happened when we shifted from the use of film to video. When film was the only way to shoot an ad, what would happen is that the campaigns would put their ads together and put them on TV. Then, particularly during the last few days of the campaign, you'd just sit back and see what happened. You did-n't have time to make any last-minute adjustments. But the advent of video changed that; with video, you could make last-minute changes and keep adjusting your cam-paign up to the last moment. That was a dramatic change in the nature of the field, but the new communication changes resulting from the Internet and the new media will be just as dramatic. Those who understand that will be successful.

Source: Reprinted by permission of Adam Goodman.

Uses-Gratification

The bullet theory and limited effects model were both message oriented, focusing on the impact of the message on the audience. The agenda-setting model was channel oriented, focusing on the priorities of the media. One theory that deviates from both of these approaches—focusing upon the audience instead—is the uses-gratification model. This approach assumes that audiences use the media to gratify personal needs related to the political campaign, a concept often summarized by saying, "What people do with media is more important than what media do to people." Thus uses-gratification research represents a movement from concerns over attitudinal and behavioral change to a focus on perceptual and cognitive changes.

By focusing on audiences instead of media messages or the source of those messages, this approach has much to offer communication students. Such an approach, however, also has inherent difficulties. The most obvious problem is that it's not really a media theory, but could more accurately be characterized as a descriptive approach to studying media. The internal motivations that drive audiences to use media are difficult to test, thus making uses-gratifications a hard theory to verify or dismiss. As a result, it often raises as many questions about media use as it answers. Still, it makes an important contribution to understanding the media by providing a valuable audience-based perspective.

Assumptions of Uses-Gratification

Studies that focus on uses-gratification begin with a series of assumptions about the media and media audiences (O'Keefe, 1976).

1. *Audience consumption of political media content is goal directed.* This statement is frequently summarized by saying that what media do to an audience may not be as relevant as what audiences do with the media. This assumption reaffirms the theory's focus on the audience.

2. *Audience members use their own initiative in linking need gratification with media choice.* Since their behavior is goal directed, audiences seek out and choose media that meet their needs. Doing this sometimes requires that they make such linkages themselves, rather than relying on the media to fully satisfy their needs.

3. *Needs may be fulfilled by sources of satisfaction other than the media.* Essentially, each individual lives in a universe in which the media are only one potential source of need gratification. Larson (1995) points out that different media compete with one another (and with nonmedia sources) to meet audience needs. Individuals may find need satisfaction in such other factors as interpersonal relationships, personal activities, employment, and hobbies. In essence, the mass media compete with a number of other sources for the attention of the viewer and reader.

4. *Individuals can verbalize their needs, media uses, and gratifications derived.* This assumption is crucial to the research aspects of the uses-gratification model. Most research based on this approach is based on self-report questionnaires from television viewers. The researchers assume the responses to those questionnaires are accurate, a critical assumption for the validity of the research.

5. *Judgments about the cultural impact of mass communication should be made only after exploring audience orientations on their own terms.* Again, the focus is on the audience, that is, the television viewer, radio listener, or reader. Attempting to draw conclusions about mass media impact have little validity, these researchers would argue, if the response of the audience and how they use the media are not considered.

Why People Seek Out the Media.   An early study by Blumer and McQuail (1969) identified five possible gratifications that people might seek from the political content of media: vote guidance, reinforcement, surveillance, excitement, and interpersonal utility. One other, personal identity, has been suggested.

Vote guidance refers to the use of the media for assistance in making voting decisions. Swanson (1976) labeled this function "decisional utility" and reported that it had the strongest relationship to exposure to the mass media. This led him to conclude that "the bases of political information acquisition are not rooted in partisan attitude protection or validation, but rather are formed in the individual perceiver's desire to understand his world and act towards it confidently with predictable consequences."

Reinforcement is a need that urges people to seek out political media messages that reinforce their existing attitudes. This is, in essence, a continuation of the selectivity hypothesis as an explanation for media gratification.

Surveillance refers to a receiver's desire to keep up with what's going on in the world, or to keep in touch with events in the world. An audience that wants to stay informed tends to engage in a lot of scanning behavior, without seeking a detailed knowledge of events. Generally, surveillance appears to lead to superficial political activity.

Excitement needs refer to those who listen to political messages for the sheer fun of it. They may view politics as a sporting event, with them as the spectators, while others are fascinated by the competitive nature of the allegorical battle. In essence, the campaign becomes political drama (Combs, 1980).

Interpersonal utility refers to our need to have information to use when talking with others. Thus the media become a source of information, providing knowledge for future discussions or arguments with others. Several subcategories have been identified, including information seeking, informal discussion needs, and opinion leadership needs (gathering information so that we can offer opinions on an issue). Swanson divided it into three sub-categories: political discussions with friends, offering advice to others, and asking others for advice.

Larson (1995) argued that some people seek out messages for personal identity needs. This need is based on the idea that we learn to identify who we are by what we view, read, and listen to. Larson argues that self-confident people meet identity needs through reading; those who are not as self-assured rely more on viewing messages. In many ways, this is an application of the "political relationship" theory to uses-gratification. The political relationship theory is discussed in the next section.

Why People Avoid Media. Just as some people use the media to satisfy personal goals, some people avoid political media for the same reason. At least four factors have been identified as contributing to this effect.

Alienation. Many voters feel powerless and left out of the political process, thus seeing no need to seek political information. This "my-vote-doesn't-matter" syndrome means that the voter has no incentive to seek political information, and therefore, rarely does. The result is a low level of political activity.

Partisanship. Highly partisan voters avoid the media for a different reason—they are highly involved in the election, but their voting decisions have already been made. As a result, they have no particular need to gather additional information on the candidates. This behavior does not extend to partisan elites, of course. They continue to seek out information that can be used for interpersonal arguments.

Relaxation. Although many people enjoy the excitement of a political campaign, many others do not. For them, political information provides little of the sought-after diversion that they need. Rather than listening to political information, they would rather engage in an activity that offers them pleasure and relaxation. Such people use television for escape gratification (Canary & Spitzberg, 1993). Political information from the media is shuffled to the back of their minds, or perhaps disregarded entirely.

Instrumental vs. Ritualistic Uses. Rubin (1983, 1984) proposed that media usage by individuals fell into two distinct categories, instrumental uses and ritualistic uses. Individuals with an instrumental orientation toward television search for what they want to watch and regard television as a tool that serves a distinct purpose (to entertain, inform, excite, and so forth). These individuals choose programs that fulfill these desires, and remain highly involved with those shows to fulfill those goals (Rubin, 1984, Rubin & Perse, 1987). In contrast, people with ritualistic television motives do not regard television as a tool but as a way to satisfy more emotional and relational needs. Some ritualistic viewers watch television for companionship, or escape (Dobos & Dimmick, 1988). Others watch out of habit or when they are bored, perhaps because more fulfilling relationship opportunities are not available.

Much of the research in this area has focused on identifying gender differences in media usage, extending research that indicates that men and women use television differently (Comstock, 1989). Men are more likely to be purposeful and goal-directed in their television watching. They plan what they will watch (Morley, 1986, 1988) and use remote controls (Walker & Bellamy, 1991) to more easily achieve these objectives (for example, to acquire information or to be entertained). Nathanson, Perse, and Ferguson (1997) described this as an instrumental viewing style, with goal-directed reasons for watching.

Women are more likely to use television to satisfy relationship (Lull, 1980; Rubin & Rubin, 1982) or ritualistic needs (Nathanson, Perse, & Ferguson, 1997). Their overall viewing patterns are less active, with justifications including using television watching to feel less lonely or because there was nobody to talk to. Thus, they are more likely to regard television as a social vehicle to spend time with others; television becomes a secondary activity around which interpersonal or emotional objectives are sought (Morley, 1988).

Men are more likely to control television watching, using the remote control to frequently change channels in search of greater variety and stimulation (Perse & Ferguson, 1993). They are also more likely than women to select programs during group viewing (Heeter, 1988) and to use the remote control to try to annoy others (Walker & Bellamy, 1991). Program loyalty, or watching programs regularly, decreases for female heads-of-households when they watch with male adults (Webster & Wakshlag, 1982). Fathers usually have the most influence in program selection and are least likely to ask others' permission before changing channels (Lull, 1982). Women are more likely to report that someone else changed the channel even though they wished they hadn't (Heeter, 1988). Even when alone, however, women may not use television purposefully. Because of domestic responsibilities (Hochschild, 1989), distracted television viewing may be an accompaniment to other activities (Perse & Ferguson, 1993).

The concept of distracted viewing has led to research on active and passive television watching. People who are active in general tend to watch cable channels (Ferguson & Melkote, 1997), supporting the theory that people who are active in general, or have more leisure time, have larger (perhaps "more active") channel repertoires. Webster and Lichty (1991) argued that program choice and media exposure are based on both media factors (availability of channels to watch) and the general leisure time of the audience. Blumler (1979) argued that such viewer activity is not an either-or condition, but is based on a number of factors. That argument may have even more weight today, given the potential of the Internet to change the way that people obtain political information (Graber, 2001).

Television and Behavior.   Some researchers have suggested that the media have an impact on the behavior of audience members, particularly in terms of aggressiveness. Research has found that people react differently to watching aggressiveness on television (Frost & Stauffer, 1987). Skill and Wallace (1990) noted that viewers may learn how to communicate aggressively by watching characters communicate on television. If so, they have plenty of role models. Most television entertainment shows include heavy amounts of aggressive behavior, with the hero of the show being the character who is most frequently aggressive (Potter & Ware, 1987). Furthermore, there is a direct link between aggression and viewing habits, with people who are verbally aggressive watching more television (Martin, Anderson, & Cos, 1997). Aggressive viewers also do not believe they are hurt by watching verbally aggressive programming, they expressed more affinity for the character, and perceived the show to be similar to real life. Heavy viewers who reported greater psychological hurt from receiving verbally aggressive messages also believed such shows were similar to real life.

Several researchers have recognized a link between personality with watching and enjoying violence on television (Atkin et al., 1979; Wober & Gunter, 1986). Leckenby and Surlin (1976) claimed that increased viewing of verbal aggressiveness leads to a greater liking and believability of verbally aggressive television shows. Rubin, Perse, and Taylor (1988) suggested that personality differences play a role in explaining such effects, with those who are predisposed toward being verbally aggressive being more responsive to shows and characters who are verbally aggressive. This is somewhat supported by research that indicates that enjoying television violence is predictive of people's verbal aggressiveness (Sebastian et al., 1978; Walker & Morley, 1991).

Strangely enough, the impact of television violence on aggressive behavior appears to be particularly strong when watching the news. Atkin (1983) found that watching real violence (such as is seen on news programs) had a greater effect on individuals' future behaviors than fictional violence (action shows and dramas). Thus, it appears that most viewers can distinguish between fictional and real violence.

Criticisms of Uses-Gratifications. Uses-gratification theory has its critics, and the most basic problem is that of measurement of needs. The theory assumes the presence of an underlying need that can only be measured as expressed behavior (usually self-report questionnaires). Thus, critics can argue that many findings under the uses-gratification model could be adequately explained by some other theoretical perspective. Littlejohn (1996), for example, points out that the theory does not focus on how the media can have negative cultural effects on the audience. Littlejohn also argues that it does an inadequate job of explaining the media's unconscious or ritualistic effects on the audience.

Campaign Implications. Despite the criticisms of the approach, uses-gratification has made some major contributions to practical campaign behavior. First, research in this area has consistently identified television as the medium that serves as the most universal needs gratifier. This finding is reflected in the heavy use of television by campaigns today. Second, uses-gratification research has consistently found that the gratification model tends to apply more to older voters than to younger voters, that is, older voters are more likely to use the media for their own purposes. Conversely, younger voters, who seem to be less goal-directed in their consumption of media, appear to be more influenced by media messages. This factor has generally led to an assumption in campaigns that younger voters are a bellwether group. In other words, if a television ad is effective, it will first show up in increased support among younger voters. Third, the model has had a major effect on making campaigns focus on the needs of the audience. The assumption of the uses-gratification approach is that the impact that campaign media have on voters depends to a large extent on the motivations of the voters to follow the campaign. Interest in the campaign determines, to a large extent, the attitude change among voters related to the campaign. Thus, to be successful, the campaign must aim to provide optimum gratification to the voters. Although media may not change any attitudes directly, failure to provide gratification could result in a loss of support.

Relational Theories

Another approach to media impact falls into the category of relational theories of media impact. These approaches assumed that the major impact of the media is the psychological relationships developed between the viewers and the persona in the media.

The Friendship Theory

Surlin's (1978) friendship theory argues that viewers consider television characters to be "significant others," or surrogate friends. This decision results from viewers' perception of cognitive similarity between themselves and the character. The result of this identification leads to watching the program that features the character more often. Once the surrogate friendship has been established, the viewers accept the point of view presented by the character (Surlin, 1974; Tate & Surlin, 1976; Vidmar & Rokeach, 1974), adopting the perspective of the character who serves as the significant other. The result is gratification, which in turn serves as a basis for watching that show more often.

The theory becomes relevant to politicians whenever the significant character addresses a political issue. Powell and Anderson (1984), for example, found that viewers who identified with a character from *Carter Country* tended to shift their attitudes toward homosexuality as the character underwent a similar attitude change on the show. In essence, a character who becomes a significant other can serve as an attitudinal anchor for political issues. This possibility was emphasized again in the 1992 when controversy erupted when Vice President Dan Quayle complained about Candace Bergen's character on the sitcom *Murphy Brown*. Quayle criticized the show for portraying the character as an unwed mother, arguing that it was not a suitable role model for family audiences. While he may not have articulated it directly, Quayle's criticism is based on the assumption that there is some validity to the friendship theory.

Political Relationships

Seymour-Ure (1974) took the relationship approach to media effects in a different direction, focusing entirely on the political arena. Although his data were based entirely on the British political system, some parallels can still be seen in American politics. Seymour-Ure argued that the major effect of media on politics was the establishment of political relationships, either at the individual, institutional, or systemic level. As an example of how the media can affect an individual relationship, he noted that the media defined an Enoch Powell speech on nonwhite immigration as a threat to Conservative party leader Edward Heath, leading to Heath's firing of Powell from his shadow cabinet position. At the institutional level, Seymour-Ure argued, the mass media's treatment of the British monarchy (an institution) made the nation's (a system) legitimacy partly dependent on that of the monarchy.

Seymour-Ure's analysis has at least two important implications for American politics. First, his argument about relationship development implies that the media made the existence of national campaigns possible (and, perhaps, inevitable). Second, and this is also a problem with his approach, he assumes that the major political action is among political elites. His most carefully documented media effects are upon elite individuals, implying that the media operate to make it more difficult for nonelites to find a way to participate in the political process. While this is frequently the case, there are numerous instances in American political history where nonelites (civil rights protesters, for example) have driven public opinion to a point where they have had some impact on public policy.

Influence Gaps

Zaller (1996) argues that people are influenced by mass communication in proportion to their exposure to messages and their knowledge of candidates. Studies that report limited effects, he argues, have been limited by methodological problems. They frequently look only at presidential campaigns, where effects tend to be smaller than in other campaigns. Such intensive campaigns create cross-cutting changes that cannot be detected when using the general linear models that most research studies use. Such models are typically applied to only a single case of mass persuasion at a time, Zaller says, processes that "virtually guarantee systematic underestimation of media impacts" (p. 37).

Zaller views each campaign as a holistic message that either reaches the voter or it does not. In a two-candidate race, that assumption generates four potential campaign scenarios: Voters may be influenced by both campaigns, neither campaign, by Candidate A but not by Candidate B, or by Candidate B but not by Candidate A. In the first two cases, in which the voter is reached by both or neither of the campaigns, the impact of the media should be negligible, creating situations in which minimal effects will be observed. However, if either candidate is able to dominate the media (scenarios 3 and 4) to the disadvantage of the opponent, the probability of media impact is high.

Zaller also argues that the media's impact will vary, based on the extent to which voters are receptors of mass media information (particularly news), a phenomenon he refers to as a "reception gap." Voters who are moderate news watchers, he argues, are those who are most likely to be converts and switch parties to vote for an incumbent, particularly if the incumbent dominates the media. The incumbent's media advantage fills in the reception gap for such voters; as they learn more about the incumbent, the likelihood of their supporting the incumbent increases. Conversely, if both the incumbent and the challenger have intense campaigns, some habitual viewers will switch to the challenger as they learn new information about that person.

Zaller is not alone in raising questions about the information gap that exists among voters. Several studies have noted that voters are often ill-informed on issues, and the media may be partly to blame for that situation. Studies have often found that news coverage on presidential elections focuses on competition and controversy rather than providing information on issues (Patterson, 1980; Patterson & Davis, 1985). Similarly, Robinson and Sheehan (1983) reported that a majority of the news coverage in 1980 failed to contain even one issue-related sentence. Such results triggered calls for more responsible coverage of campaigns by the media.

Summary

The impact of media on political behavior is a complex and ever-changing subject. The sheer volume of media exposure in modern society argues for some type of potential impact, but quantifying and specifying the exact nature of the media-audience relationship is complex. As researchers try to learn something about today's media, another theory is being developed that may invalidate many of their conclusions. Thus, academicians continue to chase the elusive answers. Still, the academic community has addressed a number of critical issues. In some instances, mass media can be used for propaganda purposes; an understanding of such techniques will make a person less susceptible to undue influence. Various scholars have debated whether political impact has a little impact or a massive impact on voters, but the answer seems to fall somewhere in between. The media can have a major impact on some voters, and a little one on others. It can influence the public's agenda on some issues, but not on others. What impact that does exist is likely mediated by interpersonal influence and the individual motivations of the voters. Still, despite all of these mitigating factors, the media are still the primary means of communication between candidates and voters. As such, it continues to play a vital role in the campaign process.

That's why consultants continue to assume that media can and do have a direct impact on electoral results. Much of the campaign budget and campaign time is devoted to media communications. Furthermore—as we will see in a later chapter—those media campaigns can often make a difference in determining which candidate wins an election. To help in that process, consultants rely upon some of the ideas developed by the academic community, and they continue to use any such idea until it doesn't work anymore, keeping in mind that the technologies of modern media are constantly changing.

QUESTIONS FOR DISCUSSION

1. What is the difference between a theory and a model? Is the uses-gratifications approach to media a theory or a model? What about agenda setting?

2. Your environmental group is attempting to build public opposition to genetically altered food grains. With only a few exceptions, you have been met with scant interest from opinion makers in the news media. Why have you had a difficult time presenting your point of view? Based on either the awareness, priorities, or salience models, how could you create a program that would improve your chances of getting news coverage?

3. Although crime has not been an issue in your candidate's campaign for state senator, recent polling suggests that voters are concerned that she has not taken a vigorous position against it. Although they still support her, that support has grown perilously thin. Is there an explanation for the voter response within the uses-gratification model? Does the model suggest a solution? Are there threshold issues about which candidates must reassure the electorate in order to be successful?

4. In polling provided to the campaign, your candidate for attorney general is running a close but weak second in an open primary, a very unusual circumstance for a Democrat. Four other Democrats are in the race. The lone Republican is ahead. Your candidate is clearly the most experienced and toughest on crime. Even the Republican president of the United States is shown making generous comments about your candidate in your television ads. What changes can your campaign make to move ahead?

PART TWO

The Campaign Team

Modern political campaigns are team activities. When an individual decides to run for public office, a team is assembled that includes professionals, family members, friends, and volunteers. The structure of the team will vary with each campaign, as will the nature of the team members. A number of specific functions are typically fulfilled by some team members regardless of the particular organization's structure. Part Two will examine those functions and the tasks associated with each.

Chapter 6 opens this part with a discussion of the campaign organization. At first glance, the day-to-day operations of a campaign look similar to that of any other organization. Beneath the surface, though, are distinct differences that are so unique to the area that an entire subfield of consulting has emerged. The modern campaign manager must form a temporary campaign organization that meshes the talents of the candidate, the candidate's family, volunteers, and professional consultants. The campaign manager is the "general" who keeps each team member focused on an assigned task.

Chapter 7 looks at campaign communication in the mass media. The key team member for this section is the media consultant, the "guru" who advises the campaign on messages, produces the media advertisements, and directs the placement of those ads in the appropriate media outlets. When a war analogy is invoked, media consultants are often compared to the air force—that member of the team who provides air cover for other campaign activities. Media consultants often work in multiple formats—television, radio, and newspapers, for example—while maintaining a consistent theme and strategic approach. This chapter examines their role and how they function within the campaign.

Chapter 8 looks at the role of direct voter contact, an activity that is less visible than mass media ads but no less important in many campaigns. If the media consultant represents the air force, then the direct voter contact team members represent the ground forces of a campaign. Telephone banks contact voters individually to identify supporters, increase voter turnout, and to communicate messages in support of or opposition to some candidates. Direct mail consultants offer services to mail letters and brochures to individual voters who have been targeted on the basis of specific demographic and attitudinal bases. The Internet has increased the potential of direct voter contact by allowing campaigns to use e-mail and web sites to exchange information with supporters.

Chapter 9 addresses the role of political speeches and the people who write them. Political speeches are the way in which the candidate personally articulates the campaign's messages and themes. The speechwriters are the communication specialists who must find a way to express the candidate's ideas in a way that communicates with the voters and maintains a message that is consistent with the overall campaign theme.

Finally, Chapter 10 examines the role of polling in political campaigns. The pollster is the intelligence unit of the team, the person who provides the team with information used to make campaign decisions. The pollster's function is really much broader than just that of conducting public opinion surveys. Most polling firms also provide other forms of communication research services, particularly focus groups. By using a variety of research approaches, the research portion of the team can provide both descriptive and qualitative information that can contribute to campaign decisions. When they've done that, the team is ready to go to work.

CHAPTER

6

Campaign Organization

In 1996, Missourians for Riverboat Gambling wanted to add slot machines to the list of legalized gambling options in the state's riverboat casinos, a change that required a referendum for an amendment to the state's constitution. Polling data indicated that the issue had enough public support to pass a referendum, but there were organizational problems.

State law was specific. Any group that wanted an amendment on the ballot was required to get a substantial number of petition signatures from at least six of Missouri's eight congressional districts. Consulting firms that specialized in petition gathering had been hired early, but they had met with only partial success. With only twenty-three days left before the deadline, about half of the state had not been reached. No signatures had been obtained from most of western Missouri, including Kansas City.

Faced with failure, the committee hired a team of political consultants to organize the process. Want ads were placed to hire workers to gather the signatures. Training materials were developed; training sessions implemented; and a centrally located headquarters established and equipped with telephones, fax machines, computers, and minimal office furniture. Finally, a payroll system was implemented to ensure that the new workers were paid on a timely basis.

Signature gatherers were provided with briefing materials that encouraged voters to sign the petition—not because they necessarily supported slot machines, but "to give the voters of Missouri the right to decide the issue." To avoid antagonizing the opposition, there was no attempt to publicize or advertise the signature campaign itself. Instead, all activities were kept at an organizational level.

In the end, a thousand petition gatherers were hired, trained, and paid to obtain a goal of 62,000 valid signatures. A core staff of twenty, working sixteen hours a day, managed the effort. The result: 147,000 signatures were gathered and the amendment went on the ballot and easily passed at the subsequent election.

This example represents the dramatic impact that the campaign organization can have on elections. While such organizational aspects are relatively invisible to the voting public, the campaign organization still plays an important role. A great campaign organization will not ensure victory, but a poor one can contribute to defeat. A better campaign organization—particularly one composed of professional campaign workers—has a better chance of winning. Or, as Medvic (2001) noted, ". . . the more types of consultants hired to assist with various aspects of the campaign, the better candidates will do at election time . . ." (p. 104).

The day-to-day management of the campaign organization is different from most other professional organizations (Steinberg, 1976a, 1976b). Several elements make the campaign organization distinctive. First, it is generally temporary in nature: a group of individuals—some professionals and some volunteers—who are brought together for a relatively short amount of time with the goal of completing a task that will lead to the dissolution of their jobs within a few weeks or months. Second, that situation is fertile ground for conflict between the various consultants, the paid vs. volunteer workers, the idealists, and the "win-at-all-costs" advisers. Third, the managers of the campaign organization have remarkably little control or legitimate authority over the others in the organization. The manager can advise the candidate, but ultimate decisions for campaign activities are those of the candidate. The manager can issue orders to others in the organization, but many of those are other consultants (who are more used to giving orders than taking them) or volunteers who can walk away from the job with little or no penalty. Fourth, volunteers are often outside the normal channels of communication within the organization (Lewis, 1999), a situation that requires the development of communication channels created precisely for them. And fifth, the campaign organization has to have constant performance reviews; an annual performance review is simply not timely enough for an effective campaign.

As campaigns have become more complex, the role of the campaign organization has also evolved—particularly at the presidential level. That organizational expansion has raised eyebrows among some critics. Several observers have complained that modern campaigns are controlled too much by political professionals (Polsby & Wildavsky, 2000; Thurber & Nelson, 2000). The role of the consultant often continues well after the campaign, providing continued influence on government even after the election is over. Consultant Dick Morris (1999), for example, continued to provide advice and consultation to the White House during most of Bill Clinton's administration.

The result, Blumenthal (1982) argued, is that campaigns have become too organized, resulting in the political environment becoming increasingly dominated by the campaign organization. Staff members from the campaign take a position on the staff of the newly elected official or remain active on the sidelines as consultants to the candidates. That action has led to a situation that Blumenthal calls the "Permanent Campaign,": after a candidate achieves election, the campaign organization stays intact to help the newly elected official make policy decisions. As a result, Woodward (1997) noted, "A concern for public opinion remains the central focus of any campaign" (p. 125). Positions on issues and legislative votes are decided on the basis of political impact. Nor is that effect limited to the primary campaign organization; all sorts of volunteer organizations that participated in the campaign can have an impact. Polsby and Wildavsky (1968) noted that, particularly at the presidential level, there is a danger that "the volunteer organizations will take on lives of their own and attempt to dictate strategy and policy to the candidates" (p. 180).

Others have argued that the role of the campaign organization has been diminished over the years. As a result of the growing influence of consultants, the professional organization has become a more dominant force in campaigns while the organizational influence of political parties has diminished (Thurber & Nelson, 2000). Campaigns of the 1940s and 1950s used the campaign organization for the latter purpose (Cass, 1962). "A veteran organizer," Key (1949) wrote, "can by his personal influence gather to the fold political cronies that he has used and who have used him in previous years" (p. 403). The consultants of the 1940s were frequently organizational experts whose expertise was who they knew rather than what they knew. "The special asset of these men is not their organizing ability or their political acumen alone," Key (1949) wrote in describing the 1940s system, "It is their intimate acquaintance with county politics and county politicians."

That focus on county politics highlights another change in campaign organizations. The increased role of the media in campaigns has altered the organizational structure of campaigns. During the 1940s and 1950s, statewide campaigns were typically organized by geography, with a state organization structured to communicate with district or county organizations (Cass, 1962; Key, 1949, pp. 403–405). Today's campaigns are more frequently organized by function, in terms of what roles or media outlets are necessary to reach the voters. Furthermore, those roles are often handled by campaign consultants, individuals who will not be directly involved in the administration of the elected official's duties.

Organizational Roles

The Candidate. At the top of a campaign organization's organization chart (see Figure 6.1) is the candidate. Some candidates are self-starters, individuals who chose to run for office for personal reasons; others are recruits, candidates who seek an office at the urging

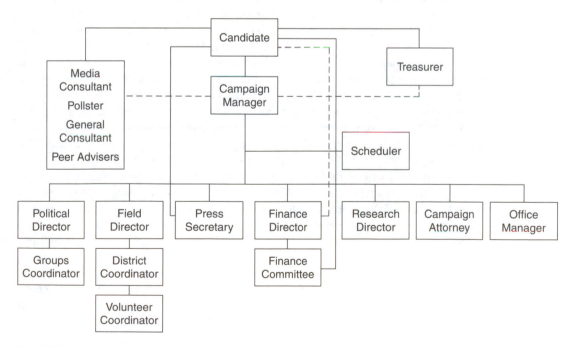

FIGURE 6.1   A Campaign Organizational Chart

of friends, neighbors, or interested third parties (Nimmo, 1970, p. 42; Seligman, 1961). Although the campaign manager is responsible for the smooth day-to-day operation, it is the candidate who is ultimately responsible for the campaign. All information is fed to the candidate through the filter of their handpicked experts and managers. The candidate is responsible for approving his or her campaign message through speeches, letters, op-ed pieces, and through statements at news conferences. Additional political communication can be inferred through the candidate's schedule. Other information about the campaign can be inferred through the candidate's personality, clothing, haircut, eyeglasses (or lack thereof), marriage (or lack thereof), religiosity (or lack thereof), and myriad other minor factors.

Candidates also set the tone for their campaigns in terms of both organizational style and temperament. Some candidates insist on micromanaging their campaigns, while others remain aloof from the day-to-day operation. Energetic candidates inspire their campaign workers to engage in a similar work ethic, while laid-back candidates might generate a comfortable and relaxed work environment. In either case, there are no models that guarantee success.

The Campaign Manager.   Overly elaborate organizations that consume large amounts of money without contributing to a persuasive message can contribute to failure. For example, a campaign that leases an airplane—seldom a cost-effective practice—may be at a competitive disadvantage. Thus enters the campaign manager. The campaign manager must be a master of cost-benefit analysis as well as the political arts. His or her job is different from that of standard business management. They are in charge of an organization that will cease operating at a known time. Even if fully successful, it will stop.

Early in the campaign, a decision must be made as to how much authority the campaign manager will have (Nimmo, 1970, p. 45). When the candidate takes a strong role in management, often the manager is weak. When the candidate takes a weak role in management, the campaign manager is strong. Either way it is up to the effective manager of the campaign to implement the campaign strategy (Kelley, 1956). This task requires the manager to negotiate the best prices for the products the campaign consumes—printing, advertising and its production, travel, and so forth. Every amount more than the minimum resources can result in a less persuasive campaign. As a result, the campaign manager will plan "minute details" for some campaign events in an effort to achieve maximum impact (Nimmo, 1970, p. 120).

The campaign manager must also motivate the staff to their best efforts during long hours with little financial reward. While many staff members may imagine themselves as members of the candidate's future staff, it is generally illegal for the candidate to promise something of value in a future public office for current labors. Generally, the staff cannot be fired, and separations can result in "sour grapes" news media reports—something no campaign seeks.

Political staffs are difficult to motivate. Some staff members are local political junkies who are drawn to the "action" of political campaigns. Others are transient to politics. Some are simply devoted to the candidate. Unless the campaign managers can convince each that he or she will learn something or that the manager has the best interests of the candidate at heart, the manager will fail.

The campaign manager must also deal with the consultants. Consultants look at the manager as someone who will get their checks mailed on time. After that, consultants hope the campaign manager will not "poison the water," causing the candidate to lose confidence. If a consultant does not start with confidence in the campaign manager, they may simply undermine the candidate's confidence.

Campaign managers who begin the process as a "best friend" of the candidate usually will not have this problem. On the other hand, "best friends" often lack the skills needed to run an effective campaign. The requisite knowledge, from effective mailing techniques to the nomenclature for advertising, is know how the average layperson does not have. Also, a less politically knowledgeable person may not have the skills needed to assist in the interpretation of survey research.

A professional campaign manager is more likely to have these and other skills, but not have the full confidence of the candidate. The average candidate fears many things about the campaign environment, not the least of which is the potential abandonment by a cynical outsider. In the final analysis, the best campaign managers run these cobbled-together organizations well only when real confidence can be instilled. Campaign managers can accomplish this with impressive resumes, lengthy hours on the job, doing a good job, and by being a good manager.

The Political Director.   The political director is charged with arranging alliances with other politicians, special interest groups, civic associations, political clubs, labor unions, environmental groups, business groups, and other groups. Political campaigns will work to consolidate natural constituencies through their political operation. For example, Republicans might attempt to ally themselves with Chambers of Commerce while Democrats do the same with labor unions. Although there are no hard-and-fast rules, these alliances are often a cost-effective means of communicating with voters. The leaders of the various groups serve as elite opinion leaders who can pass on the campaign message to larger numbers of voters. Also, the very fact of such alliances reinforces the campaign messages and counter-messages. Often during campaigns, a candidate will advertise their "endorsers" for just such a purpose.

The Field Director.   The field director is responsible for organizing activities that identify supporters and harness their energy to pass the persuasive message to others and maximize the turnout of voters friendly to the campaign on election day (Pohl, 1971, pp. 140–141). Typically, a field director will use existing political activists to find others by direct contact with voter groups by the candidate. As the campaign matures, activities begin to focus on voter identification and turnout. By creating programs, the field organization will contact voters and ask them whom they support. Lists of friendly voters are developed in this way. Beginning a few days before election day, friendly voters are contacted and urged to vote. Efforts can range from highly elaborate organizations with the creation of county and city committees with campaign representatives appointed down to the precinct, or even street levels, to merely the appearance of a field organization. The "work your base" maxim comes into play here. Many campaigns will highly organize areas where they are very strong, with little or no organization in other areas.

The Finance Director.   Most candidates have to ask others for money (Thomas, 1999, p. 68), and the finance director helps them do that. The finance director has responsibility for raising funds through direct contact by the candidate, fund-raisers, or through a finance committee. For that reason, the finance director is often a well-known (or at least well connected) member of the community "whose knowledge of the responsive sources of funds has been acquired through long observation or experience" (Key, 1949, p. 401). The finance director oversees a campaign finance committee whose members may be either a collection of the candidate's closest friends and/or supporters who have provided the larger contributors to the campaign. The main task of the finance committee is to cast an ever-wider net for fund-raising purposes.

The campaign organization is an engine that manufactures and distributes the campaign message. The fuel that feeds this machine is money, for which the campaign also has the responsibility for raising (Pohl, 1971, pp. 39–45). Some campaigns require high-test and many will run on regular. Others run dry before they cross the finish line. Without money, no campaign organization can achieve its potential, much less win its election. No amount of money can necessarily keep a campaign from losing a campaign. The campaign organization requires computers, printers, office furniture, brochures, palm cards, a letterhead, postage, posters (lawn signs), larger signs, radio commercials, television commercials, automobiles, telephones, air charters, air fares, motel rooms, personnel, and paid expert consultants, just to mention a few items. Tiny campaigns need fewer items. Huge statewide campaigns need vast resources. This function of the campaign is discussed in more detail in a later chapter.

The Press Secretary.   The first job of the press secretary is to promote the campaign message to the news media. No employee of the campaign has a greater responsibility for knowing and implementing the message on a day-by-day basis. It is virtually impossible for a campaign to be successful without a solid relationship with the news media. The press secretary is responsible for the campaign's relationship with the news media and for carrying the message to editors and reporters. It is often true that so-called free media are insufficient to elect a candidate. It is equally true that news reports that do not support the campaign message can defeat a campaign. If the press secretary is successful at his or her day-to-day job, then newspapers, magazines, television news programs, radio news programs, and the Internet will deliver the message to voters. The press secretary will often travel with the candidate to facilitate interviews on the campaign trail. The role requires the ability to write press releases and the ability to influence observers. In some campaigns, the press person also writes speeches for the candidate.

The Research Director.   There are two kinds of research in modern politics, issues research and opposition research. Issues research is the data required to support the candidate's position on a given issue. Such data can be received from recognized experts on a topic (university professors, for example), special interest group supporters, libraries, Internet research services, and other sources.

Opposition research falls into three categories: research on the opponent, research on the campaign's own candidate, and research on the voters. Opposition research is often controversial because it rather emphatically suggests that the campaign will attack its opponent (or that it expects the opponent to attack them). Such data can be as simple as a public records search for such information as tax compliance, divorce decrees, lawsuits, property holdings, education, and family. However, those can be remarkably revealing at times. One of the authors was involved in a local campaign for tax collector where a simple search of the public records revealed that one of the candidates had not paid his property or business taxes; that fact became a focal point of the campaign and led to that candidate's defeat.

Opposition research can also include hiring private detectives or professional opposition research consultants. The advantage of professionals is that they tend to know where to look for information, are more discreet in their searches, and offer better protection to the campaign. Also, their work product tends to be in a form that can more easily be used by campaign media consultants. For incumbents, the research focuses on their political record (particularly the voting record of legislators), but other issues also come into play. The authors have been involved in campaigns in which opposition research uncovered such facts as:

- A wealthy candidate who was claiming an agricultural exemption on his home as a means of reducing property taxes;
- An incumbent legislator with a criminal record, including one arrest for indecent exposure;
- Another incumbent who had written a letter to the parole board in support of the release of a convicted rapist who was the son of a major campaign donor.

Major campaigns also hire professional opposition research consultants to investigate themselves. Such practices allows candidates to understand how their public record can be interpreted by their opponent and thus allows them to anticipate potential attacks. That information is then used to prepare defensive responses that explain those sensitive portions of the record from the candidate's point of view.

Research on the voters is typically done with polls or focus groups (but is not limited to those techniques) and is discussed in another chapter. All campaigns, regardless of their budget, can engage in such basic voter analyses as investigation of voting patterns, past voting turnout, and demographic correlates that might affect the campaign (Denton & Woodward, 1985).

The Campaign Attorney.   Modern campaigns are often regulated by state and local or federal authorities with a maze of rules ranging from campaign contributions and expenditure limits to the details of when and how to make campaign reports. Also, the campaign interacts with a variety of electronic advertising media that are, in turn, also regulated by a litany of legal requirements. Campaigns, from time to time, will work to get an opponent's negative ads off the air by either threatening a lawsuit or actually suing the opposition campaign. A campaign attorney will facilitate these undertakings.

The Campaign Office Manager.   An office manager is the day-to-day boss of the campaign staff. This person is essential to controlling the routine expenses of the campaign from day to day and keeping records suitable for expenditure reports, including the payroll. This person is not necessarily somebody who is politically savvy or overly involved in political activities. However, he or she must be someone with excellent organizational and management skills, the same skills that would be essential to the day-to-day management of any business or organization.

The office manager also has the task of coordinating office functions with a staff that is often composed mostly of "professionally committed party regulars and citizen volunteers" (Denton & Woodward, 1985, pp. 55–56). Those volunteers are often women, young people, and older adults—a subset that works remarkably well together in the political environment, perhaps because they tend to be so focused on telephone sociability goals (O'Keefe & Sulanowski, 1995). Volunteer workers bring their own motivation to the job, but maintaining that motivation for the duration of the campaign can be a challenging task, one that is much harder than that of a typical office manager. If they so choose, those volunteers don't have to come to work when they don't want to.

The Campaign Scheduler.   A major campaign asset is the ability of the candidate to communicate through speeches, presentations, and interviews and to demonstrate the campaign message symbolically through the nature of a campaign appearance. Good campaign schedulers have a knowledge of the campaign message and the resources available to demonstrate that message. The authors have illustrative experiences:

- A candidate holding a news conference on the banks on the Mississippi River, in the shadows of a grossly polluting chemical plant to demonstrate his commitment to environmental ideals.
- A candidate speaking to striking union workers to demonstrate his commitment to safe working conditions.
- A candidate visiting a school to demonstrate her commitment to higher education.

To maximize the candidate's time, a scheduler is necessary. The scheduler represents the point of contact with the candidate for those outside the campaign. The scheduler makes all travel and logistical arrangements to accommodate events. Among the second-tier positions in the campaign, this is one of the most difficult and most stressful of all roles. It requires somebody with the organizational skills of a CEO and the political tact of a diplomat. The candidate's time will become a major commodity, and the scheduler is responsible for ensuring that time is spent in productive ways. That frequently means turning down invitations from friends, supporters, and financial backers; those refusals have to be made in a tactful manner.

The Campaign Treasurer.   Most campaign authorities require the appointment of an individual who is responsible for keeping the campaign's financial records. The treasurer is often also responsible for maintaining the official records of the campaign and complying with the relevant campaign finance laws. A treasurer will often act as campaign controller, as well by being the authorizing signature on major expenditure checks for the purchase of advertising time, printing, and so forth.

Consultants and Peer Advisers.   The final category of campaign organization are the consultants. In major campaigns, the consultants are part of an "inner circle" (Thomas, 1999, p. 22)—one that may also include friends and peers of the candidate—who are involved in major campaign decisions. Most of the consultant roles are discussed individually elsewhere. These people often deal directly with the candidate but depend on other members of the organization for information and logistical support. Much of the work product of the campaign organization filters upward to these consultants. They frequently get a great deal of internal recognition and financial rewards, while internal campaign workers may work for little or nothing.

This is a typical, though not the only, campaign organization. Smaller campaigns, particularly those at the local level (Thomas, 1999), adapt by having one person fill two or three of the functions, or they do not fill the slot at all. In some campaigns, the candidate is also the campaign manager, or the office manager is called campaign manager. Larger campaigns often add elaborate staffing to functions. Presidential campaigns will have all of this, and will have campaigns in each of the fifty states that will be a smaller version of the national campaign staff.

Winning campaign organizations often inspire candidates to continue their successful efforts in office. Such efforts rarely work. After the 1992 presidential campaign, the Clinton-Gore administration announced it would continue the intensity of the campaign, using the same people in their management of the White House. Within a brief period of time, it became clear that the needs of public administration were not amenable to the emotional, intense styles that typify political campaigns.

The Public Interface for the Candidate's Ideas

Even in relatively small local races for state legislature, the candidate must become accessible to hundreds of thousands of voters. For individual voters this means finding the answer to questions: Does he or she agree with me? Is he or she my kind of person? For the candidate, accessibility means communicating on a wide variety of fronts, including group-to-group and person-to-person interaction. Nimmo (1970, p. 122) called these techniques "organizational media," or, "the offices within the campaign organization that communicate with voters on the candidate's behalf." They include such elements as precinct workers, speakers' bureaus, endorsement groups, and—in modern campaigns—the webmaster. The actual impact of these techniques on election results varies. Precinct and other operations that affect voter turnout can have an impact in close elections; furthermore, a grassroots organization can be the most cost-effective means of communicating with voters in a small geographical area (Berrigan, 1982). Speakers' bureaus have little impact on the level of support and are used primarily to maintain morale among workers and supporters (Nimmo, 1970, p. 123). Endorsements may not sway many voters, but they typically increase the network for distributing the campaign message.

The campaign manager, meanwhile, must focus on communicating most messages through the news media and finally through advertising media. This role places unique strains on political campaign organizations. Voters, even voters who identify themselves as members of the same political party, hold vastly different positions on issues. A campaign organization that does not understand this will face difficulties. In general, campaigns react to the multifaceted nature of voters through ambiguity. Ambiguity can be expressed through demonstrations of the ways of the things that voters have in common, such as family, views on crime and punishment, and even minor things like opinions about haircut styles. Thus many voters are encouraged to make decisions about candidates for superficial reasons rather than issues or even self-interest. The campaign organization facilitates this process.

The General Consultant in Political Campaigns

by Mike Mann

Mike Mann is the owner of Southern Strategies, Inc., a North Carolina–based consulting firm that specializes in providing general consulting services for candidates and referendum-based campaigns.

The Political General Consultant: A person with broad general knowledge, expertise, and skills in all political disciplines who sells that knowledge to groups and individuals seeking to influence the outcome of political and ballot initiative campaigns.

Political consulting as a profession is a relatively new field. Although around informally since the first group of upright walking monkeys decided to turn their pack into a tribe and their pecking order into the selection of a chief, it was not until the second half of the twentieth century that it became a recognized profession and, in fact, an industry.

> **General Consulting Rule No. 1:** People do what they are inspected to do, not what they are expected to do.

In the early days, encompassing the 1950s and '60s, political consulting was dominated by public relations firms and a few media consulting firms. It was, however, during this time that a new political animal began to appear on the scene, the professional campaign manager. Of course campaigns had always had managers, but they were usually a friend or family member of the candidate and the management role was a "one-shot" deal, usually filled by a volunteer. The professional manager usually started out as one of those volunteers, liked politics, managed a successful campaign, figured he or she (although mostly "he" in the early days) could make some money at it, let it be known that they were available, found a demand, and voilá, the professional campaign manager was born.

The demand for political consulting grew rapidly during the 1970s and '80s. Accompanying that demand, or preceding that demand, depending on which side of the chicken-and-egg theory you come down on, was a huge increase in the availability of political money. Anyone who has passed Political Science 101 understands the formula: "d + $ = mec" (demand + money = more expensive campaigns). Of course, the purpose here is not to determine which came first or to allow our discussion to deteriorate into some philosophical debate over the good and evil of money and politics. Rather, I bring this up merely to point out that, during this period of time, more money became available for politics and this turned political consulting into a growth industry.

This increased demand for services and the increased availability of money allowed for and even prompted an influx of new and talented people into the political consulting profession. The profession became more creative and more progressive. Political consulting took on an identity of its own. The profession began to diversify and, with the diversification, naturally, came specialization.

Public relations firms, with their "package-and-sale-soft-drinks" mentality, could no longer handle the unique and special needs of modern political campaigns. The political media consultant was born, attuned to confrontation and with the ability to understand a message and to rapidly produce TV and radio spots. These airwave warriors are simply too aggressive for the "namby-pamby" sensitivities of the typical public relations firm. Political polling, which had been done by large national public opinion survey companies whose focus was primarily to determine long-range consumer trends, were replaced by young, aggressive consultants. These young consultants usually came from the academic community and understood not only the math and statistical theories, but also how to apply and interpret them in a political context and how to produce their product in a rapidly changing political environment. Also emerging, developing, and spinning off during this period were other areas of political consulting specialties such as direct mail, telephone banks, opposition research, fund-raising, list management, grassroots organization, signature collection, candidate training, and so forth.

By the late 1980s and early 1990s, political campaigns—particularly upper ballot, statewide ballot initiatives, and major coordinated campaigns—had become so complex, so involved, so technology driven, and so expensive that a new breed of political consultant slowly emerged. The general consultant role was born out of necessity. The large amount of money being spent on campaigns caused the candidates to begin to demand better and more thorough control over their campaign expenditures. The large number of consultants involved in major modern campaigns required not only control over the expenditures but also some assurance that deadlines would be met and proper coordination between the various consultants would be efficiently accomplished.

The general consultant (GC) is truly the political jack of all trades. The general consultant has typically evolved from the campaign manager role. He or she usually has years of experience in all types of campaigns. The GC must be knowledgeable in *all* facets of campaign activities to be able to successfully complete one of his or her most important tasks for the client: the production of a comprehensive strategic campaign plan. It is simply not possible to produce such a document without firsthand experience in every facet and function of a campaign.

The GC must have an appreciation for and an empathy with every staff, vending, and consulting position and role in the campaign. How can anyone expect to be a successful GC if they have never done site selection, written a script, or spent all night in a studio with a media consultant producing a commercial that must air the next day? How can anyone expect to be a successful GC if they have never written a poll questionnaire, spent time in a data collection center, or learned how to read and understand the crosstabs of a poll? How can anyone expect to be a successful GC if they have never managed a race for legislature, county commissioner, or city council? If you have never managed a political campaign, you can have no appreciation for how intense the job of campaign scheduler is. You have no idea how grueling, thankless, and humbling it is to play the role of personal aide or driver. You have no concept of the art of recruiting and directing the temperamental backbone of a campaign staff—the volunteers. You have never had the frustration of dealing with printers, mail houses, and the U.S. Postal Service, all of whom know that as a political campaign you are not a regular customer and, win or lose, you will not be around very long. If you have not managed a political campaign, you have never had the sometimes not-so-pleasurable experience of dealing with a candidate's ego, or the neurosis of a candidate's family or his or her circle of "good ole boy" advisers. If you have never managed a campaign, it is difficult to comprehend that setting up a campaign is just like setting up a business. It will require all the same infrastructure, staff, equipment, accounting services and so forth, except that on a certain date it will cease to exist. And so on and so on and so on! If you have never managed a campaign, you will probably not make it as a general consultant.

While the campaign manager is running the day-to-day, nuts-and-bolts traffic-control activities of the campaign and implementing the campaign plan designed by the GC, the GC is also busy managing the candidate. It is the responsibility of the GC to keep the candidate on track and on message, to keep the candidate out of the manager's operations (thereby avoiding micromanagement), to review all written or recorded materials planned for public consumption, to assist in the selection of all consultants and vendors, to review the activities of all consultants, and to ensure the performance of all consultants. It is the responsibility of the general consultant to conduct an ongoing audit of all campaign activities to ensure compliance with the adopted campaign plan and to make adjustments when necessary.

Source: Reprinted by permission of Michael Mann.

Political Parties

Will Rogers used to tell audiences that he was not a member of any organized political party—he was a Democrat. Some scholars agree; Mayer and Polsby (1991) argued that Democrats have more trouble maintaining party unity than Republicans. Others, however, have noted that the organizational influence of both parties has declined with the introduction of reform rules that increased the importance of primaries in selecting party nominees (Polsby, 1983). As the importance of primary campaigns has increased, the role of the party has decreased. This may be a natural evolution of the increased complexity of campaigning. Kolodny, for example, (2000) argued that "modern campaigns demand specialized, technical services that are simply beyond the political parties' institutional capacity to deliver" (p. 110). Consultants have filled that void.

Still, political parties conduct the function of political campaign organizations during periods when the candidates are not active, that is, between elections. The political parties have political directors, field directors, press secretaries, finance directors, and so forth and so on. During campaign seasons, political parties fade into the background, or in the case of presidential campaigns, become an appendage.

The relationship between the candidates and the parties is sometimes adversarial in nature, because their goals are not always synonymous. The candidate's goal is usually to gain a personal victory through the electoral process by gaining popular support; the party's goal is to push an ideological agenda through the attainment of political power. Those different goals sometimes create conflicts between the ideological purity of some party loyalists and the pragmatic goal of the individual candidates. As Safire (2000, February 14) noted, sometimes a ". . . clubby set of single-issue power brokers prefers to float out to sea in a Viking's funeral than to present a candidate who can appeal across party lines and energize swing voters."

Summary

The campaign organization serves as the vehicle by which the candidate communicates with voters, both through the mass media and on a one-to-one basis. The organization may be a close-knit small circle of friends and advisers, an informal collection of volunteers committed to a candidate, or a nationwide hierarchy that includes volunteers and political professionals. Large or small, professional or amateur, that organization becomes the public interface for the candidate's message.

Successful campaign organizations fulfill multiple functions that include financial, legal, and communication elements. Large campaigns may involve a number of individuals with well-defined roles, each one handling a key function. In smaller campaigns, functions may overlap, with a single person handling multiple duties. Either way, the functions must be fulfilled. If not, the campaign will fail to communicate its ideas to the voters. In a democracy, the candidate with the best ideas should ideally win; realistically, that doesn't happen unless those ideas are communicated to the voters. That responsibility rests with the campaign organization, particularly the candidate and the campaign manager.

Although their role has changed, political parties still play a major role in campaign organizations. They are the major organizational source during nonelection periods. The increased use of primaries as a means of selecting party candidates has led to an increased use of candidate-based organizations. Still, once the primaries are over, some members of the various candidates' organizations may be incorporated into the party's organization. Meanwhile, the party itself gears up to provide organizational support to the nominees of its party.

Either way, though, the organizational principle remains. The campaign organization represents the candidate. How well it represents that candidate can affect the election outcome.

QUESTIONS FOR DISCUSSION

1. What type of person would prefer to be a campaign manager rather than a candidate? What type would prefer to be the candidate? Why?

2. One trend during the 1990s and in 2000 was the development of political and campaign shows as a genre of popular entertainment. Television shows such as *Spin City* and *The West Wing* offered a glimpse into the inner workings of a political organization. Why are such programs entertaining? What is interesting about campaign organizations?

3. What happens if a candidate serves as his or her own campaign manager? Are both roles compatible, or does success at one inhibit success at the other?

4. Your best friend is running for lieutenant governor, and he asks you to run the campaign for him. As campaign manager, which of the following is your first task? Why?

   a. Create a finance committee and schedule a meeting.
   b. Create a campaign plan and campaign organization chart.
   c. Send a news release announcing formation of the campaign.
   d. Write a stump speech for the candidate.
   e. Hire the staff.

5. The two primary functions of a political campaign are communications and fund-raising? How are they related? How do they influence other campaign activities such as scheduling, record keeping, polling, and press relations?

6. Political campaigns are different from most other kinds of organizations. What are those differences, and why do they exist?

7 Campaign Communications in the Mass Media

In 1934, Upton Sinclair surprised the political establishment by running a strong campaign for governor of California. Before the campaign, Sinclair was primarily known as a muck-raking author whose targets were often the big businesses of the day. Politically, he was an avowed socialist, an ideology that also scared California capitalists. But his antiestablishment attitudes set well with an electorate looking for someone to lead them out of the Great Depression, and his EPIC ("End Poverty In California") program offered hope.

Alarmed by Sinclair's growing public support, his opponents united to launch a massive public relations campaign against him. The players included some revered names in politics (Earl Warren), advertising (Albert Lasker), and political consulting (consulting pioneers Clem Whitaker and Leone Baxter and Nixon consultant Murray Chotiner). Also joining the fray were some of Hollywood's biggest names, including Cecil B. DeMille and Louis B. Mayer.

Hollywood provided film shorts, the consultants provided strategy and tactics, and the politicians served as the "mouthpieces" against the Sinclair campaign. Business interests supplied as much as ten million dollars to the effort in what was called the first "public relations blitzkrieg" in campaign history. When the dust settled, Sinclair had lost the election to Frank Merriam. Sinclair's attempts to mount a political comeback in 1936 ended with a second, resounding defeat, but his legacy on political campaigning endures. As Mitchell (1992) noted, "The 1934 governor's race in California showed candidates the way from the smoke-filled room to Madison Avenue" (p. xii).

Today, all major political campaigns are media campaigns, dominated by media consultants who serve as an advertising agency for the political campaign. Candidates for federal office often spend more on broadcast advertising than any other campaign activity (Fritz & Morris, 1992), and most political campaigns spend 70 percent of their budget on television advertising. By definition, therefore, the media consultant is responsible for more than two-thirds of the entire budget and virtually all of the direct communications of a campaign.

The Effectiveness of the Process

One issue that dogged media consultants for years was whether media campaigns had any effect on elections. The entire approach of the limited effects model argued that the media had little, if any, effect on elections. According to this approach, most voters have either partisan attitudes that will guide their voting decisions regardless of what political ads might be aired. Although most limited effects models can be traced to the 1940s and 1950s, this approach was still considered viable by some observers into the 1970s. In an analysis of the 1972 presidential election, for example, Patterson and McClure (1976) argued that the candidates' ads had little effect, influencing only 3 percent of the total electorate. They did, however, argue that early ads might be important because it reaches the voters before they have made voting decisions.

Cundy (1986) was slightly more optimistic, reporting that ads can influence viewer perceptions of candidates, underscoring the significance of early advertisements to enhance a candidate's image and to act as an inertia factor, diminishing the impact of subsequent propaganda efforts. Still, this approach considers ads to be more effective for inducing resistance to persuasion than actually achieving real attitude change.

Another significant body of literature supports the idea that voters seek information from television ads. Walker (1987) surveyed voters regarding all channels of communication and found that television received the most exposure and received the highest credibility marks for both issues and candidate images. Chaffee and Kanihan (1997) compared the ways individuals gain information in order to make political decisions and concluded that television use far surpassed newspapers as a source of political decision making. Martinelli and Chaffee (1995) surveyed new citizens to determine how they sought information for voting; recall of television ads had the greatest predictive strength. Furthermore, most voters consider campaign advertisements to be more informative than newspapers and television news programs (Kern, 1989; Patterson & McClure, 1976). Also, advertisements typically convey more information than do candidate debates (Just, Crigler, & Wallace, 1990).

Both candidates and consultants work under a pragmatic assumption that the media do indeed influence voters. Consultant Dane Strother (1999, p. 186) calls television commercials "the B-52s of a political campaign. They can virtually carpet bomb a community or state; the political landscape is inexorably altered in their wake." Strother's argument overstates the case, since sometimes the number of voters influenced by television may be small. Still, they are a significant subgroup. In many elections, that small number of only 3 percent (reported by Patterson and McClure) is still enough to swing an election.

Subsequent research has supported this assumption, reporting that political ads are clearly important for late-deciding or previously uninterested voters. Devlin (1986), for example, reported that ads were crucial to the 10-to-20 percent of the electorate who are typically reached only through television during the last stages of the campaign. The impact of advertising was succinctly summarized by Jamieson (1984), who noted, "Advertising remains less substantive than most would wish and less powerful than many fear. Nonetheless, it continues to provide an important channel of communication for candidates and a source of information for voters" (p. xxvi).

Schools of Consulting

Kern reported that political media consultants tend to be dominated by one of two schools of thought, an informational school and an emotional school, or by a combination of the two, which is called dovetailing. For the informational school, the primary purpose of political advertising is to provide the voters with information about the candidates and the issues. The emotional school, which is more influenced by commercial advertising techniques, relies on simple, repeated ideas to create an psychological image of the candidate for the voters.

The dovetailing theory argues that ads are most effective if the issue and the image side of their overall message are complementary. This dovetailing concept goes beyond the verbal messages of the ads and is considered most effective if visual and linguistic elements of the ad also reinforce each other (Kern, p. 24). Today, most practicing political consultants seem to subscribe to this dovetailing concept, and research has consistently supported that school of thought. Indeed, it is often difficult to distinguish between issues and images within a political ad.

Research has consistently reported that viewers learn about issues from political ads, but the persuasive impact of those messages goes beyond the learning of information. Joslyn (1986) argued that issues are selected for ads primarily for the purpose of building character and image. That conclusion is consistent with other research that found that the purpose of ads that stress issues content can in fact be that of building an image of the candidate (Bennett, 1977; Rudd, 1986). Ads based on this dovetailing approach typically contain three components: an entertainment device designed to arouse and hold the viewer's attention; a message, frequently about the character of the candidate and an issue; and, an attempt to provoke a reaction, surprise, excitement, recognition, affect, or an action message (Kern, p. 1).

Achieving that reaction may occur in a number of ways, but one of the most common is through the use of a referent. Referential spots use a symbol believed to have affective meaning for the viewer in a fashion that transfers or refers that meaning to the candidate or the opponent (Williamson, 1984). Thus, for candidates who wish to be identified as a champion of the elderly, their ads are likely to depict them in a variety of scenes with older voters. Similarly, "education candidates" are often depicted in school settings.

A more complex approach to creating affective reactions is based on an advertising technique called the "Wheel of Emotion" originally developed in 1984 by commercial advertiser Stuart J. Agres. Kern (1989, p. 31) applied this model for political ads in terms of a traditional problem-solution format ("Buy me and you will overcome the anxieties I have just reminded you about"). The wheel identifies seven negative emotions that can be aroused by political ads, along with a corresponding list of seven positive emotions. The seven bipolar emotions are: anxious-determined, fearful-satisfied, ashamed-proud, sad-hopeful, frustrated-relieved, bored-joyful, and serious-excited. The successful ad is divided into two parts. First, a negative emotion is aroused early in the spot. Second, the candidate is offered as a solution to the problem by identification with the positive emotion, which alleviates the first. Thus, to be effective, the positive emotion evoked by the ad must be the correct one to alleviate the negative emotion raised earlier in the spot.

The Tasks of the Consultant

Regardless the philosophical school to which a particular consultant may subscribe, the primary tasks of a media consultant include development of the message, scriptwriting, cinematography and videography, editing, and spot buying. The secondary tasks include acting as a clearinghouse for campaign information involving polling, news media feedback, effectiveness assessment, and coordination of all communications to support campaign advertising.

Message Development

The optimum message is constructed when the media consultant works hand-in-glove with the campaign pollster. Both parties must cooperate in the production of a questionnaire that will throw light on those issues that can produce votes for the candidate and deprive the opponent of votes. The media consultant is generally the dominant partner because of the degree to which campaign resources are devoted to his or her activities. For many campaigns, however, the pollster acts as a check-and-balance mechanism, assuring that the media consultant focuses the effort accurately. The media consultant will involve key personnel from the campaign, including the candidate, the campaign manager, the press secretary, and others, as needed. Involvement can be formalized through poll briefings, daily conference calls, and regular planning meetings. Message development continues throughout the campaign. Most campaigns plan for a "message adjustment phase" of the campaign in the form of a second or third round of survey research and focus groups to determine the effectiveness of the initial ads and the development of new and/or different advertising approaches.

Scriptwriting

The script is the first step in the production process, which will result in a finished television or radio advertisement (spot). In early phases of the campaign, scripts will be developed to introduce the candidate or issue and lay a foundation for the delivery of the campaign message. The script conceptualizes the "look" of the spot, the type of narrator, the scenes needed to support the message, and initial suggestions for music and sound effects.

Types of Political Spots.   Different researchers have suggested a variety of means of categorizing political spots. Joslyn (1986) has argued that there are four types of ads: Retrospective Policy, which look at the candidate's record; Prospective Policy, which look at the candidate's proposals; Election as Ritual, ads that appeal to patriotic and/or partisan attitudes; and the Benevolent Leader spot, an image-based ad. Diamond and Bates (1988) also categorize political ads into four categories. Their typology includes Name identification spots, used early in the campaign; Argument spots, which present the candidate's position on issues; Attack spots, which focus on the opponent; and Positive Visionary appeals, used in the latter stages of the campaign.

We will assume a typology based on five categories: biographical spots, issue spots, attack spots, comparative spots, and inoculation spots. Biographical spots introduce the candidate to the voters; they may include elements of early childhood, education, family, community involvement, political and nonpolitical achievements, logotypes, and campaign slogans. Issue introductory spots serve to acquaint the voters with the facts of an issue, to put it into play, and to remind the voter of the problem. Attack spots are primarily negative messages about the opponent or the opponent's record. Comparative spots present a positive image of the candidate contrasted with a negative image of the opponent. An ad produced by George Stevens for John McCain's 2000 presidential campaign illustrates this type of ad. The spot, called "New Low," argued that Bush had reached a "new all-time low" in attacking McCain's record on assisting veterans. The goal of the ad, one reporter noted, was to create a "contrast between one man who should be president and another who should be spanked" (Bennet, 2000, p. 52). Inoculation spots act to protect the candidate or issue from a potential weakness resulting from some past action, either private and public. Such ads usually are run after polling information reveals the weakness. They can be highly effective in protecting the candidate from future attacks. Pfau and Burgoon (1988) reported that inoculation messages that raise a candidate's liabilities early in the campaign deflect the persuasiveness of subsequent political attacks.

Cinematography and Videography

The first draft of spots are sent to the candidate and key campaign advisers for the correction of facts and approval of the concept. After some give and take, approval is given and the next phase is undertaken. The media consultant draws up a production budget that includes a cinematographer, assistant cameraperson, sound person, a gaffer (electrician), and a grip. Also included are the costs of renting a camera, lights, and other items needed to film on location. Travel expenses, including meals, accommodations, and transportation, are also factored into the budget. The campaign approves the budget and pays all or a portion of it before the beginning of the shoot.

Next, a shot list is prepared. The shot list is a list of items and scenes needed to complete the scripted spots. The production phase may also include assorted miscellaneous shots for use in a later phase of the campaign. The candidate is usually the main subject of these shots, with many showing him or her in germane locations in an office or at home. To assure the best use of expensive resources, advance work on the production phase is critical and many details must be handled. These include considerations about the locations of the production in terms of lighting, electrical facilities, permits and permissions, parking, meals, and overnight accommodations.

Film vs. Videotape.   Some campaigns make commercials using film (either 16 mm or 35 mm). Film typically produces an ad with better color and better audio, thus arguably lending the spots a better chance of achieving the campaign's communication goals. Consultants who prefer using film also argue that, through its density, subtly more information can be presented than with video. However, video production is much less expensive and is quicker. Typically, most ads that appear late in the campaign are done on video, particularly those that are aired in response to an opponent's ads. Developing digital technology now makes it possible to have an ad shot, edited, and on the air in fewer than 24 hours—a timetable that film cannot match.

Editing

This phase is also called postproduction, and here the spots are actually produced. The first step in the process is the creation of a "select reel." The raw footage (whether film or video) is viewed and usable scenes are tabbed for the select reel. All others are put aside. The spots are then assembled according to, or as closely as possible to, the previously approved script. Spots are literally built, melding scene to scene, adding graphics, logos, superimpositions, layering special effects, and adding music, sound effects, and announcer tracks. All decisions are based on strategic targeting, some more precise than others, including the music and the announcer. During the 2000 Arizona presidential primary, for example, George W. Bush used a Spanish-language announcer in ads that targeted Hispanics, with the voice-over read in Spanish (Leavitt, January 27, 2000).

When the spot is completed, copies or dupes (duplicates) are made, with one copy forwarded to the campaign for final approval. If approved, copies are then sent directly to the television stations (either through a delivery service or by e-mail). In the past, post-production services have been both time-consuming and expensive, with consultants renting studio time to finalize the edits. Some of that has been changed, however, by developments in computer technology. Media consultants are increasingly using facilities in their own offices as computer capabilities have soared and prices have plummeted.

Time Buying

Concurrently to building the spot, the media consultant is supervising the purchasing of time from the relevant television stations and cable TV systems in the target markets. Polling data will have provided information on the nature of the persuadable voters, and the time buyers design a buy based on programming that appeals to the target audience. The first decision is identification of the media market or markets that will be used. Hutchins (1999, p. 123) defines media markets as "the geographical definition of the combined viewership for an area's TV stations and the combined listenership for an area's radio stations." Media rating services often report media markets as ADIs—Areas of Dominant Influence. Although viewer ratings are assembled for all age groups, media consultants generally purchase time for viewers who are older than twenty-five. Younger voters have historically not voted in great numbers, and targeting only the twenty-five-plus age group increases the cost-efficiency of the buy.

Gross Rating Points. The media consultant's task is a combination of science and art, mingled with constant attention to detail surrounding the campaign environment. On the science side, the buying plan is often based on numerical calculations of gross rating points (often called "GRPs," or "points"). Gross Rating Points are an estimation of how many people are reached by a given spot; they are computed as the numerical summation (the total) of the ratings for all programs for which the campaign has placed (or purchased) a spot (Beville, 1988).

"Frequency" is the number of times that a typical voter is exposed to a campaign advertisement. The simplest estimation of frequency is to divide the total GRPs by 100. Thus, a total of 100 points would indicate that the average viewer would see the spot one time. Working under the assumption that the ad must be seen three to five times to be effective, then a total buy of at least 300 to 500 points is needed for the campaign to have any expectation of the ad having any impact.

Gross Rating Points, however, may not always provide an accurate assessment of audience frequency. Instead, the concept of audience *reach* must be considered. If the campaign

Interview with Raymond Strother

On Media Strategy

Raymond Strother is a Washington-based media consultant with Strother-Duffy-Strother. His clients have included presidential candidates and a number of governors, senators, and members of Congress. Strother has also served as president of the Association of Political Consultants.

Q: What is your job in the campaign?

A: I am a communicator. I have only one job and that is to find a campaign message and communicate it from the candidate to the viewer or voter in the simplest, most understandable way. It is sort of like this sign I keep here on my wall. "The greatest thing a human soul ever does in this world is see something and tell what he saw in a plain way." John Ruskin said that. To see clearly is poetry, prophecy, and religion all in one. That's a little poetic, but I think that's what it is about. It's finding something, understanding it, and communicating it.

Q: How do you go about communicating with the voters?

A: The first thing you need is a good medium. Everybody says political consulting is a television medium, but it isn't. Television is a very poor secondary medium. The most important medium is the candidate. If you don't have that candidate, there's not much you can do with the flickering lights on the television screen to change that.

Q: Don't many voters rely on . . . television for . . . information about candidates?

A: The voter is a very wise creature. The American voter is better trained in watching television than any human on earth. They can see through flim-flam. They can find character flaws that you think you have hidden. And they can see right into the soul of a human being, if given enough time.

Q: Then how do you communicate with them on a quality level?

A: You have to have a candidate—that's the first thing. Then, you have to help the candidate learn to express himself or herself in front of a camera. Even though the candidate is the primary medium, the candidate does not have the time to spend fifteen minutes with a person, look them in the eye, explain his goals, his character, his background, and his personality. He has to go to this very poor substitute—television—because if you try to see individual voters and spend the time required with them, you would only get to a hundred or two hundred voters in the course of a campaign. So, as a substitute, you use television.

Q: Do you have to have television to win?

A: Not necessarily. One of the great victories I had this campaign season was a young guy in Montana who was my fishing guide, twenty-four years old. He had read about me, and when I fished with him he was really interested in politics. He had studied political science at the University of Montana. He kept asking me questions about how to get elected and what we did. I tried to tell him. Finally he decided to run for the legislature. He called me and asked me to do his campaign. I said, "No, I'm not going to do that. I wouldn't have the time to devote to you and you would be let down." So he said, "What am I going to do?" I said, "Get a map of your district. Get the names, addresses, and phone numbers of everyone in your district and go talk to them." He said, "What do you mean, on radio?" I said, "No, no. Go talk to them. Knock on their door. Tell them why you want to be in the legislature. Tell them why you think your incumbent opponent isn't up to the job. And talk to them. That is all you have to do. That's what politics is about. It is not about television. It is not about radio. It is about communication, and you are the best person to communicate that message."

Q: What does the candidate have to do to communicate that message?

A: "First of all, know what you are going to talk about. Why are you running?" He tried to tell me why he was running, and I said, "Those aren't good reasons. Those are selfish reasons. Why are you really running?" "Well, I'm running because this guy embarrassed my girlfriend because she is a woman who cares about things and he goes to the legislature and votes against a woman's right to choose." He went on and on. I said, "Isn't that why you are running? Why don't you tell people that?" This kid occasionally called me to report. He would tell me that he knocked on doors and some people weren't nice to him. I said you just need half plus one vote, kid, to win. When I got back from the election wars, I had a note from him. He had won fifty-six to forty-four and had unseated an incumbent. He used the best medium he could: his youth, his vigor, and his idealism. Television and radio would have gotten in the way. The problem is that audiences get large when you go to Texas, Florida, or California or almost any state. You just don't have the time or resources to do what he did. So you use television. I've made a whole circle; now to get back to the same point: What I try to do is find some kind of match between what the candidate believes in and what the public agrees with him or her on.

Q: So you rely on the candidate's philosophy, rather than recommending a set of issues to them?

A: I don't believe you can give a candidate an issue and say you must believe in A, B, and C, and not D, E, and F. I just think that is foolish. I think the public is so good at discerning bull that they can see through that. What I like to do is to know the candidate. It takes a long time to know a candidate. You can't walk in and produce television or strategy for a candidate overnight. You've got to know the candidate, what they believe in, and where they are. I normally do that with a series of interviews, and I find out what they feel passionately about. You can look in their eyes and know when they are telling you something they don't really believe, but they read it in the newspaper and it sounds good. Finally, you can get to the core of what they are and who they are.

Q: How do you decide what aspects to use?

A: We usually take a poll. If we find our candidate believes in A, B, D, and G and the public agrees on B and G only, there is no reason for him to spend a lot of time and communications effort on issues that do not resonate with the voters. It is not that we are telling him what to believe in. We are not. We are trying to help him be more efficient and not talk about things that make their eyes glaze over. That's all it amounts to. It is in no way manipulation. I like to help a candidate find him- or herself—that is the first thing. What is this campaign all about? Why should you be elected? What are your strengths and your weaknesses? Then we try to shore up those things.

Q: What do you mean, "Shore up those things?"

A: There are some things you can do. If a guy looks disheveled and people want a governor who looks like a governor, you can trim him up, give him a good haircut, take his mustache off. You can get him a nice suit that fits him, you can shine his shoes. You can do cosmetic things to a guy to make him a better communicator. Then you find ways to explain his ideas. When I did the Gary Hart campaign, he would start with an idea and five minutes later he would still be talking about it. Well, the public doesn't have time

(continued)

Interview with Raymond Strother   Continued

for that. Modern communication isn't up to that. You have to teach him how to say things in a very brief way. A good political dialogue is almost like poetry. It has to be stacked with layers and layers of meaning. One stack on top of the other, as a sort of shorthand. A thirty-second television or radio commercial must convey a lot of things that are unspoken and unseen. There must be a code.

Q: Can you give us an example?

A: In the Georgia governor's race, we had trouble with white men. We had been losing the rural vote to Republicans because of racism as much as anything else. I somehow wanted to communicate that "I am one of you" without becoming racist or insulting. I used an old Southern expression at the end of two spots where he said, "I would be honored to be your governor." That's an archaic Southern expression that still resonates with many Southerners. They have heard their grandfathers say it, and they have heard their fathers say it at one time or another. It told rural people, without wearing a plaid shirt, and without changing my grammar and scuffing around the dirt and faking it, "I am explaining to you that I share your values and your culture." That was just one word, but you have got to find those trigger words that give you deeper meanings on television.

Q: That implies that your messages must be short.

A: I work with the candidate very carefully, helping them to distill and refine their message until they can answer questions about their issues in thirty or forty seconds. Until they can do that, they are not communicators, because the American public is trained to hear things now in shorter and shorter segments. I remember when I started watching movies as a child. If you watch *Casablanca,* for example, you'll find there are camera scenes that are three and four minutes long where the camera never blinks and there's no edit, where Bogart or Claude Rains acts for three or four minutes. You'll find a lot of sequences like that in old movies. But if you watch modern television or modern movies, there is very seldom a clip longer than four seconds long. On television we are putting as many as thirty scenes in a thirty-second spot. In this past election cycle, I layered images so I could put sixty or seventy images in thirty seconds—not because it is a good way to communicate, but because it is the way people are being taught to communicate with computers, computer graphics, and television editing. We have to communicate in a style the people can understand. So we teach this candidate to communicate. Remember, your candidate is the most important medium, without question, and you must hone and sharpen that candidate. And because you get elected on the totality of what you do, not any single thing, we have to teach him that there is a message in the campaign, sometimes five or six items; sometimes it is simpler than that. But everything must be framed by that message. It is a hard thing to get a candidate to go see optometrists and not talk about optometry and then go to stockbrokers and talk about stockbrokers. What they have to learn is that there is a message and that message has to be delivered to every group and you must not change it because inconsistency will kill you. So you teach this guy or this woman to deliver a message in a plain and simple way, as John Ruskin said. And to limit the message and not get off track. And take questions and answer them to the best of their ability. And not run from questions, but to find a way to take the questions asked and turn them back to the issues that matter. You have a lot of people out there with important local issues such as saving a local Pigeon River stream or something else that seems to them to be the most important thing in the world. You don't ignore those people, but you have to take them back to the broader issue.

Q: How do you develop all this?

A: We do it in several ways, usually in conversation. I spend a lot of time with the candidate so I can use their language. Invariably, that results in people saying, "You didn't write that. I have heard the man say that." Of course, he said that some other place. That's why I wrote the spot with it. I try to give people their own language back, because if you want believability, the message has to be clean and it has to be true. You use their language. If you don't use their language, you try to force them into words that won't slip comfortably over their tongues. The voter can see it.

Q: You seem to have a lot of respect for the voter.

A: The voter is damn good. Popkin wrote a book called *The Reasoning Voter,* and it says they get the joke. If they watch enough TV and see enough candidates and hear enough radio and talk to friends, they pretty soon understand who this person is. So you have got be careful not to convey an improper image or any kind of fakery or anything that is contrived. They will catch it.

Q: While you're doing all this work for your candidate, there is likely to be another consultant on the other side doing the same thing. How does that figure into the equation?

A: Not only does the nature of your opponent frame the way you approach a campaign, the nature of your opponent's consultants help the way you plan a campaign. If you are running against a stylistic consultant who tends to do the same thing, you know you are going to have to make some allowances in your campaign for that consultant. If you go into a campaign where you know the other consultant likes to use heavy negative advertising and newspaper headlines in the ads, you sculpt your campaign to accommodate that. Maybe you use the same thing. Maybe you lay down a warning barrage first about what is about to come. In some campaigns, if we know the other consultant is terribly negative, we make an early and big show asking the opponent not to go negative to set up the idea that we are going negative but we will do it only as a last resort. There is a lot of art in it; if it were just a science, anybody could do it.

Q: What other factors enter into the equation?

A: Another factor, and the biggest thing about political consulting, is luck. If you hit the right time, with the right candidate, with the right amount of money and you win, you look like a genius. Next year you do a brilliant campaign, you do everything right, everything you do is crystal clear and nice, and you get your ass handed to you. It just wasn't your time or place or something happened or the mood swung in the country. Take the Reagan Revolution in 1980. I don't know what we could have done. I lost with Bill Gunter in Florida to Paula Hawkins, of all things. Good people lost all across the country to people who only sat there one term until the people realized, "My God, what have I done?" and kicked them out of office. There is some science to it, particularly when it comes to polling and testing. But as far as production and the formulation of a message, I'm beginning to think there is more art to it than I used to.

Q: Is the media consultant the critical role in the campaign?

A: Nothing in a campaign is in a vacuum. I'm more collegial than I used to be years ago, because I've learned a lot of people have good ideas and you can learn a lot. I don't go into a campaign saying I'm going to do the media, you are going to do the direct mail, you are going to do the phones, and we are not going to communicate. I try to make it all work together. It is not because I care less, but because I care more. My ego is finally in check where I realize that I am not the all or the ends-all. I make mistakes and I don't have all the good ideas, and so your message has to work with mail, it has to work with

(continued)

Interview with Raymond Strother   Continued

phones, and it has to work on the stump. So I work with speech writers all the time. We get together, and great stuff comes out of speech writing. I remember the Buddy Roemer race in Louisiana in 1987, a young guy named Mark McKinnon (now fairly prominent) was doing press. He wrote a speech and the last line was "I want a revolution for this state." From reading that, I changed the entire campaign and called it the "Revolution for Louisiana." That is working with other people, understanding that everybody has got ideas. The campaign evolves as you go along. You have to look for new ideas. You have to be able to change as you go along.

Q: What role does the pollster play?

A: Pollsters are, to me, still the most important part of a campaign. I think a candidate is very wise if he lets his media consultant have some say in the selection of the pollster. There are some pollsters who are better for some media consultants. Some consultants want a pollster to dictate every word of a spot. They want some kind of quantification for everything they've written. I don't think there's that much magic in it, but the pollster is very, very important. He can help you find the message and then help in refining the message. After defining a message with a poll—those areas of agreement between the candidate and the voters—you have to test the message to see if it is working. Sometimes a campaign message starts out being very important but conditions change and at the end it is not very important.

Q: What's the biggest criticism that you get as a consultant?

A: The thing they harp on us most about is negative advertising, of course, with some good reason. We've seen it evolve from something very mean, very strident, very bitter to something more balanced. Negative advertising, to work, has to have some substance and some documentation. Most negative ads now have to substantiate the charge from an institution that the voters believe in. But, still the number one thing people don't like about us is negative advertising. I don't blame them. But as strong as they feel, when we poll, we see again and again that people are influenced by negative ads.

Q: Any final comments?

A: The thing people misunderstand most about our profession is our ability to manipulate voters and candidates. A candidate is not a sponge. A candidate is not a robot we can put words in the mouth of. Those candidates don't get elected.

Source: Reprinted by permission of Raymond Strother.

---

buys ten spots on a show with a rating of 10, it will have purchased 100 points of broadcast time. However, not every voter will see it even once. Instead, 10 percent of the audience will see it ten times, while 90 percent will never see it at all. Thus, a more accurate assessment of frequency is to divide points by reach, that is, the viewership as defined by the audience of a particular program or schedule of programs.

As noted earlier, most consultants work under the assumption that a single spot must be seen at least three times (or 300 points) before it has any effect. The first time an ad is seen, it is merely noticed by the viewer ("I haven't seen this one before") but its message is rarely assimilated. On the second airing, there is a recognition response from the voter ("I've seen this ad before"), and some information may be assimilated. By the third time, the information may be fully assimilated ("This is the ad about X"). Still, at this level, the voter has merely assimilated the information; any decisional response to it may require additional exposures (Webster, 1998).

Thus, any ad must have a minimum of 300 points of exposure before it has any chance of having an impact, but even this may not be enough. Traditionally, most media consultants have assumed that a minimum of 500 points are needed for the spot to have maximum impact. More recently, many have been increasing that number to 700 points, because of the dilution and diffusion of the media that has resulted from the proliferation of cable channels (Ferguson & Melkote, 1997; Heeter & Greenberg, 1988), remote controls (Walker & Bellamy, 1991, 1993), and VCR usage. Hutchins (1999, p. 125), for example, argues that "six to seven exposures weekly are required to ensure that a campaign's messages are being retained" in an "uncluttered" environment; when the airwaves are "cluttered" with an avalanche of ads, Hutchins places the minimum number of exposures at ten to twelve, or between 1,000 and 1,200 Gross Rating Points.

Any campaign that plans to do television advertising should plan on purchasing at least 500 points worth of time for each message. Any expenditure less than this would be a waste of money. Highly visible campaigns will spend even more. Congressional campaigns typically assume that they need at least 2,500 points to be effective, enough for three or four different spots. Statewide campaigns for governor or senator will use even more, with 4,000 points often considered a minimum and 8,000 points not uncommon.

Decisional Strategies for Time Buying

Given the high cost of running a campaign, the media consultant cannot afford to waste money by spending it indiscriminately. Typically, buying decisions are made using some specific criteria. Two of the most common criteria are the cost-per-point method, and the roadblock strategy.

The Cost-per-Point Method.   The cost-per-point method tries to keep costs down by constantly calculating the cost efficiency of a particular campaign program. It does this by dividing the cost of the spot by the rating it receives for the campaign's target audience. Suppose, for example, that a spot on Program A was available for $250, while one on Program B cost $400. Which program is the better buy for the campaign? It depends on the rating that each receives for the target audience. If Program A receives a rating of 5, then its cost per point is $50 ($250 divided by 5). If program B receives a rating of 10, then its cost per point is $40 ($400 divided by 10). Program B is the more cost efficient of the two for this campaign, even though its total cost is higher. Thus, with this approach, the media buyer constantly evaluates each potential placement in terms of cost and rating, looking for the combination that reaches the target voter most efficiently.

The Roadblock.   An alternative buying strategy, the "roadblock," focuses on ensuring that the campaign's ads reach as many different voters as possible. It does this by picking specific times of high viewership and buying an ad on every available network at that time. Thus, if the target audience was composed primarily of daytime viewers, then the media buyer would purchase at least one daytime spot on every station in the market at the same time. For example, the buyer could choose a time (the 3:00–4:00 P.M. time slot, for example) and purchase one spot during that time on every network in the market (ABC, CBS, NBC, Fox, WB, CNN, and so forth). Or, if the target audience was primarily composed of people who watch news programs, the buyer could purchase a spot on the Six O'Clock News on every station in the market. The result of such a strategy is that everyone watching television during that hour would see the spot at least once. Of course, to be effective, the roadblock must be repeated several times (three to seven), to ensure that the audience sees the spot often enough for it to register.

Broadcast vs. Cable.   One budgetary decision for the time buyer is how much of the television budget should be devoted to regular broadcast stations and how much to cable outlets. In the past, most major campaigns focused their attention on broadcast television, with little attention paid to cable channels. Their justification for doing this was simple; despite the audience fragmentation created by cable, networks still deliver the highest available ratings. When reaching mass audiences, broadcast television is still the most efficient means available. But that may soon be changing. Currently, cable receives less than 25 percent of typical advertising budgets, even though it accounts for 40 percent of the total television audience (Sternberg, 2000). Local candidates are already starting to realize that cable offers them inexpensive exposure to targeted local voters, and candidates in major campaigns may soon have to follow suit.

The Theory of Critical Mass.   As mentioned earlier, media buying is a combination of science and art. The scientific approach says a television spot will have its maximum impact at some point that ranges from 300 to 700 points of exposure. In reality, pinpointing exactly when that occurs is difficult, and sometimes even 700 points is not enough. National consultants such as Republican George Stevens often want their ads seen ten to twelve times to ensure that it is absorbed by the voters (Bennet, February 27, 2000). One approach to identifying the maximum impact of a spot is called the "theory of critical mass." It can be used by those campaigns that use daily tracking polls to follow voter response to the candidate or issue. Specifically, the daily polling numbers are compared to the buy schedule, and the results are monitored for effectiveness. Typically, the spot will have no recognizable impact on voter response when exposure is less than 300 points. However, at some level of exposure beyond 300 points, the spot is likely to reach a "critical mass" in which all of its information has been assimilated by many of the voters. When this occurs, the tracking polls typically indicate a small (2 or 3 percentage points) but significant shift in favor of the candidate.

Once that first shift starts, it frequently continues for two to four days, as the ad is assimilated by more and more voters. Once the shift levels off, then maximum impact has been achieved, and it is time to change to another spot. The advantages of tracking polls in this situation is that they can help the campaign identify at which point a spot has achieved critical mass. Other than deciding that at least 300 points are needed at a minimum, it is difficult to predict at exactly what point that may occur. An ad that is both dramatic in style and simple in content may reach critical mass soon after it reaches 300 points. A more complex or subtle ad may require a full 700 points or even more to reach such a level. Regardless of the true number of points needed, tracking polls provide a means of constantly monitoring the impact of a spot, thus helping to determine changes in media strategy that may need to be made.

Traffic

Traffic is that department within the broadcast station that schedules the time at which the spot will actually air. In most broadcast stations, the traffic department operates independently of the sales department. Thus, the time buyer is responsible for communicating with the traffic department to ensure that the proper ad is running at the proper time. This is most frequently done in written form, by way of fax or e-mail.

The specific instructions will vary, depending on the strategy of the campaign, but most follow a similar format: an identification of the spot by name and number, and instructions regarding its relative importance in the rotation. A simple one- or two-word name for the spot, along with a production number, is provided by the production company when the spot is sent to the station. The buyer uses this label as a referent for the traffic department, providing rotation information usually expressed as percentages or fractions. Thus, if the campaign had only one spot that it wanted to run, the instructions might read: "Run spot 'INTEGRITY' (#01) 100 percent." If two spots were in the rotation, the instructions might read, "Run spots 'INTEGRITY' (#01) and 'ISSUES' (#02) 50 percent each," or "Run spot 'INTEGRITY' (#01) two-thirds and spot 'ISSUES' (#02) one-third."

Other Campaign Media

Newspaper Ads

Given the importance that news coverage plays in most political campaigns, it often surprises outside observers that newspaper ads typically play such a minor role in most major campaigns. Presidential campaigns, gubernatorial campaigns, and U.S. senatorial campaigns rarely use them, opting instead for increased spending on television and radio. The broadcast media have an advantage for such campaigns in that they can reach more people, including passive audience members who will later become active voters.

Newspapers are highly popular among consumer advertisers. Baran (1999, p. 109) noted that more advertising dollars find their way to newspapers than to any other medium, spurred by research that indicates the newspaper is the medium most often used by consumers when making a specific purchasing decision. Turow (1996, p. 137) noted that newspapers have an advantage over direct mail and other forms of print media in that many people see the newspaper with its ads as useful, while they consider bundles of direct mail to be junk.

Given such positive demographic attributes, why is it that newspapers are not widely used by state and local campaigns? There are several reasons. First, newspaper ads are generally viewed as an ineffective communication device. DeVries (1975) ranked newspaper ads last among print media in terms of impact on votes, placing them in a position comparable to campaign brochures. This low rating occurs because political ads are often overwhelmed by the mass of consumer advertising in most newspapers. Approximately 60 percent or more of daily newspaper space is devoted to advertising, with most of that devoted to local retail advertising (Baran, 1999; Turow, 1996). Political ads can easily get lost in the shuffle of pages. Furthermore, most campaigns assume that those newspaper readers who are persuadable are more likely to be influenced by newspaper coverage than by newspaper ads, an assumption supported by DeVries's research.

Humorous and High-Concept Advertising

by John Rowley

If a political commercial can deliver a negative message, [and] limit backlash on the attacking candidate while leaving voters laughing at the opposition, a campaign communications trifecta has been achieved. Just as corporate advertising has evolved from the period of the hard sell to the soft sell to more innovative approaches, political advertising has also evolved.

Political advertising is market driven. Since the advent of modern political consulting there have been political media consultants who generate humorous, quirky, innovative, and occasionally strange spots. It has only been recently that political candidates running for all levels of political office, and indirectly the voters, have demanded a more deft approach, particularly when attacking. A high concept (using graphics, stock footage, and/or character actors to deliver a message in place of the candidate) or humorous advertising can also work in positive commercials. These commercials cut through the commercial clutter and hook voters by using apolitical imagery, language, or music. Humorous positive commercials can work for a quirky candidate in an area where voters seek an outsider (Jesse Ventura in Minnesota) or if the spots deliver a positive message while making light of the opponent or jab politicians in general.

Using humor in a positive spot often fails for two reasons: 1) Often the humorous tone of the spot makes the candidate less credible in the eyes of the voters. Nothing puts fear in the heart of a candidate like the prospect of voters laughing at them, when they thought they were laughing with them; and 2) High-concept spots may look nonpolitical and unique, but they can also make a candidate seem disconnected from voters, real people, and real issues because they do not show the candidate as a real leader and with real people. These spots are most likely to work in the context of a media campaign, such as one for governor or the U.S. Senate, with six to twelve commercials for a candidate who is well known and where a voter connection is developed with other commercials.

To find a better way to deliver attacks without leaving a sour taste in voters' mouths, media consultants are developing new ways to deliver negative information. More innovative attack commercials use computer graphics, professional actors, and a tone that is not so harsh. We call these spots "Zorro" spots. They are elegant and deadly, like Zorro's blade. This is compared with a more conventional approach that is more akin to a sledgehammer hitting a watermelon. Here are some of the elements of high-concept commercials:

Computer Graphics. One way we have coalesced an attack message with graphics was to show a computer-generated sink drain with tax money flowing down it. This delivered a message about government waste. To leave the spot on a humorous note, we also had a photograph of our opponent sucked down the drain followed by a gurgling sound effect. To link a congressional opponent to Newt Gingrich, one commercial said the opponent and Newt Gingrich were like "two peas in a pod" and showed a graphic of their heads popping out of pea pods.

Memorable Symbols. Coalescing concerns about an opponent into memorable symbols can be very effective. For example, we faced an opponent with a better "record" than our candidate so we wanted to smash his record in front of the voters' eyes. We delivered three attacks against him over video of a record player playing. At the end of the spot, we smashed the record, and our opponent's record, onscreen. On the heels of Hollywood spending millions of dollars to promote the movie *Twister,* we produced a commercial with a tornado graphic dubbing our opponent the "The Truth Twister."

Other Creative Elements. The use of actors, music, and sound effects can be critical to the success of a high-concept spot. They can also make the commercial more interesting, which will result in more people watching and fewer hitting the remote control.

Memorable Tag Lines. If you don't think a couple of words in a commercial can be powerful, we have three words for you: "Where's the beef?" Just as a symbol can synthesize a message so can a memorable tag line. Here are two examples:

> Example 1: In a congressional race, the opposition had attacked one of our congressional clients in a direct-mail piece that included what she alleged was a picture of the congressman's house. We produced a counterattack television commercial saying that our opponent was distorting the congressman's record and that this was not his house. The spot ended saying, "Why can't Marsha be honest with us? Even about where Bart lives. And Marsha, whose house is this?" We still don't know whose house it was!

> Example 2: Another memorable tag was an attack commercial against a senator who sponsored an unthinkable law that would allow someone to bring a concealed weapon onto school grounds. The spot begins with a shot of an actor wearing camouflage, toting a shotgun, and walking along a fence row. The "hunter" was an unexpected source for an attack on a pro-gun bill. This limited backlash from politically active pro-gun and pro-NRA voters. The actor said, "We value our freedoms. Like the right to bear arms. But there's one place that guns don't belong—in our schools." He goes on to cite the details of this curious vote. The tag line for this commercial, summed up what many voters must have been thinking, "Ernie, what were you thinking about, boy?"

Source: Reprinted by permission of John Rowley.

Second, newspaper ads are expensive. The cost per thousand of reaching voters through the broadcast media is often considerably cheaper than trying to reach a statewide audience through newspaper ads. Fairly large spaces are required (sold in terms of cost per column inches) for high visibility, and multiple ads are required. As a result, running a schedule of several ads requires a large budget, one that many campaigns can't afford.

A final disadvantage is a relatively long lead time required by virtually all newspapers. Most papers require submission of ads anywhere from three days to a week for the purpose of review by the management and for advance layout. Unlike television and radio advertising, in which stations are required by law to carry most ads, newspaper management may object to an advertisement and refuse to run it. Or, they may require specific changes as a condition of running the advertisement.

But newspapers do have advantages that appeal to some candidates. The biggest advantage, perhaps, is that newspapers are primarily a local medium. Schults, Martin, and Brown (1988, p. 360) noted that, with only a few exceptions such as *USA Today* and the *Wall Street Journal,* most newspapers are published and printed locally and the medium is evaluated as a local medium. This attribute is a disadvantage to statewide and national campaigns, but it makes the newspaper particularly important for local candidates. Newspaper ads rise in importance for local candidates, particularly in rural areas where weekly newspapers have a wide distribution. A single weekly newspaper, for example, will remain in the household for days, receiving multiple readings, before the next edition arrives. That provides the politician with a chance to reach a single household several times with a single ad.

Furthermore, statewide candidates for down-ballot races (secretary of state, or various statewide commissioners, for example) will often find that their races will receive little newspaper coverage. To get their name and message into the newspaper, they will need to purchase advertising. Some of these candidates focus on multiple uses of small names to reinforce name identification. Others prefer larger ads, used less frequently, which allow them to address more issues at one time. Furthermore, purchasing such a campaign ad will sometimes generate additional coverage by the media. News outlets, including newspapers, frequently cover political ads, making the ads themselves a campaign issue and thereby expanding coverage for the ad (Kaid et al., 1993).

Still, for most campaigns, newspapers are not a high priority. The disadvantage of newspapers ads for major campaigns comes from a major asset of newspapers for other purposes. Reading a newspaper requires active involvement on the part of the reader; as a result, total newspaper readership is considerably less than viewership for the television networks. Newspaper penetration in a local market is usually extensive, reaching 50 percent or more of the local households. Those households tend to skew toward higher income and older adults (thirty-five and older) who have some degree of advanced education. Those demographics also tend to have high levels of interest and information about political issues and more likely to be active participants in the political process. As such, information obtained from advertising may play only a small role in their voting decisions.

The campaign also has little, if any, control over where in the newspaper the ad will appear. This affects the demographic makeup of potential readers. Whereas campaigns can choose to advertise on a television sports program to achieve a high probability they will communicate with men of a certain age, no such guarantee is typically made by newspapers.

Occasionally, a statewide or national candidate will use newspapers, either to target a specific geographic area or to make a dramatic statement. One popular form of newspaper advertising is the insert, which is a free-standing piece of printed matter and is often distributed by candidates through newspaper deliveries. The cost of distributing the piece in this manner is sometimes less expensive than using direct mail, and the piece has the advantage of riding on the coattails of the credibility of the newspaper.

Newspaper ads, though, can sometimes cause problems for candidates (Kantrow, 1999). The 1995 full-page newspaper advertisements run by the Republican National Committee (RNC) created a financial and legal tangle for the Republican party after they offered, in the ad, to give $1 million to the first person who could prove the GOP spending plan that year would not balance the budget or would not increase federal Medicare spending 50 percent by 2002. The ad appeared in *USA Today* and a Capitol Hill newspaper and pictured RNC Chairman Haley Barbour holding an oversized, signed check for $1 million, next to the words: "Heard the one about Republicans 'cutting' Medicare? The fact is Republicans are increasing Medicare spending by more than half. I'm Haley Barbour, and I'm so sure of the fact, I'm willing to give you this check for a million dollars if you can prove me wrong." The ad included a contest title ("Million Dollar Medicare Challenge"), an entry coupon, an address to send it to, and a deadline—December 20, 1995. The Republican National Committee later labeled the offer a "parody," but not before dozens of people responded, applying for the money. One congressional aide took the Republican party to court when the RNC refused to pay him.

Outdoor Advertising

Outdoor advertising by political candidates proliferates during campaign season. The public is besieged by billboards, ads on buses, political signs, and bumper stickers touting support for various candidates. Because of their high visibility, outdoor advertising generates a great deal of discussion among political observers, with many debating the merits of various color tones, placement in high visibility areas, and the damage to the campaign because of vandalism from the opponents. The reality for most campaigns, though, is that outdoor advertising doesn't accomplish much, since such signage does not convey the campaign message.

The primary communication function of outdoor advertising is that of improving name recognition. It works remarkably well as a tool for increasing the recognizability of a candidate. And, for some campaigns, that is enough to ensure a victory—particularly for down-ballot races. Once in the voting booth, those voters who are not tied to partisan choices often vote for those candidates whose name they recognize, often not knowing that candidate's position on issues. However, if an opponent to such a campaign ups the ante by using sufficient broadcast advertising, continued reliance on signage will virtually assure a lost campaign.

In more visible campaigns (congressional, senatorial, gubernatorial, presidential), outdoor advertising has minimal utility. Its communication capability often stops at name recognition or sloganeering (Archibald, 1975, p. 230). DeVries (1975, p. 69) ranked billboards near the bottom of the factors that influence vote decisions, ranking them above only the entertainment-oriented media of movies, stage plays, and music. They are particularly useless in runoff elections; by the time a runoff campaign arrives, both candidates have already achieved a sufficient level of name recognition. Billboards can do little to increase it even more during a runoff.

Furthermore, what little impact outdoor advertising has tends to be brief. Billboards and posters are noticed when they first appear and for a week or two afterward; after that, they tend to blend into the environment as other signs and posters appear. For that reason, long-time Republican consultant Steven Shadegg (1972) recommended that all posters and bumper stickers be held back from distribution until some specific time in the campaign that called for a boost in name recognition. If billboards were already being used (they have to typically be purchased for at least one month at a time), he recommended adding a strip of new color or a slogan to them to reinvigorate their impact.

Despite the relative ineffectiveness of outdoor advertising as a communication tool, it still has some organizational and fund-raising value, particularly as a way to maintain enthusiasm among core supporters and potential contributors. Putting up signs provides volunteers with an important campaign function, triggering more enthusiasm for the candidate. Consultant Sean Reilly (1999, p. 153) calls this the "name in lights" effect: ". . . we think of people whose names are biggest as the 'stars.'" Bumper stickers provide supporters with a convenient means of expressing their support to others, and thereby increase their commitment to the candidate. The increased visibility resulting from both can be a significant aid to fund-raising. But observers should not be misled into thinking that the preponderance of bumper stickers or yard signs for any one candidate is an indication of overall vote support. Some campaigns conduct surveys of bumper stickers, checking to see which candidate is ahead; that technique is highly unreliable as a predictive technique for project-ing winners. Bumper sticker distribution tends to be a measure of organizational strength, not public opinion.

Outdoor advertising can also be used for targeting geographical areas. Sometimes the targeting can be remarkably precise. In 1999, for example, in preparation for the 2000 pres-idential campaign, the Republican National Committee placed a billboard across the street from Democrat Al Gore's presidential campaign headquarters in Nashville. The first ad depicted President Clinton hugging Gore and also offered a quote from Gore: "One of our greatest presidents." Republican officials said the intent of the billboard was to graphically demonstrate the association between Gore and Clinton, despite the vice president's rhetor-ical efforts to separate himself from the president (Seelye, 1999).

Furthermore, the high visibility generated by billboards give them the potential for some persuasive impact, particularly early in campaigns. In his 1983 rematch with incum-bent Louisiana governor Dave Treen, former governor Edwin Edwards began a billboard campaign a year before the election. Drawing on a public perception that times were not good for the state, Edwards's statewide billboard campaign read, "Hang on, Louisiana, Edwin's coming" (Reilly, 1999). Similarly, in a 2000 mayoral campaign in Selma, Alabama, challenger James Perkins, Jr. used a sign touting "Joe's Gotta Go" as the corner-stone of his campaign to defeat thirty-six-year incumbent Joe Smitherman.

Books

The 2000 presidential campaign saw the release of a number of books by and about the can-didates who were seeking the presidency, including works by George W. Bush (*A Charge to Keep*), Al Gore (*Earth in the Balance*), John McCain (*Faith of Our Fathers*), Bill Bradley (*Time Present, Time Past*), and Steve Forbes (*A New Birth of Freedom*). But such literary pennings are nothing new in politics. Their tradition goes back to 1824 and the release of *The Life of Andrew Jackson*. Numerous others have followed, most of them intent on con-veying the idea that the putative author ought to be president. In 1975, Jimmy Carter's *Why Not the Best?* contributed to Carter's image as an honest and open politician.

Nor are such books limited to those that promote a candidate's agenda. Books that attack the opposition also have a long history in politics. The 1964 presidential campaign saw two books attacking Lyndon Johnson, *A Texan Looks at Lyndon* and *None Dare Call It Treason*. More recently, Republican Peggy Noonan (2000) took a critical look at Hillary Rodham Clinton's candidacy for a New York senate seat in *The Case against Hillary Clin-ton*, which was only one of more than thirty books attacking the former First Lady (Arnold, April 27, 2000). One (Sheehy, 1999) even argued that she was addicted to her husband, for-mer president Bill Clinton. Clinton himself has similarly been the target of several attack books. Democrats are not the only targets for such missives, though. Molly Ivins and Lou Dubose (2000) aimed their literary guns at George W. Bush (*Shrub: The Short but Happy Political Life of George W. Bush*) during the 2000 presidential campaign.

Books have also been used in statewide elections, although not always successfully. Sandra Baxley Taylor's biography of former Alabama governor Fob James (*Fob*) was released in 1990 to coincide with James's comeback attempt in Alabama politics. Although he lost that campaign, he ran again in 1994 (this time without the book) and won. Similarly, Mississippi businessman Mike Sturdivant ran for governor in 1983, despite a lack of experience in any other elective office. Part of his campaign effort was a book (*Mississippi on the Move*) that articulated his major campaign positions.

The Ongoing Process

The media consultant must pay constant attention to details surrounding the campaign environment. As the buy is made, information is gathered about the opponent's media plan. Television stations are required to maintain a public file about the details of all political advertising, and make it available for public inspection during normal business hours. By analyzing the opponent's advertising buy for targets, duration, and weight (the amount of advertising in a week), the media consultant can draw conclusions about the objectives of their advertising strategy. Such information adds to the general understanding of the campaign and the campaign environment.

During this whole process, it is the buyer's responsibility to send funds, traffic instructions, and duplicates of the spots to the television stations. In recent years, consultants have attempted to apply new technologies to the process. The use of satellites to transmit the spots directly to the stations has been utilized since the early- to mid-1980s. In the mid-1990s, computer compression technology made it possible to transmit spots through a modem.

Bush's Crash Ads

The development of new technology is constantly changing the media profession. Take, for example, the tactics used by the George W. Bush campaign in New Hampshire's 2000 presidential primary—the production of "crash ads" that used footage from Bush's campaign appearances to get new ads on the air within forty-eight hours.

Media adviser Mark McKinnon and his crew trailed Bush around New Hampshire, taping virtually all of his public remarks with a digital camera. After the event, the consultants head toward a rented studio, making preliminary decisions about footage while in the car. Proposed scripts are e-mailed to campaign headquarters, and the ad is finalized in a pre-dawn editing session. The completed spots were available (usually by e-mail) at the station before the 3:00 P.M. deadline for traffic logs, where they were worked into the advertising schedule as part of the rotation (which also included more traditional campaign spots).

The speed with which such ads reach the airwaves was unthinkable a few years ago. Predigital campaigns needed a professional crew that included a cameraman and a sound man and editing would have taken longer and been more expensive. And, at least twenty-four hours was saved on the delivery process, which previously would have been limited to overnight delivery.

The process brought criticism from the press, which noted that the ads attempt to "circumvent the press by mimicking what journalists do" (Kurtz, January 22, 2000). The Bush campaign acknowledged that intent. "It's like news. . . . It allows us to present our version of the news of the day," said Mark McKinnon, Bush's media adviser. And, he added, "It has higher credibility with viewers because they know it's not scripted and it's actual footage from the campaign trail."

Source: Kurtz, H. (2000, January 22). Bush team relies on impact of 'crash ads.' *Washington Post,* p. A9.

More changes are likely to come. During the 1998 campaigns, some spots were delivered to stations by way of the Internet. Such capabilities mean that technology is shortening the time-frame that separates conceptualization of the spot and the time of its first broadcast on television or radio.

Summary

The media consultants play a major role in political campaigns. While some argue that the impact of their media spots is minimal (sometimes only 3 percent), such small percentages often make the difference between winning and losing an election. Philosophically, media consultants fall into one of two schools: informational consultants (those who concentrate on communicating issue-based messages) and emotional consultants (those who seek to touch a responsive emotional chord among the voters). These two approaches are sometimes integrated into a single media message, a concept known as dovetailing.

The primary tasks of a media consultant include development of the message, scriptwriting, cinematography and videography, editing, and spot buying. The secondary tasks include acting as a clearinghouse for campaign information involving polling, news media feedback, effectiveness assessment, and coordination of all communications to support campaign advertising.

Television and radio represent the biggest advertising expenditure of many campaigns. Other mass media that have also been used include newspaper ads, outdoor advertising, and books. Newspaper ads are rarely used in presidential campaigns, but often play a major role in local elections. Outdoor advertising can be a quick means of increasing name recognition for a candidate. Books are rarely used to communicate directly with voters, but can be used to enhance a candidate's credibility with the press and political elites. Regardless, the television-and-radio campaign must coordinate messages with the other forms of mass media used by the campaign. Logos and slogans used in television ads must be consistent with those used on billboards or in newspaper ads. Message themes articulated in the ads must be consistent with previous articulations by the candidate, including ideas expressed in books or other print media. Coordinating such communication activities becomes the single biggest task of the campaign.

Media consultants are first and foremost businesses (Johnson, 2000). The profession derives its roots from advertising agencies, which have traditionally derived their income from commissions paid by various advertising media. To offer an incentive to professional advertising agencies, advertising outlets have paid 15 percent of their total advertising expenditure to the agency. That is true of newspapers, television stations, and radio stations. In the past decade, savvy political campaigns have taken advantage of the increasingly competitive business of media consulting to negotiate lower commission rates. As Franzen (1999, pp. 300–301) noted, ". . . that fifteen percent differential isn't written in stone, and high dollar campaigns can persuade the consultant to reduce his commission." These competitive rates often range between 8 and 11 percent, with the campaign keeping what is left over to use for other expenditures (often, more television time). The actual cost of executing a buy is generally conceded to be between 3 and 4 percent of the total buy. Such costs include buy design and the administrative cost, office overhead, and personnel costs related to the function.

Media consultants also charge an up-front fee. Such fees can be as much as $60,000 to $100,000 for a major statewide or congressional campaign. Local campaigns typically have a smaller fee structure. The rationale for the fees is that not all campaigns that begin the election process come to fruition, or to the point where actual advertising is purchased. Media consultants have ongoing expenses that include personnel, office space, travel expenses, and general office overhead. This overhead requires sufficient revenues to maintain operation. Up-front fees help cover that overhead.

QUESTIONS FOR DISCUSSION

1. What is the objective of TV advertising? What if a campaign found a less expensive way to inform voters about its candidate?

2. What is the most important element in TV advertising: content, production values (how it looks and sounds), cost of the time to buy the spots, the number of spots over a given period of time, or all of it equally?

3. If a political campaign has a budget of $1,000,000, how much is the fee of the media consultant likely to be?

4. Your opponent has put up a TV commercial accusing your candidate of being for sale to the highest bidder in the political fund-raising wars. The irony is that the opponent holds every known record for fund-raising. What should your campaign do:

   a. Make a TV ad attacking your opponent as being a hypocrite;
   b. Make a TV ad that says your opponent is making false claims about you as a smoke-screen for his poor record on the issues that matter to people;
   c. Attack your opponent for having a poor record on the issues that matter to people using a series of news conferences;
   d. Ignore your opponent's attacks?

5. In your state, the television stations in the largest media market have decided they will not sell advertising time to candidates below lieutenant governor. Normally, your candidate would spend 40 percent of his media budget in this one market. Would you use your budget to place ads in newspapers and on billboards? If yes, how would you allocate those funds? What would be the characteristics of the newspaper ads and the billboard ads?

6. Halfway through the campaign, the television stations relented. How much of your remaining media budget would you reallocate to television? Why?

CHAPTER

8

Campaign Communications: Direct Voter Contact

In 1978, even as the "Reagan Revolution" was gathering to bring conservatives to power in the 1980s, an assault on organized labor was under way in Missouri. Right-to-work advocates had put an initiative on the ballot to outlaw "closed shop" contracts in the state. Polling made it clear that labor was decisively losing the battle by as much as two to one. The polls also indicated that, in a toe-to-toe, traditional mass-media campaign confrontation, the United Labor Committees of Missouri stood to lose by an even greater margin. The more voters heard of the traditional arguments by each side, the more they broke in favor of the antilabor view.

With only ninety days left before the election, labor hired Matt Reese, a pioneer of direct voter contact methods (direct mail and telephone banks), to guide the campaign. After reviewing the polling data, Reese concluded that the only chance of winning was to run a low-profile campaign while lulling the opposition into a sense of overconfidence. Reese immediately took steps to turn down the public rhetoric and the public campaign efforts by the labor campaign. He replaced that effort with a carefully targeted effort to register new voters in traditional labor families and to target prolabor households with direct voter contact messages using direct mail. Reese permitted television advertising only in the final week of the campaign, using relatively bland spots that were viewed as not particularly effective by the antilabor side. During the last week of the campaign, most observers assumed that the right-to-work referendum was unbeatable.

They were wrong. Reese's plan worked to perfection, with the prolabor side winning by a two-to-one margin. The campaign remains an example of winning by preaching to the choir: focusing on organizational targeting rather than trying to persuade undecided voters. That model is still used in many modern campaigns. While the bulk of most campaign budgets is devoted to electronic media (principally television), most campaigns also at least supplement that with other communication channels. Furthermore, some political campaigns involve situations in which electronic communication is either too expensive or impractical. Campaigns for city council districts, for example, often cover geographical areas that are too small to make a television campaign practical. Similarly, some congressional districts located in major urban areas may not use television campaigns at all. The problem is that purchasing the advertising time on television requires purchasing the entire market covered by the station, while the voting district itself covers only a small portion of that area. In those instances, the campaign will use other communication channels to reach the voters.

These direct-voter contact channels tend to fall into three categories: phone banks, direct mail, and the Internet.

Phone Banks (Political Telemarketing)

Unlike broadcasting, which reaches large numbers of unregistered voters, telephone banks give political campaigns the ability to target voters who will be participating in the election. Moreover, telephone bank targeting can be further refined through the use of computer-enhanced lists that may include such information as party registration, age, income, education, race, and voter history. Consequently, it is possible to effectively and quietly communicate a carefully crafted message that is aimed at a specific target group of voters. The callers may be a single person or several hundred people. They may be volunteers using borrowed phones or the campaign headquarters phones after hours, or professional phone banks of hired callers working under the supervision of experienced political telemarketers. In their most effective form, the phone bank is centered in one location under unified supervision with a specific goal.

Technology from a burgeoning telecommunications industry has created an extremely dynamic environment for political telephone banks. Computer dialing can detect the presence of a live voter, and connect a telephone worker to the line. If an answering machine is detected, a prerecorded message can be left. Predictive phone banks can completely automate the process to the point of using several different scripts at the same time, vastly increasing the productivity and economic viability of very large phone banks.

The Functions of Phone Banks

Armed with a list of voters and their telephone numbers, a telephone bank can make calls to target voters, to persuade voters, to "get out the vote" (GOTV), to influence early and absentee voters, or to influence legislation.

Targeting.   Targeting is typically achieved through a process known as "Voter ID." The phone bank calls voters within the district, asking a series of questions about their voter registration, likelihood of voting, and candidate preference. To the uninitiated, the question format sounds similar to that of a short poll or survey, and many respondents mistake it for such. However, there is no sampling process involved. Instead, the purpose of the calls is to reach as many people within a designated area as possible. Furthermore, the information is used differently from that of a poll or survey. Based on their responses to the questions, voters are categorized into one of three categories: supporters, undecideds, and opposition. In most campaigns, the data on the opposition are discarded or ignored. But voters who are identified as supporters and undecideds become targets for later communication, either from other phone calls or mail.

Persuasion.   A persuasive phone bank can have three potential goals: to maintain loyalty among those voters who support your candidate, to persuade undecided voters to vote for your candidate, and to dislodge voters who plan to vote for the opponent. Maintaining current support typically uses a reinforcement message; this may involve thanking the voter for the support, acknowledging the importance of that support, and providing that voter with information that might be useful to them in political discussions. Persuading undecided voters requires a strong positive message (one typically developed on the basis of polling data) that provides the voter with a reason for supporting the candidate. Dislodging supporters of the opposition typically uses a negative phone message, one that provides the voters with a reason to vote against the other candidate. Negative phone banks are extremely difficult to counter; because of their lack of visibility, the opposition is often slow to realize their existence and is thus slow to respond to them.

Voter Turnout (GOTV).   Telephone banks are highly effective at persuading supporters to turn out to vote. Usually, a concise compilation of attack and positive information is developed to remind the voter why they support the candidate, and then to remind them of where and when to vote. Often the message is tailored to specific demographic or attitudinal descriptions of the targeted voters (Burgess et al., 2000). In effect, GOTV campaigns target the marginal voter. If no special effort is undertaken, these voters typically will stay at home, and their turnout can be critical in close campaigns and campaigns against incumbents.

Early Voting.   Early voting refers to those votes that are cast before the actual election date. Historically most early voting has occurred through the use of absentee ballots, but that changed in the late 1980s when some states liberalized their early voting provisions to encourage more early, in-person voting. Typical of these were the changes in the Texas election regulations that provided for early in-person voting by any registered voter during a two-week period before an election. The first major test of the early voting process came in a 1989 special election in Texas's twelveth Congressional District, and phone banks were used extensively by the Democratic candidate Pete Geren to maximize support among early voters in the runoff campaign (Tyson, 1990).

Based on demographic data and voting trends, the Geren campaign selected 9,000 voters over the age of sixty-five for targeted phone bank calls. If they were identified as Geren supporters, they were reminded of the runoff and urged to take advantage of the early voting times and the location of the early voting boxes. The phone bank also identified voters who needed rides to early voting locations and provided those rides. That service, in effect, served as a means of setting up appointments to vote.

Geren won the election by only 1,620 votes, and the early voting totals made the difference. He won those by 3,022 votes. Similar programs have since been conducted in other states with early voting provisions, for a number of reasons. First, in highly competitive campaigns, a small numbers of voters can make the difference between winning and losing. Second, by using the phone banks, candidates can "put their support in the bank" as soon as it has been identified. Once a voter has been identified as a supporter, he or she is encouraged to vote as quickly as possible. And third, early voting programs have the potential to neutralize negative campaigns; most negative attacks occur during the last few days of the campaign, too late to have an impact on early voters.

Legislative Lobbying.   Although political phone banks have been traditionally viewed as a campaign tool, advancements in telephone and computer technology have increased the effectiveness of phone banks as a force in the legislative arena. If a party or interest group is concerned over a specific legislative issue, phone banks can encourage voter support for that position. A typical format involves a telephone call to a targeted voter, asking for his or her position on the issue. If the respondent agrees with the position held by the phone bank's client, the voter is told, "Did you know that the legislature is considering a bill to . . ." and is asked to contact his or her representative to express that opinion. If the voter agrees to do so, the phone bank can then immediately connect the respondent to the office of the targeted representative, at no cost to the voter. By continuously repeating this process, the representative can receive a barrage of phone calls in support of or in opposition to the legislation.

This is another way in which telephone banks "fly under the radar screen," in the words of one phone bank consultant. In fact, academicians often overlook this feature themselves. For example, in an analysis of 5,000 constituent letters sent to Congress during the Iran-Contra debate, Thelan (1996) found there was a distinct difference between the tone of the letters and the public opinion polls on the issues at the time, particularly in terms of the writer's attitude toward Colonel Oliver North. Thelan concluded that those communications represented the authentic voice of an American public that was outraged by the media's misrepresentation of their attitudes. What Thelan apparently overlooked was the extent to which many of those letters were the by-product of a coordinated lobbying effort, using phone banks and other media to stimulate letters to Congress.

The Telephone Bank Process

The first step in planning and executing a telephone bank effort is to define the groups with whom it is possible to effectively communicate. This is typically done on the basis of polling data that suggest groups that are persuadable and the issues that move them toward your campaign. The campaign then seeks to acquire relevant voter lists by group. For example, the campaign would design a list by demographic and/or behavioral type, for example, a list of voters, twenty-five to thirty-four years old, female, high school educated, all races, who have voted in four of the last five general elections.

The concurrent second step is message development. Perhaps the universe is uncharacteristically supportive of an opponent because its members do not know of his or her positions, and the data also indicate there would be a shift within the voter group if they learned of your candidate's position. For example: "Hello, Ms. (_____)? I'm calling for Charlie Whatnot's campaign for Congress. He wanted me to tell you how hard he has worked for all of us, particularly to keep the right-wingers from outlawing a woman's right to choose. You know Charlie trusts you to make that decision, unlike his opponent, Congressman Squishy, who wants to make that decision for you. Charlie really needs your help in the November election to protect your rights. Can I tell him you will support him in November?" _____YES ____NO ____Undecided.

The third step is to brief the callers concerning the task at hand. Emphasis is placed on delivering the message as designed and written. Many practitioners will instantly remove any caller who will not respect the integrity of the message.

The fourth step is to assess the effectiveness of the message. This is done by reviewing the results of the calling and comparing them in a general way to the poll. With respect to the prochoice message and the "calling universe," perhaps the polling data indicated that

Interview with Tony Parker

The Role of Phone Banks in Political Campaigns

Tony Parker is owner and founder of the Parker Group, a consulting firm based in Birmingham, Alabama, that specializes in phone banks and direct voter contact. His firm has worked in a number of statewide and presidential campaigns.

Q: In today's era of mass media campaigns, where do phone banks fit?

A: It's one of the tools in a candidate's tool box. In today's campaigns, the darling of the campaign is electronic media, and they want every dollar plus one. The campaign manager's decision is to allocate money for media, mail, and phone calls. If you get into a campaign that is strictly driven by the broadcast media, you can get beat.

Q: Why are phone banks a popular campaign tool?

A: Accountable response. When I call somebody, it's verifiable that I've called them; I've talked to somebody in that household; I've got information on them; and I've identified them for, undecided, or against my candidate or issue. That's very valuable data on a household level. I can direct-mail based on that. I can go back and do persuasive phone calls, based on our message, to the undecided or even the "against." It's more targeted than mass media, and it's accountable. And it's effective.

Q: Because it's so targeted, does that make it more effective in smaller geographical areas?

A: I've been hired in presidential campaigns, I've been hired in statewides for gubernatorial and senatorial candidates. I've been hired for congressionals, mayors, city councils, and issues on a statewide and local basis. It's got its place in nearly every campaign, but it can depend upon the size of the campaign and the media market. Telephone campaigns in major media markets are much more important than in smaller markets. If you're running a congressional campaign in California, you can't afford to be up on television and radio constantly. You can't afford to buy Los Angeles to cover your congressional district in Los Angeles. There are multiple districts in there. At that point, we're much more cost effective. We can touch the voter much more effectively than you can with mass media. Conversely, it works in a city council race in a small town where you don't want to buy radio and television in a small town when you're representing just 8,000 residents in a town with a population of 50,000. And it's very effective in a stealth campaign, where you have an opponent who has a lot of money and a lot of media. You can get in under the radar screen and build up support, and sneak up on them.

Q: Can you give me an example?

A: Several years ago, in a sheriff's race in Nashville [Davidson County, Tennessee], the incumbent was getting extremely high polling numbers and had lots of money in the bank. He had an antagonist, a woman who was a community leader, really involved, and who was giving him a hard time in public. He made the statement, "If you don't like the job I'm doing, why don't you run against me?" Well, she did. Her numbers were showing 20 to 30 percent likely to vote for her; he's got 70 percent. He didn't run an active campaign. When the media asked him about it, he belittled her and said she wasn't worth spending money on. I don't remember his exact words, but at one point he basically said, "It's just a woman giving me a hard time." About a week before the election, they were still 70 to 30. He didn't consider the demographics of the election. It was an off-year election, in the summer, and they generally had a turnout of about 16 or 17 percent. In the days preceding the election, we called every female in Davidson County, and read them his statement about a woman giving him a hard time. The headlines on the day after the election said, "Mysterious phone bank wins upset of the century." She was underfunded, and the polls showed her with less than a majority. But she won about 60 percent of the vote that was cast that day. We had targeted our voters, we were under his radar screen, and we beat him.

Q: What was the turnout?

A: About 18 to 20 percent. It was higher than normal, but not a lot. We affected turnout by three or four points, maybe. But they were all our voters. While he was saying she was somebody that he shouldn't be concerned about, there were a bunch of people out there who didn't agree with him.

Q: So the phone bank can have multiple uses for the campaign?

A: It has its place in just about any campaign. It's very effective for identifying your base, for enlarging your base, for persuading a large undecided constituent, and—most importantly, the payoff— getting them out to vote.

Q: On an average, how much do you think a phone bank could potentially increase turnout?

A: We've got some data on that. In some cases, we've gone in and arbitrarily picked half of the precincts in an area by just systematically picking every other one. When we've gone back and compared the results, we've increased turnout by four to five percentage points in the precincts that we've called. I believe that's fairly accurate, and most elections are won by smaller margins than that.

Q: Why can it be so effective?

A: People have a lot of clutter coming in at them now, but if you can get through the clutter and get your message to them, showing them the difference between your candidate and the other candidate who wants their vote, you can make a difference.

Q: Has the number of sales calls that consumers are receiving made your job harder?

A: Yes it has. My phone calls in the mix with credit cards, "you-wanna-buys," fundraising, and everything else, it's hard to get through. But we're still effective, and it still works.

Q: Do you think it will become harder in the future, and, if so, will that change the nature of the business?

A: It is harder, already, and it has affected the nature of the business. People screen their calls through answering machines. It makes it harder to get through to them, but it's still effective.

Q: Does that make phone banks more or less important to a campaign than they used to be?

A: I think it's more important now. The average individual receives thousands of advertising messages every day, from billboards, television, radio, magazines. You're constantly receiving messages. It's basically background noise, and if you can break through it with an effective message, you're going to win.

Q: What techniques do you use to break through that clutter?

A: Our program starts with the traditional voter ID, persuasive calls, and GOTV (get out the vote). We also offer IVR and grassroots phone calls for legislative issues.

(continued)

Interview with Tony Parker Continued

Q: What is IVR?

A: Integrated Voice Recording. We can integrate a recorded message, in the candidate's or anybody else's voice, into our computer system and match that with targeted, computerized phone calls. It's an old game, but a new phenomenon in the way it works now. They've had voice recorders now for years, but they've been very primitive. IVR marries broadcast quality voice messaging with computerized dialing, and with a computer that can distinguish dial tones, live voices, and answering machines. You marry those things together, you've got a pretty powerful force. We've had several examples of it working. In November 1998, we called the entire black head-of-household population in Georgia the day before the election. We used Bill Clinton's voice. The entire black delegation got reelected, and it helped to promote Democrats all through the state, not just the black candidates. We used it in Cynthia McKinney's [Dem. Georgia] in 1996; she had been redistricted out of a majority black district into a majority white district, and the Democratic leadership had run a candidate against her in the primary. But she won. We used Isaac Hayes's voice. He happened to live in her district, and was well known. His message was that she's been good for the district, the state, and the country; was doing a good job, and send her back. That went out to targeted females, eighteen to fifty, and all black households. You can be very creative with it. It doesn't replace live telephone banks. It's an adjunct to them. We do the traditional voter ID and persuasive calls, and then we turn around and use the IVR either before the live GOTV or the day of the GOTV.

Q: Does it have other applications?

A: We've also used it to chase a mail piece. Say a councilman sends out a mail piece on crime. A few days later, after most of them have had a chance to hit the households, his voice—through IVR—comes on and says, "Hello, this is John Doe. I'm running for city council and I just wanted to know if you got my mail piece on crime, because I think this is a very important issue in our community. If you agree with me, I would appreciate your vote. If you have any questions, please call my campaign headquarters." We chase the mail pieces. And it works. The candidate gets phone calls. The candidate likes it, because he doesn't trust the mail pieces, and I give him statistics back on how many heard the whole message, how many were live, and how many were answering machine. The system is sophisticated enough that, if it gets an answering machine, it waits until the beep before it starts rolling the tape. Even if the person doesn't answer the phone, they can get the message.

Q: Do things like IVR help break through?

A: It's a new toy, a new tool. Right now, it's very effective. I assume that the polish will come off of it in a few years, and it'll become just another tool. Right now, it's hot because it's new and the public is not expecting it. It's kind of neat to have a political personality or an entertainment personality on your phone, even if it's a recording.

Q: How does the grassroots legislative program work?

A: If there is an issue being considered by the legislature, we can call voters. If they agree with us on an issue, we can ask them if they'd like to call their legislator about it, and we can connect them immediately, at no cost to them. And we're set up so that we can call his office directly. If that line is busy, the system automatically rolls over to another number. If that's busy, we go to another. And if that's busy, we can go to his district office. We can connect them to the legislator or one of his representatives while we're on the phone with them, and they can let the legislator know how they feel about that issue.

Q: Look ahead to the next ten years. What changes do you see?

A: I think there will still be targeted messaging, and there's still going to be electronic media. But I think you're going to see it more integrated. We're going to be able to overlay how we're touching voters much more effectively, through e-mail, IVR, telephones. Also, as life gets more complex, I think we're going to go back to some more basic techniques. We're going to see more knocking on doors and the personal touch again. I think we're going to get to an electronic overload where the personal touch will be more effective.

Source: Reprinted by permission of Tony Parker.

the campaign should be getting 80 percent "yeses." If the bank is only getting 50 percent yeses, the message is likely ineffective. It is then adjusted and reassessed.

Concurrent with message adjustment is the process of compiling the results. Those who answer "Yes" are added to a database of those who will be called or otherwise contacted in the waning days of the campaign to remind them to vote. Those who answer "No" are discarded; if they are unresponsive to this message they will not support your candidate. Those who answer "Undecided" are added to a later contact list to be called after the main list is completed. These will be mailed a solicitation, perhaps signed by the candidate asking them to be considered. This is a classic telephone bank. It may be augmented by recruiting "YESes" as headquarters volunteers, as financial contributors, as precinct workers, or as workers in a programmatic effort to further aid the campaign.

Other Types of Telephone Banks

Telephone banks can be used to assist in the management of large numbers of influentials. Perhaps the campaign has recruited a large finance committee. In an effort to maintain communications with them, the campaign arranges for three or four callers to call them with an inspirational message and to remind them of specific deadlines. In this way, the campaign can closely coordinate with its key organizations.

Specialty calling can be undertaken. It is possible, using new technology, to leave messages with and only with targets who have telephone answering machines. This was developed to deal with the problem of the increasing use of voice mail type–answering devices in general use. It is possible using the technology to use a recording of the candidate's voice as the message, "Sorry I missed you, because I really need your support next Tuesday. If you get a chance give a call. . . ."

A "blind" telephone bank, or "push poll," is a telephone bank that, more or less, obscures the sponsor of the call while providing, more or less, a very negative message about the opponent. As mentioned in the chapter on polling, its goal is persuasion, not information. Although presented in a format similar to a public opinion survey, its intent is to impart information, not gather it.

Interview with Gerry Tyson

Phone Banks and the Future of One-on-One Campaigning

Gerry Tyson is president of The Tyson Group, a Fort Worth, Texas–based consulting service that specializes in providing phone bank services for Democratic candidates. His clients have included a large number of gubernatorial, senatorial, and congressional candidates.

Q: What do you see as the role of phone banks in today's campaigns?

A: Today, phone banks are of increasing importance to political campaigns, because of diminishing voter participation. Phones provide campaigns with a more intrusive form of communication, which is what they need to get people to participate.

Q: How has that role changed over the past few years?

A: Today, candidates are using phones even more than they have in the past. Ten years ago, we would make one GOTV [get-out-the-vote] call per voter for a candidate, and that would be it. Now, we often make four such calls on behalf of one candidate. In the case of a Texas congressman last year [1998], we made seven phone contacts over a three-week period. Campaigns with sufficient money are using every conceivable means to pierce that veil of indifference that the voters have put up.

Q: Is it possible that campaign techniques are contributing to that veil of indifference?

A: Are we becoming too intrusive? That's possible. In a Los Angeles school board campaign this year, we made so many phone calls to one group of voters, that 75 percent of them were not answering their phones. Of course, the opposition was calling too, and that added to the number of calls they were receiving. We were being too intrusive, and they were getting too many calls. It grew until they apparently developed a siege mentality.

Q: Do you think the campaign process has contributed to that mentality?

A: Possibly. Any form of negative campaigning, including phone calls, can give the voters a siege mentality. There will be a time, somewhere in the future, when campaigns will appeal to voters on a more positive level. But it's not happening now. Right now, negative campaigning works. As long as it continues to work, campaigns will use it. But it is also driving some voters out of the process.

Q: What do you see as the future of the phone-bank industry?

A: In the future, there will be some form of voice communication for voters, but it will not be like what we have today. It will probably be combined with the Internet or some other form of multimedia communication. I don't know exactly what form it will take, but I can see a point in the future where voters get up in the morning and go to the refrigerator for a glass of orange juice. When they get there, there will be a red light flashing, telling them they have a message, perhaps from a campaign. The voter can go online and choose from several options: to discard the message, to open it immediately, or to put it in a cache to open later. They can also choose the format of the message, perhaps a text form that they can scan through quickly, or an audio version, or a full video-audio version. And there will be at least one option which will allow them to talk to a live person. That will be critical. Whatever format develops, it will have the option of speaking to a live person. Some form of voice communication will continue to function in political campaigning.

Q: Does that mean that the future of political communication is more one-on-one communication?

A: No. There will always be something valuable about the collective audience. Some events, the state of the union speech, for example, will continue to attract a collective audience and will be mass communication events. But the developing technology will increase the capability of one-on-one communication, including voice communication.

Source: Reprinted by permission of Gerry Tyson.

The Weaknesses of Telephone Banks

Telephone banks take considerable time to make phone calls. A persuasive bank might take two or three weeks to make its initial callaround. When the opponent gets wind of the message, he or she can plow under the message of the phone bank in a matter of days with an electronic advertisement. Using telephone banks exclusively, therefore, is a risky undertaking. Using them in conjunction with electronic advertising, analogous to "air cover," reduces the risk. Electronic advertising is often aimed at main persuadable publics. For an opponent to attack your candidate's telephone banks to get you to abandon an effort to attract persuadables is risky. At worst such attacks on obscure targets can result in a catastrophic outcome by leaving the great field uncovered.

Telephone banks are susceptible to special problems. The caller's accent and dialect can immediately sour a voter. For example, a caller with a Brooklyn accent is unlikely to be able to persuade a voter in Tennessee. It is considered generally ineffective to have whites call African Americans or to have African Americans call white voters. This fact has led some telephone bank operators to design blind telephone banks where African American callers call upscale voters with a false message from the opponent. The resulting anger and/or confusion may satisfy a given campaign dynamic.

Direct Mail

Long-time political consultant Matt Reese (1975, p. 162) once said, "You have four ways to contact the voter, . . . and the intelligent campaigner uses all four of them in proper ratio." Reese's fourth option, direct mail (the others were media, personal visits, and telephones), is an often overlooked and maligned form of mass communication with voters, yet is an important communication tool. Together with phone banks, direct mail makes up the discipline of direct voter contact. Direct mail often supplements phone banks and electronic advertising, but many campaigns will also use it as a stand-alone means of communicating with highly targeted audiences. Either way, it can be an effective campaign tool.

In high population locales where television time is very expensive, programmatic direct mail campaigns may replace television advertising because it is more cost efficient. In such cases where television advertising is very expensive and the relative number of voters is small (for example, the Los Angles media market and a race for city council), direct

Case Study: Election Day in Florida, 2000

November 7, 2000. Voters went to the polls for one of the closest presidential elections in American history. At the end of the day, neither Republican George W. Bush nor Democrat Al Gore could definitely be declared the winner. The outcome depended on the results in Florida, where Bush had an early lead in raw votes while the Gore campaign was poised to protest the voting process in at least one Florida county—Palm Beach.

Sometimes overlooked in the hoopla that followed was that of the role of phone banks in the process. In an unusual move, the Democratic party hired a phone bank on election night to call thousands of voters in Palm Beach to raise questions about the disputed ballot and to urge them to contact local election officials. The Democratic National Committee paid TeleQuest, a Texas-based firm, to make the calls and describe the problem to voters in the area. "If you have already voted and think you may have punched the wrong hole for the incorrect candidate, you should return to the polls and request that the election officials write down your name so that this problem can be fixed," the calls said.

The confusion resulted from the design of the ballot in Palm Beach. The Gore-Lieberman ticket, listed second on the ballot, was assigned to the fifth punch slot on the ballot. The second slot was assigned to Reform party candidate Pat Buchanan, and news reports indicated that some Gore voters were mistakenly voting for Buchanan.

The party had been making routine Get Out the Vote calls all day, but they shifted to a crisis management call on short notice. Those calls started shortly before 6 P.M., EST, giving TeleQuest only one hour to make the calls before the polls in Florida closed. During that hour, they made 5,000 calls, contacting 100 voters who had not yet voted and identifying 2,400 who said they felt they had made a mistake on the ballot.

Source: Solomon, J. (2000, November 11). "Florida, we've got a problem." *Birmingham News,* pp. 1A, 6A.

mail is the preferred means of communicating with voters because of the massive expense of the alternative. In other instances, direct mail is used to communicate with key, marginal voter groups with a persuasive piece delivered in the regular mail. Campaigns that use direct mail usually use many mailings to accomplish the goal of capturing a vote, thereby approximating the advertising effect of television.

When multiple mailings are employed, some campaigns will use direct mail for the distribution of attack messages and/or responses to attacks. As a response, or refutation, mechanism, direct mail is generally ineffective; but it works well as an inoculation tool to combat future attacks from the opposition (Pfau et al., 1990). Direct mail has also been used in voter turnout programs, with some success. Schmidt and Schmidt (1983) analyzed direct mail by four Republican candidates in the 1982 elections, noting that the most successful letters were those that used only two compliance-gaining techniques. They attributed the success to the brevity of the two-message format: the short letters were easier to understand and more straightforward.

The sophistication of the use of direct mail tends to vary dramatically. Ringer (1986) analyzed the differences between the language of direct mail used by national and local political campaigns, finding three key differences: national letters were more emotional and personal in style, while local letters were shorter, more general, and maintained a more professional style; letters from national campaigns were easier to read than local campaign letters; and national letters contained multiple persuasive devices—compliance appeals, explanations, and warnings—while local letters concentrated only on explanations. Ringer attributed the differences to writing style—the national letters appear to have been written by professional consultants, while most of the local letters appear to have been written by volunteers with little experience in direct mail. That was probably an accurate assessment, but his conclusions might be different today. The 1990s saw an increasing number of local campaigns that employed direct mail consultants, and that trend is likely to continue.

Direct mail is costly, with the campaign incurring costs at four different levels: list development, design, assembly, and postage. Voter lists must be obtained in a format that can be used to address the mail. In its simplest form, this is a collection of address labels, but it can also include computer disks or tapes that can be used to address envelopes, letters, personalized messages, and so forth. Such lists can be vetted to produce the desired subgroup. For example, a campaign can request a list of elderly voters from their list providers. They may want, however, elderly voters, older than sixty-five who live in a particular geographic area, and who also have college educations. Each subgroup, while reducing the total number of a given mailing, will increase the unit cost of its list. The reason is simple: more computer work is needed and is therefore more expensive. And, as always, to achieve a subgroup sort, the entire master list must be run through the computer. Some political consultants are dealing with this problem by maintaining their own lists through cooperative arrangements with computer service bureaus; or by having their clients maintain such lists. Advances in small computer technology in recent years has made it possible to handle and manipulate very large lists, particularly when located on CD-ROM. Such systems, however, require well-trained operators and managers to assure effectiveness, which affects costs upward.

The second step is to design the mailing piece. For some campaigns, this can be as easy as printing a letter on campaign stationery. Nearly every political consultant advises candidates to use heavily produced, graphically communicative designs that will catch the attention of the voter, punching through the junk mail with which it arrives to the voter. The design incorporates the campaign logo and message. The targeted message is developed on the basis of survey research like any other large investment of the campaign. Cutbirth and Rasmussen (1982) examined more than seventy examples of direct mail used for fund-raising during this period. They identified four major content norms, which typified most such letters. Typically, they first begin with a startling or dramatic opening statement that is intended to motivate people to read the letter. Second, there is an early introduction of an enemy, either a specific individual (the opponent) or an abstract group. Third, there is an attempt to assure the reader of the credibility of the organization sponsoring the letter, typically by casting the sponsoring organization as a defender of some traditional value and thus ensuring that their support will be put to effective use. Finally, there is a closing appeal for financial assistance.

The third step is assembly. Larger campaigns use "mail shops." A mail shop is literally an assembly line that puts the mailing together. Their task includes printing the mailer, affixing labels, and bundling the finished products by zip code and carrier route (to facilitate mail delivery and comply with postal regulations).

In most cases, the fourth step—postage—is provided through bulk mail permits arranged by the campaign directly with the U.S. Postal Service, a process that reduces the mailing costs. Sometimes, though, campaigns prefer to use full postage (often with commemorative stamps), based on the assumption that voters are more likely to open a stamped envelope than one bearing a permit. Because of the added expense, stamped mail pieces are more likely to be used for fund-raising letters; permit-imprinted pieces are heavily used in the final days of a campaign, using headlines and designs that are eye-appealing. Most readers simply scan printed material. Loken (1983) found that only 14 percent of the target group had read a community campaign mailing, and only 20 percent remembered receiving it. To be effective, the mail piece must have a memorable headline that quickly and clearly conveys the campaign's message. That gives the piece a potential impact, even if discarded by the voter, who must at least glance at the headline to decide whether to read it or not.

Direct mail can be used to supplement and complement television advertising. While using the look and feel of the campaign's electronic advertising to capitalize on its weight, such mailings may hone the campaign message for subgroups that might otherwise disturb the larger audience. In other cases, when attacking the opponent, for example, pains may be taken to give the mail a completely different look so as to reduce possible negative blowback on the campaign's larger financial investment, television advertising.

DeVries (1975) estimated that direct mail has a potential impact of 3.3 percentage points among ticket splitters, a rating that puts them above billboards (2.1) but below television ads (6.8). Still, the impact of direct mail can vary widely, and its effect can sometimes exceed that of the broadcast media. The 1970 Michigan gubernatorial campaign of William Milliken monitored its advertising effectiveness using experimental test precincts throughout the campaign. Their research indicated that direct mail was totally ineffective in the early stages of that campaign; later, however, during the same campaign, the mail resulted in a 9-point swing for Milliken among undecided voters, while television was relatively ineffective (DeVries, 1975, pp. 78–81).

DeVries's data came from the early 1970s, a time when many consultants were starting to appreciate the value of direct mail as a communication tool. At about the same time, consultant Richard Viguerie (1975) called direct mail "campaigning's sleeping giant" and parlayed his expertise with the medium into a fund-raising and communication mechanism that could be used to target and activate voters with strong conservative leanings. The primary use of direct mail was to simultaneously raise funds for a media campaign while also developing a list of conservative voters who could be targeted for other campaigns. The success of direct mail campaigns became obvious to most political observers during the early 1980s when it was used as a potent weapon by groups associated with the religious right, often in conjunction with broadcast media (Kitchens & Powell, 1986).

Cyberspace: The Internet and Political Communications

Jesse Ventura helped put the Internet on the map as a political force in 1998 when he used the web to organize his successful independent campaign for the governorship of Minnesota (White, 2000). Since then, nothing has fired the imaginations of political operatives and academicians in recent years more than the Internet and its possibilities as a means of communication with voters. As the *New York Times* (Kelley, 1999) noted, "The Web page is the new whistle-stop, a way for candidates to carry their messages daily to more people than they can reach on the campaign trail." Larson and Psystrup (2000) believe ". . . the Internet promises to change politicking by involving more citizens in the democratic process"

(p. 159). Selnow (2000) noted that the Internet "threatens to upset the balance (of power) by granting users the power to send information cheaply" (p. 205). It might be particularly important in engaging more young people to the political process (Owen & Cutbirth, 2000) and has the potential to be a significant channel for the exchange of political information (Hacker et al., 1996; Whillock, 1997). As Republican Jim Nicholson (2000), chairman of the Republican National Committee, noted, "Two decades ago, voters were passive receivers of information, dependent upon the judgment of editors and reporters to decide what was newsworthy. But the Internet changes that, offering interested voters the ability to go online and actively seek out the information they desire." Initially, the role of the Internet has been that of a supplemental campaign medium (Benoit, Benoit, & Hansen, 2000), but it has the potential to be much more. Tedesco, Miller, and Spiker (1999) noted that the Internet feeds a desire for information. Selnow (1998) called it a "master medium" that includes text and photos like newspapers, audio like radio, and video like TV. The Net offers distinct opportunities for audience adaptation and the personalization of campaign messages. The audience size has been constantly increasing is potentially interactive. By the 1998 elections, more than two-thirds of those running for political office had web sites (Selnow, 2000).

Politics on the Internet

Political web sites rise up and die with each new election, but some seem to have staying power. Here are a few web addresses that provide political information.

Campaigns & Elections magazine, the official publication of the American Association of Political consultants—*www.campaignline.com*

Congressional Biographical Data—*http://bioguide.congress.gov/biosearch/biosearch.asp*

The Democratic Party—*www.democrats.org/index.html*

Evote—*www.evote.com*

Get Heard—*www.getheard.org*

Kaiser Family Foundation Study—*www.kff.org/content/2000/3058*

NetPulse—*www.politicsonline.com*

Project Vote Smart—*www.vote-smart.org*

The Republican Party—*www.rnc.org*

Speak Out—*www.speakout.com*

Vote.com—*www.vote.com*

Washington Post online—*washingtonpost.com/wp-dyn/politics*

Web White and Blue (The Markle Foundation)—*www.webwhiteblue.org*

Young Democrats—*www.yda.org*

Young Republicans—*www.yrock.com/home*

Youth-e Vote—*www.youthevote.net*

Still, others have been skeptical. Davis and Owen (1998) questioned both the accuracy of political information on the Net and the quality of its public affairs reporting. Political web sites tend to be highly partisan in nature (Benoit, Benoit, & Hansen, 2000), a factor inhibiting a full discussion of issues. Furthermore, the Internet appears to have a split political personality; Internet users tend to be political liberals, but most political content on the web is conservative (Hill & Hughes, 1998). Such a dichotomy reflects the concerns of Goldzwig and Sullivan (2000) on the role of the Internet in local communities, particularly for those who were "socially and economically disenfranchised" (p. 53). Boyle (2000, p. 27), furthermore, argued that the Internet "will be used mostly by journalists and others with an existing investment in the campaign, while undecided voters are likely to continue receiving information from traditional sources."

Davis (1999) agreed, noting that the press and politicians have adapted to the Internet and are using it to maintain the status quo. At first, political campaigns used web sites as a sort of proof that they, as candidates, were up to date, "with it," and able to deal with the problems of the twenty-first century. With the explosion of web sites and the vast improvement in modem technology, cyberspace is becoming more directly useful to political campaigns. Campaigns have established web sites as virtual bulletin boards on which they post a wide range of information about their candidates, including: candidate biographies, candidate travel schedules, downloadable photographs, radio ads and TV ads, press releases, position papers, fund-raising information and fund-raising pitches, attacks on opponent's positions, specific contact information (e-mail addresses, regular mail addresses, telephone numbers) for staff and local volunteers, links to web sites whose positions coincide with the candidate's, and links to newspapers and television web sites that have written or produced favorable pieces about the campaign or an unfavorable piece about the opponent. Some sites offer "fill-in-the-blank" e-mail that supporters can forward to their friends. Still, each campaign designs its Internet presence to reflect the candidate's or the staff's individual approach. In 1992, for example, Bill Clinton used the Internet primarily for posting campaign information, while Perot's campaign was more likely to use it as a means to post opinions (Hacker et al., 1996).

Campaigns regularly check one another's web sites for information, particularly about issues and travel schedules. A campaign can often thus intercept where and when the opposing campaign will make an appearance to discuss an issue. With this information the campaign can prepare an answering statement or press release that can be handed out at the opponent's appearance.

The press has also found the Internet to be a source of news, and some candidates have taken advantage of that. In 1999, George W. Bush became the first presidential candidate to make updated lists of campaign donors available online. Similarly, Arizona senator John McCain made news when he used his web site to criticize congressional pork projects (Kelley, 1999).

Radio commercials and television commercials are increasingly transmitted to broadcast outlets through the Internet, resulting in time and cost savings. The Internet is a vast research resource and most campaigns use it to access both free services such as the Federal Election Commission and various news media paid subscription–only sites such as Lexis/Nexis and the more prosaic Encyclopaedia Britannica. While not all information about a given individual or a given issue exist on the Internet, at least a good start can be made with a relatively small expenditure of time and effort.

Interview with Max Fose

Making the Internet Work for You

Max Fose served as Internet manager for the John McCain for President campaign. In that capacity, he saw the McCain campaign set new records for online fund-raising (more than $6.4 million) and for online recruitment of campaign volunteers (more than 142,000).

Q: What role does the Internet play in campaign communications?

A: The Internet provides an unfiltered channel for communicating with the electorate. You don't have to go through the news media, and you don't have to go through the party. Because of that, it brought new people into our campaign. And, it'll bring new people into the party, if they will use it.

Q: What are the advantages to the campaign?

A: You drive down costs and increase effectiveness. The Republican National Committee spends thousands of dollars to mail information to their supporters. If you do it online, you can save that money. And the more of your supporters that you can reach with the Internet, the more you save. We signed up 142,000 volunteers. The Republican National Committee would love to have that many people on their e-mail list. Most of the news coverage that we got off the Internet was based on the fund-raising. Nearly every news story mentioned it. But that was only one use of it for us. Even without the money we raise, it would have been cost effective because of the money it saved. We distributed literature over the Internet that the volunteers paid to print out. We were able to stay in contact with our volunteers on a daily basis without spending postage. Our petition drives in Maryland were costing us $10 a signature; we got more than 4,000 from the Internet and it cost us nothing.

Q: Why did the campaign put such an emphasis on an Internet presence?

A: John McCain knew early on that he had to do something different to have a chance. He told us to be creative, take chances—we have nothing to lose. If it doesn't work, so what. We're not expected to win. Let's role the dice and see what happens.

Q: What did you do that made it so successful?

A: We had a four-step Internet strategy. First, we wanted to educate the voters about the candidate. Our issues sections were the most highly visited section. People wanted to know where the candidate stood on the issues. Second, we asked them for their e-mail address, that allowed us to communicate back to them. Everybody who contacted us got an e-mail reply. Third, we asked them for a contribution. And fourth, we tried to turn virtual people into real people on the ground.

Q: How did you do that?

A: The Internet became a virtual staging ground for most of our grassroots efforts. Once a day, we asked people to do something for the campaign, and we kept them informed about the campaign. Many of our online volunteers were more informed about the campaign than the staff. The people on staff were so focused on their own jobs that they'd lose track of what was going on elsewhere in the campaign. But our online volunteers knew. When we asked for money, they knew why we needed it.

Q: How do you get people to donate over the Internet?

(continued)

Interview with Max Fose   Continued

A: You have to ask them. You can't just put a link on your home page for contributions. You can't just put your URL on your campaign brochure and expect people to visit your site. We asked them for money five times on our home page.

Q: Did you expect the Internet to be a successful fund-raising mechanism for you?

A: No. In fact, when we started, they told me that any money raised from the Internet would be gravy. I was once told that I could even keep whatever we might happen to raise. But we raised more than $6.4 million. When you add the matching funds from the federal government, it actually totaled more than $10 million. That was 27% of our total budget.

Q: Why was it so successful as a fund-raising mechanism?

A: It's the closest thing we have in politics to an impulse buy. It's cheaper, quicker, and cleaner than traditional fund-raising. It's also new money—71 percent of those who contributed were not regular contributors to political campaigns, and 30 percent had never given money to any campaign. In the two days after McCain won the New Hampshire primary, we were taking in more than $30,000 per hour through the Internet, with no problem. At the same time, we were getting donations over the phone in the traditional manner, but not as much. We had all of our phone lines tied up and we couldn't work those fast enough. With the Internet, there was no problem.

Q: How did you get people to visit your site?

A: You can't just put up your web site and expect people to visit it. You've got to give them a reason to visit it. You've got to drive people to your site. It's like commercial market sites. People don't shop online, they go there to buy. And people don't shop for politics online. They go there looking for something. You, or the candidate, has to do something to get people to visit the site.

Q: How do you do that?

A: First, the web site has to be integrated into your communication platform. In the McCain campaign, everybody directed people to the web site. If someone called in for information, the receptionist would direct them to the web site. Second, the web site should become your communications platform. When Senator McCain got attacked for writing a letter in support of one of his supporters, he didn't try to respond to the attack. All he did was post the letters on the Internet. When he was asked about it, he'd say, "I have nothing to hide. The letters are on my web site." I bet that 99 percent of the people never read the letters, but they assumed that if he'd put it on the Internet then he must have had nothing to hide. Third, earned media drives traffic to the site. After the win in New Hampshire, at every media appearance, Senator McCain asked people to visit his web site. We raised $2 million in four days following New Hampshire. Just before that primary, Senator McCain asked if we were ready for election night. I told him that if he won, we would need a bigger server. We spent $40,000 upgrading our server, and it was the best investment we made. I wish I could get that kind of return out of my investments. During the four days following New Hampshire, we were taking in money at the rate of more than $30,000 an hour. Senator McCain started calling in regularly for an update. When we gave it to him, he would pass it on to the reporters. Coverage just multiplied.

Q: How did you keep all the information on the site up to date?

A: We provided links through our site to the local sites, and we set up those sites so that the local information could be updated by local people. That way all of the information didn't have to come through us, and we could get new information on there quickly.

Some of the local representatives would keep a list of endorsements, and put those on the sites as they came in on a daily basis. I never saw those at all. In the words of Tip O'Neill, "All politics is local," and the Internet is the ultimate local organizational tool. You have the ability to make the Internet as local as possible.

Q: What was the most useful aspect of the online program?

A: The volunteers we recruited and the money we saved. Some times we'd ask people to print out flyers, at their expense, and take them to a campaign rally or event. Sometimes we'd ask them to print out campaign literature and distribute it for us. We also used them as a volunteer phone bank. We had ninety-two hundred volunteers who made phone calls into primary states for us. We'd give them a list of ten voters in a state, and they would call them, identify whether they were for us or not, and then file a report on the call with us. In New York, we used the Internet volunteers as part of a national lobbying effort to get us on the ballot there. A number of public policy groups are doing the same thing. In Virginia, as we approached the deadline, we didn't have enough signatures to qualify on that ballot. We asked them to download a petition form, sign it, and send it back to us. That made it possible for us to get on the ballot in Virginia.

Q: What was the least useful portion of your site?

A: The press releases. It had the fewest number of visitors. Apparently the voters weren't interested in what we were putting out in our press releases, and the press didn't really use them either. Apparently reporters still prefer the traditional channels of getting information. The people who visited it the most were people from the Bush campaign.

Q: A lot of the things you did required highly targeted messages. You make it sound like the Internet is more like an interpersonal communication device rather than one for mass communication.

A: In a way, it is. You can personalize messages down to the individual. By using cookies that record their individual information, you can tailor messages so that the information each person receives will be information that's useful to them and their lifestyle. The potential for reaching voters on a one-to-one basis is great.

Q: But that's what they used to say about direct mail, when computer technology allowed you to create personalized mail for each recipient. People quickly reached the point where they could recognize that, and they became rather jaded by it? Will the same thing happen with e-mail?

A: It could. We don't really know what's going to happen. But right now it looks like we can do a far better job of tailoring our messages to individual voters.

Q: What role with the Internet play in future campaigns?

A: I don't know. You're going to have to constantly work to be on the edge of the technological curve. Looking back at what's available now, I see all sorts of applications that we could have used. I think that video is going to be important. We did an online town hall meeting with Senator McCain that was essentially a live video. He was on-camera, and we took questions over the Internet that he answered. You also have to integrate the web site into your entire campaign organization. The network news organizations have already starting doing that. All the networks now use their time on the air to brand their URL. And the stories you read there are often longer than what's in the newspaper. They haven't taken advantage of the local angle yet. Campaigns will have to do the same thing. The web must be the first thought—not an afterthought—of the campaign.

Source: Reprinted by permission of Max Fose, Partner, Integrated Web Strategy.

E-mail is a very fast way to communicate with campaign insiders. Moreover, because it is relatively easy to use, the circle of those included for such communication is large when compared with traditional systems. There are also many Internet-based fax services. The campaign can send one memo or newsletter that can be faxed to many thousands of others. Finally, web sites are able to reach non-English-speaking voters who desire detailed information if the campaign uses a web-based translation program.

While some politicians are still leery of technology, some are using it as a way to let constituents be in touch with them. For the technologically savvy, e-mail is an easy and convenient way to contact their representative, easier than mailing a letter. For the politician, it ensures public input on a regular basis. U.S. Senator Conrad Burns (Rep. Montana) used the Internet as his personal multimedia station, offering a live, weekly video and audio broadcast to answer questions from constituents. Florida Governor Jeb Bush's fondness for e-mail was disclosed to the public in a June 1999 news report. The next day, Bush was inundated with 500 electronic messages—five times the number he usually received in a day (McPherson, 1999).

The 2000 elections saw an even bigger increase in Internet campaigning (White, 2000). In Pennsylvania, Governor Tom Ridge established a web site for his reelection campaign that attracted more than 150 visitors a day (Tomlinson, 2000). In North Carolina, Republican gubernatorial candidate Richard Vinroot greeted his web visitors with a survey; respondents could obtain the results by providing the campaign with their e-mail address and Zip code—information subsequently used for targeting purposes. Others asked the visitor to sign up and to provide the e-mail addresses of three friends as well.

Individuals can also use Internet web sites to parody politicians (Lowy, 1999). There were at least four anti-Gore web sites during 1999, but the parody site that drew the most attention was the "gwbush.com" web site that parodied Republican George W. Bush's official web site (www.georgewbush.com). Bush's campaign responded by filing a complaint with the Federal Election Commission, a move that prompted a reporter to ask the Texas governor whether the parody site should be shut down (Black, 2001). When Bush replied, "There ought to be limits to freedom," his quote became the buzz of the Internet for weeks.

No other campaign technology is growing as fast as the Internet. Some remarkable endeavors may be accomplished by using it. During the Bush-MacKay campaign for governor of Florida in 1998, the campaigns were very active in using the Internet for rhetorical volleys. Typically, one campaign would post a campaign position on its web site. The other campaign would research and craft a response, often within an hour. The result was that campaign exchanges occurred entirely in one news cycle. Both campaigns would make the news media aware of the exchange through e-mail, faxes, or telephone calls.

One advantage of the web is that much more information about a given issue can be made available. There is no practical limit on the length of issue papers, allowing for access to the entire text of speeches, legislative proposals, and organizational details (Browning, 1996). Furthermore, web site visitors spend an average of eight minutes browsing through any public official's site; that is considerably more voter attention than can typically be obtained by any other political medium (Kelley, 1999). Phone banks, for example, can typically maintain a voter's attention for only forty-five seconds, while television ads are usually limited to thirty seconds.

The Internet has proven to be a successful fund-raising tool. John McCain's presidential campaign raised $6.4 million over the Internet in 2000, a number that accounted for more than 25 percent of his campaign budget. Contributors like the ease with which it can be done (using a credit card) and the ability to make donations based on recent campaign activities. Campaign contributions can react instantly to daily news with a response that can be translated into immediate financial support. That can be particularly true for candidates who lack institutional support or a strong initial base. In 1999, Bill Bradley faced an uphill battle against Vice President Al Gore for the Democratic nomination for president. In the first half of the year, the Bradley campaign signed up 15,000 volunteers and raised more than $200,000 through mostly small contributions over the Internet; at one point, the Internet was bringing in an average of $7,000 a day for the Bradley campaign (Kelley, 1999). On the Republican side, John McCain's presidential efforts raised more than $100,000 from online contributions in the early days of his campaign, and half a million dollars came in within a few days of his victory in the New Hampshire primary from online contributions alone. In the state of Washington, Republican John Carlson's challenge of incumbent governor Gary Locke included a "LockeSmith" web page to "help unLocke Washington." Voters who signed up through the site were asked to raise $500 in 100 days.

As a vehicle of mass communication, though, the web is still problematic. Davis and Owen (1998, p. 254) noted that it is still in "an adolescent stage" and has yet to reach its full potential. Cassidy (2000) argued that the Internet's promise of increasing voter interest ". . . wrongly assume[s] that civic participation is a function of access to technology, when it is more likely to be related to much deeper social issues" (p. 57). Part of the problem is that it is passive, which means that the voter has to seek it out. A 1999 study by Nielsen Media Research and CommerceNet reported that nearly half of American adults were online, a significant number but far short of the pervasiveness enjoyed by television. Furthermore, nearly 40 percent of those online do not bother using the web at all, and most others do not seek out political information. In a time when voters are increasingly turning away from TV advertisements (which are very easy to view), turning on a computer, finding the correct web site, and then reading several pages of issue-related material seems unlikely at best. As Curtis Gans (1999), director of the Committee for the Study of the American Electorate noted, "The Internet is a fragmenting medium, in which everything is self-selected. If you're not motivated to go to a particular site, it doesn't matter that the site exists and is wonderful."

In fact, the web seems to serve elites who can afford computers and have the needed personal interest and the time needed to access it. If anything, the Internet has lured the cream of viewers away from television, resulting in further fracturing the group of habitual voters available to receive campaign messages. Twenty-nine percent of Internet users have decreased their reliance on television for political information, while their newspaper usage has dropped by 18 percent. Other researchers (Coffey & Stipp, 1999) predict that TV usage will decline even more in the future as more viewers turn to their personal computers.

Another problem is credibility of information. As Selnow (2000) noted, "Much of the information on the Web is undocumented, put up for no other reason than that someone has a wild idea and $25 to set up a Web site" (p. 220). This problem is accentuated by the fact that many people don't realize that web site information can be uploaded with no editorial control or review by legitimate media outlets. Voters who have become highly media savvy about television, radio, and newspapers have not yet developed those skills for the Internet. As Selnow (2000) noted, "They have learned to draw a distinction between the *New York Times* and the *National Enquirer,* but many have not yet understood the difference between one Web site and another" (p. 226).

Commercial advertisers generally rate the Internet lower than television but higher than direct mail as an effective advertising medium (Huang, Leong, & Stanners, 1998). Its advantages are its ability to convey information and detail at little cost. Furthermore, it seems to be most effective for people who are verbally oriented, while voters who prefer visual media appear to be hampered by the interactive nature of the Internet (Benzjian-Avery, Calder, & Iacobucci, 1998).

There is a feeling that the Internet has a big future in campaigns (Bush, Bush, & Harris, 1998), but exactly what it will do remains unclear. As Selnow (2000) said, "The role of the Internet in American politics is presently uncertain but potentially promising" (p. 204). Surely, the lines between television, radio, computers, and telephones will be blurred. At the very least, all these instruments (and more) will be combined in the same machine. What may or may not happen is conjecture, but it will take the combination of instruments at a minimum in order to achieve a true mass media communications effect. If such a fusion of technology does take place, the effect will be powerful beyond imagining.

The Internet has shown that it is a vehicle that can deliver political communications and have an effect. It has made huge strides as a device to draw together the main players of a campaign—the candidate, the staff, the volunteers, the opponents, the news media, and public officials (DeFleur, 1997; Garrison, 1998).

Summary

While television and radio ads are the most visible communication efforts of many campaigns, they are far from being the only communication channels used by modern campaigns. Many campaigns, particularly those at the local level, may be conducted entirely through alternative media.

When campaigns move away from using the broadcast media, the media they most frequently prefer are telephone banks and direct mail. Both phones and mail allow for more precision in targeting than is available from television ads, and both approaches can communicate a candidate's message without generating high profile messages. As a result, many campaigns devote a major amount of their financial resources to both means of communication.

The growth of the Internet has provided an increased opportunity to use online media to both communicate with voters and to organize supporters. Currently, the Internet's potential has exceeded its actual use in campaigns, but that is likely to change quickly. Future elections will likely see an expansion in Internet campaigning.

QUESTIONS FOR DISCUSSION

1. The incumbent mayor, an African American, is being challenged in a primary by a former African American mayor and a white city councilman. The voters in the city are about 53 percent African American and 42 percent white, with the rest Hispanic and a few of Asian descent. Design a telephone bank program for the incumbent that maximizes his support among all groups. How would you create a telephone bank program for the white candidate that maximizes his support among African American voters? Create one for the African

American candidate that maximizes his support among African American religious and community leaders. In each case, assume that the incumbent is a former get-tough police chief; the former mayor is widely considered to have been corrupt even though he was never charged with a crime; the white candidate is a young politician who is considered to be a reformer.

2. A candidate for governor discovers her opponent has an accused child abuser as a member of his education issues steering committee. Design two approaches that bring this fact to the attention of the parents of school-age children.

3. Your candidate has spoken out on the issues using television commercials. Using the Internet, what can be done to extend the effect of the message? What role would e-mail play?

4. Your job as the campaign's field director is to harness grassroots support. During a presidential primary in the South, your opponent has launched a vicious attack ad on television in a midwestern state. Your job is to use the campaign's e-mail list to generate an effective grassroots reaction and drive the ad from the airwaves. Describe your resulting program in detail.

5. Can the Internet facilitate a substantive exchange on issues? How? What is the likelihood that the campaign that has more sophisticated features such as streaming video and audio will more favorably impress voters on the basis of its visual features instead of the merit the argument?

6. Name five ways to acquaint voters with the name of your web site. Why is this necessary?

CHAPTER
9

Political Speeches

On December 5, 1955, Martin Luther King, Jr. stood before 4,000 people in Montgomery, Alabama. The civil rights movement was at a critical juncture. Rosa Parks had been arrested four days earlier for refusing to give up her seat on a Montgomery bus, and the crowd that had gathered was primed to do something to express their disapproval. King inspired the audience by comparing the Montgomery situation to the biblical exodus of the Israelites from Egypt (Selby, 2001), proclaiming, "Now we are reaching out for the daybreak of freedom and justice and equality." The speech was the mobilization call for the Montgomery bus boycott, the first of numerous civil rights protests led by King and other African American leaders. Selby (2001) argues that the speech was a critical element of that protest, with King's inspired oratory mobilizing the protesters and instilling in them a conviction that they would succeed. Years later, that conviction was rewarded at the political level with the passage of the Civil Rights Act of 1964.

Not all political speeches have such a dramatic impact. Some observers, in fact, approach the topic of political oratory with an obvious touch of cynicism. Writer George Orwell (1949, p. 363) once described political speeches as ". . . the defense of the indefensible." Corcoran (1979, p. xv) complained that political speeches are often used "not to convey information, but to conceal or distort it . . . , (bearing) no relationship to the organization, coherency and clarification of information and ideas."

Such comments aside, though, political speeches are an integral part of the campaign process. As Martin Luther King, Jr. and others have demonstrated numerous times, political speeches can play a vital role in inspiring and uniting people around a common cause. Furthermore, as Trent and Friedenberg (2000) noted, "Speechmaking is fundamental to political campaigning. The politician cannot reasonably expect to campaign without continually facing audiences" (p. 182). Speeches are used for a variety of reasons that extend beyond pure transmission of information. They also serve important roles in political leadership and governance (Campbell & Jamieson, 1990; Hart, 1987). Their use comes closer to what Graber (1976) describes as "political linguistics," a means of creating, sustaining, and communicating political reality and of directing or constraining action toward that reality.

Words matter. The meanings of words can make a difference in people's lives. Spoken communication can spell the difference between a venture's success and failure. Colleges and universities often encourage (and sometimes require) that their students take at least one course in public speaking. Corporations spends thousands of dollars to train their executives and junior executives to obtain those skills. In the face of such widespread training, political speeches become an easy target for criticism. Jamieson (1988) complained that speechwriters interfere with the open debate of political issues: "When a politician enters a forum clutching a text," she wrote, "public discussion is likely to be replaced by declamation" (p. 216). Indeed, political speeches are usually inherently biased, with candidates using the public forum to promote their agenda or their version of events. Others associate a lack of integrity with political speeches, particularly those written by a professional speechwriter. Sometimes even the candidates feel guilty; as Jamieson noted they "are reluctant to confess that the words they speak are not their own" (p. 210). Regardless, in a modern political world, speeches and speechwriters are a necessity for major candidates.

The nature of the media is partly responsible. The modern press corps requires that advance copies of speeches be available, and the text of televised speeches have to be put into the TelePrompTer in advance of the actual delivery. Both features require a written text (Jamieson, 1988, p. 211). Furthermore, particularly for presidential speeches, carefully prepared speeches, with each word carefully chosen, are necessary to ensure that the speech is not misinterpreted (Bormann, 1960; Campbell & Jamieson, 1990, p. 10). As Noonan (1998) noted, ". . . a president really can't be winging it a lot because everything he says . . . has implications, sometimes serious ones" (p. 124).

The sheer number of speeches that an elected official must deliver prohibits them from writing each one. Presidents may give numerous speeches every day (Jamieson, 1988, pp. 212–213), creating a need for more than half a million words every year (Bonafede, 1972). Elected officials simply don't have enough time to do all that writing themselves. They must have a speechwriter to help articulate those ideas. The speechwriter's function is not to change the speaker's platform but merely to communicate those ideas to others. How they do that will vary with the writer and the candidate. Jamieson (1988) noted that the major job for George McGovern's speechwriters was to "replace his long, complex sentences with shorter ones" (p. 212). For some, it may be a relatively simple task of organizing the candidate's ideas around a major theme. For others, the candidate must focus instead on developing rhetorical techniques that can communicate the candidate's ideas to the voters.

The Nature of Political Speeches

Part of the criticisms come from the inherent differences between political speeches and other forms of public speaking. This book assumes that those differences include the following features.

■ *Political speeches are more complex than most other forms of public speaking.* Issues such as abortion, civil rights, economic theory, and international relations have generated years of debate and argument, far too much for any such issue to be addressed in a single speech. Although a thirty-minute speech offers more time to discuss an issue than does a thirty-second commercial, it is still rarely enough time to go into the details of a complex topic. Typically, the political speechwriter doesn't even try; instead, they are content with defining and examining an issue or situation in limited terms (typically those that are most beneficial to them). Political speakers will often describe the problem in emotional terms without seriously examining its solutions.

■ *Great political speeches are often developed more than written.* Jamieson (1988) wrote that ". . . those who study a modern president's speech are analyzing not a single person but a syndicate" (p. 217). Indeed, several people may contribute to the development of a political speech over an extended period of time. Candidates often take preliminary drafts of their speeches and try them out on small audiences. Some aspects may be pretested with focus group or polling research, but even these are not typically implemented until they have been tried on small audiences. Over time, a number of people may contribute by helping to refine the wording, delivery, and organization of the speech until it becomes a natural extension of their campaign activity.

Ronald Reagan became active in politics in the 1960s in California, but he started working on his stock campaign speech in 1954 (Ritter, 1968)—a decade earlier. Special event speeches often incorporate and refine successful elements of campaign speeches; John F. Kennedy's inaugural address, probably the product of speechwriter Ted Sorenson, included a polished version of a line previously used by Kennedy in a Labor Day campaign speech in Detroit (Carpenter, 1999, pp. 14–15). The memorable line today ("Ask not what your country can do for you. Ask what you can do for your country.") started out as: "The new frontier is not what I promise I am going to do for you. The new frontier is what I ask you to do for your country." Similarly, in 1968, Richard Nixon campaigned during the general election with a speech that had first been honed during his primary campaign (White, 1969, p. 378). Nor is such refinement limited to candidates; issue advocates often take a similar approach in developing their message. Martin Luther King, Jr.'s "I Have a Dream" speech is best known for his delivery of it at a giant rally in Washington, D.C., but King had previously previewed the same theme at a less well-known event in Detroit (Smith, 1999).

■ *Political speeches are part of a process, not an individual event unto themselves.* Bitzer (1968) places persuasion in the context of the rhetorical situation, contending that a rhetorician must create a fitting response to a situation. The political speech is illustrative of that situational approach. Political speeches are only one element of a larger rhetorical process, one in which the entire goal is to communicate with a mass of voters. A classroom student develops a speech with the intent of making a grade on a specific assignment, while a corporate sales presentation may be aimed at getting an immediate response. Political speeches must take a broader view, planned to play a vital role within the context of an entire campaign. They are written to provide verbal support for the paid advertisements. A sentence or paragraph may be inserted that makes little sense at the time to a local or outside observer but may be there for future strategic purposes—either to set up a later strategic move, for use in a later advertisement, or to "bait" the opposition into making a strategic mistake. During the 2000 New Hampshire primary, George W. Bush frequently inserted new lines into his speech, responding to the issue of the day. His campaign taped those lines and edited them into a "news actuality" commercial for use forty-eight hours later. In Buddy Roemer's 1987 campaign for governor of Louisiana, Roemer's campaign speech included the phrase, "I hate Louisiana politics, but I love Louisiana. That's why I'm running for governor." That phrase was first used in the campaign speeches, and later appeared in his television spots.

■ *The audience for political speeches extends beyond the immediate crowd.* Traditional speech preparation emphasizes the importance of audience analysis and adaptation, presenting the speech using language and a delivery style that is most effective for the immediate audience. Political speeches can rarely do that, aiming instead for an extended audience, or composite audience that is highly heterogeneous (Myers, 1999). At the very least, the campaign speaker must remember that an extended audience is monitoring the speech, an extended audience composed of voters, the press, and the opposition. Noonan (1998) argued that the press is the most important of these extended audiences. "[E]very speech a candidate or leader makes is serious and important, because every speech is an opportunity to succeed or fail in front of an audience that just may include the press," she wrote (p. 115). That's why, she noted, political speechwriters must "be devoted to keeping an eye on the press—what will interest them in a speech, what will impress them" (p. 133), since the press communicates the ideas in the speech to the rest of the extended audience.

Because of this extended audience, politicians frequently use a discrete campaign audience as a means of reaching a larger target, even if that message is not well received by the immediate audience. In 1999, for example, while campaigning for the Republican presidential nomination, George W. Bush criticized his own party for its lack of compassion to the poor and needy. The speech, made during the Republican primaries, was not well received by its immediate Republican audience, but it did generate a positive response from a crucial general election target—independent voters. Bush was willing to take criticism from the immediate audience in order to broaden his appeal to general election voters.

■ *The success of a political speech is often judged by its sound bites, not by its overall impact.* Noonan (1998) defines the sound bite as ". . . the little snippet of videotape that television news shows use when they show a politician talking . . ." (p. 88). Both scholars and consultants have criticized this aspect of modern political rhetoric for placing more priority on thirty-second messages than on thirty-minute speeches (Kern, 1989; Noonan, 1998). Others argue that sound bites can be an effective way of synthesizing the ideas behind a speech. Jamieson (1988), for example, commented on "the ability of a small unit of discourse to stand for an entire piece . . ." (p. 91), and in a latter work she argued that sound bites and slogans can be effective at communicating the candidate's ideas (Jamieson, 2001).

Since the target audience for a political speech extends beyond the immediate audience, its success depends on the message of the speech reaching that extended audience. The press rarely passes along the entire speech to its news audience, opting instead for quick summaries that include a limited number of quotes (usually just one). As Jamieson noted, incumbents must "say or do something that is concise, memorable and relevant to the day's news agenda" if they have any hope of getting news coverage for their issue (p. 214). Special emphasis should be placed on the word "concise." Jones (1988, p. 53) notes that TV stations typically use only about ten seconds of what the speaker says. To politicians, it often seems even shorter than that. Speechwriter Peggy Noonan (1998) recalled one incident when Ronald Reagan's frustration with sound bites surfaced. While reviewing the text of a speech, he said, "You know, I'm going to give this whole long speech but they're going to show two seconds of me and then Lesley Stahl's gonna stand there giving her version of what I said . . ." (p. 90).

Maybe so, but those sound bites become the memorable part of the speech, the cornerstone by which they are remembered and identified by both the press and the public (Carpenter, 1999). Few people remember John F. Kennedy's entire inaugural address, but they do remember its key line: "Ask not what your country can do for you. Ask what you can do for your country." While many voters missed George Bush's speech at the 1988 Republican convention, many of them can still recite his key line: "Read my lips. No new taxes." The bites chosen by the media may not be the ones hoped for by the campaign. During the 1976 presidential election, while campaigning in the New York primary, Jimmy Carter responded to a question about housing in the suburbs by saying, "I see nothing wrong with ethnic purity being maintained. I would not force a racial integration of a neighborhood by government action. I would not permit discrimination against a family moving into the neighborhood." One television network (CBS), focused on the phrase "ethnic purity" from that quote, creating an issue that dogged the Carter campaign for weeks (Schram, 1976, pp. 143–144).

There's nothing particularly new about the idea behind sound bites. They've been used in American politics since the Revolutionary War. Patrick Henry aroused a nation with his "Give me liberty or give me death" line, and other slogans have been used by numerous politicians through the ages. Jamieson (1988) describes such lines as "a memorable statement that capsulizes the speech and serves as the hook on which we hang it in memory" (p. 90). But there is an important difference between those early slogans and modern sound bites. In modern campaigning, those short phrases may be all that the voters ever hear of the speech. As Jamieson noted:

> Good reporters search for the news segment that reveals as much of the whole as possible. But where, in the past, the audience experienced the event or the whole speech and used the synecdochic statement as a memory-evoking digest, now the audience is often not exposed to the whole for which the part stands. When this occurs, the part simply stands for the part (p. 112).

Problems can also occur if the speechwriter focuses too much on sound bites. If that occurs, the speech may sound like a series of sound bites and little else. That's why Noonan (1998) argued that speeches need sound bites, but the speechwriter should ". . . never ever try to write one" (p. 88). Speeches written around sound bites, she argued, are boring, lack coherence, and have little to say. Instead, she emphasized the need of the writer to have a topic worth talking about. If the topic is worthwhile, she argued, good sound bites will naturally occur. "Great sound bites of political history are great *sentences* and *phrases* of political history . . . ," she wrote, "they weren't trying to self-consciously fashion a phrase that would grab the listener. They were simply trying to capture in words the essence of the thought they wished to communicate" (p. 93). Instead of writing sound bites, she recommended reviewing the speech after it is written, looking for lines that would work as a sound bite:

> If a sentence jumped out at me . . . , I'd make sure that it ended a paragraph or started one, so that when producers got the written transcript of the speech before it was delivered they'd be more likely to notice it, underline it, listen for it. If I saw a sentence that I thought producers might like, but I didn't want them to choose, . . . I'd make sure it was surrounded by sentences and therefore less noticeable (Noonan, 1998, pp. 90–91).

Still, even this process recognizes the importance of sound bites in modern campaigns. As Jamieson (1988) noted, "The speaker who is able to reduce situations and issues to synoptic statements . . . exercises the power that comes from helping to shape the media's definition of key events. The speaker unable to do this will cede control of the event to those who can or to the media" (p. 114).

■ *Sound bites from a speech may be open to multiple interpretations.* Slogans and memorable lines often employ language with a variety of positive connotations. The multiple meanings that can be attached to the phrases allows for the audience to become a participant in the persuasive process. John F. Kennedy's classic line ("Ask not what your country can do for you . . .") illustrates this point. The final version was actually somewhat more ambiguous than the version it replaced, allowing for multiple interpretations. Some people viewed the quote as a call for self-reliance and a challenge for citizens to stand on their own. Some others saw it as an indictment of the welfare state. In the end, it meant many things to many people, a typical attribute of a successful political speech. Martin Schram (1976) gave a similar assessment of Jimmy Carter's discussion of the amnesty issue during the 1976 presidential election: "Carter on amnesty. It is not an answer; it is an art form—carefully constructed so as to diffuse the emotions of the subject and come up with something for everyone" (p. 97).

■ *The effectiveness of the speech can be enhanced or diminished by the candidate's delivery of it.* The importance of delivery is a staple in basic public speaking textbooks. Its role is intensified in campaign speeches. How the candidate delivers the speech is central to the impression formed by the voters. Ronald Reagan, for example, converted his skills as an actor into superb presentation skills of his speeches. He rehearsed every presentation and always reviewed his stump speech before every appearance. As Michael Deaver, Reagan's communications adviser, once said, "Reagan felt that his job was the speech. Everyone in the campaign had a job to do, and his was to communicate his vision, and the way he did that was through his speeches" (quoted by von Drehle, 2000). Presentation skills are particularly important to presidential candidates; the voters' ideal image of the presidency is someone who speaks eloquently, coming up with the right word or phrase, without being packaged to do so. A professional actor such as Ronald Reagan can succeed at both of those sometimes contradictory goals, but others have problems. George W. Bush, for example, generally opted for a "homespun delivery"—"complete with stumbles and swallowed words"—because he felt that such an approach conveyed both sincerity and authenticity (von Drehle, 2000). For major occasions, candidates must also learn to use a TelePrompTer for delivering the speech. This device displays the text of a speech on transparent panels positioned on each side of the podium. Experienced speakers scan a passage with one glimpse and stare directly at the audience or camera while tossing out the sentences in a conversational tone. Few can do that effectively. Both Ronald Reagan and Bill Clinton were masters of its use.

The Speechwriter and the Process

Speechwriters have been on the American political scene from the beginning of the nation. George Washington considered his own speaking style to be awkward (Brigance, 1956), so Alexander Hamilton, James Madison, and John Jay ghosted some of his orations (Einhorn, 1981). Andrew Jackson got help with his speeches from his secretary of state, Edward Livingstone (Gunderson, 1960). Woodrow Wilson had help from Robert Lansing (Fleming,

1959), while Raymond Moley wrote Franklin Roosevelt's 1933 inaugural address (Jamieson, 1988, pp. 201–204). Given such a tradition, it's not surprising that in today's political world, major candidates don't decide if they will use speechwriters—merely how they will be used.

Trent and Friedenberg (2000, p. 174) note that each candidate faces two different decisions regarding campaign speeches: which audience or audiences should be addressed and what messages should be used. Audience selection is partly a matter of targeting (which groups are potential supporters) and partly a matter of broader influence (what message will an appearance to this group send to those who are not there). Identifying those target groups and the messages is often the job of the pollster. Expressing those concepts is the job of the speechwriter.

The ideal speechwriter has superb rhetorical skills and can write in an easily read, conversational tone that includes vivid and quotable phrases; add in versatility in subject matter and the capacity to work under pressure, and that person can be a political speechwriter (Persico, 1972). Speechwriters in the past were more likely to come from a journalistic background rather than a rhetorical background. The nature of the journalist's job requires them to write constantly, and they work daily to hone their conversational style. Journalists also have a better appreciation of what sound bites would appeal to other journalists. Rhetoricians usually have a better sense of the persuasion process, but are less practiced at the use of conversational writing.

The speechwriting process typically starts with a conference attended by the candidate, the campaign manager, the issue experts, the media consultant, and the writer (or writers). Sometimes these conferences will be held on a regular basis; at other times, the meetings may be called as needed. After the meeting, a first draft is developed. It is then checked by the issues experts and other campaign consultants for accuracy, and edited (or rewritten) to conform to the candidate's style. This process is repeated until both the candidate and the experts are satisfied with the product. That product, by the very nature of its development, is a complete expression of the campaign, but not necessarily an ideal one. Ronald Reagan's speechwriter, Peggy Noonan (1997), has written of the problems that a writer faces in crafting a speech that is acceptable to the speaker and their aides. The result may be a compromise, but it is usually at least a well-considered compromise.

A basic decision to make during this process is the nature of the arguments to be used in the speech. Three general options are available—positive arguments, attacks, and defensive arguments (Benoit, Blaney, & Pier, 2000). Positive messages (or "acclaiming") are those messages that praise the candidate or their party. Attack messages or those that focus on negative information about the other candidate or party. Defensive messages are those that respond to an attack from the opponent. Consultants generally prefer to use the first two, and defensive arguments are generally reserved for situations that require an apology. In normal campaign discourse, most consultants recommend responding to an attack with another attack, rather than a defense. Regardless of which approach is used, the writer needs information on what the candidate has previously said on the topic and research data to support the arguments (Schram, 1976, pp. 181–182).

Trent and Friedenberg (2000) note that most political campaign speeches are written as "speech modules," short segments that can be reassembled and adapted for use in a variety of situations. Shadow and Peck (1999) note that, in terms of organizational structure, the typical speech module aims to gain attention, describe a problem, present a solution, and visualize a solution. These four elements correspond to the first four elements of the classical "motivated sequence" organizational pattern for persuasive public speeches. The motivated sequence represents a five-step organizational pattern: gain attention, describe a need, offer a solution that will satisfy the need, visualize the impact of that solution, and suggest an action that the audience can take. For the purposes of individual speech modules, that last concluding step is not needed. Instead, it is reserved for use in the conclusion of the speech, when the suggested action is to support, vote for, and/or donate money to the candidate.

Message Framing

Message framing is news priming on a holistic level. If the media accept the way a candidate has framed an issue, then subsequent coverage of that issue tends to be beneficial for that candidate. Most academic research on framing has focused on news coverage, with the results indicating that the way the media frame an issue can have a major impact on public opinion and voter behavior (Devitt, 1997; Gamson, 1996; Gitlin, 1980; Graber, 1987; Iorio & Huxman, 1996; McCombs & Shaw, 1993; McLeod & Detenber, 1999). More specifically, framing can have an impact on candidate credibility by framing voter attributions of blame or praise (Iyengar, 1996). Framing works because political attitudes are expressions of underlying arguments recalled from memory (Chong, 1993, 1999; Kelley, 1983; Zaller, 1992).

While researchers have focused on the role of the news media in the framing process, the role of the speechwriter in this process sometimes gets overlooked. An effective speechwriter understands that the speech will serve as an initial framing device that will influence press coverage. If the speechwriter can influence which underlying arguments are recalled from the speech, then the frame will be successful. But, "all frames of reference do not lead to the same response" (Chong, 1999, p. 220). The frames chosen by the speechwriter must be carefully chosen to elicit the desired response.

On a campaign level, framing is achieved with the campaign theme. Miller (1999) noted that campaign themes attempt to construct a reality by framing the interpretation of external events and providing a suggestion as to how the electorate should decide the election. The theme expresses an attitude, defines the rhetorical situation, and provides a mechanism for addressing external aspects of the campaign. A campaign theme, then, acts as a controlling concept, naming and revealing attitudes toward events, providing a "strategic answer" to questions posed by situations (Burke, 1973, p. 1). The frame simplifies external events, defining them with cues for decision making. Bill Clinton's 1996 campaign theme, "Bridge to the twenty-first Century," framed the election context as a decision about the future. It simultaneously expressed confidence in his earlier programs, optimism, and excitement about the ambiguous future of the next millennium (Miller, 1999). Ronald Reagan's "common culture" evoked benevolent capitalism and civic virtue as elements of the cornerstones of the American myth (Patterson, 1999). When he needed a political scapegoat, Reagan often framed the federal bureaucracy as a "benign political scapegoat" that could be the target of his verbal assaults (Braden, 2001).

Word Choice

Framing is also affected by word choice. Careful attention is placed on choosing the right word or words to use in a speech. Words can simultaneously create labels, convey a speaker's feelings on a topic, and signal emotional distance between the speaker and the issue (Fraser & Gordon, 1994). Given that complexity, the goal of the speechwriter is to select the "right" word: "the word that does exactly what you want it to do, and nothing else" (Perlman, 1998, p. 129). In some instances, the search for the right word is so critical that drafts with blanks inserted will be circulated, so that multiple suggestions for the right word are obtained. There is nothing new here. Mark Twain once wrote, "The difference between the almost right word and the right word is really a large matter—It's the difference between the lightning bug and the lightning."

Speechwriters generally avoid long words that may be hard for the speaker to pronounce and harder for the audience to understand. As Noonan (1998) noted, ". . . big things are best said, are almost always said, in small words" (p. 54). Long words can also create other problems. She recalled a speech on volunteerism that she wrote for President George H. W. Bush. Her first draft included the phrase "muscular altruism," referring to the need for people to lend a hand and help others. Campaign aide John Sununu vetoed the term (rightly so, she says), "Because it sounds like a disease" (p. 37). Use of the phrase could have made the president the target of ridicule.

Once a word or phrase is identified, it may be used repetitively as part of a process known as "staying on message" (Norris et al., 1999). The authors worked on one campaign in which the guidelines for a candidate's radio interview included working in the phrase "fiscal conservative" three times. During the 2000 presidential election, George W. Bush never attacked Al Gore for "lying" when he made statements that were incorrect, but he repeatedly said the vice president's behavior was "disappointing"; similarly, Bush never talked about spending "cuts" to reduce government expenditures, but always used the word "savings" as his euphemism (Bruni, 2000). During the 1980 New Hampshire primary, Ronald Reagan's consultants countered concerns that Reagan was too old (then sixty-nine) by using the phrase "oldest and wisest" in speeches and in conversations with reporters, thus putting a positive connotation to the age issue. Deborah Tannen (2000) noted that George W. Bush's campaign rhetoric was filled with words that would appeal to women voters, including references to "children," "dreams," "hope," "love," and "hearts." In a December 1999 speech on tax cuts, Bush referred to "children" or "child" eleven times.

Sound Bites

Two content darlings of public speeches, examples and illustrations, play a relatively small role in political speeches. They are still used because the use of examples and illustrations add interest and clarity to speeches. But while such elements are favored by live audiences, they are often eschewed by the press. They simply take too long to replay on the evening news. Instead, the content darling of the media is the sound bite, a short concise statement that reflects a candidate's message in a memorable manner. As Jones (1988, pp. 31–32) noted, the secret to getting an idea broadcast on television is to "condense, condense, condense" until you have a statement that can be said in twelve seconds or less."

A variety of techniques are used, but four tend to dominate: the antithesis, the metaphor, the quotation, and the anaphora. The antithesis is perhaps the most memorable of these techniques. It involves the positioning of words with opposite meanings, either in a parallel or inverted format. Antitheses come in a variety of formats. The simplest is the single antithesis, where a single set of antonyms are used to express the statement. The antiwar slogan of the sixties, "Make love, not war," fits this category with the antithesis created on the words "love" and "war." A double antithesis positions two sets of words in opposition. Democratic consultant James Carville's admonition that "We're right, they're wrong" fits into this category. In the double antithesis, each key word in the first half of the statement is followed by similarly placed antonyms in the second half. This format is diagrammed as ABAB: "We're (A) right (B), they're (A) wrong (B)." Roemer's "I hate (A) Louisiana politics (B), but I love (A) Louisiana (B)" is another example. More recently, in his 2001 inaugural speech, George W. Bush praised his opponent Al Gore for a campaign that was "conducted with spirit and ended with grace."

An inverted antithesis takes the word and reverses their order to that of an ABBA format; John F. Kennedy's most famous quote falls within this category: "Ask not what your country (A) can do for you (B), ask what you (B) can do for your country (A)." Carpenter (1999, p. 39) noted that the impact of an antithesis is influenced by balance, brevity, and placement. Balance requires that approximately the same number of words and antonyms be in each of the dual phrases. Brevity is important because brief statements are easier to remember. Placement is important because the second half of the statement has the strongest impact; the crucial point of the message ("Ask what you can do for your country") should come in the second phrase of the line.

Carpenter (1999, p. 83) describes the metaphor as a form of "rhetorical shorthand," an attribute that makes it particularly useful for sound bites. In one short word or phrase, a metaphor can evoke essential meanings with relatively few words. Although a variety of metaphors are available for the rhetor, political speechwriters are more likely to use one of three versions—synechdoche, metonymy, and the archetypal qualifier. Synecdoche is the use of a part of an object to represent the entire object, much like teenagers who refers to their "wheels" when talking about their car. Metonymy uses a tangible object to refer to an intangible concept. Winston Churchill's use of "blood, sweat, and tears" served as a tangible reference for suffering. Similarly, George W. Bush used two metaphors as a means of contrast in his inaugural speech: "Through much of the last century, America's faith was a rock in a raging sea. Now it is a seed upon the wind, taking root in many nations."

Archetypal qualifiers are metaphors that have commonly accepted connotations. Common uses of this type include those founded upon references to disease, the appeal of light and the avoidance of darkness, high and low, and changes of season. Thus George H. W. Bush referred to a "thousand points of light" to refer to volunteerism as a program that could "illuminate" the nation. Similarly, Bill Clinton used the last line of his acceptance speech at the 1992 Democratic convention to cast himself as the candidate of optimism; his approach was to refer to his childhood home in Hope, Arkansas, closing with the line, "I still believe in a place called Hope."

Quotations are popular among political speechwriters, but they have to be used judiciously. Too many quotes can be interpreted as the words of a candidate who has few original ideas, while too few might indicate a candidate who is not well educated. A few, though, carefully placed and used, can simultaneously increase a politician's credibility by demonstrating that their knowledge of a subject exceeds their own opinion on it. Furthermore, the source of the quote can be used to identify with an audience. Candidates who speak to predominantly black audiences, for example, almost invariably use a quotation from Martin Luther King, Jr. Quotations can also provide an eloquent way of opening or concluding a speech. When Peggy Noonan wrote a speech for President Reagan in the aftermath of the

Challenger explosion, she closed with words from a sonnet by James Gillespie Magee to honor the astronauts who had "slipped the surly bonds of earth to touch the face of God" (Noonan, 1998, pp. 82–87).

Quotations can make profound points. When Florida gubernatorial candidate Buddy MacKay was addressing a crowd in a joint appearance with President Bill Clinton in the midst of the Lewinsky scandal in 1998, he quoted Dr. Martin Luther King, Jr. "In the end it is not the words of our enemies we will remember. It is the silence of our friends." In a sentence, MacKay made his feelings known with great emotional depth.

Anaphora is a technique in which a sequence of sentences begins with the same word or phrase. Martin Luther King, Jr. used this technique effectively in his "I Have a Dream" speech, with that phrase serving as the starting point for several expressed dreams. Similarly, George W. Bush's 2001 inaugural speech (by speechwriter Mike Gerson) used an anaphora based on the word "citizen": "I ask you to be citizens. Citizens, not spectators. Citizens, not subjects. Responsible citizens, building communities of service and a nation of character."

Humor

Mario Cuomo once began a speech to the New York Press Club by relating last-minute advice from his wife, Matilda. "I know they're a tough group, but don't be intimidated. And don't try to be charming, witty, or intellectual. Just be yourself." That introduction is an example of the effective use of humor in a political speech. It establishes a positive start to the speech, diffuses any perception of arrogance on the part of the speaker, identifies the speaker as a witty person (Chang & Gruner, 1981), and establishes a mood that will make the immediate audience more receptive to the rest of the speech. Noonan argued that every political speech needed humor near its beginning because it provided a "quick victory" for the candidate and "shows the audience you think enough of them to want to entertain them" (p. 11). Files (2000) argues that humor has become one of the standards by which voters judge major candidates, particularly those running for president. "Humor has become another proving ground, especially for anyone who wants to be president," he wrote. "Besides handling stand-up at the annual Washington dinners of powerful media barons, politicians and lobbyists, politicians are expected to appear on the late-night Leno and Letterman shows, as well as on 'Saturday Night Live'" (p. A24).

Much of the candidate-based humor is directed at themselves. At the 1994 Gridiron dinner, Al Gore had himself wheeled to the speaking stand on a handcart, thus poking fun of his reputation for stiffness. At the 2000 dinner, he acknowledged the controversy over White House fund-raising with the question, "This isn't a fund-raiser, is it?" The second primary theme for campaign humor is an attack on the opponent. These humorous attacks typically use "gotcha" one-liners, such as Al Gore's campaign line that claimed George W. Bush "thinks fettuccine al fredo is the Italian prime minister."

Humor, when done well, can also become the sound bite that is replayed by the press. One highlight of the presidential debates between Ronald Reagan and Walter Mondale was Reagan's joking approach to the age issue by insisting that he would not make an issue out of his opponent's "relative youth and inexperience." Humor can also be an effective device for inducing inoculation against persuasion; once people start laughing at an opponent or concept, it is difficult to alter their opinions in the future (Powell, 1975). But jokes that don't work are disasters; during the presidential debates leading up to the Iowa caucuses in

2000, Steve Forbes tried several jokes that were unsuccessful, either because of missing on a punch line or missing the timing on his delivery. There's a lesson there: not everybody can use humor effectively in political speeches. Noonan (1998, p. 106) warns that politicians should be particularly wary about using sarcasm in their speeches; they rely heavily upon effective delivery and might still be misunderstood. Sarcasm that backfires can be particularly harmful to a candidate.

Case Study: George W. Bush's Stump Speech

While campaigning for the Republican nomination for president in 1999, Texas governor George W. Bush used the same stump speech in nearly every public appearance. As the *New York Times* (1999, November 1, p. A1) noted, his adherence to the script "captured the caution, discipline and careful choreography behind his front-running candidacy" and "spells out . . . the personality he wants to project, the place on the political spectrum he wants to inhabit and the priorities he wants to set."

The speech included self-deprecating humor (an observation that his decision to marry his wife, Laura, was probably wiser than her decision to marry him), philosophical middle ground (the need to wed conservative principles with compassionate impulses), indirect criticisms of incumbent Bill Clinton ("I will not—I will not—use my office as a mirror of public opinion"), and a buffet of issues (endorsement of tax cuts, focus on education, free trade, promise to help children).

Most of the language in the speech was well tested, with much of it used previously in 1996 and 1997 during his campaign for the Texas governorship. But the testing of the phrases went beyond the field testing in the previous campaign. Before it was used in the presidential race, videotaped snippets of a previous speech were presented to focus groups in the West, Midwest, and South. Speechwriter Michael Gerson used the results of that research, plus transcripts of previous speeches, to produce the final stump speech that Bush actually used.

Bush, though, was actively involved in the development of the final product; Gerson went through sixteen versions before Bush approved the final one. That final draft, however, included some phrases that did not test well in the focus groups; they remained because Bush wanted them there and he felt comfortable using them.

The length of the speech varied from fifteen minutes to forty-five minutes, depending on the audience and situation. Some elements would be omitted for shorter presentations; others added for a specific audience. Speeches in agricultural states included a section on farming, while metropolitan audiences heard about his thoughts on computers and technology. But, as the *Times* noted, "The big lines and peak moments rarely change."

Those big moments included:

- A comment on free trade: "It is the fearful who build walls. It is the confident who tear them down."
- The value of education: "Failed schools create two societies: one that reads and one that can't; one that dreams and one that doesn't."
- And a humorous aside directed at those who support his opponents: "If you're for one of my erstwhile opponents, that's O.K. Just don't work too hard."

Source: Bruni, F. (1999, November 1). For Bush, an adjustable speech of tested themes and phrases. *New York Times,* pp. A1, A14.

Types of Campaign Speeches

The Stump Speech

The stump speech is the basic campaign speech used by candidates in most campaign appearances. Nimmo (1970) described it as "the prepared speech repeated endlessly . . ." (p. 119). Reporters who follow a candidate quickly identify those elements that are common to all appearances, and those common elements quickly become old news to veteran reporters. In fact, one way to identify the key components of a presidential stump speech is to compare press coverage of the speech by local reporters and by national reporters. The national reporters typically do not cover the stump material, reporting only on new elements added to the message. Local reporters, though, often provide detailed coverage of the entire speech.

An ideal stump speech is really a collection of topics usually generated by survey research from which the candidate pulls those that are most appropriate for the immediate audience. Ronald Reagan's initial stump speech was contained on a file of three-by-five notecards; he would select a series of cards for use at any specific appearance, resulting in the use of different material at different places and varying the length according to the situation (Ritter, 1968). Each speech was different, and yet themes and ideas were consistently repeated. Nimmo (1970) noted that stump speeches are not designed to sway voters' attitudes or to provide an in-depth view of the candidate's position. Its principal purpose instead is credibility enhancement. "By quoting facts and details on a variety of issues the candidate leaves the impression that he possesses the knowledge, sophistication, and acumen to hold public office" (pp. 119–120).

The Issue Speech

The purpose of an issue speech is threefold: to define the candidate's position on an issue, to frame the issue in a manner that is advantageous to the candidate, and to generate positive news coverage for the candidate on that issue. Issue speeches are often presented at occasions that are associated with the issue selected. Thus, a speech on increasing the minimum wage might first be presented to a labor union, while one on changes in capital gains taxes might be offered to a business group. For that reason, the speechwriter must compose the speech with both the immediate audience and the extended audience in mind. The presentation must be organized well and argued coherently, so the immediate audience will attend to and follow its content. It must also contain a condensed version of the issue proposal (preferably in a sound-bite format) that will make it easy for the press to provide coverage.

A number of different formats can be used for issue speeches, but the most common approach is relatively simple:

1. State a voter-held premise about the issue ("Education is the key to our future")
2. Link the issue to the position ("Your governor must take the lead in improving our schools")
3. Link the candidate to the position ("John Doe will make sure that gets done")
4. Support the argument with:
   a. the candidate's record on the issue ("As a legislator, I sponsored the bill that raised teachers' salaries to the national level"), or
   b. a proposal on what to do ("I'll put together a statewide lottery with the funds dedicated to improving education")

5. Appeal for support, with that support linked to the issue ("But I need your help. Vote for me in November, and together we can improve education in this state.")

   To generate coverage of the speech, the candidate must have something newsworthy to say. That decision is often based on how much risk the candidate is willing to take. The more risk involved in the message, the more likely it is to receive coverage and the more legitimate the message becomes (Garlick & Mongeau, 1992). But taking too big of a risk opens the candidate to criticism. The candidate must also evaluate the degree of rigidity he or she will hold on an issue; the politician who appears too rigid is seen as too ideological, while the one who shifts too often is viewed as an opportunist who lacks values (Denton & Woodward, 1985, p. 11).

The Event Speech

Politicians are often called upon to make speeches at special events, such as political conventions, holiday celebrations, or celebrations to honor other people or historical figures. Speeches at party events are often full of praise for the party's candidates and attacks on those of the opposition (Benoit, Blaney, & Pier, 2000), but speeches at nonpartisan events are more complex. The event offers a chance for positive publicity, but the focus of the news coverage is likely to be on the event rather than the candidate. Any overt attempt to take advantage of such events often creates a backlash. The general rule here is that the speech should be written to focus on the event rather than the candidate, a goal that will naturally benefit the candidate if done well. To do otherwise is to risk the development of a self-serving image.

   Combs (1980) used the terms "political ceremonials" and "political rituals" to describe many such event speeches. Political rituals, he noted, can dramatize the cohesion of a political group, separate it from another political group, and link "the group to a guiding myth" (p. 25). Some—including the inaugural addresses, State of the Union addresses, and farewell addresses—are institutional in nature and serve specific purposes (Campbell & Jamieson, 1990). The inauguration ceremony, for example, comes complete with an inaugural speech. The ceremony itself is a ritual of political succession that invests the new president with power, duty, and privilege (Mair, 1962). Not all political rituals involve political speeches, but many do. The speakers may be "long-winded orators" who speak on predictable topics (Combs, 1980, p. 28), but even cliches can serve a communicative purpose. After all, the very nature of political rituals is to celebrate political symbols (Duncan, 1968), and ritualistic speeches provide that opportunity.

Playing Defense

Since a candidate's image plays a critical role with the voters, an attack on that image can prompt a self-defense speech (Gold, 1978). Such speeches have a long history in American politics, but the modern era of media-based apologies can probably be traced to Richard Nixon's "Checkers" speech. Nixon, besieged by charges that he had misused donations from campaign contributors, went on television to defend his actions; the only gift he had accepted, he claimed, was a puppy his family had named Checkers.

   From the consultant's perspective, the best guideline for responding to attacks is "The truth is the best defense." The first action is to discuss the action with the candidate,

The Top Ten Cases of Political Foot-in-Mouth Disease

by Jim Kitchens

One complaint commonly heard in the press is that politicians never really say what they think or feel. They are all merely parroting "spin doctors"—consultants such as myself—to help them put the best light on any situation.

As someone who has spent twenty years working in politics, I want to personally assure each and every one of you that the political consultants are not in control.

Nope, we wake up and read the headlines with the rest of the proletariat and with much the same reactions: "They said that?"

In fact, I have spent noncampaign years collecting my top ten "oops" quotes: evidence of political foot-in-mouth disease that no spin doctor could possibly cure.

10. *"I am not a crook."* Tricky Dick wasn't quite tricky enough to avoid this blooper. Advice: If a politician says this out loud, he is a crook. And if he is a smart crook, he should be content with stealing the public blind, rather than stealing the public blind and expecting them to like him, too.

9. *"I have had lust in my heart."* Then-presidential candidate Jimmy Carter, quoted in *Playboy* after being asked if he had ever committed adultery. Advice: Next time, Jimmy, just say no.

8. *"It's OK to cut down all the trees . . . Jesus is coming back soon and the world will end."* Former interior secretary James Watt on whether logging should be allowed in national parks. Advice: No high-level appointments without a high-level psychiatric exam.

7. *"I think the people want to hear what I have to say."* H. Ross Perot, on why he bought thirty minutes of television air time. Advice: Never underestimate the voters' intelligence or overestimate their interest. Political candidates should remember that the person who most wants to hear them talk lives in the mirror.

6. *"I swear to tell the truth."* Lieutenant Colonel Oliver North. Advice: Make sure your staff recognizes something before they publicly swear to it.

5. *"Today I announce my candidacy to run for president of the United States."* Former vice president Walter Mondale, announcing his intention of running against wildly popular incumbent Ronald Reagan. Advice: There is no suitable advice for a suicide mission.

4. *"I am tired of your unfounded accusations. If you think I am unfaithful to my wife, then prove it."* Presidential candidate U.S. Senator Gary Hart to the press. Advice: Never challenge the press to prove that something they think is true is actually true, when you already know what they think is true, is true.

3. *"I've never seen anything like it."* President George H. W. Bush, upon being shown a grocery store price scanner. Advice: If you want to help a candidate make friends outside the Beltway, take them out and show them a few new things like ATM machines.

2. *"P-O-T-A-T-O-E."* Vice President Dan Quayle. Advice: Never put a candidate in a position that confirms a nine-year-old really might do a better job of running the country.

And the number one "OOPS":

1. *"I did not have sex with that woman . . ."* President Bill Clinton. Advice: The president's trousers should be surgically attached and removed only after he leaves office.

Source: Adapted from: Kitchens, J. (1999, July 10). A bad case of foot-in-the-mouth disease. *Orlando Business Journal*, p. 63. Used by permission of James T. Kitchens.

identify the facts in the matter, and develop a defense based on those facts. If the candidate denies the action, or provides some justification for the action, then a variety of options are available. Most of these have been described, under a variety of labels, by a number of communication scholars.

Kenneth Burke's (1973) theory of dramatism states guilt as the primary motive behind such speeches. The major means of not accepting such guilt, according to Burke, was a process he called "Victimage." Victimage, or scapegoating, discards the guilt by transferring it to someone other than the accused. Scott and Lyman (1968) identified two other types of account behavior for self-defense speeches: excuses and justification. Excuses involves admitting to a wrong act but not accepting full responsibility for it. Scott and Lyman identify five subtypes of excuses, one of which is scapegoating. The other four can be added to Burke's limited list—accidents, defeasibility, biological drives, and justification. A candidate uses an "accident" argument when they claim that unexpected factors influenced the behavior or act. Defeasibility is used when a candidate argues that they could not have committed an action because of a lack of knowledge or completed it because of a lack of will. The biological drive category is better known as the "I couldn't help myself" argument. Justifications are perhaps the most complex form of excuses; in this approach, the candidate accepts responsibility for the act, but does not accept the fact that the act was wrong.

Benoit, Gullifor, and Panici (1991) identified four types of defensive speeches, those based on denial, evasion of responsibility, minimization, and mortification. Denial claims that the speaker had no responsibility for the act, evasion tries to reduce responsibility for the act, and minimization tries to reduce the salience of the act. Mortification occurs when the candidate admits the wrongful act and asks for forgiveness.

Ware and Linkugel (1973) identified four types of rhetorical self-defense: Denial, bolstering, differentiation, and transcendence. Their definition of denial is similar to that of Benoit, Gullifor, and Panici (1991), which is that denial occurs when the candidate disassociates him- or herself from the act. Bolstering attempts to offset the source by associating the speaker with something for which the audience has positive affection. Differentiation takes the speaker's image out of a negative context in the hope that it is the context and not the speaker that caused the displeasure. Transcendence tries to place the object of disapproval in a more favorable context.

A similar taxonomy was identified by Kennedy and Benoit (1997) when they examined Newt Gingrich's defensive rhetoric following the controversy that erupted after he signed a multimillion dollar book deal; they identified five strategies used by Gingrich: denial, good intentions, bolstering, attacking accusers, and corrective action.

The Apology—The Mea Culpa

"The truth is the best defense" maxim applies to the apology also. Voters are more tolerant of wrongdoing than many candidates might realize, and they are particularly tolerant when a candidate is willing to accept responsibility and acknowledge wrongdoing. However, their tolerance is strained if a candidate denies an action and later facts reveal the denial to be a lie. When an apology must be given, the simplest and most effective approach is to say, "I shouldn't have done it and I won't do it again." The technical term is mortification, which is the admission and acceptance of wrongdoing (Burke, 1973, p. 39). The goal of the speech is to seek forgiveness, and—more often than not—it usually works. Such a speech shows that the candidate is human, and voters are willing to forgive—particularly if it is a first offense.

Apologies are effective but not necessarily easily elicited from candidates. Benoit, Gullifor, and Panici (1991), for example, noted that Ronald Reagan dealt with the Iran-Contra controversy by first using denial; after that his arguments shifted to the justification of his actions as being well-intentioned. After the release of the Tower Commission Report detailing the activities, though, Reagan finally issued an apology—one based on mortification (acknowledging that he had traded arms for hostages) and victimage (announcing changes in people and policy to prevent a similar event from happening again). Benoit, Gullifor, and Panici noted that the latter approach was the most effective.

Case Study: How Not to Do a Mea Culpa

California congressman Gary Condit had a problem. In the spring of 2001, a government intern named Chandra Levy mysteriously disappeared. Although the police quickly eliminated Condit as a suspect, his prior relationship with Levy became public knowledge. While the police conducted their investigation, Condit had little to say on the matter and offered information only when directly asked. By late August, his reticence was hurting his chances for reelection. (He lost the primary election the following March.) The congressman and his campaign staff decided it was time to go public.

Time magazine writers Michael Duffy and Nancy Gibbs (2001) noted that Condit's mea culpa speech should have been an easy one to write. Their recommended speech:

> I did a stupid thing, America. In an attempt to protect my family and Chandra Levy's, I kept my mouth shut when I should have gone immediately to the police. I shouldn't have waited for them to come to me. These are mistakes I will carry with me for the rest of my life, and I am deeply sorry.

Such a speech would have been an example of "mortification,"—an admission and acceptance of wrongdoing (Burke, 1973), a classic mea culpa that is often effective. Condit, however, chose not to use that approach. He defended his previous positions instead and attacked the media for attacking him. That approach backfired. As *Newsweek* noted, "The media criticism of his performance . . . was unrelenting, and the public reaction wasn't much better." An NBC poll showed that only 2 percent believed he was concerned about Levy, while 93 percent said he was protecting himself politically.

Such negative public reactions can often occur if a politician approaches a mea culpa with a combative rather than a contrite attitude. As *Time* writers Duffy and Gibbs concluded, "If the Congressman was hoping to sound contrite about his relationship with missing intern Chandra Levy, he might have tried saying he was sorry."

Sources: Duffy, M., & Gibbs, N. (2001, September 3). How not to rebuild a reputation. *Time,* pp. 34–35.

Hosenball, M., Breslau, K., & Jackson, B. (2001, September 3). From bad to worse. *Newsweek,* pp. 20–23.

The Nonspeech

Speechwriters sometimes write speeches that are never given. Sometimes these are written merely as a draft of ideas, a starting point for the discussion of how issues or themes are addressed. More often, these are anticipatory in nature, written for situations in which the outcome is not yet known. For example, two speeches are typically written for election night—one should the candidate win and another if he or she loses. Presidents often have disaster speeches ready for tense situations that could go awry, hoping they will never need to use them. In 1969, for example, William Safire (1999) prepared a speech for President Richard Nixon's use if Neil Armstrong and Buzz Aldrin became stranded in space during the historic first trip to the moon.

Speeches that are not used are not necessarily wasted. The writer typically files them away, using its prepared material for a later situation that is more appropriate. On other

The Speech Not Given

William Safire wrote a speech for President Nixon to deliver in 1969, in case the Apollo XI astronauts were stranded on the moon. It never had to be delivered.

The request for the speech came not from Nixon but from astronaut Frank Borman, NASA's liaison to the White House. Borman called Safire to say, "You want to be thinking of some alternative posture for the president in the event of mishaps." When the stunned Safire did not respond, Borman added: "Like what to do for their widows."

Borman then explained that the most dangerous part of the trip was not landing on the moon, but in launching it back up to the mother ship. If that failed, Neil Armstrong and Buzz Aldrin could not be rescued, Mission Control would have to cut off communications, and the doomed astronauts would be left to starve to death or commit suicide. Nixon aides H. R. Haldeman and Peter Flanigan told Safire to proceed with a plan for that tragic contingency.

On July 18, 1969, two days before the astronauts reached the moon, Safire recommended a contingency plan. In the event of a disaster, the president should telephone each of the widows-to-be. After NASA cut off contact, a clergyman would perform a ceremony equivalent to a burial at sea, commending their souls to "the deepest of the deep" and concluding with the Lord's Prayer. A draft of a speech for the president was included with the plan. Here is a selection from the speech:

> "Fate has ordained that the men who went to the moon to explore in peace will stay to rest in peace," the speech began. "These brave men, Neil Armstrong and Buzz Aldrin, know there is no hope for their recovery. But they also know that there is hope for mankind in their sacrifice. . . . In ancient days, men looked at the stars and saw their heroes in the constellations. . . . In modern times, we do much the same, but our heroes are epic men of flesh and blood. Others will follow, and surely find their way home. Man's search will not be denied. But these were the first, and will remain foremost in our hearts. . . . For every human being who looks up at the moon in the nights to come will know that there is some corner of another world that is forever mankind."

Safire based the final line of the speech on lines from a poem by Rupert Brooke, who died in the British royal navy in World War I. "If I should die, think only this of me: That there's some corner of a foreign field that is forever England."

occasions, private distribution of a never-delivered speech can have positive benefits for the campaign. One of the authors once wrote a speech for a candidate to use at a rally honoring a civil rights leader; a last-minute change in the schedule resulted in the speech never being presented, but a copy was distributed to some of the participants. That led to an important endorsement for the candidate.

Influencing the Situation

How important is control of the immediate speech environment? Quite important, judging by how much emphasis consultants and candidates place on influencing that environment. Campaigns typically go to great lengths to generate large crowds for campaign appearances; if numerical numbers are expected to be low, the appearance will be scheduled for a smaller location so that the crowd will at least appear to be larger. Collateral material is distributed and placed in strategic spots (within range of the television cameras) to enhance the festive and optimistic mood of the event. What about hecklers? They're okay too, if properly placed. George Wallace used to insist that hecklers be placed closed to the stage, making it easier for them to verbally attack him. Wallace felt confident in his ability to outwit the hecklers and knew that the television cameras would capture the entire exchange for the evening news.

Campaigns also choose the music that will be played at such events. That's nothing new. Franklin Delano Roosevelt campaigned to the strains of "Happy Days Are Here Again," a tune that reflected the optimistic promises of his campaigns following the sad days of the Great Depression. More recently, candidates have been choosing pop or rock songs to represent their campaigns. Decisions on which song or songs to use are carefully made. The song can't be too popular (people will get tired of hearing it) and must be politically correct (McFetters, 1999). And, most important, it must underscore the campaign message in a positive manner. Thus, both Ronald Reagan and Bob Dole campaigned to the beat of "God Bless the U.S.A."; Bill Clinton relied heavily on the Fleetwood Mac tune, "Don't Stop Thinking About Tomorrow"; And George W. Bush opened his campaign for the 2000 presidential election with "Signed, Sealed, Delivered, I'm Yours" Most of those worked well, but some candidates have run into problems. President George H. W. Bush wanted to use "Don't Worry, Be Happy," but songwriter Bobby McFerrin publicly said he didn't support Bush. Similarly, Bruce Springsteen objected to Reagan using "Born in the U.S.A.," a song he had originally written as the plaint of a Vietnam veteran.

Summary

Political speeches are an integral part of the political communication process. They reflect the candidate's expression of ideas and form the basis for mass media messages. Still, they differ from many other forms of public speaking in terms of how they are developed, written, presented, and used. Many political speeches are developed over time, as different units (or modules) of the speech are written, tested, and rewritten as the expression of a message on a particular issue is refined. In the process, though, political speeches offer verbal opportunities for candidates to define their positions on issues, speak out on current events, defend their records, and offer apologies for misdeeds.

The format for such speeches will vary, ranging from the rough informality of a stump speech in a small town to solemn occasions that involve the death of citizens. The political speech may be an informal presentation to a small group of supporters, introductory comments at a press conference, or formalized statements delivered in a televised public address. In any situation, the political speech plays a vital role as a primary source of material that is reported by the media to the voters. As a result, the political speech speaks to both its immediate audience and to an extended audience, conveying messages that can have an important impact on framing issues and defining the images of political candidates.

QUESTIONS FOR DISCUSSION

1. At its best, political rhetoric is the politician's voice and the voice of his or her campaign. Analyze examples from one particular campaign and try to identify to what extent the rhetoric of the campaign was a key part of the campaign plan? Were there any examples that you believe were simply a reaction to unexpected circumstances on the campaign trail? The random musings of the candidate? The result of careful research?

2. A candidate expresses a popular desire in a well-received speech. Behind the rhetoric, however, there is little to suggest the sentiments expressed by the candidate have any grounding in the candidate's own life and experiences. Can such a speech be successful? How can an opponent attack such rhetoric? Can you cite an example?

3. A candidate in Pennsylvania for the U.S. Senate suggested that if criminals have a right to an attorney, why can't the people have a right to quality health care. Is this an effective argument? Why or why not?

4. Special interest groups, speechwriters, political consultants, candidates, their spouses, supporters, and contributors: Which of these is likely to be a source of political rhetoric? Which of these is likely to be a source of *good* political rhetoric?

CHAPTER

10 Political Polling

The authors once met a local political activist who opened the conversation by saying, "I don't believe in polls." She then recounted the story of a local tax referendum that she led, noting that she campaigned in the wealthy section of the community by talking of how the area would benefit from a better school system. When campaigning in the low-income areas, her message focused on the structure of the tax—it would be paid by wealthy families. She summed up her story by smiling and saying, "We passed that without ever doing any polling."

No polling? Perhaps. But she did engage in audience analysis, and that is essentially what polling is—audience analysis (Gunter, 2000; Ruddock, 2001). With a small local electorate, one with which she was highly familiar, she was probably correct to reject formal polling. Her narrative indicated, however, that she did adjust her message to different target audiences based on her perceptions of those two audiences. Had she done a poll, the pollster would have recommended the same strategic approach that she used.

She didn't need a poll because she already understood her electorate well. Candidates in major campaigns lack that capability. A person from a wealthy Texas family may run for president, but it is unrealistic to expect that person to understand the problems faced by Hispanics in California, coal miners in Kentucky, ranchers in Montana, or African American voters in Mississippi. Polling fills that knowledge gap, providing a way for the candidate to analyze large and diverse audiences within the electorate. The resulting data are used for planning, evaluating campaigns, and developing campaign strategies (Ferguson, 2000). As the sophistication of the data-gathering process increased, candidates found a variety of uses for the information. First, polling provides a view of public opinion that can be compared with those of the candidate. Second, polling provides a basis for the expenditure of scarce campaign resources. Finally, a campaign can discover the standing of its candidate compared with an opponent.

Scientific polling in political campaigns began in the late 1930s, a development that coincided with a nationwide increase in the use of scientific approaches on communication variables. By the 1960s, polling techniques were used regularly in presidential campaigns. Veteran political pollster Bill Hamilton traced the beginnings of modern strategic campaigning to the successful use of telephone surveys in the 1970s (Hamilton & Beattie, 1999, p. 95). By then, most statewide candidates were regularly using polling techniques. By the early 1980s, several national polling firms had formed their own telephone banks, while several independent phone facilities were also formed for the purpose of conducting telephone surveys. Meanwhile, the use of polls had expanded to congressional candidates. By the 1990s, their use expanded further, with many local candidates starting to use polling services.

The news media also joined the bandwagon, with an increasing number of newspapers and television sources regularly using polls as a means of reporting on campaigns. From 1984 to 1988 alone, the number of news media polls on campaigns tripled (Taylor, 1990, p. 261). Some argue that the release of such polls helps to construct public opinion, rather than just measure it. Generally, though, research indicates that polls can affect the perception of public opinion, but do not create a bandwagon effect that induces undecided voters to side with the probable winner (Daschmann, 2000). For that reason, political campaigns seldom release their data, even when they would report positive information for them. Instead, they prefer to use their polling resources to validate campaign messages and to discover the movement of public opinion on key campaign issues, information they would prefer that the opposition not have. When they do release information, it is highly selective, with information favorable only to their side typically released. As a result, those news outlets that wish to have polling data often gather their own data. The effect is that the news media regularly release their polling data showing who is leading and by how much, and political campaigns seldom offer theirs unless there is a vast and potentially destructive difference between their numbers and the media's numbers.

Types of Political Polling

Although most people use the terms interchangeably, there is a technical difference between a political poll and a political survey. A political poll is a relatively short questionnaire with a descriptive purpose; its intent is to describe voter attitudes and intentions with relatively simple questions. A political survey uses a longer questionnaire and seeks more in-depth information about attitudes and predispositions. The differences between the two are most apparent in the benchmark survey and a tracking poll. The benchmark survey seeks in-depth information about the voting public, with the intent of using that information to develop a campaign strategy. Tracking polls are a way of "keeping score," to know who is ahead at any given point in the campaign.

Benchmark Survey

The benchmark survey is an initial survey taken by the campaign to assess the political environment and develop a campaign strategy. The benchmark is a specific type of cross-sectional survey, which is a survey that studies a cross section of a population at a particular point in time (Stacks & Hocking, 1998, p. 237). It makes no attempt to measure or observe changes among voters. It is more interested instead in obtaining a description of the attitudes and beliefs of the voting population as a whole, and identifying any demographic or psychographic differences among those voters. It is typically conducted early in the campaign (sometimes as much as eighteen months before the election).

Tracking Polls

A tracking poll is considerably shorter than a benchmark, usually consisting of only ten to fifteen short questions that can typically be asked in less than five minutes (frequently, only two or three minutes). Its primary goal is test ballot assessment, which is to learn which candidate is leading and by how much.

The most crucial part of the tracking poll is the test ballot ("If the election for Position A were held today, would you vote for Candidate X or Candidate Y?"). It gives the most direct test of the relative success or failure of the campaign, serving as an index of which candidate is ahead at that point in the campaign. Tracking polls may also test the campaigns' major messages to identify possible reasons for success or failure. The last set of questions typically included in a tracking poll are demographic questions about the voters themselves—age, partisan preferences, income level, ethnic background, gender, and geography. Each of these demographic factors represent something that can be used by the campaign for targeting purposes.

Tracking polls fall into two broad categories. The "One-Shot Track" is a short, cross-sectional descriptive study. It takes a cross section of the voting population and describes their attitudes and voting intentions at one specific time during the campaign. The Moving Window Track ". . . provides the campaign with the most stable and accurate measure of a trend line and the base for timely strategic decision making (Hamilton & Beattie, 1999, p. 102). The "Moving Window" ("Rolling Average" or "Rolling Sample Survey") is an example of a cohort trend longitudinal study—a survey technique that gathers observations over time with the sample drawn from the same subgroup universe (Stacks & Hocking, 1998, pp. 238–239). In the case of a political moving window track, that subgroup is voters. The moving window allows for constant polling to gauge the effect of the opponent's ads, the effects of the candidate's ads, and assessments of whether new ads are needed for the campaign.

Like the one-shot track, the moving window track does not provide causal information. It lacks the presence of an external control group for making causal inferences. Still, while caution should be used in interpreting the data from any single day (John, 1989), moving windows offer the pollster multiple options for analysis (Moore, 1999). It is considerably more precise than a one-shot track because it allows the pollster to draw conclusions about which factors occur at which time. That additional information increases the reliability of the informed judgments made by the pollster and the other participants in the campaign. When something happens that causes a dramatic shift in voter responses, that shift can be detected immediately. That, in turn, allows for a quicker and more effective response on the part of the campaign.

Other Polls and Surveys

A number of pollsters use a variety of names to describe other polls and surveys that have specific purposes. Two of the most common are strategy adjustment polls and Vulnerability surveys. A strategy adjustment poll is a relatively short questionnaire used to assess the effectiveness of the campaign's strategy, with the information used to make any necessary adjustments in that strategy. Hamilton and Beattie (1999) refer to this type of poll as a "brushfire survey," adding that they ". . . should be conducted when a strategic decision needs to be made" (p. 102). The questionnaire is typically midrange in length (about ten minutes), longer than a tracking poll, but shorter than a typical benchmark survey. The focus is on questions that measure the images of the candidates, their relative test ballot strength, and any refinements in issues that may need to be reassessed.

Vulnerability surveys are similar to benchmark surveys in terms of length, but differ in intent. This questionnaire is designed to measure the likelihood that an incumbent can be defeated by a strong challenger. If the vulnerability survey indicates the challenger has a chance, it can help them develop a strategy for the campaign and assist in their fund-raising efforts. Sometimes, the vulnerability survey is done on behalf of the incumbent with the intent of identifying potential points of weaknesses; in those cases, the incumbent typically uses the information to reduce those weaknesses before a challenger has an opportunity to take advantage of them.

Exit Polling

One popular form of polling for media outlets is exit polling. Exit polls are on-site surveys conducted on the day of the election with voters as they leave the voting booth. Their purpose is to identify for whom they voted, and what factors influenced their voting decision. For campaign purposes, this is relatively useless information; the campaign is over, and it is too late to use the information for strategic adjustments. However, these data can be useful to media outlets by allowing them to project winners before the polls have closed and to provide some type of insight as to why one candidate won and another lost.

Exit polling is not a foolproof system. It is subject to the same margin of error (usually plus or minus five percentage points) that limits regular polling approaches. Furthermore, since it is physically impossible to have interviewers at every voting site, the validity of the system depends on the representativeness of those voting precincts that are selected for interviews, which introduces a further possible margin of error. Those precincts or election districts are often chosen on the basis of turnout in previous elections, without considering whether the nature of the precinct has changed since that time. Even if representative precincts are chosen, if those precincts do not have voter turnout rates consistent with the election as a whole, its results may be invalid. Given all of these problems, it is really remarkable that exit polling is as effective as it is. Most of the time, the national networks get it right, and correctly project probable winners. Still, they occasionally miss. In 1984, for example, the national networks projected Senator Jeremiah Denton (Rep.-Ala.) to win reelection; when the votes were finally counted, Democratic challenger Richard Shelby narrowly defeated him. In 1996, incumbent Senator Bob Smith, Rep.-N.H., was declared the loser, but he narrowly won reelection. In the 2000 election, exit poll projections for Florida led to a series of wrong predictions by the television networks. Early on election night, all of the major networks declared Al Gore the winner; they subsequently rescinded that and later credited the state to George W. Bush's win column. Eventually, they withdrew both predictions; the vote count was so close that it took weeks to decide a winner.

Focus Groups

A focus group is a group of people who are gathered together at a common location to discuss some topic under the direction of a moderator (Merton, 1987; Merton, Lowenthal, & Kendall, 1990; Stewart & Shamdasani, 1990). Krueger and Casey (2000) note that focus groups are about listening. When used properly, the process improves listening, the results can be used to benefit the participants, and those participants leave with a good feeling about having been heard. In most cases, the size of the group is relatively small (usually ten to fifteen participants). As a result, data from focus groups lack the generalizability of similar responses obtained from a poll. That weakness aside, in-depth information can be obtained. In essence, polls and surveys provide a "quantitative" assessment of a political situation. Focus groups provide "qualitative" data about the same event (Denzin & Lincoln, 2000; Morgan, 1988; Silverman, 2001). Joseph Glick (1999, p. 121) noted, "The strength of the focus group is that it allows people to be people." Surveys can tell a candidate what is happening and focus groups can tell them why. As Hansen et al. (1998) noted, the semi-structured nature of the focus groups allows the researcher ". . . a potentially much richer and more sensitive type of data . . ." (p. 258).

Two factors are critical to the success of a focus group: a good research question and a good facilitator. The research question is essential, because it is unlikely that the researcher will elicit useful information when they do not know what they are seeking. The research question guides both the development of the group discussion and the selection of the participants, who are usually selected on the basis of some demographic or psychographic criteria (undecided voters, ticket splitters, and so forth).

Similarly, the facilitator is a key person in the process (Glick, 1999, p. 119). The facilitator's job is to encourage discussion by all participants, guide the discussion along the topic of interest, but not to influence the discussion in any manner. He or she often has a guide or a questionnaire to remind them of the information being sought, yet they must use some personal research skill to guide the discussion without letting the questionnaire become an artificial part of the process. As the discussion progresses, the facilitator must ask effective questions to draw out a group, and then refine those questions based on the group's responses. Doing that requires a skillful moderator, who can then produce useful information. As Glick (1999, p. 117) noted, "When nonconsensus and disagreements are encouraged, two things generally emerge in group discussion: opinion becomes nuanced in ways that begin to reveal underlying thought frameworks, and people often invoke powerful images. . . ."

Facilitators often have materials with them that can be used to stimulate discussion. The most popular of these are copies of television ads, with group participants serving as critics and explaining their responses to the ads. The pollsters and other campaign officials typically monitor the entire process. The monitoring frequently occurs at the same time as the discussion, with the researchers and campaign officials observing the discussion behind a one-way mirror. In addition, the entire process is videotaped, providing for frequent viewings at a later date to verify conclusions.

As mentioned before, because of the small sample size, the representativeness of focus group results is questionable. The general rule of thumb is that you need at least two groups, for comparison purposes, with ten to fifteen participants in each group. Usually, though, the campaign is not looking for generalizable answers. Instead, the goal of focus group research is to obtain new insights into the electorate and their views, which works to supplement the work of the media consultants. For instance, focus groups have led to the development of campaign slogans, using terminology provided by the focus group participants. Or, campaign ads may be reedited based on the participants' comments. Other times, focus group discussion can lead to the development of new ideas or messages that are subsequently tested with survey research (Wimmer & Dominick, 1994, p. 148).

The most common uses of focus groups in political campaigns are to pretest television ads, monitoring audience responses to presentations, and identifying audience language habits that can be used in campaign messages. One Republican pollster who frequently used focus groups is Richard Wirthlin, who provided data for former president Ronald Reagan. Every time Reagan gave a televised speech, Wirthlin had focus groups watching and using hand-held devices to record their responses to the speech, second by second. Wirthlin used the resulting data to identify what worked and what did not work for each speech. The information was then used in preparing the next speech (Taylor, 1990, p. 218).

Focus groups have limitations. Wimmer and Dominick (1994, p. 149) argue that, considering the small sample size and qualitative methodology, gathering quantitative data are inappropriate for a focus group. Along this line, most academicians argue that focus group data should be viewed as only preliminary data that should be verified with more in-depth research.

Another problem is their representativeness. Focus groups consist of volunteers who are often provided monetary incentives to participate. Such groups may not be representative of the overall population from which they were selected. That is particularly true if those participants are "professional subjects," who are constantly used by research organizations for a number of projects. Once someone volunteers to participate in a focus group, the research organization often keeps the name (complete with phone number and demographic data) on file. When they need another participant with those demographic criteria, the research organization may first call people who have participated before, creating a sample of people who are frequently used for similar research. Constant repetition of this process leads to focus groups composed of unrepresentative samples.

The Process of Political Polling

Questionnaire Development

The process of political polling begins with the questionnaire development. Typically, the pollsters and the candidate (and media consultant) discuss the issues and circumstances surrounding the campaign. As a result of the discussion, the pollster develops a first draft of questions to test these relevant factors. This is followed by subsequent rounds of discussions and revisions until all parties are satisfied that the questionnaire will provide the information sought.

Guidelines for Writing Questions.   Designing a questionnaire requires that the pollster be careful in constructing and writing the questions themselves. Questions need to be direct, clear, and unambiguous. Furthermore, unless there is a specific reason for testing audience biases, most questions should be phrased in an unbiased manner. This can be difficult, because many candidates prefer only to phrase questions from their own perspective, not that of their opponent. Still, the pollster has been of little use to the campaign if the survey does not provide unbiased information.

Most pollsters use some version of forced choice options or Likert-type questions. Forced-choice options are closed-ended questions that limit respondent options (such as "Yes" or "No"). Likert-type questions expand the options slightly to cover a broader continuum of responses, but still offer limited options (such as "strongly agree, somewhat agree, undecided, somewhat disagree, or strongly disagree").

Other techniques have sometimes been attempted, but with limited success. Some pollsters use a "feeling thermometer," in which respondents rate candidates and issues on a scale ranging from zero to one hundred. Generally, most voters have trouble making such fine distinctions. Research, in fact, indicates that voters make their most optimum distinctions about candidates and issues if the options are limited to no more than nine intervals. Furthermore, some voters interpret the zero to one hundred scale differently; some view it as if it is an academic scale. As a result, the midpoint of "fifty," which should be an average rating, is considered a "failing grade" by some respondents.

Zaller and Feldman (1992) oppose both the Likert-type scales and alternative scales like the feeling thermometer, arguing that attitudes on issues are particularly difficult to measure as precise preference points. They argue that issue positions may be based on a number of considerations that might move them toward any number of positions on an issue. These "considerations" are underlying arguments that are recalled from memory and may vary with time (Chong, 1993). Zaller (1990) also argues that responses to survey questions are influenced by the political sophistication of the respondents, and that pollsters err by giving the same weight to the responses of uninformed voters and the responses of political sophisticates. The only way to counter this, they argue, is to measure attitudes within a range of possible responses that are either acceptable or not acceptable to the voter. From an academic perspective, Zaller and Feldman have a valid point. From a consulting perspective, attempting to measure attitudes within ranges of responses is expensive and may produce limited additional information for the client. Few candidates are willing to pay for the extra expense to do so.

Several different types of survey questions are often employed. These include the greeting, the screen, favorability ratings, test ballots, issue questions, message questions, open-ended questions, and demographic questions.

The Greeting.   The greeting is a brief statement that introduces the interviewer to the telephone respondent and leads to a question about their interest in responding to the survey. Typically, the greeting starts with an introduction ("Hello, I'm John Doe, . . .") and identification of the research unit (". . . and I'm calling from JLP Research"). As Stacks and Hocking (1998) noted, these two elements serve "as a credibility inducement and provides indication that the project is important" (p. 251).

Next is an explanation of the project ("We're conducting a survey on politics within the state.") coupled with a request for assistance ("Would you mind taking a few minutes to answer a few questions?"). Typically, before the person can answer "yes" or "no," an additional inducement is provided by mentioning the short amount of time involved and the importance of the call ("The questions will only take about five minutes, and your answers could help us understand the state better.").

The Screen.   If the respondent agrees to participate, the next job for the interviewer is to determine whether they qualify for the survey. This qualification element is operationally defined by the survey's screen, a question that verifies their eligibility. For political polls, the minimal and basic screening question is one that asks whether or not the respondent is a registered voter; if not, the phone call should be terminated. Most pollsters add additional screens, however, depending on the nature and circumstances of the campaign. These might include questions regarding whether the respondent plans to vote in the election, and the likelihood of their doing so. Because of the possibility of embarrassing someone who does not vote, these questions are often asked in a manner that makes it socially acceptable to say they will not vote. Thus, instead of asking, "Are you going to vote in the upcoming election?" the screen is instead phrased, "As you know, the state will be holding its election for statewide offices in November. Do you currently plan to vote in that election, or do you expect that you will be unable to vote in that election?" If the person qualifies under the screen, and agrees to participate, then the rest of the survey can be completed.

One factor that can influence the results is the inclusion of people in the sample who will not vote. Even with a carefully worded screen, some people will misrepresent their voting intention and participate in the survey. Such overreporting generally does not affect the results of the data (Katosh & Traugott, 1981), except in the case of race (Sigelman, 1982). Blacks are more likely to overreport than whites (Abramson & Claggett, 1984, 1986, 1991; Hill & Hurley, 1984), although some (Silver, Anderson, & Abramson, 1986) argue that the difference is slight. At least one regional difference has been identified, with white voters in the South more likely to overreport than white voters in other parts of the country (Bernstein, Chadha, & Montjoy, 2001). Those people most likely to overreport their voting intention are those ". . . under the most pressure to vote . . . , the more educated, partisan and religious, and those who have been contacted and asked to vote for a candidate" (Bernstein, Chadha, & Montjoy, 2001, p. 22).

Favorability Ratings.   The first questions asked on many political surveys are favorability questions designed to measure positive and negative evaluations of candidates. Favorability ratings are typically phrased as, "Do you have a very favorable, somewhat favorable, somewhat unfavorable, or very unfavorable opinion of Candidate X?" Voters who are unable to offer an opinion on a candidate might be coded into one of several other categories ("unsure," "don't recognize," and so forth). Campaigns monitor favorability ratings for themselves and their opposition closely on tracking polls, since communication impacts often show up on these ratings before they are noticed in the test ballots.

Favorability questions are usually among the first questions in the survey for two reasons. First, they are relatively easy to answer, particularly if you begin the survey with high-profile candidates. If the respondents can answer the first few questions easily, it tends to create interest in the survey and increases the chances that they will participate for the duration of the questionnaire (Wimmer & Dominick, 1994, p. 119). Conversely, if the survey starts off with questions that the respondent feels they cannot answer, they will feel pressured to give a response for which they have no real opinion (Bishop, Tuchfarber, & Oldendich, 1986); many subsequently hang up. Second, since favorability questions provide a baseline measurement of image, it is important to get those responses before any questions are asked that might affect those images. Voters' feelings about political leaders tend to exceed their knowledge of those leaders in that they are quite capable of expressing an opinion about a candidate even if they know little about that person. Furthermore, those feelings are often indicative of voting intention (Blais et al., 2000). Surveys sometimes provide information about the candidate that might be previously unknown to the respondent, and that could, in turn, affect his or her image of the candidate. If the favorability questions are asked after that information has been provided, then the responses to the questions will be influenced.

Test Ballots. The most frequently cited questions on a survey or poll are usually the test ballot questions ("If the election for Position A were held today, would you vote for Candidate X or Candidate Y?"). The test ballot gives the most direct test of the relative success or failure of the campaign, serving as an index of which candidate is ahead at that point in the campaign. Its true value to the campaign varies, though, depending on when the survey is taken.

The question is nearly always included in early benchmark surveys, typically being omitted only for candidates who do not want people to know they are considering a campaign. Despite the frequency with which it is cited, though, the test ballot provides relatively useless numbers in these early stages of the campaign. Early test ballot numbers are heavily influenced by the extent to which each candidate is recognized by the voters, leading to inflated numbers for candidates with high levels of name recognition. Furthermore, both candidates will spend the rest of the campaign trying to (and often succeeding in) changing those numbers; the candidate with the best test ballot numbers tries to increase his or her lead, while the person in second place tries to move ahead of the candidate in first place.

Another version of the test ballot, one that frequently appears on vulnerability surveys, is the "definite reelect" question: "If the election were held today, would you definitely vote to reelect Candidate X, like to consider someone else, or would you definitely vote against Candidate X?" This version of the test ballot is used when testing the vulnerability of incumbents. It can be used even when there is no known opponent for that incumbent. Responses give pollsters an indication of the size of core support and core opposition to the incumbent.

The test ballot is also one of the most frequently misinterpreted numbers in the poll, since the candidate who is ahead in the polls is not always the one who is winning. This paradox is created by a phenomenon known as "the incumbent's undecided vote." When a well-known incumbent is included in the test ballot, the undecided voters tend to vote heavily against the incumbent. Why? Because they're not truly undecided—they've already decided that they don't want to vote for the incumbent. They are merely waiting for more information from the challenger before deciding whether that challenger is an acceptable alternative. In most cases, undecided voters eventually vote for the challenger. Thus, for incumbents, the goal is to get above the 50-percent level on tracking polls. Incumbents who cannot reach that level are susceptible to defeat.

Mood of the Electorate. These questions are designed with the intent to identify underlying trends that can have an influence on the election. The classic question of this type is the standard "right direction–wrong direction" question, which is used to measure satisfaction with the political system. A typical wording is, "Generally, do you believe things in America are headed in the right direction, or have things gotten off onto the wrong track?" Similar questions can be used to measure satisfaction with the economy, education, the judicial system, or any other political battleground.

Issue Questions. Issue questions are intended to measure voter reactions to the major political issues of the day. Although the question formats vary considerably, the most common techniques for measuring issues are in terms of support or opposition of an issue, agreement or disagreement with a position, or forced choices on major positions. Support and opposition questions generally use a Likert-type approach such as "Do you strongly support, somewhat support, somewhat oppose, or strongly oppose requiring a three-day waiting period for the purchases of handguns?" Agree-disagree approaches identify an expressed position related to an issue to see whether the public agrees with it. Again, it typically uses a Likert-type scaling technique, such as asking respondents whether they "strongly agree, somewhat agree, somewhat disagree, or strongly disagree" with the statement: "Any attempt to limit handgun purchases interferes with the public's constitutional right to bear arms." Forced-choice issue questions offer a variety of positions and ask the respondents to pick the one that most closely aligns with their own. An example: "Do you support efforts to require a three-day waiting period for the purchase of handguns, or do you consider such efforts an infringement on the public's right to bear arms?"

Controversial issues that delve into a person's values are often difficult to test (McCarty & Shrum, 2000), particularly when it comes to measuring minority opinions. Noelle-Neumann's (1974) "spiral of silence" model hypothesized that people whose opinions are not congruent with the national majority may be reluctant to discuss those issues in public. Research indicates the premise is particularly true when talking with a stranger, such as someone conducting an interview over the telephone (Salmon & Neuwirth, 1990). Responses to controversial issues can also be altered by the words used to test the issue; questions related to poverty, for example, carry emotionally laden implications if words such as "welfare" are used (Fraser & Gordon, 1994).

Image Questions.   Some survey questions measure specific areas of the candidate's image, an area that Hamilton and Beattie (1999, p. 99) refer to as "personalities." Although the format of image questions can vary, many use an "agree-disagree" format or a rating format, such as one to ten, which provides a range of possible image dimensions.

Message Questions.   Frequently, the candidate and/or the media consultant will test messages that might be used in the campaign. Furthermore, the campaign can often anticipate the messages that the opposition is likely to use. Both elements are included in the survey so that the candidate and the consultants have some estimate of the relative strength of each message. Message questions are sometimes phrased in an "agree-disagree" format, looking for versions that score significantly more than a majority of "agree," or even, "strongly agree," responses. Another version is the "more or less likely to vote for" approach, which ask, "Would you be more or less likely to vote for a candidate who . . . ," with the specific message used as a tag line. Potential attack messages against the opposition are also tested. As Hamilton and Beattie (1999, p. 99) noted, "Researching the arguments against the opposition helps determine what voters see as 'fair' and what they feel is out of bounds, what they see as critical to the office or extraneous."

Projective Questions.   Some pollsters use projective "what-if," questions that are intended to give them some idea as to how the campaign might play out. From an academic viewpoint, this approach is highly questionable. From the consultant's view, such questions are often inaccurate, highly speculative, and ineffective. Their major campaign purpose is to provide some sort of reassurance to someone associated with the campaign, but the data themselves are often hard to interpret. That's because the voters themselves don't know exactly how to answer such questions and provide a response only because they are required to do so. Such questions epitomize the problems associated with multiple considerations and political sophistication raised by Zaller (1990). The past is more knowable than the future, and voters are more likely to make judgments on information that is retrospective than is prospective.

Open-Ended Questions. One problem with most survey questions is that the respondents can only answer what is asked. When only closed (or forced) option questions are used, the pollster cannot identify what other issues or factors may be operating within the electorate. One way to counter this problem is to use open-ended questions that allow the respondents to express an opinion with no guidance from the pollster. The most common open-ended question is the "most important issue" question ("Overall, what do you think is the most important issue facing the nation today, the thing you would like to see the president and Congress deal with and try to solve?"). The open-ended format allows for an unlimited range of responses, which can go beyond the scope of what the politicians are directly dealing with at any one point. That gives the pollster a chance to analyze those voter concerns that are not yet on the table of the government agenda. Open-ended questions are also used as "probes" when more information is needed to explain responses to a forced-choice question. For example, a favorability rating for a candidate only provides positive or negative ratings for a candidate, with no explanation as to why the voters hold those attitudes. Following a favorability question with an open-ended probe ("Why do you feel that way about Candidate X?") can expand the campaign's understanding of that attitude.

The disadvantages of open-ended questions are that they generally provide less information than can be developed from structured questions; furthermore, the results are less reliable in assessing the impact of attitudes on campaigns (Rahn, Krosnik, & Breuning, 1994). Miller and Shanks (1996, p. 503) noted that structured survey questions provide a clearer picture of the sources of voters' preferences because they are not hampered by the ambiguity of open-ended questions and the uneven or incomplete data that often result.

Demographic Questions. Demographic questions measure attributes of the respondents such as age, income, party affiliation, gender, and ethnic background. They are usually delayed until the end of the survey, and they serve three purposes. First, they allow the pollster to stratify the sample and verify its representativeness. Second, crosstabulations of the results, by these demographic questions, are the primary statistical analyses for the survey. Third, the demographic breakdowns provide crucial targeting information to the campaign.

Sampling

Ideally, political polling is a scientific process for describing the attitudinal and demographic makeup of a voting population at any given point in time. Polling is based on the mathematical principles of sampling, a process that projects that the responses of a representative portion of the electorate can be used to gauge the responses of the electorate as a whole. The accuracy of any political poll, though, will depend upon the extent to which the sample represents the actual voting turnout on election day. For that reason, the use of some means of random sampling is essential, and a variety of techniques have been developed for that purpose. Still, there is no such thing as a perfect sample technique. All have limitations, although most are minor.

Random Digit Dialing. Random digit dialing involves the use of a computer to dial phone numbers using a random process. Researchers who lack a computer with this capability can substitute a *random numbers table* and achieve the same effect. This process has advantages in that the researcher cannot deliberately bias the sample in any manner and that households with unlisted numbers can be included in the sample. Its disadvantage is that many middle- and upper-income homes now have multiple phone lines coming into the house, while lower-income households have only one. This creates a risk of biasing the results against lower-income households.

Computer-Generated Lists. One approach for generating a random sample is to have a computer select the telephone numbers from the telephone books of the sample area. Lists generated with this approach use some multiple (usually ranging from 10 to 20) of the projected sample size as the basis for the list generation. Thus, if the target sample size for the survey is 600 registered voters, then a list of 6,000 randomly selected telephone numbers (if a multiple of 10 is used) is generated. The multiple numbers increase the efficiency of the telephone, since all numbers used are known to be associated with active telephones (that doesn't happen with random digit dialing). The disadvantage of this approach is that it does not reach unlisted numbers (again, creating a potential bias against lower-income households). That is often corrected by randomly changing one number (plus or minus one) to some of the phone numbers on the list.

Stratified Random Sampling. The most common approach, regardless of how the list is generated, is to use a process called stratified random sampling. In this approach, the pollster predetermines how many responses are needed in each category of one major demographic variable (usually geography), and then respondents are randomly selected from within each of the subgroups of that category. As the survey progresses, calls are monitored to ensure that they correspond to the projected participation on one other variable (usually gender). After the survey is completed, the other demographic variables are tested to ensure that each category of those factors are adequately represented. This approach is the preferred choice of most pollsters because it guarantees that certain groups within the population will be sampled. As Hansen et al. (1998, p. 241) noted, stratified random sampling "allows for the appropriate representation of different groups in the population" to ensure that the sample represents the population under study.

A variation of the stratified random sample is "cluster sampling." Cluster sampling involves the development of computer-generated lists of "clusters" of people with similar demographic characteristics based upon the stratification criteria. A pollster conducting a statewide survey of 600 registered voters would create a computer-generated list of 600 clusters of voters (with ten to twenty-five names matched with phones per cluster), with those clusters corresponding to the stratification criteria of the survey. One name from each cluster would be interviewed for the survey. Cluster sampling has the advantage of being relatively immune to problems created by low response rates, which come from people who refuse to answer the phone or participate in the survey. Theoretically, as long as at least one person from each cluster participates in the survey, the response rate will not affect the validity of the sample.

Interviewing

Most political polling involves the use of telephone interviews and professional callers. Professional interviewers know to read the questions as they are written, know when to repeat questions that are not understood, and know to refrain from commenting or reacting nonverbally. Even then, there will be problems, because not everyone reached by telephone will agree to respond to the survey. Yu and Cooper (1983), in an analysis of surveys reported in academic journals, found that the average completion rate for telephone surveys was about 72 percent, and that that estimate applied only to those who did not refuse to participate during the greeting or screening stage. Phone banks that specialize in political contacts often reach an 80 percent rate when dealing with lists of registered voters, but their success can drop if a general population list is used. Furthermore, the completion rate of the interview goes down as the length of the interview increases. Wimmer and Dominick (1994, p. 121) recommend that telephone surveys be limited to a maximum of twenty minutes in length, since there is a significant increase in the breakoff rate (hang-ups) when interviews exceed that length. Electronic surveys have to be even shorter, since it is easier for people to hang up on a machine than another human (Havice, 1990).

Data Analysis

Data analysis for a political poll is considerably simpler than similar types of analyses conducted for academic polls. The basic level of analysis is a simple crosstabulation, with crosstabs conducted on each individual survey question. The independent variables for the analysis are typically the demographic questions and the test ballot. The primary statistical analysis used is the Chi-Square (χ^2), but this statistic is often not reported to the campaign. Instead, the data analysis is provided to the campaign in the form of tabular columns (banners) that identify, by frequency and percentages, the responses of the overall sample and of each demographic subgroup. Sometimes additional analysis, such as linear regression or discriminant analysis, is necessary to provide the campaign with more specific information about the data (Kitchens & Powell, 1975), but the use of such techniques is not a common practice.

Level of Confidence and the Confidence Interval

At its core, political surveys are a simple mathematical process of counting responses. Since the numbers obtained from that process are obtained from only a sample of the population, those numbers are only estimates of how the total population would have responded. Thus, those numbers are useful only to the extent that they can be compared to probable numbers that would exist in the target population if you could count the responses from everybody. Two statistical concepts allow that comparison to be made: confidence level and margin of error.

Confidence level (or level of confidence) refers to the extent to which the pollster has confidence that the findings obtained from any one particular survey will fall within a specified interval. The width of that specified interval is referred to as the margin of error. The minimum level of confidence for social science research is usually 95 percent. Table 10.1 provides examples of how the margin of error varies, depending upon the size of the sample. Note that as the sample size increases, the margin of error decreases. Thus the margin of error for a sample of 300 is ±4.9 percentage points, but that drops to ±4.0 for a sample of 600. The margin of error for a sample of 1,000 is ±3.1 percentage points, and that for a sample of 1,200 would be ±2.8 percentage points. Reducing the margin of error any lower than

TABLE 10.1   Selected Sample Sizes and
Corresponding Margins of Error

Sample Size	Margin of Error (%)
300	5.7
350	5.2
400	4.9
500	4.4
600	4.0
800	3.5
1,000	3.1
1,200	2.8

that requires considerably larger sample sizes. As a result, few surveys employ sample sizes larger than 1,200. It simply becomes cost prohibitive, with relatively few resulting benefits. Such larger sample sizes can typically be justified only if there is some specific need to analyze some of the subgroups in more detail.

Report Writing

The utility of polling information largely depends on the pollster's ability to interpret the numbers and provide that interpretation to the campaign. This is typically done in a written report. Report styles vary, depending on the preference of the pollster and the campaign. At a minimum, though, most reports include a summary of conclusions and a set of crosstabs that report the frequency of responses to each question from each respondent in a particular demographic category. The harder task is assigning meaning to the numbers. Sometimes small numbers may be a sign of a bigger or growing trend. Democratic pollster William Hamilton notes that the public may exhibit a "low-grade fever" for change that may have a dramatic impact on eventual voting behavior (Taylor, 1990, p. 224). In October 1989, for example, President George H. W. Bush received a 75 percent positive rating in a Time/CNN poll, even though most voters (between 72 percent and 86 percent) consistently opposed his public policy agenda. By 1992, that discrepancy had grown to the point that the incumbent president was eventually defeated by his opponent Bill Clinton.

What Can Go Wrong

Any number of things can confound the results and lead to unreliable poll numbers. The most common problems are sampling errors, question framing, ordering effects, and interviewer effects.

Sampling errors are perhaps the most common mistake. If the sample in the survey is not representative of those voters who will vote on election day, the survey is likely to be inaccurate. That can easily occur. In some instances, the respondent selection process was not truly random, leading to skewed results. Other times, the pollster may use a stratified random sample based on turnout patterns of previous elections; if those turnout patterns are altered in future elections, the survey will be inaccurate. In addition, the sample can be affected by the use of improper screening questions. Some media surveys, for example, screen only for "head of household" or for "registered voters." Most pollsters believe a more accurate sample is generated by what is known as a "tight" screen in which only "probable voters" are selected for the survey. Even then, overreporting can occur if nonvoters get through the screen.

Question framing is another major factor that affects the results (Box-Steffensmeier, Jacobson, & Grant, 2000; Hansen et al., 1998, pp. 244–246). Ideally, questions used in the survey should be clear and simple, requiring a minimum amount of effort on the part of the respondent. Lengthy questions create confusion, with the respondent often forgetting the first few options by the time the last ones have been recited (Wimmer & Dominick, 1994, p. 109). Responses can also be influenced by the verbs used in the question; people often agree with questions that ask whether they believe something should be "allowed" or "forbidden," regardless of the topic (Holleman, 2000).

Biased questions use words and phrases that have positive or negative connotations to the voters. For example, consider the question: "Do you favor or oppose spending more money on welfare?" That question often receives a majority of negative responses because of the negative connotations associated with the word "welfare." Conversely, if that question is phrased with a positive connotation ("Do you favor or oppose providing more money to the poor and needy?"), it will generate an undue number of positive responses. The goal is to use neutral language to obtain an unbiased response ("Do you favor or oppose increasing the budget for health and human services?").

Another question format that can influence survey results is the use of leading questions. Some leading questions may be based on a defined frame of reference, a process that will change the response. Kinder and Sanders (1990) noted that a person's response to a candidate or issue can be altered by manipulating the priority that the respondents give to different arguments or considerations. Such processes frame political issues to the advantage of the candidate, creating favorable poll results that might be used in efforts to mobilize current constituencies (Jacobs & Shapiro, 1994).

In addition, double-barreled questions should be avoided. Double-barreled questions are questions with two parts, creating a situation in which the voter may respond to either or both ideas separately. For example, a question such as, "Do you support the president's efforts at gun control and his attempts to fight crime?" is double-barreled. The voter might have different reactions to the president's efforts on gun-control and his anticrime program, even if one is part of the other. The result could be poll numbers that reflect some unknown combination of the two attitudes.

A third factor that can alter survey responses is an "Ordering Effect" or "Context Effect." Ordering effects refer to the impact of question placement on voter response. As Hansen et al. (1998) noted, ". . . where a question is placed both in a numerical sense but also in a contextual way, can impact on the meaning of the question and the results (p. 246)." Wimmer and Dominick (1994, p. 120) called this problem "question contamination," in reference to the impact that one question might have on subsequent questions. The respondents use the information from an early part of the survey to answer questions in a later section (Todorov, 2000), thus biasing the responses to the latter. Ordering effects can influence the responses to both attitudinal questions (Schuman & Presser, 1981; Tourangeau & Rasinski, 1988) and some demographic questions such as race (Martin, DeMaio, & Campanelli, 1990). Suppose a survey, for example, included a series of questions aimed at voter attitudes toward education; if those questions were followed by another series asking them which issue they considered to be the most important problem facing the state, an undue number would likely answer "education." Another example of an ordering effect was reported by Morrison (1986) in his study of public attitudes toward the BBC, in which response differences were attributable to the ordinal placement of the questions. As noted earlier, favorability ratings and test ballots are typically placed in an early ordering position on the questionnaire, to avoid the impact of any other questions on those results. Conversely, demographic data and personal or sensitive questions are generally placed near the end of the questionnaire. This allows time for the interviewer to establish a rapport with the respondent, and the other responses have already been obtained should the respondent choose not to answer the personal questions.

"Interviewer effects" refers to those responses that are produced as a result of the behaviors of the interviewer. Research has indicated face-to-face interviews can be influenced by the type of clothing worn by the interviewer (Hickson & Stacks, 1992; McPeek & Edwards, 1975), his or her ethnic background (Finkel, Guterbock, & Berg, 1991), a number of nonverbal cues (such as nodding, smiling, or tone of voice) and by verbal cues (Conrad & Schroder, 2000). Most political surveys are conducted by telephone, which at least eliminates those factors related to the personal appearance of the interviewer. But telephone interviewing does not eliminate all interview effects. Gubrium and Holstein (2001) note that, even over the telephone, the respondents' answers can be influenced by their perception of the interviewer and the interviewer's perception of the respondents. Additional control can be obtained by using professional interviewers who are not connected to the campaign. Preferably, the telephone personnel who conduct the survey should not even be aware of which candidate is paying for the survey, thus limiting their ability to influence the results. Another technique is to use callers who do not know any of the candidates. This is frequently done by subcontracting the phone calls to a phone bank in a state different from that of the campaign.

One common demonstration of how interviewer effects alter a poll can be seen with the use of "volunteer" polling. To save money, some low-budget campaigns will sometimes use volunteers to conduct their own in-house polling for the campaign. This approach invariably overinflates support for the candidate. Even if extensive training is conducted for each of the volunteers, it is still impossible to eliminate all of the subtle cues that they will give to respondents. Consequently, the survey results will be tainted.

The Ethical Controversy Generated by Political Polling

From the consulting perspective, polling has a positive impact on political campaigning. It provides campaigns with a sense of audience analysis, or at least an impression of the public's perception toward any number of issues. Still, several observers have criticized polls, arguing that the poll results have too much impact on campaigns and candidates. Taylor (1990) argued that polling has had a negative impact on the political process because "politicians have become increasingly dependent on the technologies of political market research . . . to guard against ever uttering an unpopular word in public (p. 218)." Taylor quotes Democratic pollster Stan Greenberg as saying, "The dialogue has become more sterile because the campaign ads are designed to repeat back to voters what they already know."

Interview with Bill Hamilton

Polling in Modern Political Campaigns

> *Bill Hamilton, who died in early 2000, was a pioneer in the polling profession, starting his firm in Miami in 1964 and moving it to Washington in 1969. He was a founder of the American Association of Political Consultants, a former president of it, and honored as International Consultant of the Year in 1992 and with the Lifetime Achievement Award in 1998. Many of Hamilton's methodologies have been adopted as standards in the polling industry. In addition to international politics, and media and public affairs research, some of Hamilton's clients included senators Eagleton, Talmadge, Bayh, Bentsen, and Breaux; former Speaker of the House Tip O'Neill; and governors Askew, Graham, Edwards, Brown, Babbit, and Barnes. His firm, Hamilton Beattie & Staff, has offices in Washington, D.C., and Amelia Island, Florida.*

Q: What is the role of polling in modern political campaigning?

A: From a strategic standpoint, polling is at the center of campaign decision making. Polls have become even more central than they used to be. We know how to collect data better and analyze it better; and the need to focus the message, particularly on the most persuadable voters, has become even more critical. The only way you get that information about message and targeting is through polling.

Q: What does polling do wrong in a campaign?

A: It makes the candidate happy or sad, and then they quit looking at the poll—that is a big danger. Often a poll gives only top-line information to less experienced consultants and managers, who just look at the basic information and don't go deeper into the analysis.

Q: By "top line," do you mean the overall results?

A: Yes, or even the first cut at the crosstabs. That's particularly true late in the campaign when decisions are made so quickly. It's understandable then. But we have the same problem with our benchmark polls, which we conduct ten to fifteen months out. That's plenty of time to do a more thorough analysis of the data. But we give the top-line results to the client as soon as the tabs come in, decisions are made too quickly, and we seldom analyze what it all means. That also suggests that we don't stress the kind of research design that would provide more in-depth information. That's one of my big hangups, not designing the benchmark to provide in-depth analysis and then following through. As pollsters, we ought to start looking toward more in-depth analysis, not just faster analysis and top-line numbers.

Q: What sort of extended analysis would you like to do?

A: At a minimal, once you've looked at the crosstabs, I'd run them again after the first client conference, and I'd run more multivariate analysis. At Hamilton Beattie & Staff, we are trying to use some value analysis using CART. And we're using factor analysis for some of our segmentation. All of this simply takes time. You can't do it, of course, when you start tracking, but you can do it fourteen months out. What that does, if you know you've got the time, is allow you to design a more thoughtful and in-depth study for your benchmark.

Q: How do media consultants respond to this concept?

A: I don't know that they've seen very much of it yet. We're just starting to do it. The media consultants to which I've sent my designs are starting to like it, and they're asking for refinements. In a sense, I'm allowing them to help design the process. But I don't think they've seen very much of this kind of analysis in a campaign situation.

Q: Essentially their overall goal is to simplify the message. Does this help them do that?

A: It makes it hard for me initially to explain how it helps them. Basically, I have to tear the electorate apart, piece by piece. In putting it back together, I figure out the thematic to the campaign, what is the best message for the campaign, and what are the best sub-messages. I can't just ask people if they agree or disagree with a given value statement, take that result, and say, "This is our theme." That's just not a deep enough look into the American psyche. The electorate is either too uninformed or their values too over-lapped to let one single question tell you how to best communicate with them.

Q: Some people have noted that polling has become more frequently involved in lower-level campaigns in the past few years. Do you see that change occurring also?

A: Absolutely. That's one of the reasons we now have so many pollsters in the business, an expansion and fractionalization of our market. The only way we could grow was for our market to move down the importance and size level of campaigns. There's more money in campaigns today, polling is getting its piece of that action, and it's getting it at state senate, house, and county commission levels. Now who actually pays for polling at the lower level is a little bit different. You usually don't have a state senator or state repre-sentative paying for their own poll. Instead, a House caucus or an interest group pays for a set of surveys that somehow find their way into the strategic development on the campaigns they care about.

Q: In those types of races, there has to be some sort of evaluation regarding [the] relative merit of doing the survey. At what point does it become cost efficient to do one, as opposed to taking the money and spending [it] on something else?

A: I'll give you two situations. In the best situation, polling should be no more than 8-to-10 percent of your campaign budget. If you don't have that much to spend on the rest of the campaign, you shouldn't do a professional poll. If you truly need the polling infor-mation, you should either figure out a cheaper way to do the campaign, or a cheaper way to do the poll. That's one answer. The other answer: suppose you've got a race that's only going to spend $50,000, but you really need to know if there's a chance to win, because you (as House Speaker or director of an interest group) could put that money into another district in another part of the state that looks almost as good for your group's perspective. But you don't know in which district you've got the best chance of winning. In that case, the party or group might spend $7,000 to $10,000 on a poll, so they can know which race gives them their best chance of winning control of that particular legislature.

Q: Critics sometimes criticize polls, saying that politicians govern by polls instead of with leadership. Do you agree?

A: I do not think that is erroneous.

Q: Is that good or bad?

A: When I'm thinking about the system in general, it bothers me that we have different kinds of politicians now than just twenty years ago. I remember a statement that Sena-tor William Fulbright made to me after I presented him with the results of our poll showing him trailing Governor Dale Bumpers. Fulbright said, "I guess we need to go out and talk to those courthouse crowds, and we'll get the advantage back." In other words, he was not afraid of the poll numbers; he was set to go out and campaign the way he normally did, feeling that his style and leadership would win the day. You have few

(continued)

Interview with Bill Hamilton   Continued

leaders like that today. Today we have leaders whose entire environment is determined by the top-line opinion numbers. They know where people are on the abortion issue, gun control, and whether they want foreign aid. They (the candidates) don't really change positions on these issues, but the numbers determine how and whether these issues become part of the dialogue in the campaign.

Q: What can pollsters do to change that, or can they do anything?

A: I'm not sure they can. First, the media outlets now control most of the public polling environment. Second, once a professional pollster becomes involved in a client's campaign, it is a fight—a contest— to win against at least one other option. You're hired to provide the best advice to beat the other option or candidate and win for your client. When I'm in a campaign, I am, in a sense, a valueless-oriented professional. That's not totally true, but you take on that role. We're much like lawyers, who don't tell their client, "I think you're guilty so I'm not going to give you a fair shot at a trial." We give the same professional effort to do—within some set of norms or rules—whatever it takes to win.

Q: What are those "rules of the game"?

A: That's a problem, because those rules are not really established yet. The attorneys have their norms and rules of the game, which have been established over the past thousand years. Ours, for political pollsters and consultants, are not quite established yet. That's why we have this constant flap about negative campaigning or "who's an evil consultant." But I do think that we can't do very much about that, because we're in the game to win.

Q: Do you think that polling has contributed to negative campaigning or would it exist in the absence of polling?

A: All we did is make it more effective. We've had negative campaigning forever, and some of it was horrible. The attacks against Grover Cleveland, in either campaign, were just incredible. If polling has done anything, it has begun negative, rather attack, campaigning earlier in the process and given us a guide as to when you really need to do it to win. It has made it clear to many candidates, early in the campaign, that regardless of how much they try to make themselves the good guy with positive, issue-oriented campaigning, they cannot defeat the other guy without bringing down his popularity. A candidate can drive his own popularity from 30 percent to 60 percent, but if his opponent begins with 70 percent and stays there, he will probably lose. As a candidate, would you "attack" under those circumstances?

Q: Project ten years down the road. What will the polling industry be like then?

A: Over the last fifteen years, there's been very little change, quite frankly. We've changed the speed with which we have to make decisions, because of the speed in which campaigns and communications operate. And technology advances have driven this development. What we haven't done is take more time to design and analyze our benchmark survey. I think that's going to happen. You don't need constant information early in the campaign; the voters don't change that much before Labor Day. But in earlier campaigning, you are dealing with segments of the electorate. Studying and understanding those segments in ways that are more in-depth than we do now is something that's going to come. Candidates are going to start asking more frequently, "You say I need this strategy. Then how do I deal with the teachers, with union members, and suburban soccer moms, or 'soft' voters from the other party? Tell me about each one of those. Tell me how to approach and communicate with those people prior to getting into the actual campaign."

Q: What about tracking late in the campaign?

A: I don't think that's going to change much, except that there's going to be even more requests for the regularized tracking that we perform. I don't agree with overnight *reporting* of tracking numbers. I *do* agree with regularized nightly tracking, using rolling averages. I like to roll the base every three days, instead of every day, because I don't think voters change their minds every day. I think you would have to have a thousand points on television every day with a very evocative ad in order to change opinions enough to accurately measure opinion change over twenty-four hours. So I don't think you ought to track and report every day, but I do think you should report two, maybe three, times a week. And you should spend more on those polls at that point in time, because that's when you're spending your major communication dollars, either in mail or television.

Q: If there was anything you could change about the industry, what would it be?

A: I would do more of what Raymond Strother is trying to do as president of the AAPC, something I've been doing for fifteen years—training young consultants. We need to give them a context of professional training, so they will understand where they're going, and where we've been. If they're pollsters, they'll at least understand what a fund-raiser goes through, what a manager needs from a poll. Or if they want to go into direct mail consulting, they'll understand polling, or how to fit their message with that of the TV consultant. That way we develop a group of consultants who understand the entire industry even though they come through their training with specific specialties. What happens is that kids get into the business just because they think, "Hey, this is neat, and I think I can make a lot of money here." They're not trained, have no perspective, and they don't understand the system. They don't understand the marketplace in which they operate. That marketplace—the free democratic process—is the most unique marketplace in the world. It's a different marketplace than selling one pain reliever against another. There's a different set of rules and a different outcome on society. You need some time to think about that, and you need this seasoning early. Otherwise, I think we will end up with a group of people in the second and third generation of our consultants who are cynical, nonideological, apartisan, with only profit driving their professional performance.

Q: You seem to be addressing the problem of infighting among consultants in a campaign. Are you saying that if consultants understood the role of the other consultants better, that infighting might decline?

A: That's only part of it. If everybody had a set of common experiences, the process will be more efficient, effective, and pleasant. That's why campaign retreats are good to get consultants together with their candidate; they bring together some common experience and give each some understanding of the other's perspective and how they will perform in the campaign. But you're never going to change *all* the infighting, because if you're a big-deal consultant in this business you're somewhat of an egomaniac. That's the only reason you're in this business. We can say we're in it because we love the process, and I think a lot of us are. But all of us are also in it because we're manipulative control freaks. We think we can manipulate people, get them to think like us, and we enjoy doing that. That's why we're in the business. When you put any four of us in a room, you're going to have clashes.

Source: Interview with William R. Hamilton. Reprinted by permission of Ann Hamilton.

Such attitudes are not particularly new. Former President Harry Truman similarly lambasted the use of polls during his term in office. "How far would Moses have gone if he had taken a poll in Egypt?" Truman asked. "What would Jesus Christ have preached if he had taken a poll in the land of Israel? What would have happened to the Reformation if Martin Luther had taken a poll? It isn't polls or public opinion of the moment that count. It's right and wrong and leadership." Dionne (1991, p. 311) gave a similar assessment of focus groups, but the comments could easily be applied to polling research. "The focus group may be the perfect symbol of what has happened to democracy in America. Insofar as 'the people' are consulted by political leaders these days, their reactions are of interest not as a guide to policy but simply as a way of exploring the electorate's gut feelings, to see which kind of (usually divisive) message might move them the most. The approach to politics is not even Machiavellian; it is Pavlovian."

Others argue just the opposite. Jacobs and Shapiro (2000) question whether political leaders base decisions on public opinion or poll data. They argue instead that politicians increasingly ignore public opinion in favor of their own views and those of their major supporters. The result, they would argue, is politicians have become less responsive to public opinion than in the 1960s and 1970s, while the use of polls has increased over the same span of time. Similarly, Fishkin (1995) complains that the voice of the public is often never heard by political elites. Herbst (1998) agreed, concluding that many political elites reject the voice of the people as uninformed or nebulous.

Ryan and Wentworth (1999) argue that polling has a negative impact on news coverage of political campaigns, with the media ". . . focusing more on who is ahead and who is behind than the substance of political issues" (p. 81). Research supports that criticism. The number of poll-related stories has increased in recent years. Stories about polls have also been given a higher priority within newscasts, and reporters have increasingly defined campaigns as based on the success of the candidate's campaign activities, as measured by polls (Craig, 2000). One reason is that many reporters are not well informed on the issues themselves, and coverage of polls is easier to do. Others argue that the public is also more interested in the ups and downs of political careers, or relative changes in candidate positions in the polls, than they are in specific issues. Regardless of the cause, though, today's media (newspapers, magazines, radio, the Internet, and TV) do indeed have a strong focus on "horse-race" coverage, with many media outlets now conducting their own surveys (thus creating their own news).

Herbst (1998) questioned the validity and neutrality of polling. She argued that the validity was in question because the impact of polls is based more on the assessment of political elites (journalists, political activists, legislative staffers) than upon the attitudes of the mass public. The neutrality of polling is also open to criticism, she added, because numbers do more than convey neutral information, but also serve as a basis of authority. Those numbers can be influenced by the manner in which public opinion is measured. Political polls often work within a "file drawer" model that incorrectly assumes that attitudes are stored in memory and retrieved when a question is asked during the survey (Tourangeau, Rips, & Rasinski, 2000). That model leads to surveys that ask questions that the respondent may have never considered. When that occurs, the survey may be creating and constructing an attitude for the respondent, rather than measuring it. Fishkin (1995) recommends a technique he calls a "deliberative poll," in which a large representative sample is gathered at one location; he polls the participants only after one or two days of intense discussion and education on an issue.

Cantril and Cantril (1999) identified a "mixed signals" effect that is often present in polls, noting that public opinion polls often produce contradictory results. Not only will polls from different candidates have different numbers, but contradictions often exist within the same poll. Voters will often, for example, say they oppose an increase in taxes while supporting increased government spending. They attribute the phenomenon to a subgroup of voters called the "ambivalents." They also identified another subgroup (largely conservative Republicans) called the "steady critics," who have little confidence in government but are highly involved in politics. Their responses can also send mixed signals in a poll.

Former Democratic pollster Paul Maslin believes polling has contributed to the rise in negative campaigns. As quoted by Taylor (1990, p. 218), Maslin said, "It's like taking a shot, because you can see the way they [negative ads] move the numbers. The techniques have gotten so refined, the weapons so powerful, that if you don't use them, you'll lose. . . ." Maslin's comment seem to echo the pragmatics of polling in modern political contests. The ethical issue to be addressed is not whether to use them, but merely how to use them in an ethical manner. Polling is merely a sophisticated form of audience analysis—a basic skill taught in nearly all communication courses. If audience analysis is important for other forms of communication, why not for political campaigns? Political candidates have a right and, ideally, an obligation to consider the beliefs and values of the people they represent. In a time when a single officeholder may represent thousands or millions of people, polling provides a means of assessing those beliefs and values.

Pseudopolling

One form of polling sometimes used in unethical ways is the category known as "pseudopolls." These include call-in surveys, push polls, and cyberpolling.

Call-in Surveys

Call-in surveys are a popular media feature in which the public is provided a question and asked to phone in their responses, a technique first used by ABC News during the televised Carter-Reagan presidential debate on October 28, 1980 (Frankel & Frankel, 1987). While call-in surveys can produce interesting results, they have no scientific validity and may contain substantial errors (Gerhard, 1990). The sample is a process of self-selection rather than a random sample. Although call-in poll participants are demographically similar to the population as a whole, they are more opinionated than telephone survey respondents (Cotter, Perry, & Stovall, 1994) and more likely to be activists with a prochange mentality (Bates & Harmon, 1993). Furthermore, participation in some call-in surveys costs money (sometimes fifty cents or a dollar per call); that monetary intrusion biases political responses for Republicans, who are typically more able to afford the call and spend the money. Finally, call-in surveys cannot control how many times a particular person responds; any one person could make multiple calls to the computer, and they could get their friends and relatives to do the same. If a call-in survey addresses a "hot" issue, its results are more likely to indicate the relative organizational strength of the candidates than it is their popular support. Unfortunately, despite their problems, call-in polls tend to be credible to media audiences.

As many as one third of newspaper readers believe they are credible sources of information, especially for readers with less formal education (Gerhard, 1990).

Push Polls

Push polls are not polls at all, but merely a questionable form of phone bank persuasion. This approach takes advantage of the public's familiarity with the polls by calling a respondent under the pretense of conducting a poll. Once the person agrees to participate, they are read a list of questions designed to imply negative information about an opponent. Thus, instead of eliciting unbiased information from the respondents, the survey is merely used as a form of negative or smear campaigning.

A typical push poll was used in the 2000 South Carolina Republican presidential primary by George W. Bush. A phone bank in Houston, Texas (Voter Consumer Research), called South Carolina voters and asked a series of carefully scripted questions. The initial questions were simple and straightforward—Will you participate in the Republican primary? How much attention have you paid to the Republican race? Are things better or worse in the country?—but the later questions were used as a means of providing negative information on Bush's competitor John McCain. The questions were not really questions, but merely messages disguised in a question format that attacked McCain's position on tax cuts, told the voters McCain had been reprimanded by the Senate Ethics Committee, and argued that his campaign finance plan would give more influence to unions and to the press (Yardley, 2000).

An earlier example emerged in a 1996 issue debate in Texas over the tobacco issue. A tobacco company (Phillip Morris) hired Public Opinion Strategies, an Alexandria, Virginia, firm to develop a push poll against the state's attorney general, Dan Morales, who was preparing to file a lawsuit against several tobacco companies. The script "included more than a dozen negative statements about Mr. Morales's record as attorney general" and the resulting information was used in an attempt to get him to drop the lawsuit (Van Natta, 2000).

Cyberpolling

Cyberpolling is a relative newcomer to the field of pseudopolling. It relies on voters providing their responses to the pollster through e-mail or some other online technology. Pollsters Gordon Black and Humphrey Taylor used the Internet to conduct polls for the 2000 election (Terhanian, 1999), with varying results. The Internet provides for surveys composed of larger samples, while computer technology allows for an almost instantaneous tabulation of results. That can provide a polling service that is both faster and cheaper than conventional methods while also attaining a similar level of reliability and validity. Other web sites, such as speakout.com and survey.net are being developed as a way of offering voters a direct means of expressing their opinions. The number of sites available for that purpose is likely to increase in the future, even though their main purpose is entertainment instead of research.

Cyberpolling has the same problems as call-in surveys—difficulty in controlling the sample in a systematic manner (Couper, 2000). The response rate on e-mail surveys is dramatically lower than those of both telephone surveys (Taylor, 2000) and mail surveys (Couper, Blair, & Tripplett, 1999; Schaefer & Dillman, 1998). While efforts have been made to correct that problem, their success has not yet been dramatic (Dommeyer & Moriarty,

2000). Furthermore, even if the response rate problem is corrected, cyberpolls still do not provide a sample that is representative of the general population (Flemming & Sonner, 1999; Taylor, 2000). Currently, 92 percent of the public can be reached for polling purposes by telephone, but only 48 percent of households are currently connected to the Internet. As a result, online surveys tend to overrepresent males, college graduates, and young voters (Flemming & Sonner, 1999). Finally, responses to online surveys are heavily influenced by the design of the web page (Dillman et al., 1998) and the layout of the questionnaire (Smith, 1995).

Such problems may not mean that cyberpolling is doomed to the survey trash pile, though. Some problems may merely be growing pains that are eventually eliminated or reduced. Some researchers are already working to develop systematic methodologies for the web that can provide a consistent means of evaluating its data (Schaefer & Dillman, 1998). The Harris Poll Online, for example, has the potential of providing longitudinal data from panel studies that can be useful in identifying attitudinal trends (Couper, 2000, p. 482). But most of the online surveys currently available fail to reach such levels of sophistication. The voting public will have to learn to separate trivial and entertaining surveys from those that develop sophisticated methodology.

Summary

Polling and survey research has become an integral part of modern campaigns, one that is so integral to the process that the informed voter should have a basic understanding of its role in the democratic process (Asher, 1992). What began as new technology for presidential elections during the 1970s has since become standard practice in most major campaigns. Its use has gradually filtered down to lower-level elections, and is now commonly used in many state and local campaigns. Most successful campaigns use polling, and those that do not are at a strategic disadvantage.

Is that good or bad? Some critics complain that modern polling techniques have motivated political candidates to alter their campaign practices. No longer do they lead the voters on issues of concerns; they merely follow the voters' concerns instead. Polls are used to identify voter priorities, and those priorities are mouthed back to them in the campaign. In its most essential form, though, polling is merely an extended form of audience analysis. It provides the political rhetor with an understanding of the attitudes and values of the audience to be addressed. Such a function has always been performed in political campaigns. In the past, though, candidates would go out to talk with voters individually to seek their feedback, with no way to ascertain whether what they were hearing was representative of all of their constituents. Polling provides more precision to that effort. The function hasn't changed, merely the precision with which it is done.

Even some of the critics of polling accept its utility. Sociologist Alan Wolfe (1998) prefers to use ethnographic methodologies in which in-depth interviews are conducted with a large number of participants. Such methodologies, he believes, move beyond poll data and provide a better understanding of the people's beliefs (p. 278). Still, even he noted that ". . . America is rightly guided by its polls; besides the results of the previous election, . . . politicians have little else to go on in formulating their views than the polls . . ." (p. 277). After all, to represent the public, they should have at least some sense of what the public believes.

Q U E S T I O N S   F O R   D I S C U S S I O N

1. To what extent do political polls shape and influence public opinion instead of merely measuring it? How and why might this occur?

2. Some political theorists argue that the success of democracy rests upon public opinion. If so, to what extent does political polling add to or detract from a successful democratic process?

3. Political polls usually make no attempt to survey the entire public, but only the voting public. To what extent does this add to or detract from the democratic process?

PART THREE

Campaign Concerns

During any political campaign, a number of issues and concerns will arise that must be addressed. Many of these will be campaign specific, with too many variations to discuss in this book. However, some general elements typically must be addressed by all campaigns. Some of these factors represent campaign thresholds or contingencies, conditions that must be achieved if the campaign is to be competitive.

Chapter 11 discusses a major communication concern of the campaign: press coverage. Press coverage of presidential campaigns has the potential to influence the outcome of the election. Coverage of statewide elections can influence what issues candidates discuss, and which candidates are best known to the voters. At any level, press coverage can have an impact on whether a candidate is viewed as a legitimate contender for a position. This chapter will discuss press coverage in terms of the factors affecting press coverage, topics covered by the press, and the types of events that can generate press coverage. The campaign team member who is most heavily involved in this aspect of the campaign is the press secretary, and special attention is devoted to that role.

Chapter 12 looks at the financial side of politics. Political campaigns are often massive money machines, with part of the organization raising funds while the rest spends it. Money is more than just the fuel of the campaign organization, though. Campaign fundraising can have a persuasive impact that influences press coverage, bestows legitimacy on a campaign, and reduces the competition. The financial side of politics represents a threshold that must be met if a campaign is to be effective, but it is also at the center of an ethical debate that should be addressed. This chapter looks at those elements and their impact on campaigns, candidates, and the political process.

Chapter 13 looks at the role of interpersonal communication from several viewpoints. Interpersonal communication is a key part of the opinion leadership process, with citizens discussing their views with friends, neighbors, and coworkers while refining their voting decision. Interpersonal communication plays a key role in the diffusion of information from political elites to the public. Communication between candidates and political elites influences legislation and other public decisions. Political lobbying illustrates the role that interpersonal communication can have in the drafting of legislation. Legislative cue-giving looks at the impact of interpersonal communication on legislative votes, as one lawmaker talks to another.

Chapter 14 looks at a specific way of analyzing campaigns: critical events analysis. Critical events analysis is the study of major discrete events that test the relationship between media and politics. From a campaign perspective, critical events analysis is a rare convergence of academic and consulting perspectives, albeit each approaches the topic from a different perspective. Scholars seek to identify major events—debates, convention speeches, major public appearances—that can influence a campaign. For consultants, critical events are predictive factors, points and events within a campaign that can be anticipated to have a major impact; special care and attention are given to preparing for them.

This book ends with Chapter 15 and its discussion of ethical questions in political communication. Included in this discussion is a look at several different types of unethical behaviors in campaigns, the controversy surrounding negative campaigning, and the role of consultants. The chapter ends with a section devoted to the primary goal of the book: becoming critical observers of the process. We hope that by the end of Chapter 15, the reader will feel more qualified to make critical and ethical judgments about the political campaign process.

11 Press Coverage and Media Relations

If he had to campaign today, George Washington might not win the presidency. He didn't like to make public presentations, sometimes writing his presidential speeches but never delivering them. And, forced to wear uncomfortable dentures, he had trouble smiling in public. All in all, he would not have made a good media candidate.

Compare that to the press campaigns of Bill Clinton. During his eight years in office, Clinton was beset by both financial and moral controversies that threatened his presidency and triggered an impeachment process. During it all, Clinton maintained relatively high ratings with the public, enough to remain in office for two full terms. Kurtz (1998) attributes Clinton's success to a highly effective team that effectively influenced press coverage to the president's advantage. Their primary techniques were the use of controlled leaks, carefully worded briefs, and avoidance of some questions. Simple techniques, really, but ones that allowed the Clinton administration to control the scope and coverage of news stories.

In today's political environment, saying that someone is both a "good candidate" and also "effective with the media" is unnecessarily redundant. Television is the "window on the world" through which most people follow political activities (Ansolabehere, Behr, & Iyengar, 1993). In most major campaigns, the candidate must have media-friendly characteristics to even be considered as a contender. Altschull (1995) argues that the power of the news media includes a social control function that influences campaigns and public policy. Nimmo (1970) noted that news coverage influences voter impressions of the candidate's credibility and character (p. 130). Neuman, Just, and Crigler (1992) see it as a vital agent in the construction of political meaning. Gunther and Christen (1999) found that voters rely on news coverage as a source for assessing public opinion. Chaffee, Zhou, and Leshner (1994) found that news coverage, including coverage of special events, interviews, and talks shows, added to the predictability of election outcomes. Simon (1996) found that newspaper use is related to the likelihood that a person will vote in an election, while Leshner and McKean (1997) noted that TV news played a critical role in providing knowledge about candidates. Gunter (1998) noted that the media have at least an indirect impact resulting simply from the pervasive assumptions that the media make about society, and the effect is particularly strong for television news (Wilson & Howard, 1978). Ryan and Wentworth (1999, p. 80) noted, "Whatever the magnitude of the effect on voters' behavior, media coverage now plays a major role in political campaigns."

There is nothing new about that concept. Campaigners have long recognized that voters placed more credibility in news coverage of the campaign than they did in the campaigns' self-created propaganda. Campaign efforts to take advantage of that trend have also been part of the process for centuries; supporters of both John Adams and Thomas Jefferson printed ads disguised as news (Seib, 1994). But the complexity of modern news organizations have made the task considerably more complex. Multiple factors go into a decision by a news organization when they must consider how much coverage should be devoted to a candidate or an issue. Some argue that the best coverage goes to those who are most adept at playing the "media game" (Ansolabehere, Behr, & Iyengar, 1993). Inevitably, some are covered while others—including some that might be of equal importance—are not; those who understand and adapt their message to the press are more likely to get press coverage and the credibility that is associated with it. As Sigal (1986, p. 15) noted, "News is not what happens, but what someone says has happened or will happen."

One role of the consultant is to plant the seeds for stories that will increase positive coverage for their client. Hamilton Jordan, a consultant for President Jimmy Carter, expressed the consultant's view: "Stories in the *New York Times* and *Washington Post* do not just happen, but have to be carefully planned and planted" (quoted in Schram, 1976, p. 67). German (1995) recognized the rhetorical edge that could be gained in the press by power and rhetorical skills, skills that Duffy (1997, p. 117) referred to as "the role of rhetorical artistry in gaining desired news coverage. . . ." Journalists, she added, can get ". . . caught up in the fantasy themes and rhetorical visions produced by (public relations campaigns of) corporations and powerful interest groups, (and) the underlying ideologies they represent are rarely questioned" (p. 130).

Shogan (2001) went even further, arguing that the modern press plays the role of enablers by allowing candidates and their consultants to use the press to abuse the political process. Didion (2001) agreed, calling the entire process one of "political fiction" that resembles Hollywood more than an American democracy. National politics, she argued, is a carefully choreographed drama that is created by political professionals (politicians, consultants, reporters) for the consumption of a public that has little impact on the drama. Similarly, Bennett (2001) describes political press coverage as the "politics of illusion." Political news, he argued, is a romanticized version of events that hide the actual political circumstances involved. "Indeed," he wrote, "the mark of skill in the political trade is the ability to make the public version of a situation convincing, no matter how far removed from actuality it may be" (p. 114). At the very least, then, an understanding of political campaign communication requires an understanding of how politicians and candidates interact with news organizations for the purposes of news coverage.

Factors Influencing News Coverage

Candidate Credibility

Perhaps the single most important factor influencing coverage of a candidate is the credibility of the candidate. With only rare exceptions (when a candidate is so outrageous that he or she is interesting for example), news organizations provide little coverage to candidates whom they perceive as having little chance of winning an election. In most cases, their assessment of candidate credibility is based on two factors: previous political experience and financial support. Experience through serving in previous political positions provides automatic credibility to most candidates, particularly if one is the incumbent officeholder in a "stepping-stone" position. For example, the press will nearly always provide coverage to gubernatorial candidates who are incumbents in such positions as lieutenant governor, attorney general, or secretary of state. Congressmen who decide to run for the U.S. Senate have a similar, out-of-the-starting-gate credibility with the press. Experience is not limited to experience in public office; it can also be applied to public experience at dealing with high-profile issues. For example, individuals who have spent most of their career promoting education, might choose to run for a public position related to that issue. Their long-time career in that arena would be enough to bestow automatic legitimacy to their candidacy, thus ensuring press coverage.

Perhaps the biggest factor that can establish credibility with the press for a candidate is that of financial resources. Press coverage of candidates tends to correspond to how much money they spend during the campaign. Any candidate who demonstrates an ability to raise significant financial resources becomes a legitimate candidate. Similarly, any candidate who has enough personal financial resources to finance his or her own campaign will similar receive significant press coverage. In 1992, for example, Independent presidential candidate H. Ross Perot received extensive media coverage despite his small chances of winning the election. His personal fortune guaranteed his ability to mount an extensive campaign, regardless of its odds for success, and thus led to heavy coverage by the press. At the state level, self-financed candidates have sometimes been successful, with successful businessmen who were political novices winning election as their state's governors (for example, John Warner in Kentucky and Fob James in Alabama).

Nature of the News

Newspapers and the broadcast media cover things that are "newsworthy," but not necessarily things that are "news" and/or "worthy." The press is more likely to cover a story about an individual than it will one about an issue, something that Jamieson and Campbell (1997, p. 41) called the "tendency to focus on people rather than processes." News is also a daily commodity. Roughly the same amount of time and space is devoted to news each day. Unfortunately, not as much happens on some days as it does on others. On slow news days, reporters are looking for stories to cover, and an energetic candidate's chances of getting coverage increases. Even then, though, reporters are also more likely to be event driven rather than issue driven; for example, they are more likely to report on a protest against an insurance company (a one-day event) than to report on issues related to the insurance industry.

Reporters are also drawn to conflict, so candidates and groups seeking coverage often look for ways to express their issue as a conflict. A candidate complaining about unfair labor policies has less chance of getting covered than does a group that calls for a labor strike against a company. A strike is an event representing conflict; a candidate's press conference is merely rhetoric. The attractiveness of conflict for reporters leads to another maxim of news coverage: "Typical news is not news." Reporters prefer nontypical, unusual, out-of-the-ordinary stories. As Jamieson and Campbell (1997) noted, "Resource-poor groups often have to depend on deviance and disruption in order to receive media coverage" (p. 47). Candidates face a similar dilemma, but are sometimes successful in overcoming this barrier by looking for unusual ways to dramatize their campaigns. Florida's Lawton Chiles launched a political career that took him to Florida's governorship and to the U.S. Senate by walking the length of the state as "Walkin' Lawton." Florida's Bob Graham campaigned with Work Days, eschewing normal campaign activities once a week to work eight hours in a normal job. TV news is highly visual in nature, so television reporters are more likely to cover events that offer interesting visual footage or stories for which they have available footage. Candidates sometimes provide prepackaged feeds to meet that requirement, or they choose highly visual locations for a press conference.

Finally, the last word that can be used to describe news is "easy"—easy to write, easy to understand, and easy to cover. A typical news story is short and simple (Jamieson & Campbell, 1997, p. 69). A newspaper reader will scan through it in a matter of minutes. A major television story may only be forty-five seconds long. Reporters are going to be more likely to cover stories that can be condensed into a brief time span. They are also more likely to cover a story that can be easily and quickly covered. That usually means stories that are on assigned beats, or those that can be developed and put on the air or on the front page quickly. As Jamieson and Campbell (1997, p. 47) noted, "Reporters . . . have a low tolerance for the long haul of a complex story that may take years to develop."

Nature of the Office

In the eyes of the press, all political offices are not created equal. Some warrant more coverage, and therefore more scrutiny, than others. As Jamieson and Campbell (1997, p. 61) noted, "An event is more likely to be covered and published if it involves people in positions of authority. . . ." Candidates for federal office, incumbency, and the population base of the electoral district all influence the extent to which an election will receive news coverage (Havick, 1997). As a result, some topics that are not newsworthy in some campaigns can receive extensive coverage in others. For example, a decision by a candidate to adopt a dog as a family pet is usually not newsworthy information; however, if that candidate is the president of the United States, it may become a national news story.

Location

In assessing the potential impact of news coverage, one question frequently asked by consultants is, "Where are the cameras?" The location of a press conference or interview can have a dramatic impact on the credibility of the information, the amount of coverage, and the performance of the candidate.

The first two factors—credibility and coverage—are interrelated. If the press views the information as credible, then the amount of coverage devoted to an issue will increase. The reverse is also true: more coverage increases credibility. For example, a candidate who wants to address the issue of waste in highway construction would increase his or her chances of getting press coverage by holding a press conference at a location that demonstrated the problem, such as at the end of a paved road that connected with no other road. The use of such a location provides a visual demonstration of the message and also provides television crews with interesting footage that can be used in the newscast.

The location can also be critical to the performance of the candidate. Most candidates feel more comfortable, and thus perform better during television interviews, if they are in familiar surroundings. Furthermore, the toughness of questions from reporters tends to lose its edge when they ask those questions on the candidate's home territory. During a 1987 congressional campaign in Tennessee, front-runner Bob Clement was sued for alienation of affection by a man who claimed Clement had an affair with the man's wife, thus leading to their divorce. Clement denied the allegations, but reporters had more questions. Rather than holding a news conference to address the allegations, Clement and his wife together met with reporters individually, in their home, and answered their questions on the charges. Despite the stress associated with responding to such charges, Clement was perceived as at ease and honest during the individual interviews, and the press shifted their attention to whether his opponents might be behind the allegations. Their investigations subsequently revealed that one of the opponents had indeed been behind the charges, and Clement went on to an easy win in the campaign.

Location can also have an impact on which reporters cover a candidate. After Al Gore moved his campaign headquarters from Washington, D.C., to Nashville, Tennessee, the campaign found that it was subjected to less press scrutiny. After revelations that Naomi Wolf consulted with the campaign, offering advice on how Gore could appeal to women as a "alpha" male, the Washington press leaped on the story. But Gore's campaign representatives in Nashville found that they could continue campaigning and ignore the issue, because none of the local reporters asked about it.

The 2000 presidential campaigns also demonstrated how location can affect candidate performance. During many of George W. Bush's early TV appearances, questions from reporters ". . . caused him to send a panicky look into the camera" that contrasted sharply with the "easy charm" exhibited during his first appearance on CNN's *Larry King Live* (James, 1999). Much of the difference was due to the location of the camera; instead of speaking at a press conference, where Bush often felt like a open target, the Larry King interview was conducted in "the warm, woody setting of a Nashville saloon." Democrat Bill Bradley made a similar use of location to soften his image. During some early campaign events, Bradley often sounded aloof and abstract. Those negative tones disappeared, however, when the ex-professional basketball player shot baskets at Madison Square Garden with Ed Bradley for a *60 Minutes* interview and when he sat on the court for an interview with Wolf Blitzer on CNN's *Late Edition.*

Candidate-Reporter Relationships

One factor, sometimes unspoken, that influences political coverage is the relationship between reporters and the candidates. Weaver and Wilhoit (1980) noted that candidates and reporters often have a symbiotic relationship that benefits both partners. The candidate provides the reporter with useful information, while the reporter provides the candidate with coverage. Some reporters simply like some candidates, as individuals, more than they do others, and this can create an unconscious bias in coverage. Such an effect is nothing new. Crouse's (1974) analysis of presidential reporting noted that reporters riding the campaign train with Franklin Roosevelt shared a relationship with the president that is often absent in the modern era of negative press coverage. Furthermore, such positive relationships still exist in the world of political journalism, though they may be increasingly rare. During the 2000 presidential campaign, Republican senator John McCain gained the respect of the national press by his accessibility and willingness to bluntly answer questions (Mitchell, 1999). Cornfield (2000) noted that maintaining good relationships with reporters remains an important factor, even as the nature of information dissemination changes. "The Internet enables you to bypass the news media more easily than ever. But that's no cause for poisoning relations with them," Cornfield wrote. "They can still help you compensate for weaknesses in name identification . . . , cash, incumbency and reputation with your targeted audience" (p. 55).

Indeed, a negative relationship can also be engendered, with predictable results. President Richard Nixon was never the darling of the Washington press, but he did nothing to change that relationship. Instead, the Nixon White House attempted to dominate the press through harassment. Some reporters had income tax returns audited after they published an unfriendly story, while others were barred from the White House newsroom (Crouse, 1974). That antagonistic relationship hurt Nixon when the Watergate scandal begin to unfold.

Objectivity can be impaired even if the candidate is not the source of the news. Journalists rely heavily on confidential sources within campaigns and bureaucracies for information. Sources are often built up over years through the development of interpersonal relationships, and reporters often have to trust their source for the veracity of that information. In most cases, that trust is well placed; the source would not violate the relationship by intentionally providing false information. Still, that source can have a crucial impact on objectivity by guiding reporters to some stories and avoiding others (Turow, 1992, p. 159). Furthermore, the relationship can potentially influence the slant on the story, a decision that can significantly influence public reaction to the news; Gunter (1998), for example, found that the slant of a news story had a direct effect on perception of public opinion and an indirect effect on perceptions of changes in public opinion.

Objectivity is a rather recent ideal in journalism; in the past, reporters were often open in their bias toward candidates (Schudson, 1978, p. 157). During the Truman administration, the president constantly attacked the press for their lack of objectivity, while the reporters who covered him openly considered him incompetent and over his head in the White House (Mitchell, 1998). At lower levels, money sometimes exchanged hands as a way of sealing the reporter-candidate relationship. Grover Smith, press secretary to Senator John Sparkman during the 1950s, reported that rumors abounded that some reporters were soliciting bribes, particularly television crews and their cameramen, with the word reaching the campaign through their advertising agencies. In that instance, Smith reported that he stopped the requests by passing word back through the ad agency that any requests for bribes would be reported to the FBI (Smith, 1999).

Objectivity can create its own bias, however. In an attempt to maintain objectivity, some reporters may go overboard to report divergent views—even absurd ones. By reporting a dissenting view, they maintain the appearance of objectivity, even if the opposing view lacks merit. As Joseph Turow (1992, p. 158) noted, ". . . the routines of objectivity are not the neutral recording instruments journalists like to believe they are."

Pack Journalism

Generally, reporters report what other reporters report. As Jamieson and Campbell (1997, p. 50) noted, "Hard news reports events linked to issues prevalent in the news at the time." Granted, each reporter strives to have a unique angle, a different development, or some new information on the issue of the day. But, with rare exceptions, such angles are merely variations on the same topic. During the 1970s, for example, television news relied heavily on newspaper coverage for prioritizing which stories the broadcast outlets would cover (Shaw & McCombs, 1977). Today, because of competition, each TV network monitors the others closely, and any issue covered by one is quickly picked up by another, with the agenda of one news organization influencing the others (Roberts & McCombs, 1994). Such a mentality led to dominant issue coverage at various times in U.S. history—civil rights in the sixties, Watergate in the seventies, and the Clinton-Lewinsky controversy of 1998–1999. Pack journalism also extends to candidates and others who are already in the news; any specific news event is more likely to be covered if it involves people who have been newsworthy in the past (Jamieson & Campbell, 1997, p. 61). New candidates, as a result, sometimes find it difficult to get news coverage; once they get coverage from one news source, however, the other outlets usually follow suit.

Pack journalism also shows itself in the realm of breaking news. The desire to be first with new information often produces errors, but those errors may stay within the process for an extended period of time. Once an error has been reported as a fact, other news sources repeat the error. It may eventually become an accepted "fact" for audiences that don't know better. In many instances, that mentality comes not from the reporters themselves but from editors. Crouse's (1974) analysis of news coverage of the 1972 presidential campaign found that many of the reporters on the campaign had a story refused or questioned because the wire service did not carry a similar report. Such uniformity in coverage can create a uniform, but not necessarily accurate, image of the candidate.

Some candidates take advantage of the pack journalism mentality. The most common technique for doing so is the use of "spin doctors" who interpret news events in a manner beneficial to their candidates. The goal of the spin doctor is "spin control," a term popularized during the Reagan administration. Maltese (1994, p. 215) defines spin control as "twisting (a story) to one's advantage, using surrogates, press releases, radio actualities, and other friendly sources to deliver the line from an angle that puts the story in the best possible light." Spin doctors are most effective at spin control in the area of breaking news. Coverage of breaking news is considerably more difficult for reporters (particularly TV reporters), because they often lack the time to verify how other media outlets are covering the same story. That offers spin doctors a chance to define the story positively for their client, hoping that other news outlets will pick up on the same spin.

News Priming

Iyengar and Kinder (1987) argued that the media establish standards used by voters to evaluate the government, the president, and political candidates. These standards are developed as a set of expectations that are used as the basis of judgments of the political activity that the voters see and hear in the media. This theory was subsequently supported by research regarding extensive 1986 media coverage on the Reagan administration's covert diversion of funds to the Nicaraguan contras. Voters' evaluations of Reagan were strongly linked to the amount of coverage that the issue received (Krosnick & Kinder, 1990). The news priming function is the primary reason that elected officials and candidates want to dominate the media agenda (Perloff, 1998, p. 218).

Reporters themselves can become victims of news priming, sometimes falling into the habit of reporting events not in terms of results but in terms of expectations. If previous news coverage has indicated that a candidate is expected to win a primary, then victory in that primary is not particularly newsworthy. Reporters instead look to see whether the victory was by a margin that was bigger or smaller than anticipated. If the margin of victory is too small, then the "win" may be treated as a "loss" in the resulting news coverage. Consultants typically participate in this process by trying to deflate expectations before an event and making positive comparisons with the expectations on a post hoc basis. Even in the absence of such expectations, consultants consider news priming to be an important factor in spin control.

Topics for News Coverage

Events

During nonpolitical months, most news outlets (broadcast and print) assign reporters to "beats" based on topics (such as crime, health, city government, and so forth). That typically changes during election time, with most reporters assigned to cover specific candidates—not topics or issues. The natural by-product of this approach is an increased emphasis on coverage of campaign events like appearances and speeches rather than issues. Schram (1976, p. 207) described the media event from the candidate's perspective:

> A media event is a by-product of the performing arts that is often without cultural, social, or even aesthetic value. It is the sort of thing that does not necessarily look impressive in person—it may, in fact, look perfectly ridiculous and may even *be* ridiculous. But if it guarantees that the candidate will get in one of the local news shows that night, then it is good.

Jamieson and Campbell (1997) explained why such events appeal to the press: "An event is concrete and discrete; ordinarily it can be explained clearly in a limited time or space. A single event is more likely to be intelligible and to be a novel, dramatic event involving specific individuals" (p. 46). The media event meets both the visual and time criteria for the press, providing them with a story that is relatively easy to report.

Issues

Overall, the media has a relatively poor record of covering political issues, generally making it a lower priority than covering the campaign itself (Ryan & Wentworth, 1999, p. 81). Even during nonelection times, the media's success at covering issues is questionable. Keefer (1993, p. 412) concluded that "the news media serve to hinder—rather than facilitate— citizen participation" in the policy-making process. Another concern is that coverage of personal issues may replace coverage of campaign issues. Recent elections have not reduced the criticism. Shogan (2001) chastised himself and other reporters for their tendency to cover personalities instead of issues during the 2000 presidential election.

Most political candidates also believe the press should provide more coverage of issues—as long as it is their issue. This is particularly true of candidates running a single-issue campaign, regardless of the issue topic. Most political consultants tacitly accept the findings of agenda-setting research and its importance to campaigns. If their issue of choice becomes the major news story of the campaign, their chances of winning will increase. Thus, a Republican campaigning on an antitax campaign is always enthused about any news coverage related to taxes. Similarly, a Democrat campaigning on a prolottery campaign always benefits from coverage of lottery issues during the campaign. The effect of such coverage decisions can be dramatic. By putting issues in the public spotlight, the media can influence party preferences (Brosius & Kepplinger, 1992) and influence the actions that people take on those issues (Roberts, 1992).

Scandals and Controversy

The news media salivate over a political scandal. Like a moth drawn to a bright light, the media will quickly focus on a scandal, even if getting too close to the scandal can damage the media itself. During 1999, when controversy broke out over Republican George W. Bush's possible use of drugs, one reporter noted that "the frenzy that is gripping the Washington press comes from the merest whiff of scandal" (Fillipelli, 1999). Sabato (1991) described the trend as a "feeding frenzy" in which journalists destroy a candidate. Similarly, Patterson (1994) has argued that the focus on scandals has made the political system ineffective by destroying trust in political institutions.

In most cases, neither the candidates (both the target of the scandal and the opponent) nor the media look good during scandal coverage, since nobody appears interested in a serious discussion of the campaign. The candidates focus on spin control, trying to put the scandal in the best possible light for themselves and the worst possible for their opponents. The press focuses on sensation, often offering serious issues only as justification for sensational images and controversy. As Yardley (1999) noted, "It is a shootout in which there are no good guys" (p. 6C).

The Horse Race

Ryan and Wentworth (1999, p. 81) have noted that the news media's emphasis on polls has led to a horse-race approach to political coverage, with the media focusing more on which candidate is ahead and who is behind than on the issues of the campaign. Such coverage is so intensive that it can have a greater impact on the outcome of an election than coverage of policy issues (Serini, Powers, & Johnson, 1998). Johnson (1993) noted that the press generally follows a two-step phase in campaign coverage, focusing initially on general indicators of candidate strength and then shifting to event-specific horse-race coverage. There are several reasons for this type of campaign coverage. First, it's relatively easy to do. Relative positions in the polls are fairly easy stories to write and report, requiring little investigation into issues by the reporters themselves. Second, many viewers and readers like this approach. Early studies of the uses-gratification theory identified "excitement" as one reason that people seek out political issues. Political junkies often view campaigns as the ultimate sporting event, played on a statewide or national field, with poll results giving the "score" at various points during the campaign. Many critics, though, question the value of horse-race coverage, arguing that it detracts from coverage of issues and encourages self-centered voting patterns (Capella & Jamieson, 1997). Increased focus on who's winning means less coverage on important issues that could affect the voters.

Personal Lives

During the 1884 presidential campaign, Grover Cleveland was beset by accusations that he had fathered an illegitimate child. Cleveland's only response to reporters who approached him about the issue was "Tell the truth," and most reporters did not pursue the matter. Not so today. Modern campaigns often represent a "politics of intimacy" (Parry-Giles & Parry-Giles, 1996) in which a candidate's personal life is considered fair game. During the 2000 presidential campaign, candidates were asked a multitude of questions that had little to do with the issues of the office, but a lot to do with what they did in private. During Hillary Rodham Clinton's campaign for the U.S. Senate from New York, a radio talk show host in Buffalo asked the First Lady if she had been "sexually unfaithful" to her husband (Hu, 2000); Clinton called the question "out of bounds," but answered it anyway (she denied the charges). Topics considered appropriate by reporters ranged from the sometimes controversial to the mundane, including questions about their sex lives, religious views, physical and mental health, income, advisers, friends, favorite books, movies, and political philosophers.

Two issues seemed to be raised by this type of political reporting. At what point do reporters cross the line, delving into matters that are none of their's or the public's business? To what extent does such intrusion keep highly qualified candidates from even running for public office? The latter is difficult to answer; during the Clinton-Lewinsky controversy, Republican governor George W. Bush speculated that he might not seek the Republican nomination for president if he and his family would have to be subjected to such scrutiny, but he ultimately decided to run anyway. Right or wrong, though, the press seems intent on examining candidates' private lives, and the pressure to do so increases with the increased visibility of the office being sought. Candidates who run for public office today have to expect some news coverage of their private lives.

Some public figures, in fact, take advantage of this effect by using their public exposure to increase coverage for issues that are of interest to them. The most obvious situation in which this occurs is with the presidential first ladies, some of whom fought to protect their privacy while others used their public recognition as a forum for favorite issues. Some, such as Barbara Bush, become celebrities in their own right (Wertheimer, 2000). Eleanor Roosevelt became a famous public figure whose public persona was quite distinct from that of husband Franklin Roosevelt (Lash, 1971); by using the public exposure that came with her position, she was able to promote the causes of a number of issues that concerned her. Conversely, Betty Ford's personal bouts with alcohol started out as a private problem that evolved into a public crusade for others to seek rehabilitation (Gutgold, 2000). Other first ladies, such as Edith (Mrs. Teddy) Roosevelt (Hastings, 2000) and Lou Henry (Mrs. Herbert) Hoover (Atkinson, 2000), sometimes fought against public intrusion into their lives, preferring instead to focus on a sense of home life for themselves and their families.

Campaign Advertisements

Campaign ads sometimes become news, particularly if they are sufficiently controversial or targeted toward a specific group. Over the past few years, in fact, coverage of campaign advertisements have increased. This factor can be both a boon and a bane to campaigns. On the positive side, news coverage of the ad can extend the message to larger number of voters. On the negative side, "when the message is aimed at one constituency, it can backfire if it is replayed in the news and critiqued by press pundits in the view of other groups of voters" (Stone, 1999, p. 150).

In the past, media outlets have done a relatively poor job of evaluating campaign advertisements. During 1988, for example, 17 percent of newspaper coverage focused on campaign advertising content, but less than 2 percent of it dealt with the accuracy of advertising claims (Jamieson, 1992). One innovation of campaign coverage during the 1990s that attempted to deal with this problem was the introduction of "adwatches," a name for news coverage of campaign ads. The idea behind the adwatch program is an admirable one. Given the impact that campaign advertising has on elections, the media have a responsibility to report on those ads, including a recounting of any inaccuracies that might be present. Unfortunately, reality often misses the ideal of this goal. Between 1972 and 1988, network news coverage of ads were often negatively slanted (Kaid et al., 1996). Since then, most television news coverage has been neutral; however, when there is a slant, it is largely negative (Kaid, Tedesco, & McKinnon, 1996; Tedesco, McKinnon, & Kaid, 1996). Newspaper adwatches tend to be neutral in focus (Tedesco, McKinnon, & Kaid, 1996), providing little evaluation one way or the other to the reader.

Generally, adwatches seem to have minimal impact on voter decisions. Geiger (1993) found that adwatches usually produced no effect. In other instances, adwatch coverage can mitigate the intended effects of the candidate's ad. Capella and Jamieson (1994) found that adwatch coverage of a 1992 Pat Buchanan attack ad against George H. W. Bush caused viewers to consider the ad as less fair and less important, and they were more likely to have a negative view of Buchanan than of Bush. Still, the latter effect tends to be an exception. More often than not, the effect of adwatch coverage of an ad is to enhance the sponsoring candidate. O'Sullivan and Geiger (1995) found that the enhancement effect was particularly pronounced when the adwatch supported the claims in the ad. The impact seems to be more pronounced with negative ads than with positive ones (Ansolabehere & Iyengar, 1995), even if the adwatch coverage criticizes the ad as unfair. Pfau and Loudon (1994) reported that critical adwatches can produce a boomerang effect, further enhancing the ad itself. Jamieson may have explained why in her study, which found that, after viewing an adwatch, voters remembered the ad itself better than the corrections made by the media commentator. Another possible explanation is that adwatch coverage may help to legitimize false or misleading advertising claims by airing messages in a credible news environment (Jamieson, 1992; West, 1993).

Narrative Examples

Modern television news focuses heavily on the use of a narrative story line, a trend that has contributed to the increased use of the horse-race coverage mentality mentioned earlier. Apart from horse-race mentality, though, much political coverage focuses on the narrative element. Many individual political stories use a narrative example, or exemplar, to drive home the point of a story. Brosius and Bathelt (1994) defined exemplars as illustrative single cases used to reflect an issue being discussed. On broadcast television, their use is almost an art form. A story on the loss of rural lifestyles might be prefaced with a few statistics about farmland development, but the meat of the story would likely be an exemplar: a story of a Midwest farmer who was losing his farm to encroaching development. Such narrative examples have a strong impact on both personal opinions and perceptions of public opinion (Daschmann, 2000).

Types of News Coverage

Straight News

The most frequent form of coverage available to politicians, candidates, and campaigns is that of straight news. The story is reported, hypothetically in an unbiased manner, and presented as information that will keep the readers and listeners informed. As noted before, consultants are unofficial proponents of the agenda-setting hypothesis, particularly its news-priming implications, so most make conscious efforts to seek such coverage (Ansolabehere, Behr, & Iyengar, 1994). Success in achieving news coverage is typically referred to as free media, or earned media. The latter term, although somewhat pretentious and inaccurate, is particularly popular among consultants, since it indicates they have done something on behalf of the client to generate coverage for them.

Regardless of whether that coverage is defined as "free" or "earned," the hope of every candidate is that their stories are not only covered, but covered in a way that is beneficial to them (Graber, 1987). The easiest indicator for this is placement of the story in relation to others (Nimmo, 1970, p. 130). They hope that newspapers will give their positive stories front-page treatment. Their prayer is that negative stories are buried with small headlines, somewhere in the back of the paper. Whether in the newspaper or on radio, placement of the story is critical. The lead story on TV news is often used as part of the promos, or teasers, used to entice viewers throughout the night to stay tuned to the news. As a result, lead TV stories tend to get more coverage than others that are on the same night. Similarly, individuals with only a minimal interest in politics might scan the front page of the newspaper.

Editorials

Consultants usually assume that editorials and op-ed (opinion) pieces in newspapers have little direct impact on election outcomes. Few people read the editorials, and those who do tend to be politicos who have already decided how they will vote. Still, endorsements can have an impact on down-ballot campaigns. Furthermore, newspaper editorials can have a major, indirect, impact if the campaign chooses to use editorial content in its campaign advertisements. Being able to cite a newspaper brings instant credibility to a television ad, and candidates love to use headlines as a visual association for a verbal message.

One particular form of editorial that draws a great deal of attention is the editorial cartoon, a visual and humorous part of the editorial page (Brinkman, 1968; Carl, 1968; Riffe, Sneed, & Van Ommeren, 1985; Wheeler & Reed, 1975). Some scholars view cartoons from a historical perspective (Steakley, 1983), while others consider them merely a social barometer that reflects public opinion (Penner & Penner, 1994). Still, a significant number of scholars view political cartoons as a form of persuasion that can influence public attitudes (Morris, 1993; Turner, 1977). Morris (1993) identified three communication functions of the cartoon: condensing a complex issue into a single image, combining elements from different domains into one, and domesticating (making the abstract or distant seem familiar). Some have argued that such rhetorical functions imbue political cartoons with the ability to change public opinion (Brinkman, 1968) and influence perceptions of political figures (Bosdorff, 1987). At the

Free Media Relations: The State of the Fourth Estate

by John Rowley

> *John Rowley is a Democratic media consultant with Fletcher & Rowley Consulting, a Nashville-based media firm with a nationwide clientele. Fletcher and Rowley have both worked as reporters and campaign press secretaries, and have written and produced political advertising in more than 275 political campaigns.*

For nonpresidential candidates, media coverage is dying a slow death. "Free media" coverage becomes scarcer each election cycle. News departments, reporters, candidates, and political consultants must all take their share of blame for the degenerated state of the American political debate. However, the principal problem is that the print and electronic news media rarely cover substance in political campaigns.

Most media outlets do market research to determine what brand of news will attract attention. People tell researchers they don't want local political news. With the exception of the creme de la creme (*New York Times, Washington Post, Los Angeles Time, Boston Globe,* and a few others), media organizations are obliging voters' lack of interest in politics by providing less coverage of local political stories.

Like the private sector, political campaigns are a marketplace. Supply and demand are powerful forces. There is currently a great demand from the media for political campaigns to provide controversy or to give "inside baseball–type" information such as polling data and campaign strategy. Candidates, as a result, are supplying more press releases about polls and fewer positive policy proposals. Candidates who offer new ideas are continually punished with scant coverage of their proposals or by being patently ignored. If candidates are rewarded by talking strategy and attacking the opposition, this is what more campaigns will do.

This approach is destined to prove Walter Lippmann correct in his assessment that "football strategy does not originate in a scrimmage; it is useless to expect solutions in a political campaign." If the media ignore candidates who stay positive and talk about the issues, while rewarding candidates who attack and offer insider information, it is clear what more candidates will do (and their political consultants will recommend): ignore the issues, spin the media, and attack the opposition.

Managing a Media Crisis

A media relations crisis is a rare event in a political campaign. However, when a crisis occurs, it is often the only interaction between a campaign and the news media that could mean the difference between winning and losing.

There are a myriad of campaign crisis: A well-documented lie. An illicit affair. An ethical uproar. A grand hypocrisy. A torrid tale from a candidate's wayward youth. A campaign's tour de force blunder.

It should not escape us that Bill Clinton faced all of these crisis, some of them repeatedly, as a presidential candidate and as president. Although war stories of Clinton's survival of crisis now seem mythic, he has been equally legendary at his crisis mismanagement in the early stages of his most memorable moments of truth.

Like many candidates facing a media crisis, part of Clinton's problem was that he responded before he had reviewed all the facts. When candidate Clinton's problems erupted with the draft, with Gennifer Flowers, and with drug use, Clinton didn't have all the facts or selectively forgot some of them. As a result, some of his early denials made each crisis much worse and extended the life of the story. Clinton's consultants and campaign staff, though talented, were flying blind

(continued)

Free Media Relations: The State of the Fourth Estate   Continued

because they didn't have the information they needed to manage the media and to limit the life span of the stories.

Looking at Clinton's political perseverance, we are reminded of the adage that the master is not always the best teacher. Bill Clinton is the greatest political survivor in the television age of politics. However, we would not necessarily go to Van Gogh to understand postimpressionism, to Mozart to learn opera or to Michael Jordan to sharpen our jump shot. The bottom line is that Bill Clinton is an excellent model for how to salvage a campaign and a presidency after dramatic media relations mistakes. He is not a good model for preventing and stopping crisis before they spiral out of control.

If a candidate has a devastating problem in their background it will surely bubble up over the course of a tough, high-profile political campaign. If a candidate and the campaign know about an explosive problem, preparation can breed perseverance. The following are some of the tenets of effective political crisis management.

Candidate: Research Thy Self. A professional research consultant or someone who is not a close friend of the candidate should complete an exhaustive review of his or her public record. This "self-research" can prepare a candidate, the campaign, and the candidate's family for damaging stories months before they rock the front pages. The most prepared campaigns will draft responses to anticipated attacks written months in advance so the campaign is ready to move fast and decisively at crunch time. Amazingly, it seems that President Clinton went into the New Hampshire primaries of 1992 with scant self-research available to his campaign team.

"Just the Facts Ma'am." When a bad story breaks or an opponent aggressively attacks, campaigns should say little or nothing until all of the supporting documentation is assembled and evaluated. This period should ideally be a few hours as the campaign gathers itself and crafts the response. Most mistakes in a crisis are made in the first couple of hours because of a quick response without accurate information.

If That's Your Story, Stick to It. Crisis communication is no time to freelance or attempt to work in a flashy ad-libbed quote. Once the facts are clear and a message crafted, the candidate and the campaign spokesperson should not deviate from the script. Reporters' invitations to speculate or hypothesize about possibilities and motivations should be ignored. Once the facts are clear and the message is written, stick to it.

Speed Kills Bad Stories, Speed Wins Elections. Unless all necessary information is not available, campaigns must aggressively counter and document their side of the story in the first news cycle. If stories run with the negative information about the candidate without the campaign's most compelling response in the news story, the negative information may be imbued in the voters' minds.

Taking Tough Questions off the Table. Political operatives who help candidates survive crisis think like reporters, not like candidates. Before delivering a prepared statement or holding a news conference, determine what the most ticklish questions will be and attempt to preempt them in the prepared statement. This will begin to pivot the debate onto your terms and possibly avoid extensive debate with reporters that can lead to mistakes and a statement that deters from the campaign's message.

They Call It Spinning. We Call It Aggressive Followup. If a hard-nosed reporter appears to be inclined to do a damaging story, there is more work to do. The campaign communications director should continue following up to make the campaign's points, to provide additional documentation, and in some cases to provide more access to the candidate to answer unanswered questions.

Don't Let the Media Uncover "The Rest of the Story." If other troubling information is sure to be revealed in the wake of the crisis, the campaign should preemptively release it on their own terms. It will always be bigger news, with more prominent play, if a media outlet has uncovered a news nugget than if a contrite candidate releases the embarrassing information. This will also likely shorten the life span of a negative story. A few years ago, one of our clients was about to be eviscerated on the front page of the *Washington Post* for his hawkish talk in office and his dovish actions during the Vietnam War. By releasing the information himself, this candidate moved the story from Page 1 to 18-A and prevented it from being more than a one-day story.

Liars and Their Offices Are Soon Separated. If the truth hurts, lies hurt more. Candidates can avoid questions, ignore inquiries, or change the subject. But they should never lie. Lies in politics are almost always uncovered by reporters, political enemies, or by one-time political friends who are now political enemies. If a lie is uncovered, the reporter will never forget it. If a lie is told, political enemies will meticulously document it and use it against the candidate in the future.

Promoting Positive Proposals

The hardest thing to do in politics is to get a lengthy story done on a new idea or positive policy proposal. The best way to maximize coverage of a new idea or proposal involves three elements. In order of importance to the media, they are 1) using an interesting visual element; 2) developing a memorable name or catch-phrase; and 3) proposing a good, new idea.

The Visual. No matter how great an idea, if it does not have a compelling visual element, your average candidate will receive limited television and print coverage. The best press conference doesn't need any spoken words to send the message. In Bill Clinton's 1996 campaign, he signed an environmental bill at the cusp of the Grand Canyon. What he said could never match the dramatic visual.

The Sizzle. A memorable name and creative language always help a policy proposal. We worked for a candidate whose office implemented an innovative program that would prosecute the worst criminals the fastest while saving tax money. He dubbed it the "Rocket Docket." One compelling phrase aroused interest and told the people what they needed to know about the initiative.

The Substance. Candidates who have real solutions that are salable in a campaign are the stuff of which winners and long-term political success stories are made. Being the "ideas candidate" can help a candidate get good reviews from editorial boards, if not good news stories.

Delivering a Negative Message

Candidates attack through the news media to drive up the negative impressions of their opponent by creating controversy and conflict. Here are a few principles for candidates going on the offensive:

Hypocrisy Detector. If the attacking candidate is even half as guilty of the same offense as the candidate being attacked, the strategy should be reevaluated. For instance, how can you attack a candidate for raising taxes twelve times, when you voted to raise taxes six times? If a candidate has devastating vulnerabilities, a counterattack exposing a hypocrisy or a lie of their attacker is usually their only hope to change the subject and divert attention.

Walk in the Other Candidate's Moccasins. As an attack press release or press conference is planned, the campaign team should spend some time walking in the other candidate's moccasins. They should think about how they would respond to the attack and develop their side of the story. Even though we would like our opponents to be demons, most are not. For instance, a congressional

(continued)

Free Media Relations: The State of the Fourth Estate   Continued

candidate was attacked once for missing an important vote on the minimum wage. It turns out he missed the vote to be with his wife while she gave birth to their first child. Ouch. The only thing worse than the media not covering your attack is dealing with the backlash and loss of credibility that results from getting it wrong.

Seeing Is More Important than Hearing. Stories need a compelling visual element. Much of the voter research we have done shows that the most persuasive form of communication a voter receives is television news about the candidates. Because of this fact and because it is still the most powerful political communication medium on the planet, most campaign news relations should be targeted toward the television stations.

Use Humor. Negative statements should be sprinkled with bon mots when possible. If you can deliver the negative information about your opponent and leave voters laughing at them, you have achieved a work of political communications art. In working in the governor's race in Louisiana, it was discovered that our opponent bought David Duke's mailing list and hid it from the public. Our candidate put out a statement that our opponent had redefined the term "Louisiana Purchase." It made the point and it made them laugh.

Use a Spokesperson to Limit Backlash. For negative statements, a campaign spokesperson should deliver the message instead of the candidate. The more voters see a candidate on the offensive the more likely an attack will hurt the attacker as much as they hurt the attacker's opponent. By using a spokesperson whenever possible, a campaign limits backlash against the candidate.

Candidate Preparation

For medical doctors working with patients and for spin doctors advising candidates on media relations, the Hippocratic oath applies: "Do no harm." The first rule of candidate media relations is to not make any mistakes. Elections are not won or lost as a result of candidate generating a great positive news story or delivering a pithy positive quote. But a number of elections every year turn upon one mistake a candidate made in an interview. That is why the best candidates not only have ideas and are good communicators, but they practice their responses to the toughest questions before the red light of a TV camera is on and tape is rolling. Newt Gingrich may have said it best, "Practice the big truth so you can say it in thirty seconds on television."

Source: Reprinted by permission of John Rowley.

very least, their structure and intent fall within the realm of traditional rhetorical form (Medhurst & DeSousa, 1981), and several scholars have approached them from that perspective. Bosdorff (1987), for example, looked at the rhetorical implications of political cartoons attacking former presidential cabinet member James Watt. Similarly, Holm argued that political cartoons about the Clinton-Lewinsky sex scandal had a positive impact on Bill Clinton's image because many of the drawings identified him with the common man. That factor could have contributed to keeping Clinton in office despite the threat of impeachment.

Not all scholars agree with this approach. Despite their humor and political insight, political cartoons are often ignored by the average voter and misunderstood by many. Those who most appreciate political cartoons tend to be political insiders, a trend that prompted

Bormann, Koester, and Bennett (1978) to conclude that cartoons were essentially inside jokes that few people understood. Research generally supports the latter conclusion (Carl, 1968); average readers often miss the point of the cartoon. Still, when the point is driven home, a political cartoon does so in a graphic and memorable way.

Sunday News Shows

In national politics, some of the most influential news television occurs on Sunday mornings (when few people are watching television) on interview shows such as NBC's *Meet the Press,* CBS's *Face the Nation,* and ABC's *This Week with Sam Donaldson and Cokie Roberts.* As TV commentator Roger Simon (1987, p. 4) once noted, those shows are all based on the assumption "that important political and government figures, faced with vigorous questioning, just might slip and commit news."

The format of the shows are similar. Each has a reporter or reporters directing questions at public officials or other newsworthy individuals. In most cases, those guests are either high-ranking administration officials or people who are in leadership positions in Congress. The oldest of the shows, *Meet the Press,* made its debut in 1951. For the remainder of that decade, the questions were gentle, with reporters typically showing respect toward their guests. Simon (1987, p. 5) noted that, in the beginning, "persistent follow-up questions were somehow considered bad manners." Today, tough questions are the rule, not the exception. Furthermore, appearances on the shows may offer little opportunity to reach undecided voters; the audience tends to be made up of active voters (Hofstetter et al., 1994), most of whom have already made their voting decision.

So why do politicians agree to participate? First, they want to get exposure for themselves and their ideas. Despite the small audience, all of the Sunday interview shows generate a great deal of spinoff coverage. Comments made on the show are reported on the evening television news and distributed in print to all of the major newspapers. An effective interview on any of the shows can dramatically increase recognition of an issue, pushing it to the forefront of the media's agenda.

Second, most of the guests are not afraid of the tough questioning. Most, if not all, have been interviewed thousands of times before they make their first Sunday-morning appearance. Their interview-response skills are often just as well developed as the interview-questioning skills of the reporters. As Simon (1987, p. 6) wrote, "If they don't want to say something, it is hard to make them say it."

The Role of the Press Secretary

The press secretary is the major conduit of news and information between the candidate and the news media. As Perloff (1998, p. 69), noted, "It is a dicey job," one in which verbal missteps can have serious consequences. The role is such an integral part of today's political communication process that it is easy to forget that it is a relatively new role. For decades, most statewide campaigns did not bother to use one. Even at the presidential level, the position did not formally exist until the administration of Herbert Hoover (Nelson, 1998). Stephen Early's performance during twelve years as Franklin Roosevelt's press secretary generally defined how the job should be handled, at least in the eyes of the press (Mitchell, 1998).

Gradually, the role of the press secretary filtered down to other campaigns. Grover Smith served in the function of press secretary for Senator John Sparkman (Dem.-Ala.) during the 1950s. At the time, however, senators had no official press secretaries, and Smith's official title was "research assistant." Smith eventually organized the first press secretary association for the Senate, and got recognition for the group when newsman David Brinkley agreed to speak to them. Smith subsequently arranged for the official contact lists for each senator to include a person in each office who was identified as the press secretary (Smith, 1999).

In most modern campaigns, the role is distinctly separate from other campaign functions, with the press secretary acting as both manager of the message and "messenger boy" (Grossman & Kumar, 1981, p. 130). The press secretary serves as a conduit for information to the press, keeping reporters alerted to the candidate's schedule, scheduling press conferences, and writing press releases for standard announcements. As a conduit, the press secretary serves as a gatekeeper between the candidate and the press. Using that "gate" to control access to the candidate requires a careful balance. Too much can be detrimental, offering too many opportunities for negative press; too little can be even worse, creating an antagonistic relationship that also leads to negative coverage.

Although approaches to the role can vary, depending on the personality of the individual, most press secretaries aim for a positive working relationship with the press with the intent of maintaining that relationship through the ups and downs of the campaign. As a result, some campaigns use both the campaign manager and the press secretary in "good-cop/bad-cop" roles. When the campaign feels it is necessary to criticize the press, the criticism is more likely to come from the campaign manager; that way, the criticisms do not hinder the press secretary's working relationship with reporters.

As a conduit of information, the press secretary has several options for passing information on to the press. "On the record" refers to those comments that may be quoted in the press and the name of the source identified. If the information is released, "on background," the quote can be used but the source cannot be identified by name—only by status or position ("a source close to the president said . . . ," for example). "Deep background" has even more control; reporters can use the information provided by the press secretary, but they cannot attribute it to a particular source. Some information is given "off the record." In those instances, the reporter is not to use the information in their story at all; it is provided merely to help them understand the larger context of an issue or situation.

Some information may bypass the press secretary entirely through the process of news leaks. Leaks are used on premature information that the source wants the press to have, but which they are unable to disclose through normal channels ("This reporter has learned . . .").

The Impact of New Media

The expanding role of the Internet in modern society has the potential to dramatically alter the way that people get their news information and how they interact with government officials as a result. The Internet offers a mechanism for bypassing traditional news sources. As such, it has the potential to bypass the gatekeeping function of the press, providing more news on more topics than has previously been available to the public. The Internet has already had at least two dramatic effects on news coverage. First, it has accelerated the news cycle, that range of time in which a story is presented to an audience. Television and news-papers have traditionally operated on a twenty-four-hour news cycle, giving readers and viewers a summary of one day's events at a time. The Internet operates on a much faster cycle, with something become "old" news sometimes within a matter of hours. Second, the Internet has led to an increase in the sheer volume and availability of news. Those who wish to keep up to date on current events, including political events, can do so at any time of the day. Kovach and Rosentiel (1999) noted that this "never-ending news cycle" has had at least one negative impact on news, with a "journalism of assertion" replacing the traditional approaches of verifying information before broadcasting it.

The potential of the Internet as a news source has so far outstripped its reality. One reason is that news sources have yet to understand fully how to use the Internet to convey political information. Musso, Weare, and Hale (2000) analyzed municipal web sites and found that most lacked a clear mission, provided few effective features, and had little infor-mation that would be useful to those who might log on to the site. The second reason why the Internet has not reached its news potential is that most users don't consider it a primary news source. Internet users log on to web sites primarily for entertainment, and rely on newspapers as their major source of news (Althaus & Tewksbury, 2000).

Summary

Despite the incursions of new media such as the Internet, the impact of media coverage will not dissipate anytime soon. Candidates will still be judged by many voters on their ability to deal with the press, the information that many voters get will continue to come from the press, and candidates will continue to be chosen, at least partly, on the basis of "their media-friendly characteristics" (Ryan & Wentworth, 1999, p. 80). That's why modern campaigns devote a significant amount of resources to developing and maintaining relationships with the press.

That relationship is a complex, ongoing process that is constantly in flux. News cov-erage of a candidate can be influenced by a number of factors. While some of those factors are under the control of either the campaign or the reporter, many others are triggered by events in a campaign environment over which neither the candidate nor the reporter has control. The resulting news stories can appear in a variety of formats with a number of dif-ferent effects. Naive candidates can find their personal reputation damaged by selective reporting of facts about their past. Experienced candidates may find their pet issues are overlooked in favor of other issues that have grabbed and kept the media's attention. And, with the advent of the Internet as a new means of dispensing news information, the news cycle as been compressed into a shorter frame of time. Not surprisingly, the role of the press is growing increasingly complex in modern campaigns.

QUESTIONS FOR DISCUSSION

1. Your candidate has planned a series of news conferences highlighting his environmental proposals. The first one goes well, but on the way to the second event, the candidate's auto-mobile is sideswiped by a patrol car driven by a deputy sheriff. Will the accident or the news conferences result in greater news coverage? Why?

2. In 1992, Bill Clinton, beset by charges of womanizing, placed second in the New Hampshire primary. He described himself as the "comeback kid," and the news media generally treated his performance there as a victory. What role did "expectations" play in this perception? If you had been campaign manager for one of Clinton's opponents, what effective spin could you have used that might have led to a different interpretation?

3. On the night before election day, a television station carried the story that your candidate for mayor had been killed in a traffic accident. The story was false, and the report was corrected in the next news cycle. How can such a report damage your campaign? As campaign manager, what would you have done to deal with this story? What responsibility does the television station face?

4. Abraham Lincoln is cited as an example of a candidate who would have great difficulty winning the modern presidency. As his campaign manager, how would you muster arguments in his favor? What campaign preparations would you undertake to focus the news media on his strengths: his good sense of humor, strong values, and excellent political leadership skills? How would you spin a story on his lack of media skills? How would you get the media to cover the "Lincoln" issues?

12 The Role of Political Money

Political novice John Corzine altered the political landscape of the 2000 Senate election in New Jersey when he entered the election with a reported net worth of $300 million and vowed to spend as much as he needed to get elected. "Money has been a dominant theme in the New Jersey Senate race since Mr. Corzine announced his interest a year ago," wrote one reporter (Halbfinger, 2000). "His willingness to pay any price was cited by nearly every candidate who eventually withdrew, among them the governor, Christine Todd Whitman, a Republican, and Democrats Michael Murphy, Frank Pallone and B. Thomas Byrne."

For the academic community, political communication is an exercise in the democratic process in which different ideas compete for public support. For the consulting community, campaigns are a business. Not surprisingly, money is a pivotal factor in the consulting role, while it is often criticized by the academic community. Consultants focus on bending the constantly changing rules of the game so they can simultaneously do a more effective job for their clients and make more money for themselves. Academicians, meanwhile, often bemoan the role that money plays in modern campaigns.

The media might adopt both views. Their editorial departments toss out criticisms of the role of money in campaigns while their advertising departments eagerly compete for political advertising. A typical editorial comment notes that the presidential elections are likely to be won "by whichever candidate can get the highest number of wealthy people to write $1,000 checks," while adding, "This is no way to run a democracy, and it is a result of our sorry system of campaign finance" (Judis, 1999). Still, while the editorial department and television commentators rail at the system, as much as 70 percent of the money collected by campaigns is spent with those same media outlets.

An occasionally overlooked aspect of the financial side of politics is that the concern over money also creates problems and arguments within the campaign. Even though fundraising plays a critical role in their careers, many candidates despise fund-raising. When former Illinois senator Paul Simon retired from politics, he cited the dislike for the almost daily routine of soliciting those contributions necessary to run for reelection. Many candidates have a similar distaste for seeking money, creating another potential source of internal conflict between the candidates and their consultants. While the candidate resists additional fund-raising activities, the consultants may be pressing for more money to use in more projects. Given that scenario, it is hardly surprising that Franzen (1999, p. 300) noted that ". . . many of the difficulties that arise between consultants and their clients revolve around money." The consultants argue for another round of media or another program as necessary for success, while the candidate projects the resentment they might face from donors who have already been more than generous with their contributions. Internal conflicts between consultants also often revolve around money. Most of the campaign budget typically goes to the mass media consultant, a situation that can build resentment among the other vendors. Polling, direct mail, telephone, and organizational consultants often find themselves fighting for the remaining dollars. Success at getting those monies helps to finance their business through another campaign cycle. Failure to win the fight gives them an easy explanation as to why any particular campaign did not win.

The reality of modern politics, though, requires some means of dealing with such conflicts, since money is an essential and necessary ingredient for most campaigns. As Perlmutter (1999, p. 2) noted, "It is extremely difficult to run for higher office in America without an enormous war chest filled with one's own money or that of wealthy friends and partisans." The fact is that money buys the means of political speech. Without money political messages cannot be tested by pollsters; advertising spots cannot be created; ad time cannot be purchased; staffs cannot be hired; campaign schedules cannot be kept, and money cannot be raised. Without adequate funding there is less political speech. For the candidate who wants to win, money is an ever-present reality.

This means a fund-raising plan is essential to the campaign. Even those candidates who enter the process full of idealism will eventually learn about the financial side of politics. They enter the profession as civic-minded idealists who believe their views can have an influence on public policy. By the end of their first campaign, they have a healthy appreciation for the role of money—either because they had to spend so much time raising it, or because they were defeated by a better-financed opponent. For their messages to prevail, the candidate must have at least enough money to communicate those ideas to the voters (Broder, 1999). That means that fund-raising starts early, with presidential candidates typically starting their fund-raising efforts more than a year before Election Day (Drinkard, 2000).

The Role of Political Money

A sometimes overlooked aspect of political communication is the rhetorical effect that money has on the campaign (Jones, 2000). An effective fund-raising program provides at least four rhetorical advantages to a campaign by enhancing credibility, attracting media attention, increasing subsequent fund-raising, and diminishing the opposition. Early fund-raising is critical to candidate credibility. Early success draws media attention to the campaign, bestows legitimacy to the campaign efforts, and puts pressure on the competition to raise a comparable amount. The media attention can create a mushrooming effect; journalists tend to cover campaigns in direct relationship to how much money the candidate raises, and the increased visibility created by that coverage can spur even more donations. As the bank accounts start bulging, the pressure to compete drives some competitors away.

The most dramatic recent example was Republican George W. Bush, who used the rhetoric of money to drive out and finally overcome his primary competitors and win the 2000 Republican nomination for president. Elizabeth Dole dropped out of the race, citing her inability to compete with the record $70 million raised by the Bush campaign. More than a year before the Republican convention, *USA Today* (Lawrence, 1999) cited the inevitability of Bush's nomination and quoted Larry Markinson, of the Center for Responsive Politics, on the rhetorical impact of Bush's campaign war chest. "It really shows the power of the purse," Markinson said. "The funders have decided who the next nominee is going to be six months before anyone casts a vote. The reality of these numbers has to be brutal for the other Republican candidates."

Jennifer Steen, of the Scholars Network of the Citizens' Research Foundation at the University of California at Berkeley, called political money a "self-fulfilling prophecy" that drives out competition. "The perception that a millionaire can buy victory exerts a chilling effect on electoral competition, discouraging would-be candidates from entering the fray," she wrote (Steen, 2000). That conclusion was based on data analyzed from four congressional campaigns over four election cycles that pointed to an "unmistakable pattern": "the richer the candidate, the fewer the opponents."

For reporters and editors, the amount of money becomes a scorecard by which candidates can be judged. Each side is so sensitive to the rhetoric of money that the release of any such information by one side often prompts a similar salvo from the other. When New York mayor Rudolph Giuliani's Senate campaign reported that it collected $12 million in 1999 for his 2000 campaign against Hillary Rodham Clinton, Clinton, who had refused to release her fund-raising totals at that point, announced she had collected $8 million during the same time period. As the *New York Times* noted, "It was emblematic of the pronounced role of money in the race that the advisers then sought to explain why her total was not higher, pointing out, for example, that she had been raising money only since the summer" (Levy, 2000).

Strategic decisions on the use of campaign finances can also have a critical impact on election outcomes. In 1996, Republican candidate Bob Dole started his primary campaign early in an effort to win the nomination with a growing momentum that could carry him to a November victory. Unfortunately, his campaign ran out of money before the primary season was over. Bill Clinton, meanwhile, was spending millions of dollars on ads touting his political agenda and building a lead among key constituencies that Dole was never able to overcome.

Sometimes the rhetoric of money can exceed its political impact, particularly in self-financed campaigns. Data from the Citizens' Research Foundation, a campaign finance research center at the University of California at Berkeley, have consistently found that millionaires who finance their own campaigns face an uphill battle in winning an election (Steen, 2000). As Steen noted, "Self-financers usually don't win. When they do, it isn't their money alone that puts them in office" (p. B1). Several factors contribute to this conclusion, including the millionaire's lack of political experience and their lack of a political network. Her study of five election cycles (from 1990 to 1998) found that only six of thirty-eight non-incumbent Senate candidates who financed their own campaigns with at least $1 million had won their campaigns, a success rate of only 16 percent. Meanwhile, 49 of the 155 non-incumbents who raised $1 million or more in contributions won their elections (a 32 percent success rate). Differences in House races were even more dramatic: The success rate among those who raised a million dollars (67 percent) was more than three times that of millionaires who used their own money to campaign for Congress (21 percent).

Rules of the Game

Candidates cannot merely enter a campaign and immediately start to raise and spend money. Modern campaigns play by a sophisticated, complicated, and often confusing set of rules. Federal candidates (presidents, senators, and members of Congress) must adhere to federal laws that are monitored by the Federal Election Commission (FEC). State and local candidates have a different set of rules, although many of those local regulations are patterned after the federal guidelines. Although there are some exceptions for local regulations, the relevant laws generally fall into three different categories: limits on contributions, limits on spending, and reporting requirements (Schotland, 1992).

Campaign Contributions

Federal law limits contributions for federal elections—campaigns for president, U.S. senator and the U.S. House of Representatives—to $1,000 from individuals and $5,000 from political action committees (PACs). Once any election is completed, the contributor can donate again for the next election. The implications of this is that, for some candidates, the actual ceiling on individual contributions for one election cycle is $3,000, not $1,000. A contributor could donate $1,000 to the candidate's primary campaign, another thousand to the primary runoff, and still make a third donation for the general election. With the same setup, political action committees could potentially donate $15,000 to the campaign—$5,000 for each of the three elections.

Finally, the financial books close in each phase except in one important respect. Funds may be raised for a primary or runoff or general election to the extent of debt. If a campaign owes money at the end of any of these periods, it may continue to raise money to pay off that debt. Often a financial contributor of a beaten opponent will contribute to a winner by helping to raise funds to pay off earlier debts. Potential contributors who might not want their support known might pledge a later contribution to pay off debt. The same contributors may then contribute in subsequent phases of the campaign.

Spending Limits

The goal of spending limits is to create a more level playing field for candidates. Ideally, the winner of the election should be the candidate with the best ideas, not the one with the most money, and spending limits are an attempt to provide more parity on this front. However, neither the federal nor local governments may unilaterally limit expenditures for all candidates. Candidates may spend their own money without limits. In *FEC* v. *Buckley,* the Supreme Court held that doing so would be to interfere with those candidates' right to freedom of speech. As a result, spending limits can be placed only on those candidates who choose to raise their funds or, in the case of presidential campaigns, those who accept matching funds from the government. If the candidate accepts governmental funds, or otherwise chooses not to use personal funds then the government has the right to place rules on how those funds are spent.

Congressional and senatorial candidates are typically not eligible for matching campaign funds, unless they qualify under regulations for their individual states. As such, there are rarely any spending limits for those races, only the individual contributions limits. For presidential candidates who choose matching funds, the first $250 of each individual contribution can be matched by federal funds. In the 2000 presidential primary campaign, for example, candidates who accepted matching money were limited to spending $40.5 million during the primary campaigns (that amount varies with each election). If the candidate chooses not to accept matching money, they are not bound by any spending limits. During the 2000 election, for example, Republican George W. Bush raised more than $70 million in individual and PAC contributions; he chose not to accept federal matching funds and spent much of that total during the primary season. Democrat Al Gore accepted federal funds and was limited to the $40.5 million ceiling on primary expenditures.

In presidential elections, the general election campaign officially begins after the parties formally nominate candidates at their conventions in the summertime. That portion of the presidential campaign is funded by taxpayers. In 2000, the Democratic and Republican candidates each got $67.5 million, and both were prohibited from using other funds. Theoretically, a candidate could refuse the federal money and raise money under the same rules as for the primaries. That has not yet happened.

State and local candidates have a different set of rules, which often vary dramatically from state to state. About half follow the federal model and offer either full or partial public financing of statewide elections. Others require candidates to raise their own funds but have contribution limits similar to those for federal elections. Still others allow unlimited contributions but have strict reporting requirements. Reporting requirements also apply to spending the money, with some states limiting expenditures until an initial report has been filed. Others require reports at specific times, with enforcement penalties varying from state to state. The bottom line for the consultant is that he or she must become familiar with the local laws as quickly as possible. Not surprisingly, the most valuable volunteers the campaign can recruit are local lawyers and accountants who are willing to research the legal and financial aspects of the campaign game.

Reporting Requirements

To enforce campaign contribution laws, both the federal and state government rely on specific reporting requirements for monitoring purposes. Reporting requirements are strict, even those elections that are not subject to contribution limits. For that reason, most major campaigns employ both a lawyer and an accountant to make sure that the account books are in proper shape and that all reports are made in a timely manner. Keeping those books requires a sophisticated set of records. In federal elections, for example, the $1,000 limit is cumulative for each individual campaign. A contributor who donates $500 early in the campaign can later donate another $500, but not more than that. When a contributor reaches a cumulative total of $1,000, he or she has given the most allowed for that election and is not allowed to contribute again until the next election cycle begins. Thus, the campaign's accounting system must be sufficiently complex to keep up with individual contributions and the cumulative total of each individual's contributions.

Circumventing the Rules

The basic regulations provide only a broad framework for the legal side of campaign finances. Campaigns often look for ways to adhere to the letter of the law while expanding the amount of money they are legally allowed to raise and spend (Adamany, 1990). A number of avenues have been used for this purpose.

Interview with Joe McLean

Raising Political Money

Joe McLean is a partner in McLean-Clark, a consulting firm that specializes in fund-raising for candidates of the Democratic party. They have provided fund-raising services for a number of statewide and congressional candidates. The firm has offices in Washington, D.C., and in Murpheesboro, Tennessee.

Q: What's it like to be a political fund-raiser?

A: Well, it's a job.

Q: What type of a job? What do you have to cope with that you don't in some other jobs?

A: It's like any job. You work hard and hope for the best. There is an impression that people have that politics is glamourous. The fact is that it's really hard work, particularly fund-raising. You don't raise money by going to big glitzy events. You raise money by asking for it. It's hard work, it's competitive. If there's any key to it, it would be hard work and good information management.

Q: What do you mean by information management?

A: You have to decide who you're going to ask and how you're going to ask them, and then you have to keep up with the information. When you ask them, you have to keep up with what they say and what you've done to collect the money. It's a lot like sales.

Q: But you don't have a product that you can give them.

A: You're selling them good government.

Q: How do you see the role of fund-raising in campaigns? Is it the fuel that keeps the engine running?

A: No. I don't view it that way at all. In the old days, when I first started doing campaigns nearly thirty years ago, campaigns were about going down to the courthouse and getting the county executive and the sheriff to support you. They would get other people to support you, and you'd win because they supported you. Nowadays, there's virtually no machine politics in America anymore. Nowadays, it's about giving people a reason to vote for you, telling them what you want to do and why it's important that you be elected. It's communication. In my opinion, that's much better, because voters are more engaged—or, at least they should be more engaged—on the decisions that we as a nation, county, or city have to make. So campaigns are about communication. The most effective way to communicate, obviously, is person to person—going door to door and shaking hands. But if it's not a small city alderman's race, you're not going to see all the voters and talk to them. Certainly not within a time period in which they will remember you when it's time to go to the polls and vote. People don't like to think about politics very much. They don't think about politics. The average high-information person thinks about politics less than five minutes a week, and that's somebody who reads the paper every day. The average citizen doesn't think about politics hardly at all. So you must communicate with people in a manner that's relevant to their lives and within a time period in which they are willing to think about politics. Most people don't want to think about elections until it's close to the election. Obviously you can't do that as an individual. So you have to pay to communicate. Just like McDonald's and General

Motors, we have to communicate to people with the vehicles available to us: television, radio, direct mail, phone banks. And it costs money. So what you do is you turn money into message into votes. I would recommend to you a 1980 or '81 study undertaken by the JFK School [of Government] at Harvard, at the behest of the House Administration Committee to study the effects of the Federal Election Campaign Act. They determined that the problem with politics wasn't that there was too much money in politics, the problem was there isn't enough. We're not able to effectively communicate a message on the issues because we don't have enough money to spend. We're left with quick thirty-second commercials and cheap shots with negative campaigns. It's dated—it's several years old—but nothing has changed. Its principles still apply. Human nature hasn't changed.

A: Then you're arguing that the influx of money into campaigns has been good for democracy, not bad for it.

Q: Absolutely. And here's one other thing to think about. As there has been a move for campaign finance reform, as the federal donation limits have been reduced due to inflation, and as the states have put limits on campaign contributions, there has been a concomitant rise in independent expenditures. I'm not talking about just soft money for the parties, although that is certainly one symptom or issue. I'm talking about things like the "Harry and Louise" ads—companies or individuals spending millions of dollars, not just to influence elections, but to influence legislative votes, to drive the political agenda. We have a representative democracy in this country. It's worked very well for us, although it's still quite an experiment. It's only a little over 200 years old, and nobody really knows whether it will work or not. But we do know that our representative system has served us well so far, and I would say that campaign finance reform strikes at the heart of representative democracy because it makes elections less relevant and independent expenditures more relevant. What we're beginning to engage in is an experiment in direct democracy. You can look at California to see the effects of the initiative decision out there. California schools are a disaster. Post–Proposition 13, California schools are among the worst in the nation because they have no money. Nobody knows whether you can run a country the size of the United States via direct democracy. We know we can sorta run it with representative democracy.

Q: Why can't you do something to limit the soft money and independent expenditures?

A: How are you going to communicate? The voters don't really want to listen to you anyway. They don't want to think about the issues facing the country. Why do we not have national health reform in this country? Why do we have a system of privatized, nationalized medicine? There's no bureaucrat on the federal payroll who's harder to deal with than an HMO bureaucrat. We've privatized national medicine because we tried to reform the medical system, and the insurance companies and the HMOs spent a fortune on issue-based ads to turn the American people against those initiatives. Right or wrong or indifferent, these people didn't make campaign contributions to elect members to Congress who would agree with their position on it, they went straight to the people in an exercise in direct democracy. It's not unusual. Particularly in Washington, we see a lot of television ads driving straight at an issue.

Q: That's going to occur whether there's money going into campaigns or not.

A: Didn't use to. Didn't have to. Don't misunderstand me. Just because all this happened just after campaign finance reform, I don't believe that's what caused it. But I do believe it was a direct result. That and the emasculation of the political parties. There is

(continued)

Interview with Joe McLean   Continued

not a lot of party discipline; you can't hold the ideological line. We have fifty-three different political parties here in Washington. Every member of Congress—house member or senator—raises their own money and looks out for themselves pretty much. In fact, soft money is one way to get back some party discipline.

A: Could soft money increase the power of the parties?

Q: It could be, a little bit. Both the Republicans and the Democrats use coordinated campaigns now as a funding and organizational vehicle (primarily funding vehicle) for voter contact activities and get-out-the-vote. More and more they're using them to drive messages, to communicate with the voters.

Q: What about the ethical issues surrounding fund-raising?

A: The money in a political campaign is the cleanest part of the campaign. It's all public record. There's a paper trail on every penny you raise and spend. Even with soft money, there's a paper trail on it. The parties have to keep up with that. I support reporting soft money. I support keeping up with where this money comes from. But here's the problem. When you're talking about soft money, we talking about money that the parties spend, there's not much question about who it is. If it says paid for by the Democratic party, you know who put that ad on and you know why it's there, and you can take it at face value or not. And voters are not stupid. Sometimes voters don't pay attention, but boy, when they do pay attention they're really smart about ferreting out who's telling the truth. What bothers me are the 527 organizations who have no controls at all. They can raise money from any source in any amount. If you had $100 million, you could spend $99 million of it as "The Committee for Good Government" to denigrate a candidate. You could say that Candidate X has been charged with felonious assault against small barnyard animals and that he beats his wife. You could say anything you want, because, first, he's a public figure, so it's very difficult for him to sue you; and second, he may not even know who you are because your committee is just a sham name. There are no regulations on you at all. You can do whatever you want. You're protected by the First Amendment in what you say and how you say it. The Supreme Court has said that money is speech, so it's absolutely in the dark and there's nothing you can do about it. That's what I fear and that's what I think that campaign finance reform leads to.

Q: So you think campaign finance reform increases that type of hidden campaign?

A: I know it does. Just look around. We're seeing it right now. If you could take your $99 million and legally support candidates who feel the way you do, you'd be a lot more likely to do that than you would to just put it on TV and crucify somebody. Sometimes you hear goo-goo, good-government liberals [who] say these people are buying influence. That's not true at all. It's obvious that they've never been through the process of raising political money. Agreeing with somebody on the issues is a precursor, the first step, for consideration for a contribution. We have to already be with them before they'll agree to consider a contribution. Then, the thing that really makes them decide to do it is "winnability." What actually moves the money is winnability. It's not a matter of influence, it's a matter of confluence. When they're willing to make a contribution, we already agree with them.

Q: If you could change the law, how would you change it?

A: If I could change the law, I would increase the contribution limit, and I would be serious about disclosure. I would increase the penalty for nondisclosure and for incorrect disclosure. I would certainly want to increase the penalty for making a contribution in the name of another. And I would open things up. Understand that the unions are at a huge financial disadvantage. They can do checkoff and reverse checkoff on their members, and they can use their union dues for soft-money contributions, but that's really all they have. Corporations and the business community as a whole is larger than the union community and they have a lot more avenues for moving money. They can get PAC contributions from their executive and administrative personnel. They can raise money from their stockholders. They can communicate with their solicitable class in any way they want. They can not only engage in political communication with those people, but they can ask them to send money to politicians or to contribute to an independent expenditure campaign. They have tremendous financial power that they can bring to bear, and they do. The amount of money just spent on the trade agreement with China was staggering. We'll never know how much it was, but we do know that it moved votes. Now, we have a First Amendment obligation to allow people their freedom of speech in a free society. And if you hold that the key to an effective democracy is an informed electorate, then they ought to be spending that money on it. So I don't have all the answers. I don't know exactly what to do. I know that every time we've messed with the campaign finance system, the law of unintended consequences bites us hard.

Q: Are you saying that past reforms have increased the amount of money spent?

A: It's not the amount of money that's spent, it's the effect on political outcomes.

Q: Give me an example.

A: The trade relations is a good example. There was a tremendous amount of money spent on that, and it affected the outcome. But the voters don't really understand how it works. Health care is another good example. The only people who can't be sued in America are HMO executives, and that's because there has been a tremendous amount of money spent, all of it sub rosa, to skew the debate on health reform. Now I'm not an advocate of national health care, but there is an argument for it. But the voters have never heard that view, because the other side of the argument has never had enough money to do anything with it.

Q: So what does that do to the political system?

A: It subverts the system. In our democracy, in almost every case, the ends do not justify the means. The process by which you make a decision is as important as the decision that's made.

Q: But, you seem now to be agreeing with those who question the role of money in campaigns.

A: In traditional political campaigns, there is virtue in spending more money instead of less. Diminishing marginal utility of political money kicks in with a vengeance in a political campaign. The voters only want to hear about the campaign for the two or three weeks before the election. Unless it's a bigger race, like a presidential race, it's a really short cycle. They'll only watch so many ads before you turn them off. If you buy a 1,000 gross rating points a week for five weeks, you've saturated the electorate. You've spent all the money you can on TV. So you go buy radio but, again, there's only so much radio that you can or want to buy. There's only so many pieces of direct mail that you can or should send. There are only so many phone calls you can or should make. If you did everything you could possibly do in a campaign, you could only spend a certain amount of money. And, the last dollar is much less valuable than the first dollar. The first 700 gross rating points in a week are critical; the last three or four hundred

(continued)

Interview with Joe McLean   Continued

rating points in a week have diminished utility. And that holds true for all the different types of communication. There's only so much money that you can spend.

Q: But that implies that, for the system to work, both candidates need some money to communicate.

A: I think it's vital that both parties have money to communicate. For the electorate to make good decisions, they have to be informed. For them to be informed, we've got to jam it down their throat, because they won't take it otherwise. The voters won't actively go out and get the information. We have to engage the voters in the issues, and it takes money to do that. It takes lots of money to do that. It's why General Motors and Procter and Gamble spend millions of dollars every year on advertising. They have to engage people who really don't want to think about their product. If we spent on political campaigns what Procter and Gamble—not the whole industry now, but just Procter and Gamble—spends on just advertising soap products, the average congressional race would cost about five million dollars. Right now, though, the average House race is not a half million dollars. Winning House races average about a million dollars now. And that's just compared to one company, not the whole industry.

The reason why people notice it is that people always see companies like McDonald's on TV. They're actually running about 150 gross rating points a week. But they don't have the same challenge that you have in a political campaign. They just want to keep you remembering their brand name. What we have to do in politics is more complicated. We have to get them to recognize the candidate, like the candidate, and engage in a specific behavior for the candidate, at a specific time. And we have to do all of this within a relatively short time frame. So during that time, we're on the air with a 1,000 gross rating points, and that makes people notice it. It looks like we're spending a lot of money; actually we're not spending enough money, but we're spending it all in a short amount of time.

Source: Reprinted by permission of Joe McLean.

Hard Money vs. Soft Money.   The most common method for circumventing the rules—as of this writing—is through the distinction between "hard money" and "soft money." Hard money is the designation used for donations made to the candidate or the campaign; hard money is subject to all the restrictions of the campaign finance laws. When the campaign is actively engaged in activities aimed at seeking voter support or actively requests that voters vote against a particular candidate, it is required to spend hard money on those efforts.

Soft money refers to donations made to the candidate's party rather than to the candidates themselves (Corrado, 1997; Magleby & Holt, 1999; Smith, 1998). Soft money is usually donated by corporations, labor unions, and wealthy individuals. As long as it is donated to the party and not to individual candidates, soft money is not regulated and can be given in unlimited amounts.

There is also no limit on how much of this sort of soft money can be spent. The only limits on soft money are how it is spent. Soft money is viewed as the party's money, not that of the candidate. Theoretically, soft money can be used to promote party activities and party views, but is not supposed to be used to actively solicit votes for any specific candidate. It is supposed to be used only for getting out the vote and other general political activities. From a practical perspective, however, it is often used to a candidate's benefit by coming just short of using forbidden words, such as "vote for" or "vote against." In essence, such ads can say "Congressman X is one of us. He supports us with his vote by opposing abortion on demand and gun control. He supports us in the U.S. House of Representatives." A hard money ad can say, "Congressman X is one of us. He supports us with his vote by opposing abortion on demand and gun control. Vote for X and keep him in the U.S. House of Representatives."

One of the most open uses of soft money during the 2000 elections came from the Virginia-based Republican Majority Issues Committee, which sought to raise $25 million in donations that ranged from $500,000 to $3 million while promising its donors that they would remain anonymous. Such an approach is legal, provided that neither the group nor its ads explicitly tell voters which candidates to vote for or against, the committee receives no guidance from Republican congressional or party leaders, and it does not coordinate its efforts with any of the candidates it supports. If a group meets those three requirements, it is not required to register with the Federal Election Commission and, as a result, not required to report its donors nor restrict the size of donations from individuals.

When using soft money, the campaigns walk a fine line adhering to the legal requirements while maximizing expenditures. Some of the techniques they use include:

Staff Transfers.   Once a candidate has received the party's nomination, they typically shift most of the campaign staff to the party headquarters. That allows campaign workers to continue to draw regular paychecks without any of the funds counting against the hard money spending limits.

Consulting Services.   Many consulting services are not considered to be direct efforts to solicit votes. Polling is considered a form of research that is separate from the advertising efforts. Voter turnout programs can be organized to help all of the party's candidates, not just individual candidates. Consequently, payment for such services can come from the party, thus giving the campaign more room to operate under the spending limits.

Issue Ads.   While soft money is—theoretically—not supposed to be used for campaign ads, both parties have frequently done so under the guise of "issue ads" (Magleby & Holt, 1999). Issue ads are legal; both parties have the right to communicate their position on issues that they deem important. To be within the legal guidelines, however, the ads cannot solicit voter support for a candidate. Typically, the parties get around this requirement by simply using the issue ad to address a campaign theme deemed important by the campaign, and then merely omitting the traditional "Vote for Candidate X" line at the end of the ad.

The first major use of issue ads came during the 1996 presidential campaign when both Bill Clinton and Bob Dole used their national party organizations to buy millions of dollars worth of TV spots. The Clinton ads, paid for by the Democratic National Committee, ran almost continuously for more than twelve months before the election in key markets and totaled more than $46 million dollars; the Republicans joined the fray later and spent a similar amount.

Multipack Ads.   Some states have regulations that allow for soft money to be used for candidate advertisements as long as more than one candidate is depicted in each ad. The regulations vary, but a typical requirement is for a "three-pack," which means at least three different candidates must be mentioned in the ad. The intent of such regulations was to allow party advertisements that argue for the election of a partisan "team" of candidates, but both parties have used the law to support individual candidates. The technique is simple. The thirty-second ad is designed with twenty-six seconds devoted to the targeted candidate; the names and postage stamp–sized photos of two other candidates (sometimes candidates who have no opposition) are flashed during the final four seconds to make the ad a legal use of soft money.

Both issue ads and multipack ads skirt the intent of the original law, but the candidates generally go unpunished because of the ambiguity of the amended versions of the laws. In 1998, auditors at the Federal Election Commission ruled that both Clinton and Dole had exceeded their spending limits by using the soft money ads, but the commission decided not to pursue enforcement because of the vagueness of the legislative requirements (Drinkard, 2000). The practical effect of that decision was to give the presidential candidates of both parties almost total control of the budgets of their party's organization.

Third-Party Independent Expenditures.   Despite the limits on campaign donations and expenditures, most court decisions have interpreted the freedom of speech principle to mean that the government cannot limit the political activity of groups who wish to participate in the political process as long as the group's activities are not coordinated with those of a campaign (Magleby & Holt, 1999). As a result, starting in the late 1970s, the involvement of friendly interest groups in campaigns has increased dramatically (Smith, 1996). Kitchens and Powell (1986) reported on early third-party campaigns by New Right organizations on behalf of Republican candidates. Since then, as Drinkard (2000) noted, "They have grown more active with phone banks and ads that praise candidates who agree with them and rap those who don't." The 2000 campaigns saw such activities on behalf of candidates from both parties. The AFL-CIO, the Sierra Club environmental organization, and several abortion-rights groups spent millions to help Democratic candidates, while the National Right to Life Committee, the Republican Leadership Council, Americans for Tax Reform, and several other groups did the same for Republicans.

PAC and Candidate Donations.   Contributors who have donated the limit to the candidate of their choice can still make donations to group and individual political action committees. Those PACs, in turn, can potentially donate up to $5,000 to an individual candidate. Furthermore, contributors can also donate the legal maximum to other candidates, even if those candidates have no competition. Those unchallenged incumbents can then legally donate their collected funds to other candidates within their party who do face opposition. Consequently, many powerful incumbents maintain major fund-raising organizations; by raising huge sums of money, they discourage challengers from taking a serious look at them while simultaneously raising funds that can be used by other candidates with tougher campaigns. By using their money in that manner, incumbents can become "political benefactors" to other candidates in their party (Baker, 1989).

Fund-Raising Techniques

Techniques for raising campaign funds are unlimited, but a few tried-and-true tactics have been employed for a number of years in various combinations. Among the most common are host events, direct mail, online contributions, and bundling.

Host Events

A favorite fund-raising technique at all levels is the hosted fund-raiser. In most cases, the event is treated as a social occasion in which a select few have an opportunity to mingle with the candidate and to show their support for the campaign. The host is a major donor who typically sets an example by making a sizable donation to the campaign. At the local level, the event may include informal receptions, teas, or coffees (Thomas, 1999, p. 68–72). As the size of the campaign grows, so does the guest list and the formality of the event. At statewide or presidential levels, the event may be a dinner with a celebrity guest speaker (or, in some cases, several), with rival campaigns touting their various celebrity donors. During the 2000 Democratic primary, Al Gore was supported by actors Kevin Costner and Chevy Chase, musician Quincy Jones, and TV executives Norman Lear and Grant Tinker. Republican George W. Bush counted actor Chuck Norris among his financial supporters.

In May 2000, the Democratic National Committee set a one-day fund-raising record of more than $23 million with its "Gala Tribute to President Clinton." The event featured a visit from the president and performances by singer Stevie Wonder and actor-comedian Robin Williams. Ten unions donated $500,000 each to the event, twenty other groups or individuals anted up $250,000. Other tickets sold for as little as $50 each.

The prime example of a hosted fund-raiser for an individual candidate belongs to the losing Democratic contender in the 2000 campaign, Bill Bradley. Bradley listed actors Tom Selleck, Paul Reiser, and Steve Guttenberg among his supporters, but his most visible supporters were former professional basketball players whom Bradley knew from the days when he played the game. A number of those former players collaborated to host a fund-raiser for Bradley at Madison Square Garden that garnered more than $1.5 million (Dao, 1999).

Direct Mail

Richard Viguerie's (1975) description of direct mail as a "sleeping giant" is based largely on the capacity of the medium for raising money. During the late 1970s and early 1980s, Viguerie's consulting firm raised millions of dollars for Republican causes and candidates using direct mail. But Viguerie has not been alone in using direct mail for political fund-raising. In the 1972 presidential election, the Nixon campaign raised money using a mailing list of 65,000 contributors, while Morris Dees developed a mailing list of 165,000 names to raise money for George McGovern and Jimmy Carter (O'Leary, 2000).

Justification for a direct-mail solicitation are limited only by the imagination of the candidates and their consultants. During the 2000 Republican primary, Arizona senator John McCain sent out 40,000 letters before his wife's birthday, asking supporters to send a special birthday contribution to his campaign; the approach raised more than $63,000. California's Republican congressman Jim Rogan used a similar approach, but in reverse; the letter to

Bradley's Sports Heroes

In their never-ending search for campaign funds, candidates sometimes use celebrities to help them attract the cash. While raising money for his 2000 presidential campaign, Democrat Bill Bradley, a former professional basketball player, effectively used his connections to sports for that purpose.

Bradley started by recruiting his former college teammate at Princeton, Rick Wright, as finance director. Next came his former roommate on the New York Knicks, Dave DeBusschere, who hosted a fund-raiser on Wall Street at Mickey Mantle's sports bar. Others who joined his effort included Los Angeles Lakers coach Phil Jackson, and Washington Wizards owner Abe Pollin, who raised $500,000 at a brunch.

The biggest single fund-raiser of this type came in November 1999 when Bradley hosted a "Champions and Legends" extravaganza at Madison Square Garden that drew 5,000 people and raised $1.5 million with a program that included Julius Erving, Bob Cousy, Moses Malone, and Kareem Abdul Jabbar (Dao, 1999).

Nor were the celebrities limited to sports. Also attending were director Spike Lee, rock musician Bruce Hornsby, and actors Harvey Keitel and Ethan Hawke. The *New York Times* called it "one of the largest, slickest and most unusual political fund-raisers in memory."

To promote the event, several stars appeared on the talk show circuit on behalf of Bradley on the morning that it was held, with basketball stars appearing on *Face the Nation* (Julius Erving, Oscar Robertson, Dave DeBusschere), *Meet the Press* (Bill Russell, Jerry Lucas), and *This Week* (Willis Reed, Earl Monroe, Phil Jackson). The event itself was covered by both political and sports reporters.

Tickets were available through a ticket agency and on the Internet, leading to attendance by a large number of people who did not normally go to political fund-raisers. And, unlike many political fund-raisers, this one generated a large amount of favorable press coverage for Bradley.

---

supporters came from his wife, who included a birthday card addressed to her husband for the supporter to sign and send along with their donation. The Rogan piece was the work of direct mail consultant the Lukens Cook Company; the same company produced a piece for Kentucky congressman Jim Bunning that featured a letter written in a child's scrawl and was reportedly signed by Bunning's eight-year-old granddaughter. It included one line that read, "I talked with Miss Debbie (Grandpa's campaign manager) and Mr. David (his finance director) and they told me we must raise $50,000 to get Grandpa on TV more."

One of the most memorable uses of direct mail, though, came in a 1999 effort by the House Republican Campaign Committee. In early 1999, the committee spent more than $30,000 to send out a computerized fund-raising letter, but ran into trouble when a computer foulup mistakenly sent some of the letters to the wrong people. No problem. In June, the committee sent out another letter asking for donations to cover the snafu and to save the job of the person who got blamed for the error (Drinkard & Pound, 1999).

Online Contributions

One major change in the 2000 elections was the extent to which the Internet became an avenue for raising campaign funds. Overall, the four major candidates in the 2000 presidential election (John McCain, Al Gore, George W. Bush, and Bill Bradley) raised more

Making Lemonade out of Lemons

In early 1999, the National Republican Campaign Committee spent more than $30,000 on a direct-mail solicitation, only to have some of the letters sent to the wrong addresses because of a computer malfunction. When the mailer produced lower-than-expected returns, a second letter was sent that used the error as justification for another solicitation (Drinkard & Pound, 1999).

The letter was signed by Patty Catano, the committee's mail supervisor. She apologized for the earlier mistake, one that caused some people on the solicitation list to receive other people's mail.

"Frankly, I've never been so upset in my life and haven't slept well since this happened," the letter read. "I even thought about selling my car to help pay for my error. But the truth is, I don't have that much money saved, and my old car just isn't worth that much money."

The letter went on to ask donors to send $125 or more to help her erase the $37,358.31 cost of the previous mailing, noting that she might have to resign if she couldn't raise the money ("I am a very serious person, and my parents taught me to take full responsibility for my actions. I am hoping with all my heart that you'll find some way to help me out.")

The letter implied that Catano was responsible for the mistake. Actually, the fault lay with the consulting firm that had subcontracted for the work.

---

than $9 million from online contributions. Three (Gore, McCain, and Bradley) raised more than a million dollars each online, and one (McCain), more than $6 million. Online contributions accounted for about 25 percent of McCain's total campaign budget, but less than one-half of one percent of George W. Bush's funds came from the Internet (Noble & Kennedy, 2000).

The advantage of the Internet as a fund-raising mechanism is that it is politics' version of an "impulse buy" (Drinkard, 2000). Supporters can show their enthusiasm for a candidate by going online and using their credit cards to express their support and approval immediately. Not surprisingly, then, the biggest influxes of cash from online sources tend to come after major events. The thirteen Republicans who led the U.S. House's impeachment efforts in the Senate trial of President Clinton also used the Internet to try to raise campaign funds for Republican congressmen who supported the impeachment ("Impeach This," 2000). John McCain collected more than $400,000 online within 48 hours of his victory in the 2000 New Hampshire Republican primary (Drinkard, 2000) and more than $2.8 million in the weeks that followed (Noble & Kennedy, 2000). McCain also broadened the use of the Internet, scheduling a live online fund-raiser that was the first event of its kind—a $100-per-person "town hall" meeting online at the College of Charleston.

An additional advantage of online fund-raising is that it develops a database of individual donors who can be asked to donate again at a later date. Forty percent of the online donors were first-time givers to a presidential campaign, and the typical donation was between $105 and $115—well below the maximum level of allowable donations. To be successful, though, the candidate's web site must be designed to facilitate fund-raising activities. Jalonick (2000) noted that the three crucial elements of success were to ask them to donate, don't make them search for a place onscreen to contribute, and don't use technology that you're not equipped to handle. In essence, the web site must make it easy for potential contributors to donate their money and easy for the campaign to handle the money that comes in.

The Internet was such a major source of campaign funds in Campaign 2000 that it caught the Federal Election Commission by surprise (Whillock, 2001). The commission found itself having to issue a number of rulings on issues that it had never faced before. Generally, though, campaign web sites are subject to similar sponsorship requirements as are other campaign media (FEC Advisory Opinion #1988–2, 1998), but those requirements are not placed on individuals using their home equipment (FEC Advisory Opinion #1999–17, 1999). The most important ruling, though, for fund-raising purposes was the revision that allowed credit card contributions to be eligible for federal matching funds, with the provision that the campaign report the name of the donor, and the donor's occupation and employer for any contribution over $200 (FEC Advisory Opinion #1999–9, 1999).

Bundling

Limits on campaign contributions are also intended to limit the influence that any one contributor can have on a candidate. One by-product of the laws, however, is that the relatively low ceiling on the limits makes it impossible for the candidates to seek such contributions on an individual basis. A presidential candidate with a budget of $30 million, for example, would have to meet individually with more than 30,000 different people to have a chance to solicit funds in that amount. Campaigns handle that (and simultaneously get around the intent of the law) by using a process known as "bundling."

Major contributors are asked to provide "bundles" of campaign contributions that include their contribution, contributions from other family members, and contributions from their employees and/or business associates. In the 2000 election, for example, George W. Bush raised more than $70 million for his primary campaign; while all of the individual contributions were within the legal limit, most of that money was raised by only 200 people, super-fund-raisers who were known in the Bush camp as "Pioneers" (Hitt, 1999). Al Gore used a similar technique in the 1996 election when his visit to a Buddhist temple served as the impetus for a bundling event. Legally, there is nothing wrong with the approach, but it represents a tactic that the framers of the law had not anticipated. As a result, there is no legal requirement for the candidate or the campaign to identify who the super-fundraisers are. In fact, some reformers approve of bundling (*Nixon* v. *Carver,* U.S. District Court 518, U.S. 1033, Springfield, MO, 1996). In essence, then, bundling is a process which simultaneously makes it easier for campaigns to raise money while also allowing major contributors a chance to provide campaigns with major sources of funds. The latter factor, in essence, circumvents the intent of the campaign finance laws.

Summary

An effective fund-raising program is usually the result of a well-planned and executed program that involves a great deal of time and labor devoted to that effort. Perhaps that's why consultant Carl Silverberg (2000) described "discipline" as the most important ingredient in fund-raising efforts. If the effort is successful, the campaign gains at least four rhetorical advantages. Fund-raising enhances credibility, attracts media attention, increases subsequent fund-raising, and decreases the opposition. Early fund-raising enhances a candidate's credibility, draws media attention to the campaign, bestows legitimacy to the campaign efforts, and puts pressure on the competition to raise a comparable amount. Increased media attention can generate even more donations, putting pressure on the competitors and possibly driving some of them out of the race.

Campaign funds are raised amid a set of rules that govern campaign contributions, reporting, and spending limitations, but campaigns often use "soft" money to circumvent at least some of these requirements. Traditional techniques for raising funds include the use of host events, direct mail, and "bundling" plans in which major donors serve as surrogate fund-raisers. More recently, the Internet has provided a means of online fund-raising through which supporters can use their credit cards to make "impulse donations" to a campaign.

Overall, though, the financial side of political communication is full of potential ethical and legal potholes that can create problems for the candidate, the campaign, the donors, and the voters. As new campaign laws have been developed, loopholes have always been detected and unintended consequences emerged that have affected the campaign process (Smith, 1996).

QUESTIONS FOR DISCUSSION

1. A multimillionaire candidate for governor, who had lost several major statewide races that he had largely funded himself, was determined to be successful in a political endeavor. Beginning very early, he raised funds for his gubernatorial race from all possible sources. Seven months before the election he had raised four times as much money as all other candidates. As campaign manager for one of his opponents, what would you do to counter this financial advantage? As his campaign press secretary how to you keep news coverage of his financial success continuing?

2. Why do the news media spend so much time reporting how much money a candidate raises?

3. One candidate for governor raised more funds than were permitted under the laws of his state. As a result, his opponent received a windfall in the final two weeks of the campaign in the form of a cash payment from the state—one of the penalties placed on a candidate for exceeding fund-raising limits. As a result, in the last two weeks of the election, the first candidate was criticized for his excessive funds and poor campaign management. Meanwhile, his opponent was able to purchase more advertising and visibility than anyone expected. Was this fair? Why or why not?

4. In an open city council race, one candidate raised very little money. However, third-party advertisements supported him unanimously. Generally, the amounts of money actually spent on the campaign was the same on both sides. Was this fair?

5. Your campaign has decided to use the Internet as the major fund-raising avenue for a secretary of state campaign. As campaign manager, what strategies and tactics do you use to maximize contributions? As campaign manager for the opponent, what strategies and tactics do you use to minimize the value of those contributions?

13 The Role of Interpersonal Influence

As he arrived for work one morning, John remembered a story on the evening news the night before about a presidential candidate's position on an environmental issue. John was an assistant manager of an automotive tire plant, and petroleum-based waste was a common by-product of the production process. Would the candidate's new position on this issue affect his industry? His job? His paycheck? He would have to see what others at the plant thought.

John's inquisitiveness illustrates the importance of interpersonal influence, or opinion leadership, in modern political persuasion. Most modern theories of political influence assume that opinion leadership plays a pivotal role. Voters evaluate the opinions of others while forming their own opinions (Mutz, 1998). As they move toward and make their individual political decisions, they argue with and inform one another about the candidates and their issues (Huckfeldt & Sprague, 1995). Various theories disagree on the specifics of its role and the relationship of opinion leadership to media use, but nearly all specify a significant relationship of some type. The limited effects model views interpersonal opinion influence as a mitigating factor that limits the impact of the media. Agenda-setting views interpersonal discussions as reflective of media priorities. Uses-Gratification views "interpersonal utility" as one of the reasons that voters seek information from the news. In each case, the theory proposes a link between what voters see or read in the news and what they discuss with other voters. What people discuss with others, it turns out, may be more influential than what they receive as information from the media.

The topic represents one area of political campaign communication research in which there are major divergences between the views of academicians and consultants. Most academic research on the topic has focused on the role of interpersonal opinion leadership as it affects public opinion, an approach represented by the example at the beginning of this chapter. But the concept of interpersonal influence has a much broader view among consultants, one that includes interpersonal opinion leadership, diffusion of information, elite leaders, lobbyists, and legislative leadership.

Interpersonal Opinion Leadership

The Two-Step Flow

The concept of interpersonal influence was first introduced into modern political communication theory as an explanation of the "rule of minimal effects," or limited effects model, discussed in an earlier chapter (Klapper, 1960). Katz and Lazarsfeld (1955) suggested the "two-step flow" as one explanation for these minimal effects whereby more knowledgeable and active opinion leaders processed and passed on campaign information to their friends and associates. Berelson, Lazarsfeld, and McPhee (1954) and Lazarsfeld, Berelson, and Gaudet (1968) reinforced this view, arguing that one reason the media had a limited effect on voting behavior was because the media were subordinate to interpersonal influence. When faced with voting decisions, many voters simply did not rely on information from the media and instead sought advice from people they respected, either to find out how to vote or to reinforce a decision already made (Rogers & Cartano, 1962). Thus much political information reached the public only after it had passed through interpersonal channels. Interpersonal opinion leaders interpreted the media in light of the social predispositions of their community and passed those interpretations along to other members of the social groups. The result of these interpersonal discussions was that the media reinforced attitudes rather than changed them. Mass persuasion, it was argued, was subordinate to interpersonal influence. In this framework, opinion leaders are an essential element for the effective transmission of media information to the public. Information first reaches opinion leaders, who subsequently pass their interpretation of the information along to their followers.

Problems with that notion soon became apparent. Researchers had trouble identifying who were opinion leaders and who were not. Opinion leadership differed from topic to topic, and designating a particular person within a social group as the opinion leader became difficult. Furthermore, data from the original study by Katz and Lazarsfeld (1955) indicated that most of the interpersonal discussions generated by the media were horizontal in nature—between social equals—rather than a downward transmission from leaders to followers. As a result, researchers in opinion leadership soon shifted their focus to an analysis of social influence produced by those horizontal interpersonal discussions.

Interpersonal Utility *(Anticipated Communications)*

One approach to studying interpersonal discussion is interpersonal utility, a concept developed in the uses-gratification approach to media effects. Interpersonal utility refers to the idea that information obtained from the media serves as a storehouse of data for interpersonal discussions between friends and in the workplace. The function springs from our needs to have information to use when talking with others. The media are viewed as sources of information, outlets that provide verbal ammunition for future discussions or arguments with others. For those who actively participate in elections, interpersonal conversations about politics is a frequent activity. Election time stimulates a round of coffee-shop, e-mail, and telephone exchanges as political junkies seek to stay up to date on the latest political information. Their talk will include exchanges of information, political arguments, and issue-specific news as political activists express their views and exchange information with others (Wyatt, Kim, & Katz, 2000).

Several subcategories of interpersonal utility have been identified. Swanson (1976) divided it into three subcategories: political discussions with friends, offering advice to others, and asking others for advice. Other suggested uses have included information-seeking and opinion-leadership needs (gathering information so we can offer opinions on an issue). Nor is the interpersonal utility of political information limited to information or decision-making purposes. Voters also use political media as a source of information for informal discussion and entertainment. Political jokes are frequently exchanged in this manner. Television comedians such as Jay Leno and David Letterman become the source of new jokes that later become fodder for the interpersonal context. During 1998 and 1999, the controversy surrounding President Clinton's relationship with a White House intern eventually led to impeachment proceedings against the president; the late-night television shows, meanwhile, provided jokes that were later retold in interpersonal and work-related environments (Powell & Kitchens, 1999).

Interpersonal utility views the process from the view of the voter, not the political candidate. Voters discuss political stimuli when it is useful for them to do so, not when campaigns want them to do it. Neuman (1986) argues that voters use discussions with opinion leaders as a filtering mechanism that allows them to bypass most of the political information that comes from campaigns. As Neuman (1986) wrote, "It is unnecessary to recompile and reevaluate all the available political data when a trusted friend or colleague has already completed the task" (p. 173).

Rumors

Rumors refer to interpersonal communication constructed around unauthenticated information (Rosnow & Fine, 1976, p. 11). They can have a dramatic impact on political campaigns. Some political rumors occur spontaneously, but others are carefully constructed by consultants or other campaign agents. When they develop spontaneously, they typically reflect a group effort to define what is occurring. In those instances, Allport and Postman (1947) argue that the foundation of rumors is laid when events are important and news is lacking or ambiguous; the resulting rumors reflect a normal desire to find meaning in events, even though the attempt might prove dysfunctional (p. 144). Spontaneous political rumors often surface during times of political turmoil. For example, rumors continue to circulate regarding the assassinations of President John F. Kennedy, Martin Luther King, Jr., and Robert F. Kennedy.

In other instances, campaign rumors may be a packaged story that is deliberately planted as a political whispering campaign (Rosnow & Fine, 1976, pp. 27–29). Such campaigns are nothing new. Andrew Jackson's campaign for the presidency was tainted by rumors spread by the opposition that he and his wife lived together in adultery. Martin Van Buren was rumored to be the illegitimate son of Aaron Burr. During the 1972 presidential election, the Nixon campaign used a number of "dirty tricksters" to spread rumors about George McGovern and the other Democratic presidential hopefuls. Sometimes such campaigns can be dramatically effective; the Nixon campaign succeeded in driving Senator Edmund Muskie out of the race. The manipulative use of rumors can continue even after the elections. Government officials initiate rumors on a number of issues as a trial balloon to test public reaction. News leaks are an organized form of rumor initiation that allows officials to release information without attribution.

Political rumors can be especially powerful because of the rhetorical situation in which they occur. Allport and Postman (1947) noted that the seeds for rumors are planted when the issue is salient and information is ambiguous. The emotional content of many political campaigns, coupled with the equivocation that often dominates political speeches, provides a fertile field for rumors to grow. As a result, organized efforts to spread rumors can be dramatically effective. And, with the advent and anonymity of the Internet, campaigns have a quick and effective means of planting such information.

Diffusion of Information

One limitation of the two-step flow is that subsequent research failed to verify the existence of any two-step process in the diffusion of political information. Quite the contrary, information diffusion seemed to be more reflective of a multistep process. People receive information from the media, discuss it with friends, get more information, and exchange that with other friends. Through continuous repetition of this process, political news is diffused (sometimes gradually, sometimes quickly) throughout the general population. As Kraus and Davis (1976) described the process, "It suggests that messages flow from sources and are eventually absorbed and used by individuals just as rainwater influences the growth of plants" (p. 125). If the news is about a high-profile discrete event, the information flows quickly. Many people hear about such events by talking with others, not through the media directly (Kingdon, 1970; Ostlund, 1973). Research in this area has looked at a variety of such topics, including the spread of news about President John F. Kennedy's assassination (Greenberg, 1964; Mendelsohn, 1964), the attempted assassinations of George Wallace (Steinfatt et al., 1973) and President Ronald Reagan (Gantz, 1983; Weaver-Lariscy, Sweeney, & Steinfatt, 1984), the explosion of the space shuttle Challenger (Riffe & Stovall, 1989), and the first human heart transplant (O'Keefe, 1969). Research studies have also examined the role of the media in diffusion of information about public issues, including health issues related to influenza epidemics and HIV/AIDS, crime prevention, and the "Just Say No" antidrug campaign advocated by former first lady Nancy Reagan. Sometimes the diffusion process has been dramatic; Warren (1972) found that diffusion of information about a racial incident in Detroit led to a polarization of attitudes among whites and African Americans, with TV viewers experiencing the greatest polarization.

Rogers's (1995) work on the diffusion of innovation includes the role of opinion leadership. It suggested that new information reaches the public through a series of steps, with change occurring gradually. The new concept is typically initiated by the candidates or political elites, and then passed on to the media and opinion leaders. Interpersonal influence plays a pivotal role in the late diffusion process, because some people are skeptical and embrace new information only after getting verification from others.

Factors Affecting Diffusion

Sometimes diffusion of information occurs quickly, as with reports on the attempted assassination of President Reagan. In other incidents, the diffusion may occur more slowly or at various speeds within different social groups. Several factors appear to influence how quickly any specific piece of information spreads, but three seem to dominate: the trust in the media, the relevance of the information, and interpersonal peer networks.

Media Credibility.   Voters are more likely to pass on information they receive from the media if they trust the source to provide valid information. Deutschmann and Danielson

(1960) noted that interpersonal communication on political issues is usually a response to mass media reports; it typically occurs only after the information is first presented in the media. Stamm and Dube (1994) reported a positive relationship between high levels of media trust and high levels of involvement. Rogers (1995, p. 27) noted that those people most likely to influence others are generally more exposed to all forms of external communication.

Generally, television news has the most credibility with most voters. Stempel and Hargrove (1996) found that most people (70 percent) use local TV news as their primary source of news, followed by network TV news, newspapers, and radio. Talk radio, TV magazines, and grocery store tabloids were used less frequently as reliable sources of information. Gunther (1988) found a positive relationship between trust in television and newspapers for a moderate level of issue importance. Gunther and Lasorsa (1986) found a positive relationship between perceived issue importance and trust in newspapers.

Information Relevance.   Political junkies are more likely to diffuse political information than will the public as a whole. That phenomenon is hardly surprising, considering that research has shown that voters are more likely to discuss news in the media if the news is perceived as being relevant to their own lives (Basil & Brown, 1994). High issue relevance spurs questions about opinions and a desire to gather more information for decision making (Chew, 1994), particularly if the perceived consequences of the issue is a positive one for the individual (Rogers, 1995, pp. 30–31). Another form of relevance that affects diffusion is "personalized risk," which is an individual's belief about the likelihood of personal injury or property damage and the individual's perception of control over the situation. Taylor's cognitive adaptation theory (1983) assumes that when people get information from the media that is perceived as a personalized risk, they attempt to gain mastery over the event or its consequences. One way to handle such information, particularly if it is political in nature, is to discuss those potential consequences with others.

Relevance is also a factor that affects ideologically based issues. Miller and Shanks (1996) noted that a variety of predispositions, preferences, or perceptions can motivate voters who are strongly ideological. "This kind of activation is doubtless reinforced by informal communications among other, similarly inclined members of the same social category, as well as by more formal efforts to mobilize members of organized groups defined in terms of those categories," they wrote (p. 497).

Interpersonal Networks.   Miller and Shanks's (1996) emphasis on reinforcement within social categories also points to another critical factor: interpersonal networks. Diffusion is more likely to occur, and occur quickly, among those individuals who have active interpersonal peer networks or who live in social systems with active interpersonal networks. For diffusion purposes, Rogers (1995, p. 23) defined a social system "as a set of interrelated units that are engaged in joint problem-solving to accomplish a common goal." Social systems are often related to socioeconomic status; voters in higher socioeconomic groups generally have broader interpersonal networks. Furthermore, socioeconomic status is strongly related to public affairs knowledge, and that knowledge is increased when the individuals also have high media use and consider the information useful (McLeod & Perse, 1994). In essence, the more people you know, and the broader your range of associations, the more quickly information can be diffused to a larger audience.

Political Elites

Political observers watched with interest in 1999 and 2000 as Arizona senator John McCain ran a surprisingly strong, although ultimately unsuccessful, campaign for the presidency. Many pundits attributed McCain's early success to shifts in public opinion, arguing that his campaign addressed themes that generated frequent interpersonal discussions about him among friends and coworkers. Sometimes overlooked is that McCain's very presence in politics was at least partly due to a different form of opinion leadership: elite leaders. McCain had no ties to Arizona until he married Cindy Hensley and moved there in 1981. His wife's father, beer baron James W. Hensley, helped finance McCain's first race for Congress in 1982 (Frantz, 2000). Adding to McCain's edge was the support of another political elite, Darrow Tully. Tully, the publisher of Arizona's biggest newspaper (*The Arizona Republic*), ensured that McCain was the darling of the state's business establishment. With Hensley's money and Tully's endorsement, McCain was able to outspend and defeat better-known opponents.

That early success illustrates the role that political elites play in political campaigns. This collection of active politicos and members of social and professional groups who are active in the political process has been tagged with a number of descriptive labels including the "para-political system" (Easton, 1965), a "para-political subsystem" (Donahue, Tichenor, & Olien, 1972), and "intermediate relations and ties" (Suine & Kline, 1976). Regardless of the terminology, research has generally viewed political elites as a stabilizing force that balances the upward and downward communication between government and voters (Donahue, Tichenor, & Olien, 1972). As an upward channel, the intermediate relationships increase active participation. As a downward channel, the parapolitical ties provides a context for processing and receiving messages, thus serving as "social anchors for evaluating and contextualizing messages" (Siune & Kline, 1976).

These power brokers have an influence on public opinion that can extend beyond their financial help and personal ties. Neuman (1986) calls them political elites, a subgroup of political sophisticates who participate in political activities and "respond to political stimuli" (p. 103). They are distinguished from other voters by three variables: their knowledge of politics, the salience of political issues to them, and the complexity of their conceptualization of politics and campaigns. Despite the potential powers of political elites, they are limited by the sparsity of numbers. For the democratic process to work, Neuman argues that "it remains important to balance the specialized knowledge of the elite and the generalized common sense of the mass polity" (p. 189).

Politicians value and seek out political elites to enhance their chances of electoral success (Nimmo, 1970; Shadegg, 1972). As such, political elites become persuasive targets of a political campaign effort, resulting in them serving an intermediary role in which they are both sources and receivers of information. As a result of elites' direct contact with politicians, subordinates view the elite as a secondary source of information, someone who can obtain data and can pass them on to them. At the same time, as targets of the persuasive efforts of politicians, elites are receivers of campaign messages and not simply channels for further diffusion.

The communication process between politicians and elites differs in channel, style, and goals. In most cases, politicians prefer to communicate directly to the elite, either through personal contact or personal letters (Powell & Shelby, 1985). There is correspondingly less reliance on television or other forms of mass media. When the mass media are used, the persuasive goal often differs from that of normal campaign communication. In a process known as "laying cover," politicians or special-interest groups may use a mass media campaign in an effort to convince political elites that popular opinion is on their side. Even there, though, the ultimate argument is made through direct contact instead of through the media.

The style and goal of candidate-elite communication also differs from other campaign communications. Politicians feel less need to be friendly, representative, or easy to talk to when conversing with elites, as compared to contacts with voters (Powell & Shelby, 1985). As less attention is paid to these skills, the effective candidate is likely to increase his or her active listening skills when dealing with political elites (Joy, 2001). It becomes more important that candidates understand the elite's position on issues. Part of that shift in skill usage is a by-product of the directness of the messages exchanged in such settings, and part may come from the interpersonal channels used. The personal contact represents an affirmation of the political elite's worth, as acknowledged by the politician. Such acknowledgment may be the crucial communicative goal for both the politician and the political elites.

Still, the role of interpersonal influence is not limited to politician-elite interactions. Some groups and individuals have developed programs that target political elites for lobbying efforts. An Alabama estate lawyer who launched a campaign to repeal the federal estate tax used political elites as a crucial part of his campaign effort. Birmingham lawyer Harold Apolinsky identified fifty congressmen who were not yet supporting the bill and targeted thirty of their donors who had given the maximum $1,000 contribution. He contacted each of those contributors and asked them to call the legislators and urge them to support the repeal of the tax (Brumas, 2000).

Political Lobbying

A very specific type of political elite who is actively involved in the political process is the political lobbyist. Lobbyists are an often overlooked factor in the political process, and yet their influence likely exceeds that of any other type of political consultant. As of 1999, Washington, D.C. was the working home of more than 20,000 lobbyists. That number far exceeds the number of professionals who make their living as campaign consultants, and represents nearly forty lobbyists for each member of Congress. The money involved (more than $1.4 billion in 1999) makes even George W. Bush's campaign war chest seem small, and that number only covers the federal government. Add in the massive number of lobbyists in each state capital, and a staggering number of people are involved in the lobbying process.

Nature of the Profession

Dexter (1969, p. 4) defined lobbying as a process of addressing or soliciting support from a legislative body. Their job is simple: to have influence over legislation (Lane, 1964, p. 4) and to validate the role that their group plays in policy making. They remind legislators that they are around and that their views should be considered when policy decisions are made. They keep in touch with interest group allies and try to spur them on. The constant interaction is a means of exchanging information, developing strategy, and politely supporting and pushing other groups.

Interview with George Clark

Lobbying State Legislatures

George Clark, the Executive Director of the Alabama Industry and Manufacturers Association, has worked as a lobbyist for several years. He was a member of the Alabama legislature before that.

Q: What are lobbyists, and what do they do?

A: There are several different types of lobbyists. Contract lobbyists work for various clients who have the money to pay an individual to lobby for them. They're sometimes referred to as "hired guns," and they may be hired by a company, a coalition of companies, or a coalition of interests. Supposedly, the only limitation on their clients would be conflicts of interests with clients they currently represent or an issue that they just personally believe is something they don't want to do. That may be a personal decision on their part, or a business decision. Some contract lobbyists may say, "I'm not going to represent this particular interest, because it could hurt me financially down the road in representing the type of clientele that I want to build up." A second type are the trade representatives, lobbyists who represent a trade association; they stick to whatever their association's interests are. Third, there's a broad group of grassroots lobbyists who may or may not be compensated for what they do. They are often average citizens who believe in a particular issue. It may deal in social issues such as the death penalty, or it could be an issue like gambling, where a coalition of churches get together and lobby against a gambling proposal before the legislature. Sometimes these are one-time organizations, but we're finding more and more that are groups like the Christian Coalition, who have a loose-knit organization. It may be a year or two between issues when they come to the legislature, but they do maintain some type of organizational effort. And fourth, there's a miscellaneous category of state agencies and people on the state payroll. They're merit system employees, and they lobby for their particular department's budget. Included in that group is higher education, who sometimes get the support of alumni and friends of the university involved in their lobbying efforts.

Q: What makes a successful lobbying effort?

A: Several factors. One is the individual lobbyist and his or her contacts; if a lobbyist is well liked on a personal level, they're able to advance their issues better. Second, the amount of money that a lobbyist gives to a candidate and their reelection efforts. Third, the grassroots support behind a measure. If an issue has broad-based support, or at least well-organized support that appears to be broad-based, and you have individuals from the home district contacting legislators, that lends itself to a successful lobbying effort. And fourth, an issue that meets the "public smell test." It's a lot easier to sell something that is not going to hurt a legislator politically; it's harder to pass a piece of legislation or kill a piece of legislation if that vote will hurt a legislator when it comes to reelection.

Q: You seem to be saying that a lobbyist is not a lone wolf fighting these battles?

A: Yes. And it's getting more that way as we see more complicated issues coming before the legislature. Compared to twenty years ago, you're now seeing more coalitions of interests pooled together, with a number of associations and lobbyists coming together to get legislation passed.

(continued)

Interview with George Clark Continued

Q: Why?

A: The legislature is more diverse than it was twenty years ago—racially, socially, and politically or party-wise. Many times what you'll see on a difficult issue is that a coalition will hire contract lobbyists and work within an association as well. And they will hire people who are known to have contacts with Democrats, with Republicans, and with minorities.

Q: What difference do you see between lobbying at the state level and the national level?

A: A national issue is usually managed by one big broad-based team out of Washington. They tend to act as a coach or quarterback, and they get grassroots involvement in all the states. They'll hire a lobbyist at the state level to do limited work, to contact certain members of Congress. They may hire someone just to get one vote, but that's probably because that particular congressman or senator serves on a particular committee that's important to the issue. The contract lobbyist may be hired to advocate that particular issue to just one person. But that same activity is going on in fifty states.

Q: What about the national lobbyists themselves? What differences are there in the way a national lobbyist and a state lobbyist do their jobs?

A: One of the major differences is that the lobbyist in Washington is dealing with staff members in Congress. In the states, lobbyists deal directly with the legislator—not staff. Another difference is that you use documented reports, evidence, letters from constituents, that type of device, more than you do at the state level. At the state level, it has to be more of a personal relationship than it does in Congress.

Q: But I've also seen state lobbyists go to enormous efforts to develop information on an issue and provide that information to the legislator.

A: Yeah, but not only to the legislator. You provide it to the press as well. That ties in to the public smell test. Legislators want to be liked, and they want to do a good job. They don't want to vote for things that they'll be ridiculed for or criticized for. So it helps if you're able to educate the media so the media says good things and lends its support to an issue. Then you try to educate the legislator on the advantages of that particular piece of legislation. You develop white papers or position papers on an issue to make the legislators comfortable in their decision-making process.

Q: Why is that different from the national level?

A: At the state level, legislators depend on lobbyists for a lot of their information. At the federal level, Congress has staff that advise them on all kinds of issues, and they have the money to hire the staff to gather information. At the state level, they don't, so state legislators depend on lobbyists, to a large extent, to provide them with information. Often a legislator is confronted with different facts or different analyses that would lead you to different conclusions. Then the legislator has to decide which is accurate.

Source: Reprinted by permission of George Clark.

Despite the commonality in goals, lobbyists often differ in the way they do their job. Some rely on letters written by their constituents. Others prefer direct contact with the legislator. For all, they have the responsibility of being the eyes and ears of their organization. They must keep the members of their group aware of policy developments and legislative changes that may affect their clients. Lobbyists are the nerve endings of an interest group, and they spend most of each day carrying messages back and forth between their environment and the organization.

The profession is both maligned and misunderstood. Hamm (1991) noted that few lobbyists engage in unethical activities, and most work long hours to represent their constituents. But the negative images remain anyway, with many being seen as backroom operators with an unethical influence on the laws of the land. Contrary to that image, most try to be as visible as possible. They attend congressional hearings even though nothing much of consequence is likely to happen there. They'll make repeated visits to different Capitol Hill offices, even if they can only leave a message with a secretary. Interminable after-work receptions are a chance to exchange a word or two with legislators. One retired lobbyist was quoted as saying: "I used to get irritated when I'd see my colleagues in on a Tuesday, Wednesday, or Thursday afternoon (Congress's usual days in session). I'd ask them why they weren't on the Hill. You have to be seen. Even if the legislators don't know who you are, if they see you often enough, they'll start to feel you belong" (Checkoway, 1993).

Many professional lobbyists don't even describe themselves as such, referring to their work instead as "public affairs" or "government relations." Aberbach (1990) noted that many resent the "lobbyist" label "because of its unflattering connotations (and) also because it doesn't adequately describe what they do." As a group, they are highly educated (Salisbury, 1989). Many hold advanced college degrees in law, business, or political science.

Turnover, among both lobbyists and politicians, makes the job even harder. Turnover among lobbyists is frequent, with a great deal of movement in and out of lobbying jobs. The typical lobbyist has been in the job for five or fewer years (Orren, 1989). Part of the turnover is likely due to frustration, for theirs is a job in which most policy outcomes are determined by factors beyond their control (Salisbury, 1989). Part of the turnover comes from opportunities in other organizations; competent lobbyists frequently say that their professional contacts within the political arena makes other job opportunities available to them (Checkoway, 1993). Even when there is stability among the lobbying forces, there can still be significant turnover among the legislators with whom they must work. Each new election brings a new group of representatives, initiating a process known as "courting the rookies." When new faces reach the nation's capitals, lobbyists emerge to court these legislators. The basic forms of courting include dinners, sporting events, trips, and gifts. Trips may consist of hunting, fishing, and some trips that might include a small amount of business. Lobbyists send cards on special days, mail flowers to secretaries, give candy and cigars to politicians. Some lobbyists offer services to political officials that include massages from therapists or chiropractic services.

Tools of the Trade

Several factors contribute to their effectiveness. Not surprisingly, those factors share some commonality with other persuasive situations.

Interpersonal Relationships.   The primary communication tool of the lobbyist is interpersonal communication. Their main objective is to build solid relationships and connections with as many legislators as possible. Once a relationship is established, it becomes a
means for lobbying issues later. As one New Jersey lobbyist said, "Before I ask for anything
from them, I try to make friends" (Rosenthal, 1993). Athletics is a major tool, with many
lobbyists jogging, golfing, or playing basketball with legislators. Relationships are developed and maintained even if the legislator generally opposes the lobbyist on most issues.
Issues shift and coalitions change, and a lobbyist who may be at odds with a legislator on
one issue may need his or her support on another (Sethi, 1993). A positive relationship is
continued for as long as possible.

Credibility.   One reason that lobbyists are, as a rule, highly ethical in their professional
behavior is that credibility is an essential component of what they do. Their job is persuasive
in nature, and credibility is essential to the persuasive process. They readily admit this; the
need to protect their credibility is the top priority for the job (McCaid, 1989). If they lose that
credibility, for whatever reason, their job (and their reputation) is threatened. "Washington is
a village," Aberbach (1990) wrote. "You are known by your good name and integrity." Similarly, as one lobbyist told Orren (1989), if you mislead a member of Congress, "you can
expect a member never to listen to you seriously." Another corporate lobbyist told McCaid
(1989), "all you have is your word." The emphasis on credibility starts early during the development of the relationship. As the lobbyists get to know an individual legislator, they look
for ways to demonstrate their friendship and credibility to the legislator.

Money.   Lobbyists are a generous source of campaign contributions (Rosenthal, 1993,
p. 129) and frequently set up political action committees for that purpose. Money helps
them to elect friendly legislators, candidates who are more likely to share their philosophical leaning. Campaign contributions open doors for later lobbying efforts, and creates
obligations that a legislator can repay by at least listening to the lobbyist's position. The
money factor is not limited to campaign contributions. Lobbyists also lavish money on
entertainment for legislators—"fact-finding" trips to vacation spots, receptions, and meals.
There are a number of restaurants in Washington, D.C., for example, where a member of
Congress can enter at nearly any time, knowing that they are unlikely to have to buy their
own meal. Some lobbyist who is also dining there will invariably pay for the meal.

Research.   Aberbach (1990) noted that the lobbyists' messages are guided by one principle: "The more factual the better." Some staff members spend all or most of their time gathering information, separating the useful from the unnecessary (Salisbury, 1989), and
compiling it in a manner that is most useful to both the lobbyist and the legislators. Messages must focus on specific facts. If a lobbyist hopes to persuade a legislator to change his
or her vote on a piece of legislation, he or she must have new information. No legislator will
be influenced without factual support, regardless of how close the relationship is with the
lobbyist. Sometimes new information comes from polling data. Many lobbyists maintain
relationships with political pollsters for that purpose. If a legislator is wavering on a particular vote, lobbyists might provide them with a poll to illustrate how a vote on legislation
might affect their reelection chances. Others seek public support by focusing media attention on the issue (Yanovitzky & Bennett, 1999).

Hamm (1991) argues that the goal of the lobbyist should be to create a dependency by providing the legislator with the right kind of information at the right time. Typically, the "right kind of information" will be arguments that point out the consequences of the proposed legislation (Lau, Smith, & Fiske, 1991). Sethi (1993) noted that the optimal role for lobbyists is that they become trusted sources of information when legislators need data. For that to occur, lobbyists must become experts in their subject of concern. Once they have mastered a complex policy issue and the consequences of policy changes, they become part of the legislative process. Legislators seek them out for advice, and many lobbyists actually assist (sometimes heavily) in the writing and wording of new legislation as policy makers draw on their knowledge to solve difficult issues. Lobbyists will also help a legislator by working to get support from other legislators.

Compromise.   The lobbying profession is one in which most tasks are doomed to failure. Ideal legislation, as defined by the lobbyists and their constituency, is rarely achieved. Instead, most legislation is produced as a compromise between competing positions. Successful lobbyists recognize this fact and aggressively seek workable compromises that are acceptable to all parties (Checkoway, 1993).

The Revolving Door

One unusual aspect of the lobbying profession is the extent to which the roles of legislator and lobbyist are often a revolving door through which former legislators become lobbyists. As of 1999, 138 of Washington's registered lobbyists were former members of Congress, two thirds of whom left the Hill after 1990. Twenty-five percent of those congressmen defeated in the 1994 elections subsequently landed jobs in Washington lobbying firms. Rosenthal (1993, p. 113) noted that 20 percent of the lobbyists in California were former legislators or governmental staff workers. The advantage of the revolving door is that most legislators have an intimate understanding of the legislative process and preexisting relationships with their former colleagues. But the practice has raised ethical questions about its effect on legislation. Would legislators who might want a high-paying lobbying job after they retire be influenced in their relationships with lobbyists? Under current law, former members of Congress cannot directly lobby their colleagues for one year after leaving office. But they can go ahead and establish their lobbying position or business while indirectly lobbying on issues. Thus the effect of the law is merely to delay direct lobbying for one year.

Legislative Cue-Giving

Cue-giving research focuses on how legislators decide how they will vote. Most research has indicated that the primary cue is partisan in nature (most legislators vote in concert with other members of their party), a trend that makes the lobbyist's role even more difficult. Legislators, however, are sometimes faced with issues on which their party has no formal stance. In those instances, they may resort to personal beliefs or they may rely upon any number of other cues. Cues that could influence their vote are the position of other legislators, input from legislative leaders, influence from the executive branch, information from interest groups and their lobbyists, and attitudes among the legislator's constituents. Regardless of which specific cue influences the final decision, most arguments for voting for or against a bill fall into one of two categories—arguments based on the merits of the proposal, and warnings of the political consequences of voting the "wrong" way.

Research into "cue-giving" was pioneered by Kingdon (1973), who interviewed sixty members of Congress in 1969. The results of the survey found that most legislators followed partisan lines on noncontroversial legislation, but broke party lines to vote with the apparent majority on controversial issues. Matthews and Stimson (1975) subsequently defined cues as "any communication—verbal or nonverbal—intended or unintended" that influences voting (p. 51). They described cue-givers as colleagues with attributes of trustworthiness, similar views, friendship, and reciprocity. By the 1980s, studies in cue-giving were shifting from Congress to state legislatures, with the reporting of different results. Ray (1982), in a study of legislatures in Pennsylvania, Massachusetts, and New Hampshire, found that the most important cues were fellow legislators and interest groups. The executive branch, conversely, had little impact.

A number of studies have examined the role of friendship as a cue-giving factor. Patterson (1959), in a study of the Wisconsin state assembly, argued that legislative friendships were a function of geographic location, length of tenure, earlier political alliances, and seating arrangements on the floor. In a study of the Iowa legislature, Caldeira and Patterson (1987) demonstrated that legislators who sit next to one another tended to develop friendships. Uslaner and Weber (1977), in a study of all fifty state legislatures, found that legislators cited friends in the legislature as the largest source of cues on how to vote. Matthews and Stimson (1975) found that friendship was frequently mentioned as an attribute of friendship in the U.S. House of Representatives. Ferber and Pugliese (1999), however, in a study of the New York State Assembly, found that the influence of seat proximity was largely a function of party. Proximity tended to influence cues because members of the same party are seated together.

Ferber and Pugliese (1999), in an examination of controversial roll call votes, found little relationship between communication among legislative members and their votes. There was such a relationship on one issue—the death penalty—with members who "stuck to business" when talking with colleagues demonstrating more influence on that issue. But there was little support for other issues (abortion, health care, surrogate parenting for example). Generally, state legislators rely on party leaders for "narrow" issues, but shift to other cues on issues with a broader appeal. Similarly, in the U.S. House of Representatives, members of Congress rely on cues from staff, party leaders, committee chairs, ranking members, and other colleagues on issues that are of an internal nature to the legislature. If the issue is of a broader, external nature, however, the parties' use of cues differed according to the subject at hand.

Campaign Implications

From a campaign perspective, the importance of interpersonal communication has been widely accepted, if not always implemented. Diffusion theory, for example, is rarely used by campaign consultants. Kraus and Davis (1976, p. 125) have pointed out a number of theoretical weaknesses to diffusion research, and some of those bear directly on why consultants have generally ignored this element. Specifically, the diffusion model is primarily descriptive in nature. Research has focused on what happens to information on a post hoc basis, rather than predict how any specific information will be diffused. Lack of predictability is its major academic weakness, which also reduces the utility of the theory to consultants. Diffusion theory cannot predict when barriers might appear, how long the diffusion will take, how widespread it will be, or what stages it might pass through. Such an ambiguous conception of what might happen simply reduces its utility to consultants and campaigns.

But the general concept of interpersonal influence has been incorporated into a number of campaign efforts and techniques. Typically, campaigns first target elite opinion leaders, with major campaign efforts directed at getting their support. Still, the importance of interpersonal opinion leadership has not been overlooked. Some campaigns, including George McGovern's 1972 primary campaigns, placed a major emphasis on interpersonal communication programs (Devlin, 1973). As early as the 1960s, Republican consultant Stephen Shadegg (1972) often touted the value of interpersonal influence on campaigns. He recommended two distinctly different approaches in which the two-step flow could be used in campaigns. The "Social Precinct" program began with a mail campaign in which supporters wrote to their friends, asking them to provide advice and support to the candidate. If they agreed, they were added to a computerized list; the campaign would regularly provide those people with information about the campaign that could be used in interpersonal discussion. Although he provided no empirical support for the success of the program, Shadegg's plan aimed at reaching 3 to 5 percent of the voting public with the program. That formula was based on an assumption that each member of the social precinct was able to influence ten other voters on behalf of the candidate.

The social precinct survives today in electronic form, with many campaigns distributing such information to supporters by e-mail. In fact, the Internet offers campaigns their first capability of establishing an interpersonal network based on a global communication system (Carey, 1998). Since the modern process starts with computers, with new names and e-mail addresses easy to add, it likely sees more use today than it did in Shadegg's time. Its impact can be diminished, however, when all members of the social precinct come from the same or similar social groups. When that occurs, the "insider" information exchanged at the interpersonal level is merely a repetition of the information that each received by e-mail. Reinforcement occurs, but only among existing voters. To be successful, the social precinct program must spread its reach into a variety of social groups. The ultimate measure of its success is not the number of people who are reached, but the number of different social groups that are represented.

Shadegg's other plan, the "Block Captain" program, is also still around. The block captain is a program in which telephone workers call potential supporters in an effort to recruit interpersonal opinion leaders. When a person is contacted who agrees to become an interpersonal worker, a personal letter is sent to them. Campaign brochures are included, along with a request for the volunteer to distribute the information to the neighbors who live on the same city block. As new issue materials are developed, these may also be mailed to him or her with a request to distribute them. On election day, the telephone bank contacts each of the individual block captains again, asking them to knock on their neighbors' doors and remind people to vote. The value of the block captain program hinges on two factors, the value of interpersonal influence and its capacity to increase turnout within targeted areas. During the 1970s, Texas-based Democratic consultant Hugh Palmer adopted a variation of Shaddegg's plan and used it to start a telephone-based consulting firm for Democratic candidates. Palmer eventually used the technique in a successful campaign as a candidate himself, winning election as mayor of Fort Worth.

The use of such programs indicates that most consultants place some value on the role of interpersonal influence on political voting behavior. Most consultants generally accept its value and like to use that process to their advantage. Implementation of such programs on a large scale can be difficult and costly, however. As a result, the organized use of such programs is often restricted either to small elections or to targeted areas of a larger electorate. Ultimately, when campaigns have to reach masses of voters, consultants will focus their efforts on the mass media.

Summary

While mass media still dominate most political campaigns, the role of interpersonal influence cannot be overlooked. Interpersonal influence operates on multiple levels in political campaigns. Voters discuss campaigns with one another, seeking information or expressing a commonality of opinion in a manner that validates their lifestyles. Among political activists, interpersonal discussions are an integral part of daily conversations, but political topics will often be sprinkled into the conversations of those with even a moderate level of interest in politics. Consultants have tried to take advantage of this phenomenon by developing programs that can use voters' natural tendency to talk about politics. In the past, these programs have relied on organizational frameworks that used telephones and direct mail as the main communication channels. With the increased presence of the Internet, campaigns can now maintain one-to-one contact with supporters by e-mail.

Interpersonal communication is also a factor in candidate interactions with elite opinion leaders when the candidates seek donations and support that will legitimize their campaigns. While only a small percentage of the voters may ever see the candidate in such an informal setting, the candidate's ability to communicate on a one-to-one level can potentially influence the success or failure of their campaigns.

Lobbyists engage in an ongoing process in which interpersonal communication plays a key role. For them, interpersonal contacts with legislators is a means of influencing legislation. Although often unseen by the voting public, the communication exchanges in this forum have a major impact on legislative packages that affect the public.

Finally, legislators use a variety of interpersonal cues when deciding how they will vote on much legislation. In addition to talking with lobbyists, most legislators exchange information with their colleagues, seeking to either learn more about a particular piece of legislation or to broker deals that will be beneficial to some legislation that they support. Again, the interpersonal communication process exercises a vital role on legislation that affects the public.

QUESTIONS FOR DISCUSSION

1. In 2001, the state of Mississippi held a referendum on whether the image of the Confederate battle flag should be removed from the state flag. Those who wanted to change the flag spent more than $700,000 in their campaign, while expenditures by the keep-the-flag side were minuscule by comparison (estimated at about $10,000). Still, in the subsequent referendum, voters supported keeping the old flag by 66 percent to 34 percent. How could the effects of interpersonal influence explain why a poorly financed campaign could be so successful?

2. One of the Democratic candidates in a primary received the endorsement of a prominent Republican. The Democrat played the endorsement very prominently in advertising, spending more than the other two Democrats. However, polls taken with three weeks left showed the candidate running third among Democratic voters. The campaign manager immediately removed the references to the Republican endorsement in the campaign advertising. The candidate won the primary. What led the campaign manager to make this decision? What is one explanation for this effect?

3. The city government decides to bring to a vote a proposal to build a new professional basketball arena. Enthusiastic fans, the chamber of commerce, and city officials support the proposal. Those who oppose higher taxes and "corporate welfare" oppose the proposal. Design a campaign plan to defeat the arena that will mobilize the most opponents while using only limited financial resources. Be sure to use an interpersonal communication and opinion leadership component in the plan.

4. A proposal is made to outlaw union agreements throughout the state that require union membership. How can the unions prevent the proposal from passing, using their membership as an activist core of support?

14 Critical Events Analysis

On November 4, 1979, Iranian demonstrators overran the guards at the American Embassy in Tehran and captured a number of American personnel as hostages. When initial diplomatic efforts failed, President Jimmy Carter wrote a letter to the Iranian leader Ayatollah Khomeini, arguing that the embassy personnel were not spies and should be freed. As the press waited for presidential actions, little else was done. As press secretary Jody Powell said, "They think we're doing more than we are. They don't know how lousy our options are" (quoted by Jordan, 1982, p. 36). As negotiations dragged on, the Carter administration froze all Iranian assets in the United States, put other sanctions in place, and saw a United Nations commission formed to deal with the issue.

Nothing worked. Finally, the president attempted to free the hostages with a dramatic military rescue operation. That failed too, in an embarrassing manner, when U.S. helicopters had trouble flying in the sands of the Iranian desert. Eventually, Iran requested a $24 billion payoff for releasing the hostages. Carter refused. Unfortunately for Carter, the whole debacle continued through all of 1980—including the 1980 presidential election campaign. His inability to free the hostages was viewed as an indication of his weakness in the presidency. When the dust settled and the votes were counted, Ronald Reagan had been elected president. Iran freed the hostages on the day of Reagan's inauguration.

From a political campaign perspective, the Iranian hostage crisis would be classified as a critical event, which is an event that becomes a focal point of media coverage and thus influences the political environment. Researchers study the phenomenon using a technique known as "critical events analysis" (Kraus, Davis, Lang, & Lang, 1976). A number of research studies have used the approach, with many looking at high-profile political debates, such as the 1960 Kennedy-Nixon debates (Kraus, 1962), or provocative events such as the assassination of President John F. Kennedy (Greenberg, 1964; Mendelsohn, 1964) and the attempts on the lives of candidate George Wallace (Steinfatt et al., 1973) and President Ronald Reagan (Gantz, 1983; Weaver-Lariscy, Sweeney, & Steinfatt, 1984). Others have looked at key speeches during the campaign, including keynote speeches at the parties' conventions (Benoit, Blaney, & Pier, 2000).

From the campaign perspective, critical events analysis is a rare convergence of academic and consulting perspectives, albeit each approaches the topic from a different perspective. For the academic community, critical events analysis is primarily a post hoc process; scholars seek to identify major events—debates, convention speeches, major public appearances—that could have influenced the campaign. Identifying and analyzing those events provide scholars with an opportunity to examine the campaign process as a micro-cosm, identifying key points within a campaign and studying how they influenced the outcome of an election. For consultants, critical events are predictive factors, points, and events within a campaign that can be anticipated to have a major impact. Special care and attention are given to preparing for them.

Antecedent Conditions

Not all campaign events are critical to the success or failure of a campaign, but critical events analysis, as outlined by Kraus and his associates (1976), assumes that campaign events can have an impact when certain social conditions are present. The most common characteristics that must be present are dissemination of information about the event, either concurrently with its occurrence, or extended over a period of time after it occurs, or both; and voter interest in the event, either at the time it occurred, after it occurred, or (more often) both.

Dissemination of Information

The dissemination of information about any campaign event is usually defined by its media coverage. Such coverage frequently occurs before, during, and after the event. Anticipated critical events, such as presidential debates, receive advanced publicity from the media, extensive on-site coverage of the event, and even more extensive postevent coverage. Still, on-site coverage by the media is not essential for an event to be considered a critical one. Sometimes all or most of the coverage occurs well after the event, particularly if the event was not anticipated by the news media. The Watergate break-in, for example, received only a small amount of coverage at the time it was discovered, and it had no appreciable effect on the Nixon-McGovern presidential campaign. However, subsequent coverage over the next two years was extensive, eventually leading to President Nixon's resignation.

In some small and local elections, media coverage of a critical event may be minimal or nonexistent; dissemination of the information about the event is limited to those in attendance and to the subsequent interpersonal discussions that follow. Still, that may suffice; when the electorate is small, the interpersonal discussions that follow may quickly spread the information. The authors, for example, are familiar with one state senate campaign that was decided on the basis of a critical event that never received news coverage. In that incident, the son of the candidate got involved in a fistfight with an elderly man over the placement of a campaign sign. The event received little news coverage, but rumors about the incident spread quickly. Campaign polling subsequently revealed that the incident was the major reason the candidate lost the election, with more than 60 percent of the electorate aware of the incident.

Voter Interest

For an event to be critical to the election, it must capture voter attention. The reasons for that attention may vary. Sometimes it may result from the news-priming function of the press. The news media's advance coverage of the event may serve to heighten awareness of it, leading to close attention being paid to the event. The intense scrutiny given to presidential debates, for example, falls within this category. Speeches at political conventions play a similar role; the media often provides gavel-to-gavel coverage of major convention speeches, priming them with advance notice of what the speaker might say. The most striking example of the role of news priming in political events, though, may be the undue impact that the media place on early presidential primaries and caucuses. Typically, all of the major newspapers and TV networks provide extensive coverage leading up to and following the Iowa caucus and the New Hampshire primaries. As the first two major electoral events in a presidential campaign, these two events are critical to the success of any major candidate. Straw polls are sometimes promoted by the media to the point that they can become a critical event. Jimmy Carter used a 1975 Democratic straw poll in Ames, Iowa, as a springboard in his winning presidential campaign a year later.

Sometimes an event becomes critical because it becomes a symbolic representation of a larger issue. Martin Luther King, Jr. made this attribute a hallmark of the civil rights movement; rather than campaign for civil rights as a broad ideological issue, King based his protests on specific incidents that represented the larger issue—Rosa Parks's refusal to sit in the back of a Montgomery, Alabama, bus; sitting at a public lunchroom counter in North Carolina; a voter registration drive in Mississippi. More recently, during the 2000 presidential campaign, George W. Bush's appearance at Bob Jones University became representative of his ties to the religious right of the Republican party (Bruni & Kristof, 2000), leading to a subsequent apology from the candidate (Berke, 2000). President Clinton's decision to participate in the thirty-fifth anniversary of the Selma march resulted in extensive news coverage of that annual event (considerably more than in past celebrations) and served to highlight his concern over the fight for civil rights.

At other times, an event may play a watershed role because it plays a critical role in defining a candidate's image. During the 1988 presidential campaign, the vice presidential debate between Dan Quayle and Lloyd Bentsen included Bentsen's tart criticism of Quayle, "You're no Jack Kennedy." The line helped to define Quayle as a political lightweight, an image he was never able to overcome, and thus limited his ability to seek the presidency himself. Quayle was subsequently hurt by another critical event that hurt his image and credibility when he incorrectly spelled "potato" at a public school appearance. Nor is the damage of such events limited to Republicans. The Monica Lewinsky controversy was a critical event in the presidency of Bill Clinton. Even though Clinton survived the impeachment effort that resulted, the event had a lasting impact on his personal image as president.

Identifying Critical Events

Most studies that use critical events analysis have examined provocative events and the dissemination of information that followed them. These topics have included assassinations, speeches, and major protests. One of the earliest was a study of a parade to honor General Douglas MacArthur in Chicago, and every presidential debate since 1960 has garnered such academic attention. From the academic perspective, one purpose of this research is to identify those events that will produce the most useful explanation and prediction of social change. If the key points of a campaign can be reduced to one, or perhaps just a few, critical events, then analysis of the entire campaign or of any social change process can be simplified. In essence, critical events analysis makes the study of social change feasible.

Otherwise, the enormity of the interaction of variables and events could overwhelm any single research effort.

Given that goal, then, a key aspect of the analysis is the proper identification of critical events. Important events that made a difference in a campaign must be identified, and all must be included. Just as important, those events that had little or no impact on the campaign must be eliminated from the analysis; their presence could unnecessarily complicate the analysis with extraneous variables and information. Ideally, that filtering process is most productive if it is conducted before the event, because advance notice of an event allows for a more thorough analysis of it. Presidential debates are the most obvious events that can be routinely anticipated; not surprisingly, they are among those critical events that have been the most thoroughly studied, beginning with the Kennedy-Nixon debates in 1960 (Kraus, 1962). Since then, the debates have produced a number of memorable moments—Bentsen's dig at Quayle, Ford's miscue on eastern Europe, and Ronald Reagan's affable joke about his age when paired against Walter Mondale.

The Innocuous Critical Event: George W. Bush at Bob Jones University

Sometimes an otherwise routine campaign event can grow into a critical event, at least for a short time. Such an event occurred during the 2000 Republican presidential primary in South Carolina, when George W. Bush made a campaign appearance at Bob Jones University.

Bush's appearance at the school was not particularly unusual. Republican candidates had routinely stopped there in previous elections, seeking the support of the religious fundamentalists who played an active role in the Republicans' primary in South Carolina. Appearing there was effective. Bush successfully beat back a challenge from John McCain in South Carolina, partly with the help of the religious community in the state.

But, as the *New York Times* noted, the appearance came ". . . to haunt his campaign and challenge his claim to being a new kind of conservative eager to expand the Republican Party's appeal to all voters" (Bruni & Kristof, 2000).

The problem erupted in the subsequent primaries, when McCain used the appearance to imply that Bush implied an acceptance of the school's intolerance of other religious and racial groups, and the candidate had moved too far to the right in his efforts to appease the religious right. Those messages worked effectively to give McCain victories in the primaries that followed, and reporters continued to press Bush on the issue at nearly every campaign appearance that followed.

The governor's advisers, meanwhile, admitted they did not anticipate the reaction and were "stunned that the visit became such a huge issue" (Berke, 2000). Three weeks after the appearance, the campaign finally responded by issuing an apology that "expressed regret . . . for not speaking out against racial and religious intolerance during (the) visit . . ." (Bruni & Kristof, 2000).

Within two weeks of the apology, the issued had died down and that crisis had passed for the campaign.

Sources: Berke, R. L. (2000, February 28). Regrets well placed, if questionably timed. *New York Times,* p. A10.

Bruni, F., & Kristof, N. D. (2000, February 28). Bush rues failure to attack bigotry in visit to college. *New York Times,* pp. A1, A10.

The problem, of course, is that not all critical events can be anticipated. Sometimes critical events are planned by one of the competitors, but revealed to the public and the press without advance notice. This is frequently done through the paid media, with a campaign using an ad that aims to catch the opposition in a "surprise attack." Holding the surprise until the last minute gives the opposition less time to plan a response, and gives the press less time to thoroughly examine the issue. Another form of unanticipated critical event are campaign blunders. The frequent campaign appearances by candidates allow for multiple opportunities to make a mistake; if that mistake is documented, it can play a pivotal role in the campaign. In 1986, Alabama Republican Senator Jeremiah Denton was heavily favored to win reelection until he complained in a campaign speech that he "didn't have time" to talk to voters and also do his job. While the speech received little news coverage, a campaign worker for challenger Richard Shelby filmed the speech, and Denton's words became the topic of subsequent news coverage and a major commercial for the Shelby campaign. Shelby subsequently won the election.

Studying Critical Events

As Kraus et al. (1976) noted, "The ultimate purpose of critical event analysis is to provide a scientific explanation of how elite actions have social consequences and how certain social processes constrain elite actions or negate their intended impact" (Kraus et al., 1976, pp. 199–200). That rather comprehensive goal cannot be achieved easily or with data that only approach the event from a limited perspective. Instead, critical events analysis attempts to use a variety of methodologies integrate data collected at both the individual and societal levels. At the individual level, these might include interviews with individuals and/or a broader range of participant-observation research. At a societal level, it might include public opinion research or an analysis of societal trends. The particular methodologies used have often varied depending on the extent to which prior notice was available and to what extent political elites were involved in the creation of the event. As noted earlier, identification of a critical event cannot always be anticipated. If the importance of the event is only recognized after it occurs, then some form of ad hoc research design must be employed to gather what information is available. If political elites are involved in the planning and execution of the event, the researchers can often mine their memories for useful information leading up to the event, even if that information was not public knowledge before the event. Political elites, however, sometimes have minor roles in truly critical events. Some may be well planned, but others, such as the Kennedy assassination, are outside the control of the politicos. The methodology also has to be adjusted on the basis of how the information was disseminated. In the past, major coverage was almost an essential ingredient in the diffusion of information about a major national event, but the extent and type of coverage may vary, depending on journalistic anticipation and evaluation of the event. The advent of the Internet has led to an increase in alternative sources of information.

A Design for Critical Events Analysis

An ideal analysis of a critical event gathers four types of information, data from the locale, the public response, media output, and opinion trend indicators.

The Locale.   The goal for the researcher who studies the locale can vary, depending upon the nature of the event. Still, a few research questions seem to apply to most situations. The major ones are:

1. What happened? Understanding the event requires a re-creation of the sequence of individual events that constituted the major event. At this stage of the research, the researcher approaches the critical event much like a detective or accident investigator, first trying to get a sense of what happened before any conclusions about "why" can be drawn.
2. What was the goal of the participants? This element of the analysis is essentially a post hoc strategy analysis in which the rhetorical intent of the participants is identified. Why did they do this? What goals were they trying to achieve? This is a crucial stage in the research process; a misidentification of the participants' goals likely dooms the rest of the study to unproductive analysis.
3. Who was the target audience? This element of the process recognizes that the audience with which the event has the greatest effect may not be the immediate one. To understand the participants' intent, you must also understand whom they were trying to reach.

Answering these three questions usually involves one or more of three different techniques: direct observation, indirect observation, and focused interviews with elites. Direct observations may come from researchers positioned at the locale themselves. In the "MacArthur Day in Chicago" study, some members of the research team were stationed at points along the parade route to observe the reactions of others in the crowd as MacArthur's entourage passed by. Indirect observations may use unobtrusive data that might provide information about the size and nature of the immediate audience—how many beverages were consumed, how much trash was later collected, how many pro and anti signs were present at the event. Focused interviews with elites are necessary, though, to get a better understanding of their intent and target audience. Even that may not be sufficient for an ongoing campaign, since political strategists are reluctant to reveal their strategy while it is still being deployed. But an experienced interviewer can glean significant information about the participants' goals and targets, and that must be done to make the research valid.

Public Response.   Understanding the impact of a critical event requires an understanding of the public response to it. The issues in analyzing such responses are threefold: What is the public's perception and awareness of what happened? What sources of information did they use to form those perceptions? and Were there any perceived changes in opinions and attitudes as a result? The most common means of collecting these data is with some form of interview methodology, typically either a public opinion survey or a series of focus groups.

Collection of Media Output.   Public response to a critical event is often based on both the event and media coverage of the event. Critical events analysis thus places a major priority on collecting the media output related to a critical event. In the past, this has primarily meant collecting newspaper clippings and video copies of network news coverage. Electronic news sources have been particularly important, since—in the past—most people first heard about any one critical event through television or radio news, or from an interpersonal contact with someone who had heard about it there. More recently, the Internet has started to play a larger role in early dissemination of news about breaking events. Regardless of which medium dominates early coverage, the impact of critical events is often determined by news coverage of those events. In debates, for example, postdebate designation of a "winner" increases the likelihood that the public will view that candidate as the winner (Lowry, Bridges, & Barefield, 1991). That, in turn, has a positive influence on perceptions of that candidate's image, particularly his or her trait attribution (Ferguson, Hollander, & Melwani, 1989) and related vote decisions (Elliott & Sothirajah, 1993).

Collection of Opinion Trend Indicators. When a critical event occurs, academic researchers are often poised to quickly conduct a public opinion survey to analyze audience response. But they are not alone in their pursuit of the topic. Many news organizations and national public opinion companies, such as the Gallup Poll and Harris Poll, also follow suit. The plethora of surveys that typically result serve as a data bank for an intensive analysis of public opinion trends. These can prove crucial in developing an understanding of the event and its impact on the public.

Debates as Critical Events

The most visible of the anticipated critical events in presidential campaigns (and some statewide races) are televised debates. Debates have been major components of every presidential campaign since the Ford-Carter debates of 1976 (Hess, 1988). They are now such an institutionalized and ritualistic part of presidential campaigns that voters expect them to occur (Kraus, 2000), even though they are not legally required as part of the campaign. Furthermore, despite concerns over political malaise and lack of interest among voters, televised debates typically have a large viewing audience, larger than any other presidential campaign event (Buchanan, 1991).

Presidential debates are truly critical events. They offer candidates a chance to enhance their credibility while addressing issues that the media might have overlooked (Hellweg, Pfau, & Brydon, 1992). Furthermore, although such elements are merely one of several sources of voter information, debates typically have some type of impact on the voting public (Chaffee, 1978). For candidates, debates can orient voters about the personalities of the candidates, highlight differences in political philosophy, and focus attention on the candidates (Glenn, 2001). For voters, debates can increase interest and participation in a campaign (Buchanan, 1991; Delli Carpini et al., 1997), increase voters' information about the campaign (Becker et al., 1978), enhance their ability to discuss the campaign with others (Miller & MacKuen, 1979), and trigger increased interpersonal communication about the campaign (Jamieson & Birdsell, 1988). For the media, debate allows some reporters access to the candidates in a situation that allows for cross examination–type questioning, thus allowing the voters to see how the candidates respond under pressure (Glenn, 2001). One immediate effect is a short-term impact on the salience of issues (Atkin et al., 1989; Swanson & Swanson, 1978). In the immediate aftermath of the debate, the issues addressed by the candidates are likely to receive increased coverage from the news media and an enhanced perception of salience by the voting public. Debates can also influence the image and perceptions of the candidates, although the impact does not typically alter any voting intentions (Abramowitz, 1978).

Still, debates are not perfect forums for candidate-voter communication (Jamieson & Birdsell, 1990). Media questions can be superficial; even persistent questioning may reveal little information. Candidates often resort to repeating segments from their stump speeches or use the debate as a forum for attacking their opponent (Glenn, 2001). Voter response to these factors is often affected by three factors: the expectations of the candidates, the performances of the candidates, and the political ideologies of the voters. The expectations of the candidates often come from other elements of the campaign, depending on the image that the candidates project and the issues they discuss (Hellweg, Pfau, & Brydon, 1992). In the 2000 election, George W. Bush entered the debates following a series of campaign misstatements that had raised doubts about his ability to perform well during the debates. While his resulting performance was not particularly stellar, it wasn't bad either. He subsequently came out of the debates with an improved image with the voters.

The performance of the candidates is also a factor. Debates present the candidates to the voters for a longer and more intense view of the candidates than either news or through advertising, giving the public a chance to familiarize themselves with the candidates (Jamieson & Birdsell, 1988, p. 28). Vancil and Pendell (1984) noted that the candidates can use that opportunity to demonstrate a presidential image; if they succeed at doing that, they will typically be perceived as the winner of the debate. Candidates can also lose debates with poor performances. As is discussed later in "mistake-based critical events," a candidate who blunders during a debate can suffer serious damage. As Lawrence (2000) noted, "Mistakes are replayed endlessly on news and TV." During the Bush-Gore debates, for example, Al Gore drew negative attention from the press with a series of inaccurate statements, including the claim that he had visited Texas following a natural disaster in the state. The resulting news coverage about the misrepresentations occupied the news agenda for several days and necessitated a subsequent apology from Gore. Similarly, in 1988, Michael Dukakis lost ground when he was asked whether he would favor capital punishment for the killer if his wife were raped and murdered. Instead of expressing emotion, he listed the policy reasons behind his opposition to the death penalty (Lawrence, 2000). Mistakes are not always verbal in nature. In 1992, President George H. W. Bush was criticized for glancing at his watch during a debate, as if he were anxious for it to be over.

While the press will focus increased attention on factual errors, voters often react negatively to personal mistakes. Personal behavior during the campaigns are often evaluated through the lens of voter expectations. Hinck and Hinck (1998) argue for evaluating such responses through their politeness theory. Their work is an expansion on Brown and Levinson's (1987) theory that politeness is a universal value that operates across cultures. According to politeness theory, one standard used by voters to evaluate candidates is the expectation that the candidates maintain an attitude of respect for the opposing candidate. Any deviation from this standard makes the voters uncomfortable and can cause a negative reaction toward the candidate who violates the norm. The candidates used politeness strategies in both the 1992 and 1996 debates (Hinck & Hinck, 2000). The factor emerged again, in a negative manner, for Al Gore during the 2000 debates. At times, Gore made the voters uncomfortable with his overly aggressive debate style, his audible sighs, and his tendency to move closer to Bush when the latter was answering a question. Such moments become pivotal points in the debate because the viewers are attuned to potential violations of politeness and they view behaviors at that moment as indicative of broader values and competence. They recognize key moments when a candidate's public face is threatened, and how the candidate handles those moments affects the voters' perception of his or her competence in handling dramatic conflict within the debate.

Finally, voters' impressions of the debates are based heavily on their political ideology, position on issues, and prior support of a candidate (Martel, 1983). Despite the secondary impact that debates can have on voters' information, they typically have little effect on voter decisions (Abramowitz, 1978). Decided voters typically score their candidate as the winner. For them, the debates are more like a pep rally. Rather than changing their vote, it merely reinforces their support, particularly if the candidate meets their expectations. Even the positive impact of increased knowledge and information is tempered by the voters' predispositions. Although they generally increase their knowledge of the campaign, the voters may still misunderstand much of the information in the debate (Jacoby et al., 1986). Ultimately, debates have a pivotal role in campaigns, but their impact can be muted by other campaign factors.

The Consultant's View: Planning and Coping with Critical Events

For campaign consultants, critical events are what the name implies: critical to the election. Despite the overall complexity of preparing and running a campaign, consultants generally assume that there will be two or three critical points within a campaign that will serve a watershed function. How those crises are handled often determines the success or failure of that campaign. The consultants' view of this process, however, tends to have three distinct differences from the academic perspective. First, consultants typically approach critical events from a predictive perspective. If critical events can be anticipated, perhaps the campaign can make preparations to handle them more effectively. Some critical events are obvious—the campaign announcement, televised debates, convention speeches, and speeches on major issues. Preparation for these events is often extensive, with the candidate and the staff preparing for the event with research, review, and preparation. Research is conducted on the audience and issues that must be addressed. Topics and ideas are reviewed in discussion sessions involving the candidate, consultants, and other campaign workers. For events in which press questions are anticipated, the consultants employ role-playing, adopting the role of reporters and tossing increasingly difficult questions at the candidate. Debate preparation frequently includes at least one person who plays the role of the opponent, seeking to throw the candidate off balance with an unanticipated question or challenge.

Lawrence (2000) noted that debate contenders also typically rehearse a few "gotchas." Noonan (1998) traces the trend to 1976 when Walter Mondale criticized the substance behind Gary Hart's positions by asking "Where's the beef?" "After the success of Mondale's line," Noonan noted, "the word went forth: candidates needed to be supplied by their staff with zippy sound bites before they went into a debate or an interview" (p. 98). In 1984, Ronald Reagan faced concerns about his age with a response that he had planned in advance: "I want you to know that I will not make age an issue of this campaign. I am not going to exploit for political purposes my opponent's youth and inexperience," he said. Everybody laughed, including opponent Walter Mondale, and the issue never arose again. Jamieson (1988) noted that the line also functioned as a cover for weak performances by Reagan in other parts of the debate, particularly a somewhat rambling closing statement.

"What saves him . . . is the brevity of the light-hearted joke contrasted with the four-minute length of the final speech," Jamieson wrote. "The former lends itself to the news clip, the latter does not" (p. 113).

A different type of "gotcha" was used by Lloyd Bentsen in the 1988 presidential debate with Dan Quayle. After Quayle said he had as much experience as John F. Kennedy had when Kennedy sought the presidency, Bensten responded, "Senator, I served with Jack Kennedy. I knew Jack Kennedy. Jack Kennedy was a friend of mine. Senator, you are no Jack Kennedy." The line is still remembered as the classic example of a put-down in campaign politics. Still, such one-liners are rare in presidential debates, since it is typically difficult for any candidate to accomplish his or her goals with a single answer or line. Noonan (1998) credits that rarity to the media literacy of the voters: "The American public has become very sophisticated about such lines," she wrote, "so sophisticated that they now discount them" (p. 97).

Preparations for the candidate may include both verbal and nonverbal training. Goodman and Gring (1999), in an analysis of the 1992 and 1996 presidential town hall debates, noted that Clinton often repositioned himself so that each television image of him either included the American flag in the background (in 1992) or pictured him with the audience (in 1996). They concluded that Clinton ". . . made a conscious effort to maximize his visual impact during the town hall debates . . . ," a factor that implied that he had planned and practiced the positioning in advance of the actual debate.

A second major difference for consultants is that, from the campaign perspective, not all critical events are public in nature. The public nature is essential to the academic community and its efforts to study the public impact of critical events. Without a public component, the event can have little impact on public opinion. From the campaign's perspective, though, the campaign may experience one or more nonpublic critical events that could potentially spell the difference between winning and losing. Typically, unless the campaign is a well-documented presidential campaign, these critical turning points may never become public knowledge. Still, while the public may be unaware of them, they are critical to the campaign. These might be more accurately classified as "critical decisions" or "critical maneuvers,": deliberate choices or strategic moves that have a disproportionate impact of the rest of the campaign. Elements that fall within this category could include fund-raising decisions, endorsements, and allocation of resources. For example, the decision to seek funds from an unpopular source could have a positive impact on campaign finances but a negative one on public image. The endorsement of a major African American leader could result in the support of many of that person's followers. Campaigns are often won or lost on the basis of how resources are allocated for the campaign.

A third distinctive element of the consultant's view of critical events is that consultants often make assumptions about the probable timing of critical events. Critical points in the campaign typically occur very early or very late in the campaign. The early stages of the campaign establishes the strategic base of the campaign, and decisions that are made during this time have an effect that often lasts throughout the entire campaign. First impressions are critical; the candidate's introduction to the public often sets the tone for subsequent responses to the candidate's message. The announcement provides the first major instance of media exposure for the campaign, demonstrates the ability of the campaign to execute its basic campaign function, and provides a frame for interpreting later messages from the campaign.

The second major timing for critical events is late in the campaign, within the last two weeks of the election. Numerically, this time frame appears to be when most critical events occur for three reasons: external organizations, such as those who organize and coordinate campaign debates, often time their events for these latter stages; most campaigns save their most important strategic moves for the latter stages; and the public pays more attention to the campaign as election day approaches. Thus, during this time, the candidates must perform well in debates, execute critical moves in their own campaign strategies, and respond to similar moves by their opposition. For many campaigns, then, something happens in the last two weeks that is of critical importance. How the candidates respond to that event often determines who wins the election.

Between that early starting point and the late stages of the campaign, there is a span of time in which are produced few critical events. While the campaign must be alert to problems, this stage is often spent raising money, conducting routine campaign activities, and fleshing out the details of issues and strategies for later use in the campaign.

Mistake-Based Critical Events

One frequent characteristic of critical events in a campaign is that their impact is intensified if a candidate makes a mistake. Diamond and Cobb (1999) refer to this phenomenon as "the candidate as catastrophe." Part of the phenomenon rests in the psychological processing of negative information. As Lau (1982) noted, voters appear particularly sensitive to negative information about candidates. When that negative information is triggered by a critical event, it can have a major effect on a campaign. During the 1976 Ford-Carter debates, for example, President Ford incorrectly identified which nations in Eastern Europe were under Communist control, an error that was repeatedly pointed out by subsequent commentators. Given the importance of negative information in critical events, the goal of many candidates is often to escape from such events with as little damage as possible. As Diamond and Cobb (1999, p. 242) noted, "the battle is not to convince citizens that one's policy is *right,* but simply that it is *not unreasonable,* that a favored candidate's election . . . does not portend catastrophe."

Summary

Critical event analysis simplifies campaign analysis by focusing on major, discrete events that had significant impact on the election. The approach offers a way to view the campaign in a holistic way that might replicate the decision-making process many of the voters may go through. Several conclusions have already been drawn from previous works, many of which could be useful to the consultants in the industry.

One by-product of critical event analysis is an understanding of the importance of the message communicated by the event. Such messages are not always verbal in nature, but the impact is significant anyway. The ultimate impact of the critical event on public opinion is often symbolic in nature: what the event communicates about the people involved. In addition, those critical events that can be anticipated are likely to involve a great deal of campaign preparation and creative effort; the creative side of that equation is often directed at the message, or finding a symbolic way of having an impact on voters. In most cases, the mass media provide a critical link in conveying that message to the public.

There is, however, an implication of the watershed impact of critical events that is discouraging to both the candidate and the professional consultant. Given the inordinate effect that watershed events have on an election, the success of their campaigns are typically based on how they handle a relatively small number of tasks. Both the candidate and the consultant can perform admirably 90 percent of the time, but if their miscues occur on critical events, they are likely to lose the election. Conversely, they can both make a lot of mistakes on minor aspects of the campaign, but still perform well by winning the critical events. Because of that, the study of critical events is likely to remain an important factor for both the academic and the consulting communities.

QUESTIONS FOR DISCUSSION

1. A small down-state newspaper has reported that your opponent was asked the question, "Is withholding too much for the working man?" Your opponent answered, "What's withholding?" Is this a critical event? If it is, how do you communicate it to voters? How do you communicate it to opinion makers?

2. During a debate, one of the candidates for the U.S. Senate walked over to his opponent's lectern and demanded that she sign a pledge not to accept soft money. She refused. Later he attacked her for refusing to sign the pledge. Was this a critical event? How would each candidate spin this as a turning point in their respective campaigns?

3. In a runoff election, a self-described "law and order" candidate for attorney general is revealed to have a police record as a college student for assault. The crime occurred twenty-five years earlier and the victim and other witnesses have died. What can the candidate do to keep this information from becoming a critical event? What can the opponent do to make it a critical event?

4. During a campaign for the U.S. House of Representatives, Cold War tensions escalated when a U.S. surveillance aircraft disappeared without a trace near the borders of the Soviet Union. The incumbent made a statement in support of the U.S. Air Force and the families of the crew. His opponent condemned the Soviets and accused them of breaking international law. Is this a critical event? If yes, how can each candidate respond to the situation? If no, how should each candidate proceed?

15 Ethical Questions in Political Communication

In June 2000, the sheriff and circuit clerk of Winston County, Alabama, were accused of buying votes with money and moonshine whiskey. Federal indictments against the officeholders charged that they passed around cash to potential voters. The going rate for a vote, according to press reports at the time, was $2 or $3, with liquor tossed in as a bonus (Associated Press, 2000). Their defense for their actions was that they were merely engaging in the promotion of voter turnout, but a grand jury disagreed. Several of the participants were subsequently found guilty of voter fraud.

That case is only one example of how ethical and legal issues become involved in the political campaign process. The motivation to win sometimes drives participants to use a variety of questionable techniques that might enhance their electoral chances. Many cross the line and are clearly illegal. Others may fall within the boundaries of law, but still raise questions of ethical behavior.

Somewhat surprisingly to some outside observers, the consulting community and the academic community generally hold common views on this issue—although for different reasons. The academic community justifiably deplores unethical campaign activities as an affront to the democratic process that may succeed in overriding the will of the majority. Consultants generally share that sense of moral indignation when they see unethical behavior; in fact, their reaction may be even stronger than that of the academic community. To them, unethical behavior is both an affront to their profession, and a factor that could cause them to unfairly lose an election. Consultants who develop a reputation within the community for unethical campaigning are reviled as snakes who perpetuate the worst of the negative stereotypes of the profession while making it increasingly harder for their opponents to win an election in the face of such tactics. Where the two communities disagree is in the development of criteria for moral behavior. While the specifics of such criteria vary with individuals in both communities, a few points of agreement defining campaign ethics can be identified:

1. Philosophically, academic views of political ethics are usually based on democratic idealism, while the value criteria for consultants is campaign pragmatism. The philosophy of ideal democracy is based on the concepts of freedom of speech and the ability of the truth to dominate and win an argument—those with the best argument will win. Candidates who use unethical tactics undermine that ideal, creating a situation in which the "sneakiest" candidate might win. The consulting philosophy of pragmatic democracy is based on the concepts of communicating with the voters—those who communicate the best have the best chance of winning. From the consultant's point of view, victory can be obtained through either message advantage (winning an argument because you have truth on your side) or through rhetorical advantage (winning an argument because you can explain your side of the argument better than the other side can explain its side). Again, though, unethical tactics undermine both assumptions. Message advantage and rhetorical advantage may be lost if unethical tactics prevent the campaign from communicating with the voters.

2. The academic goal of the dominance of truth is based on an assumption of an open and equal debate of ideas. Consultants believe that the use of inequities in access is an acceptable and ethical form of behavior. Some campaigns simply lack the finances, media exposure, and name recognition to present a viable message that articulates their side of an argument. For the academic community, such inequities of resources invariably mean that the message of one side is underrepresented in the media. Consultants, conversely, view the lack of resources as an indication of lack of legitimacy. An inability to raise resources reflects the lack of acceptance of a message among opinion leaders. As a result, they feel no qualms about presenting their message in a vacuum created by a lack of opposition from the other side.

3. Academics fear that unethical campaign practices can lead to the selection of unqualified leaders and the development of faulty governmental policy. Consultants fear that unethical campaign practices could cost them an election. Long-time political consultant Steven Shadegg (1972) often preached that consultants should be careful not to let the other side "steal" elections. From the consultants' point of view, unethical behavior is not merely an attack on morality, but also an attack on the consultants' win-loss record (and, indirectly, their future income).

Types of Unethical Behavior

Unethical activities in campaigns can occur at any point in the campaign process, but a few stand out as more frequent and easy to identify. These include ballot stuffing and vote buying, scandals, conflicts of interest, dirty tricks, issue avoidance, negative campaigning, and the role of consultants.

Ballot Stuffing

The case cited at the beginning of this chapter is an example of an illegal practice known as ballot stuffing. There is nothing historically new about the practice. Lyndon Johnson's opponents claimed he won his first election because of ballot stuffing in one Texas county. Chicago mayor Richard Daley was accused of stuffing the ballot box in Illinois to secure the presidency for John F. Kennedy in 1960 (Cohen & Taylor, 2000). Similar examples could be cited from nearly every state in the union.

In the past, the most common form of ballot stuffing was "graveyard voting." Campaign workers would scour tombstones for names of people who were still listed on voter registration rolls and find a way to cast a vote on their behalf. Such actions occasionally prompt remarks from veteran political junkies who talk about somebody's uncle—a person who "voted a straight party ticket all of his life and for ten years afterward." The most common means of implementing ballot stuffing in modern campaigns is through the use of fraudulent absentee ballots. A few states have implemented "early voting" systems, where anyone can go to the polls before election day and cast a ballot. Others have retained traditional absentee ballot laws that allow people to vote in that manner if they are ill, shut in, out of the area on election day, or have jobs that make it difficult for them to go to the polling place. In close elections, both parties actively solicit absentee voters in an attempt to swing the elections. Such campaign activity can have a direct effect on voter turnout in the absentee boxes, with absentee votes accounting for as much as 10 percent of the total votes cast.

The weakness of the absentee system is that people who are ill or shut in will fill out their forms without the supervision of any election officials. That aspect makes the system open to manipulation, with unscrupulous operators filling out multiple forms and casting ballots on behalf of citizens who may not realize that they are even voting. Sometimes the results can be outrageous. In the 1994 election in Greene County, Alabama, three suitcases of absentee ballots were reportedly carried to the post office on election day. In that election, 34 percent—1,400—of all ballots cast in the county were absentees. Eleven people were eventually convicted of voter fraud after court testimony revealed that many of the ballots had been signed by the same person ("Greene County fraud," 2000). During the 2000 primaries, another Alabama county saw more than half (54 percent) of its votes cast as absentee ballots (Chandler, 2000).

Another simple way to stuff the ballot box is to pay voters for their vote. Although illegal, campaigns are occasionally caught giving money, alcohol, or other inducements for support. The Winston County, Alabama, example cited at the beginning of this chapter is typical of such tactics, with voters reportedly paid a few dollars and given liquor for their support.

While such tactics are obviously illegal, others skirt the law. Some candidates offer free postvoting parties, with food and drinks available, to those who show a form that indicates they voted. One group used voter participation as automatic inclusion in a lottery for a new sports utility vehicle. Such approaches are legal, since the voter is not required to support any specific candidate. Merely the fact that they voted, regardless of whom they supported, warrants admission to the party. Candidates, though, are unlikely to support such voter incentives for demographic and geographic areas they do not expect much support from.

Scandals

In 1998, scandal erupted in the While House when the media revealed that President Bill Clinton had engaged in a sexual relationship with a White House intern, Monica Lewinsky. The resulting controversy led to the impeachment of the president and sparked an avalanche of discussion about scandals, moral values, and the decline of ethics among government officials (Brito, 1999). Such scandals are nothing new in political life, including the presidency (Worland, 1998). During the presidency of Woodrow Wilson, rumors circulated that he had poisoned his first wife so he would be free to marry Edith Bolling Galt. Grover Cleveland served two terms (1885–1889 and 1893–1897) despite providing financial support to a baby boy who was born out of wedlock; his opponents mocked him with the chant,

"Ma, Ma, Where's my pa?" Other presidents reported to have had sexual liaisons outside of marriage include James Garfield, Warren G. Harding, Franklin Delano Roosevelt, Dwight Eisenhower, and John F. Kennedy.

What is new about modern politics is the extent to which such scandals have expanded into the personal sphere, with the walls that separate one's public and private lives collapsing (Lee, 2000, p. 45). The personal lives and scandals of officeholders have become the subject of both press inquiry (Sabato, 2000) and campaign attacks (Sabato, Stencel, & Lichter, 2000). Except for Cleveland's paternity case, the sexual activities of most other presidents were considered off-limits by both the press and opponents. That tradition began to change with Gary Hart's candidacy in 1987. Hart was beset by rumors that he was having an affair while conducting his campaign for the Democratic presidential nomination. At a meeting with the press, Hart denied the charges and dared reporters to follow him around if they didn't believe him. Reporters from the *Miami Herald* accepted the dare and later revealed the story, one that knocked Hart out of contention.

That opened the door for closer scrutiny of Bill Clinton's personal life in 1992 when stories of his relations with a number of women were detailed. Still, some aspects of the gentlemen's agreement not to discuss such matters prevailed, at least for the '92 election. The national Republican party was not openly involved in the accusations against Clinton. Instead, the charges came from local Republicans in Clinton's home state of Arkansas. Clinton's chief opponent, incumbent Republican president George H. W. Bush, distanced himself from the charges and never mentioned them in his own campaign appearances. That element of civility had disappeared by 1998 when Republicans in Congress were open in attacking Clinton's extramarital relationships.

The press, meanwhile, reported it all. The scent of such scandals often inspires a "feeding frenzy" of extensive coverage by newspapers, television, and Internet reporters (Sabato, 2000), with each hoping to "out-scoop" the others with the latest tidbit of gossip or information. The press was hampered in the 2000 election by having two major candidates—George W. Bush and Al Gore—who were not as colorful as Clinton, but they still found scandals to report. Bush was beset by rumors of drug use and a drunk-driving arrest, while Gore was targeted for questions about his fund-raising machinations. One local reporter (Yardley, 1999), in addressing the press scrutiny on Bush, called it ". . . a shootout in which there are no good guys." Yardley was particularly critical of how the press covered the Bush angle, but his assessment could apply to a number of other topics and candidates. "The parties to the immediate dispute are equally unappealing," he wrote. "On one side is the governor of Texas, whose flippancy is exceeded only by his self-righteousness; on the other side are the ladies and gentlemen of the press, whose self-righteousness is exceeded only by their hypocrisy. None of the participants is interested in serious, sober discussion of whatever consequential matters the presidential contest may entail. . . ."

The focus on scandals has also led to increased coverage of politicians' personal lives, including their health (Purnick, 2000). Janet Reno's fight with Parkinson's disease is public information. On April 27, 2000, New York City mayor Rudolph Giuliani held a news conference to reveal that a biopsy of his prostate gland came back positive. Such intrusions into the health of candidates is a relatively new phenomenon. The public never heard about (and most knew nothing about) John F. Kennedy's struggle with Addison's disease or the extent to which a stroke felled Woodrow Wilson. Franklin Roosevelt was elected to four terms as president without most voters realizing that he was paralyzed from polio. The

amount of coverage devoted to such issues probably portends that press coverage of political scandals and personal issues will continue to be a staple of the nightly news and the
morning paper. What used to be private matters have now become public issues.

Conflicts of Interest

Another major ethical question is that of conflicts of interest. The financial side of politics
is so vital that any legislature has the potential for voting on or representing issues in which
they have a conflict of interest. In campaigns, opponents are often quite willing to point out
such conflicts. Still, given the number of incumbents who face only token opposition, the
extent to which such conflicts of interest exist may be underestimated.

One watchdog group that keeps an eye on this issue is the Center for Public
Integrity. While the presidency has come under scrutiny from this group, its biggest criticisms seem to be aimed at state legislatures and Congress. The group's 2000 study of state
legislators found that at least one in five helped regulate their own business or professional interests, had financial ties to organizations that lobby state government, and might
receive income from agencies they oversaw; one in four sat on a legislative committee that
regulated their own profession; at least 18 percent had financial ties to businesses or organizations that lobby state government; and nearly one in four received income from
another government agency, often from agencies the legislature funded (Lewis, 2000). An
earlier year-long study on Congress (Lewis, 1998) traced the decision-making process on
major policy issues and concluded that "at critical forks in the road between the broad
public interests of the American people and vested interests, Congress has taken the
wrong path. That wrong path is illuminated by campaign contributions and other forms of
political lucre."

Conflicts of interest are also a potential concern for the consulting industry. Consultants work for numerous candidates, some of whom have differing political philosophies. The conflict can become critical when differing candidates take different positions
on the same piece of legislation and both solicit advice from the consultant. Whichever
side loses that debate can, often justifiably, feel that they did not receive the best possible
advice from their consultants. Some consultants handle this problem by offering services
on a very specialized basis. In addition to those who work for only one party, others specialize by issues or special interest groups—business, labor, women's issues, the environment, and so forth. This effectively reduces the number of potential conflicts, but
some will still arise. In those situations, the consultant has a professional obligation to
tell the client (or potential new client) about the potential conflict. In some instances, the
consultant should turn down a new client to avoid the conflict. At the least, if the client
knows about the conflict, he or she could then evaluate whether the consultant is the best
one for the job. In many cases, it would be to the candidate's advantage to talk to another
consultant.

Dirty Tricks

During the 1972 presidential campaign, Richard Nixon's reelection efforts were centralized
in a committee that was somewhat appropriately named CREEP, an acronym for the Committee to Re-Elect the President. A subunit of that organization known as the "plumbers"

was in charge of developing strategies that would be disruptive to other campaigns. Their tactics set the standard by which modern dirty tricks are judged. Spies were placed into campaigns, unfounded rumors started and spread, and information contrived to place opponents into unsavory situations. The resulting jail terms for many of those campaign workers dampened the enthusiasm for such high-handed techniques on such a grand scale, but some chicanery continues in most campaigns. Many campaigns continue to place spies in the opposing camps, and some dirty tricks continue.

The most common dirty trick in local elections is sign destruction. Local candidates often find that their campaign signs simply disappear overnight. A candidate challenging an incumbent sheriff in Florida discovered that his four-by-eight plywood signs had been systematically torn down and used to build a hunting cabin by the supporters of the incumbent. At least one congressman came under scrutiny when his father was arrested for tearing down campaign signs of his son's opponent. One of the authors worked in one campaign in which the candidate was appalled to find that one of his supporters was defacing the signs of the opponent. When the staff was ordered to locate and identify the culprit, the candidate was further appalled to discover that the villain was his own son.

In the past, one common dirty trick involved making rude phone calls in the name of the opponent. Voters might be awakened at midnight by a phone call purporting to be from one campaign, with the resulting conversation leading to the caller insulting the unsuspecting voter. The advent of caller ID has reduced the use of this tactic; the turnaround came in 1996 when a number of campaign workers (for a number of different campaigns) were caught with the new device. Still, the telephone remains a popular means of using unfair influence in an election, and other nefarious techniques are limited only by the imagination of those who feel compelled to do something of that nature.

Dirty tricks sometimes come with a touch of humor. During the 1960s, political prankster Dick Tuck spent much of the year creating problems for Richard Nixon's campaign. He arranged for fortune cookies at a Nixon reception to read, "Vote for John Kennedy."

The Self-Motivated Spy

People who engage in unethical behavior in political campaigns often do so for what they consider good reasons. During the 2000 presidential election, lifelong Democrat Juanita Lozano got a position with Republican George W. Bush's presidential campaign.

During September, before the first presidential debate between Bush and Al Gore, Lozano mailed a videotape, a strategy book, and other campaign papers to Gore adviser and former New York congressman Tom Downey. The videotape reportedly showed Bush getting frustrated and agitated under tough questioning—information that Lozano thought would be useful to the Gore team.

Gore's advisers, though, refused to accept the help. Downey turned the materials over to the FBI, who eventually traced them to Lozano. Although sentenced to a year in prison and fined $3,000, she did not express regret over what she had done.

Source: Romano, L. (2001, September 1). Woman gets one year for stealing Bush tape. *Washington Post*, p. 4A.

During a railroad whistle-stop tour in California, Tuck dressed as a trainman and signaled the engineer to pull away from the station just as Nixon began to speak. When Nixon visited San Francisco's Chinatown, Tuck erected banners that read "Welcome Nixon" in English but contained an anti-Nixon message in Chinese (Combs, 1980, p. 155). All in good humor? Not to the Nixon campaign, who used the actions as justification for forming their own dirty tricks squad.

Technological innovations now offer unethical campaigners with numerous other opportunities to mislead the public. Digital photography and video allow for film editing that can put candidates in places they never were and with people they've never met. Kaid (2000) noted that modern editing techniques, special effects, visual imagery, and computerized alterations can create a technological situation that "has the potential to interfere with the ability of an informed electorate to make rational choices" (p. 156). Furthermore, since the quality of digital editing can be extremely high, it can be difficult to detect such alterations. A vigilant public, a skeptical news media, and an outraged opponent are the only elements that must ultimately come into play.

Negative Campaigning

One area of political campaigning that attracts controversy is that of attack ads, or "negative campaigning." Such tactics are nothing new, going back to the early ninetieth century. Andrew Jackson's 1828 presidential campaign remains one of the dirtiest campaigns in American history. When political opponents discovered that Andrew Jackson had married his wife Rachel before the divorce from her first marriage was final, they attacked him as an adulterer. Jackson fought several duels to defend her honor, and the opposition distributed a "Coffin Handbill" that featured drawings of coffins representing men whom Jackson was accused of murdering or otherwise having done away with. Jackson responded in kind, accusing incumbent president John Quincy Adams of spending thousands of federal dollars to furnish the White House with gambling equipment.

Negative campaigns are standard practice in most modern elections (Garramore, 1984, 1985). Challengers may attack the incumbent with a "time for a change" argument (Trent & Friedenberg, 1995) or use some version of the In Man–Out Man attack strategy (Kitchens & Stiteler, 1979). Campaigns use negative ads because they believe they have an effect on voters, and research has generally supported that contention. Decades ago, tradition dictated that incumbents need not engage in negative campaigns, but that has gradually changed. Procter and Schenck-Hamlin (1996) found no difference in the types of negative attacks used by incumbents or challengers or open-seat campaigns. Others have argued that women candidates should avoid negative campaigning or incorporate strategies that "accommodate sex-based stereotypes of femininity" (Trent & Sabourin, 1993, p. 36) by softening or in some way disassociating themselves from the attack (Procter, Aden, & Japp, 1988), using humor (Kern, 1989; Taylor, 1990) or drama (Johnson-Cartee & Copeland, 1991). Procter and Schenck-Hamlin (1996), however, found no difference in the negative attacks of women candidates and men candidates.

Procter and Schenck-Hamlin (1996) called negative ads "a normative advertising form" after they found that negative political ads were remarkably similar in both substance and style across all types of political campaigns. Their finding is not really surprising, given that all of the ads that they studied were likely all made by the same small cadre of consultants. They also suggested that negative advertisements were used more to blunt an opponent's chances of winning the election than to promote the sponsoring candidate's own images or characteristics—another conclusion that would not surprise consultants. The typical negative political ad, they noted, attacked the sponsoring candidate's opponent, had the appearance of a report, used a neutral reporter to present the attack, focused primarily on the opponent's ethics, and used undocumented facts and figures to support its claims. Nor are such negative ads limited to the verbal aspects of the ad; Kaid (1996) found that 42 percent of the spots contained some kind of video editing, special effects, or other technological distortion, and such distortions were more likely to occur in negative spots.

The ethical dilemmas associated with negative campaigning tend to fall within four different categories of criticisms: fairness, appropriateness, effectiveness, and impact on the political system.

Fairness. Some critics view negative ads as inherently unfair. Negative ads may focus on a single negative factor related to a candidate, oversimplifying the argument while disregarding the totality of that person's career (Hale, 1994). Lee (2000, p. 44) argued that "any system that creates such stark contrasts between good and evil will oversimplify problems, create a language of political resentment, and . . . increase the citizen's dissatisfaction with government." For example, incumbent members of Congress are frequently attacked by challengers who claim that they have voted against some issue that is popular with the voters. However, given the multiple votes that Congress takes on issues such as social security, budgets, and tax reductions, it is nearly always possible to find a recorded vote where a member of Congress voted "against" a popular issue. Procedurally, such votes are sometimes necessary to set up a vote on a stronger version of a bill. An even bigger fairness issue is when there is little or no justification for the charge. In the 1998 Alabama lieutenant governor's campaign, a lawyer and a private investigator were indicted for paying a prostitute to say she had sexual relations with one of the candidates (Huffington, 1999).

Appropriateness. Some critics argue that the topics of negative ads are inappropriate for true political debates. Such ads, the argument goes, cross the boundary of issue debate and become personal attacks that degenerate into name calling. During the early 1980s, conservative Republican groups attacked a number of Democratic incumbents, calling them murderers because they were prochoice on the subject of abortion. The name-calling nature of the attacks negated any attempt to discuss the complexity of the moral issue itself. Similarly, Democrats often label Republicans as the party of the wealthy, an approach that does little to discuss the intricacies of economic issues.

Effectiveness. Views on the effectiveness of negative ads tend to fall into two distinct schools of thought. One approach assumes that negative ads are highly effective, with voters responding in dramatic fashion whenever a negative ad is launched by one candidate against an opponent. Others argue that negative ads are not effective and are more likely to backfire on the candidate who dares to use them. Negative ads, this approach argues, merely give voters a reason to vote against the candidate who stoops to such mudslinging tactics. Consultants generally assume that there is validity in both points of view. There is little doubt about the first position; practical experience and academic research both support the view that negative ads are highly effective. Kaid and Boydston (1987) found that negative ads effectively damaged the image of targeted candidates; furthermore, the effect was significant across party lines. Other studies have found that negative ads are effective at producing greater image discrimination and attitude polarization (Garramore, et al., 1990). Negative ads can be particularly helpful in providing a cognitive frame for voters who are less attuned to the political system (Zhang & Buda, 1999). Even critics of negative ads have noted that comparative negative ads can assist voters in making rational choices (Gronbeck, 1992).

On the other side, negative ads can go too far and create a boomerang effect against the candidate who uses them. Consultants generally assume that a candidate who gets labeled as a "mudslinger" is likely to lose the election. The problem, of course, is identifying at what point a negative ad crosses the line that separates legitimate discussion of issues from unfair allegations. For the most part, the answer is relatively easy—the voters decide. If the attack goes against the ethical values and perceptions of fairness held by the voters, they consider it mudslinging. Many times, the voters' perception of fairness may differ from that of both consultants and academicians. For example, during 1999, Republican politicians were campaigning for the impeachment of President Clinton. Their public arguments for his removal from office were based on both personal and legal factors related to his relationship with a White House intern. A majority of the public, though, considered the effort to be an unfair intrusion into private acts. The result: the Republican effort failed, and President Clinton survived the impeachment.

Conversely, George H. W. Bush used ads in his 1988 campaign that academicians tend to view as unfair. The "revolving door" furlough ad focused on a Massachusetts inmate who was temporarily released under a program supported by Governor Michael Dukakis, and who committed a felony while away from the prison. Jamieson (1996) complained that the ad "invited the false inference that Dukakis had furloughed 268 first-degree murderers who had then committed other serious crimes" (p. 461). Furthermore, she noted, the ad had racial overtones since it depicted "dark-complected convicts," with one convict looking directly at the camera who is "more dark-skinned than the others" (p. 461). The issue was visited again by the "weekend passes" ad sponsored by the National Security Political Action Committee, a group that supported the Bush campaign. This ad associated Dukakis with Willie Horton, a murderer who had raped a Caucasian woman after being temporarily released on the Massachusetts furlough program. The ad, which compared Bush's and Dukakis's positions on crime from the Bush perspective, has an announcer saying, "Dukakis not only opposes the death penalty, he allowed first-degree murderers to have weekend passes from prison." The ad cites the example of Horton's furlough, adding, "Horton fled, kidnapping a young couple, stabbing the man and repeatedly raping his girlfriend." Again, academic critics considered the ad unfair; it cited only a single incident while implying that many others had occurred (Jamieson, 1996, p. 471). The public though, at a time when crime and repeat criminal behavior was considered a major issue, responded dramatically to the ad. Public perception that Dukakis was soft on crime rose 11 points to 63 percent. From the public's perspective, it was a legitimate issue that depicted Dukakis's views on crime.

Impact on the Political System.   One of the most serious ethical issues raised by negative campaigns is their impact on the political system. Typical of these concerns is Gronbeck's (1992) allegation that negative campaigns undercut the electoral process. Ansolabehere and

Iyengar (1995) argue that negative campaigns polarize the electorate and drive people away from the polls, thus reducing political participation among the electorate. Jamieson (2001) disagrees, arguing that attack ads do not reduce voter turnout. Still, researchers have consistently reported finding high levels of apathy and low levels of public knowledge among American voters. Most critics of this persuasion argue that negative ads increase political cynicism by "turning off" voters who avoid political participation in ever-increasing numbers. The result, as *Newsweek* reporter Meg Greenfield (1999) noted, is that "politics has become less something in which people engage than something they watch."

The November 1996 election saw a turnout of less than 49 percent, the lowest voter turnout rate since 1924 (Doppelt & Shearer, 1999). Kanter and Mirvis (1989) described a process by which people become cynical in stages: a precondition of unrealistically high expectations, frustration of those expectations, followed by a sense of deception or betrayal. Unrealistic and harsh campaigns can add to this cynicism by focusing on deception and betrayal by other candidates. Critics argue that negative campaigns contribute to this cynicism while also engendering prejudice and disrupting communities (Domke, McCoy, & Torres, 1998).

Hollihan (2001) believes negative campaigning also affects those voters who remain part of the process. Negative campaigning, he argues, increases the likelihood that voters will make electoral decisions on the basis of self-interest rather than considering issues in terms of what is good for the nation. "If the candidates are depicted as primarily concerned with advancing their own interests rather than the public interest," he writes, "then why should individual voters not be concerned first and foremost with protecting their own personal interests?" (p. 182). Capella and Jamieson (1997) agree with Hollihan on the increase in self-centered decision making by modern voters, but they attribute it to another factor: horse-race news coverage. Regardless of the reason, the basic premise of both scholars is the same—when campaign decisions are made on the basis of candidate self-interest, then voters are likely to adopt a similar self-interest in making their voting decision.

Despite all of the rhetorical concern, there are few empirical data to support these allegations. Hart (2000) used a computer analysis of campaign messages to show that political campaigns are not as negative as most people assume. Furthermore, the presence of negative ads in a campaign has no impact on involvement in the election, communication behavior regarding the election, or likelihood of turning out to vote in the election (Garramore et al., 1990). Political cynicism can be a problem, but it appears to be related to a broader range of issues than just negative campaigning. Miller (1974) argued that political cynicism was associated with alienation that comes from citizens who feel they have insufficient political influence to control outcomes. Neuman (1986) attributes it to low levels of political sophistication as evinced through knowledge, salience, and conceptualization.

Some authorities view the problem as an attribute of the voters, not the campaigns. Ehrenhalt (1996) complains that the American public no longer succeeds at balancing the demands of modern life with a feeling of community, resulting in a decline in civic virtue. Similarly, Erber and Lau (1990) view cynicism as a characteristic of the voter rather than an effect of the system; political cynics tend to be voters with chronic issues and those who perceived themselves as distant from both candidates; similarly, low levels of political trust are associated with voters who think about politics as represented by the people involved in it rather than the political system itself. Cynicism is inversely related to both external and internal political efficacy. External and internal efficacy are two distinct factors (Craig, Neimi, &

Silver, 1990). External efficacy refers to an individual's beliefs about the responsiveness of governmental authorities and institutions to citizen demands (Balch, 1974; Coleman & Davis, 1976), while internal efficacy is based on beliefs about one's own competence to understand and to participate effectively in politics (Neimi, Craig, & Mattei, 1991).

Another frequently voiced concern is the possibility that negative advertising dampens the enthusiasm of qualified people to run for public office, resulting in a smaller (and less qualified) pool of candidates. There does seem to be an increased number of politicians who are more interested in personal power than in public service (Ehrenhalt, 1991), but a negative campaign does not appear to be the dominant cause. Potential candidates who decide not to run seem to be more concerned instead about press scrutiny than of negative attacks from the opposition. According to *Campaign & Elections* magazine, 81 percent of candidates surveyed say that press scrutiny keeps qualified people from running for office.

Another justification for negative campaigns is that such advertisements address issues that the public needs to know about. Negative ads frequently address character issues, the dimension that most voters consider most critical for people who hold public office. As Myers (1999, p. 305) noted, ". . . we believe possession of this ability (morality) to have a special value and expect this fact to be reflected in most people's desires." From this perspective, voters have a right to know about factors that might indicate serious moral deficiencies on the part of the people they are considering electing to leadership positions.

Efforts to Reduce Negative Campaigning

Negative campaigning has become such a common practice in campaigns that a number of groups have attacked their use. Kaid (2000) believes such reactions are unjustified. "It is often difficult to isolate the reasons that many find negative ads inherently unethical," she wrote. "There does seem to be an underlying assumption in the criticism . . . that somehow it is just prima facie unethical to engage in 'negative campaigning' or 'negative advertising' " (p. 160). Indeed, it's quite possible for a negative ad to meet all the standard criteria of ethical values: truth, honesty, and fairness. Consultants would generally argue that the best negative ads do just that—provide honest and fair information that the voters need to have before making their decision. Still, as negative tactics have increased, a number have advocated that candidates take a more positive tone in their campaigns. The most visible efforts along this line have come from the Interfaith Alliance, a Washington-based group representing Catholics, Protestants, Muslims, and Jews that asks candidates to sign a pledge ("The Framework of Civility for Political Candidates") that they will "reject personal attacks, innuendo or stereotyping in describing or referring to your opponent." Political expediency almost dictates that a candidate has to sign the pledge; in the 2000 elections, more than forty candidates for federal office, including Hillary Rodham Clinton, George W. Bush, and Al Gore, signed the pledge. But whether the pledge does much to reduce negative campaigning is questionable. In the heat of the battle, the oath may be disregarded or a justification found for not abiding by it.

The Role of Consultants

Veteran Washington journalist Jules Witcover (1999) argues that professional consultants in campaigns have altered presidential politics for the worse. Their inclusion in the process, he

Interview with Stan Adkins

The Consultant's View of Campaign Ethics

Stan Adkins is president of Adkins & Associates, a Miami-based media consulting firm. Adkins was one of the participants in a series of panel discussions on political ethics that was sponsored by the Pew Foundation.

Q: What is the difference between the way consultants and the public view political campaign ethics?

A: The public would probably like to think that people would operate under an absolute, clear cut, black-and-white, Marquis of Queensbury–type rules environment. I don't think they believe that has ever been the case, but they would like to think that it could be the case. The reality is that unethical campaigns have been around for a long time. There were arguably much worse campaign tactics used in the early 1800s than today, particularly in attacks on character and just out-and-out lies printed in newspapers.

Q: So you'd say we've made progress?

A: Yes, I think we have made progress. There is now a higher level of media scrutiny and it is more at arms length than it was then. It's at least easier to identify unethical campaigns than it was during the 1800s. Ad watches help to keep people within parameters of truth.

Q: Where do consultants fit in this ethical growth?

A: Consultants are no different than any other subset of the population. There are honest ones and dishonest ones, or at least some who lean more toward stretching the truth if not totally distorting it. Others stay between the lines, or at least come closer to staying between the lines. It is our job to try and characterize things in the best possible light for our clients and in the worst possible light for our opponents. In doing so, we push messages to limits. Does that cause a distortion? Probably, and if it's too distorted they need to be called on it. The people who call them on it, right now, are either the other side or the media. Generally, the media is pretty good at focusing on something if it truly is a lie or distortion. Last-minute dirty tricks like Nixon used—including breaking into their offices and putting out letters on other people's letterheads—are way over the line. They got caught doing it, but it didn't take away his office. Ultimately, Nixon lost his office, but not really because of a dirty trick. He lost it because of a coverup of a dirty trick. If he had admitted, "Yeah, we were trying to find out what the other side was doing, and things probably got out of hand," I don't think public opinion would have gone against him as much as it did. The public would probably have accepted it as a political thing that was no big deal and no reflection on national security or his ability to govern. But it became a character issue; his character was always in question, but until then it wasn't enough of an issue to defeat him when it came to choosing him versus the opponent.

Q: How much of a role does research play in terms of ethical considerations?

A: The level of research that is available today is astounding. We can pretty much know almost anything about a person. Certainly public records are easily obtainable, but records that you would think would be private are available to anybody who has access to the Internet. When you look at those records through a lens that focuses on somebody as an advocate for a specific position, you can focus on specific pieces of that record.

(continued)

Interview with Stan Adkins   Continued

Would you take something out of context and use it? Some people do. We would not, because we figure that someone would spin around and shoot us for doing that. It would undermine our credibility for any further messages. Those who do that typically do it very late, near the end of the campaign. I'm not sure how effective that is anymore, because it's somewhat suspect.

Q: How does modern technology fit into the puzzle?

A: It's a major concern. With photo technology and computers, people can be placed in places they never were. They can be placed side by side with other people they were never with. That has been done, and done with the obvious intent to mislead the voters. The candidate is placed with someone who is very positive or very negative to the constituency, and there's a real danger. That becomes evidence of an event that didn't occur, but to those who see it, it looks real. One of the bigger dangers out there is how technology is going to allow those without scruples to create whatever fiction they want and to have it look credible.

Q: What would you consider your personal guidelines?

A: We will not create fiction, but we will look at everything that a person has done that relates to job performance and, in some cases, to their character. Some consultants use the "Mommy Rule"—they wouldn't do anything that they didn't want their mother to see. I just don't know what Mommy is used to seeing anymore.

Q: Does "Mommy" prefer a campaign based on issues?

A: Those who follow politics would like to think of everything as a Lincoln-Douglas debate. The candidates express their ideas and you make your decision on where they stand on specific issues. It hasn't been that way for a long time. Some constituencies are motivated by a single issue, and you communicate with them on that issue. But, other than that, the fundamental equation is that people vote for people they know and people they like, in that order. If they know you and they like you, they'll vote for you. The inverse of that is that if they don't know you or don't like you, they won't vote for you. So our goal as we position communication is to increase the positive awareness of our candidate and either minimize awareness or increase negative awareness of our opponent. That's pretty much the formula. Short of there being a highly salient or volatile issue, which is seldom the case, that's it.

Q: What would you say is the public's ethical image of consultants?

A: They haven't seen many consultants. They've seen James Carville and some of the Clinton consultants. To a lesser extent, they've seen consultants who've moved into the media, but I don't think they make the connection that those people were political consultants and operatives. For most of the public, I think the term "political consultant" has a pejorative connotation. They probably think they're less than honorable, and they lead some sort of "I Spy"–type life. They probably think we're snake oil salesmen, but they think politicians are too. So, by extension, the people who work for politicians are viewed negatively. The media has done a good job of coining words like "spin doctor" that have negative connotations. It's not as if you look at a consultant and say this is a person who's helping craft a white-paper policy statement on how we're going to treat hunger and poverty in America. Yet, consultants are helping craft those messages. Most consultants that I know contemplated, at one time or another, being candidates. They got into the business because they had an interest in the process and in government and found themselves behind the scenes instead of on the stage. Many of them have genuine political philosophies and they know how to articulate them. In many instances, that's how candidates and consultants get together. There's a chemistry there. The candidate has to have some connection to the people they're hiring before they can trust them and listen to them. There should be some similarities or some level of philosophical alignment. There are a number of consultants who are just purely technical hired guns; they will do a cold and detached analysis and execute a plan, but I would like to think that there are fewer of those than the ones who have political philosophies and work for candidates who espouse those philosophies.

Q: What responsibility does the candidate have in maintaining an ethical campaign?

A: They have the ultimate responsibility. Their most common defense is, "I wasn't aware that was going on in my campaign." But they need to be aware of what's going on. The campaign is them, after all. Anything that is communicated, in particular, is them. In some cases, the mechanics of fund-raising are beyond the scope of the candidate to really know the details, just because of how it's done. A candidate asks one person to help them raise money, and that person asks twenty-five other people. The candidate may not know any of those other people, and some of them may have done something unpleasant. That's a blind side issue that candidates cannot always be aware of in advance. The best they can do is to react after the fact. But in terms of communication and strategic messages to be used, they have ultimate responsibility to say "yea" or "nay." They have to be comfortable with the statements being made. There are far too many totally reflective candidates, those who are empty suits who are interested in politics purely for their own personal pursuits. They are driven in data that says the public is interested in X, Y, and Z, and that's what they embrace. They are reflective of whatever the public believes at that moment, and they have no substantive direction of their own. There's a lot of that. That's unfortunate. It's somewhat a function of the advance in the science and technique that modern campaigns have. You can, to a very high level of accuracy, determine sentiments on issues and determine what motivates an electorate and craft a message that is consistent with that. That's unfortunate. That is not bringing the best and the brightest forward to serve. But I'm not sure that the best and the brightest want to be held to the same level of scrutiny that candidates are held to today.

Q: What do you mean?

A: The absence of privacy. There was a time, not that long ago, when there were areas of a public official's life that were private. While their private life may be an issue of character, it's not necessarily an issue of ability to govern or to be effective as a leader. What their sexual preference is, or what their sexual appetite is, would have little bearing to me on their ability to make decisions on national defense. Now the salacious part of any individual's background is more important than anything they've had to say or contribute on the substantive issues of governing. To live under that level of a microscope, because that's the story the press wants, is not something that most people are willing to accept as a reasonable sacrifice to be in public office. The sacrifice should be time, time away from pursuit of some other type of career or business. You make that sacrifice, and you serve in public office, but not to the extent of having your entire life stripped away layer by layer. And, not just yourself, but anyone around you, becomes fair game. How important was Billy Carter's beer drinking to Jimmy Carter. As brothers, did that merit the national attention? I don't think so. It is a celebrity status. The media that follows it to that level falls to a paparazzi-type standard.

(continued)

Interview with Stan Adkins   Continued

Q: Look forward ten years. Is the ethical minefield going to get more difficult?

A: I think it will get more difficult and it gets more complex. That comes back to technology. There will be so many other sources of information, via the Internet, and narrowcasting of communication to specific and very small segments of the voting population. That will allow for very narrow messages to be used. Some of that is going on now, with phones and direct mail. But soon you will be able to do that with the Internet. In ten years, most homes will have high speed cables that are fully integrated with their entertainment systems. They will get real-time data available with whatever they're watching. If they're watching a television commercial for one candidate, they might simultaneously be able to see an opponent's message. The technology will also be there to make things that are not real and to make them seem real. Hopefully, the technology will similarly exist to be able to immediately respond to that and mitigate it. But there will always be people who see the lie and don't see the story that said it was a lie. And there will always be people who don't lose their office for lying.

Source: Reprinted by permission of Jon S. (Stan) Adkins.

---

believes, has led to an increase in negative campaigning and a win-at-all-costs mentality that is detrimental to the democratic process. Similarly, Newman (1999) argues that marketing, not ideology, drives America's contemporary political system, leading to an emphasis on image over substance, personality over issues, and thirty-second sound bites over meaningful dialogue.

Whether such critics are correct in attributing negative effects to consultants may be debatable, but there is no doubt that consultants have changed the process. During the 1960s, campaign managers were usually friends or political allies of the candidate who either took a job in the administration or went back to their regular job. Today that role is handled by professionals who move from campaign to campaign. As a result, Newman argues, campaigns become dominated by people who have no ideological allegiance and who justify amoral behavior on the basis of the need to win. Denton (2000) argued that television undermines democracy because candidates use media consultants and pollsters to subvert its watchdog role. Television, he wrote, "has been co-opted by politicians as an instrument of advocacy" (p. 93). Pohl (1971) took a more moderate view, arguing that consultants were "not necessarily evil men" but merely technicians whose participation is necessary to the modern political process; still, their roles should be limited. "Technicians should make only technical decisions, like how to implement a policy," he wrote. "When they are asked to *make* policies, they exceed both their proper responsibilities and their talents" (p. xiii).

Consultants have also contributed to a political environment known as the "permanent campaign" (Blumenthal, 1980). Pollsters recommend that incumbents start their survey work up to eighteen months before the election, a time frame that gives members of Congress only six months of noncampaign activity. In 1995, Bill Clinton began running TV ads for his reelection campaign a year and a half before the election. For the 2000 presidential election, George W. Bush and Al Gore both kicked off their campaigns in June 1999.

Even in the absence of overt campaign activities, incumbents may be tempted to look at each legislative or executive move for its political impact on future campaigns. Members of Congress use the congressional franking privilege to constantly remind supporters of the good job they are doing, thus making it harder for opponents to mount a viable challenge.

Other critics have argued that modern campaigns have become rhetorical exercises in issueless politics, with voters seeking pseudoopinions to justify their choices. Cloud (1997), for example, argued that political discourse was merely the "rhetoric of therapy," and its primary purpose was healing, coping, adapting or restoring an existing order—not a discussion of issues. Such political rhetoric, she argues, distracts from real issues or flaws in the system by encouraging voters to focus on themselves and their private lives. Hart (1998) draws a similar conclusion, arguing that television trades political wisdom for five lesser emotions: intimacy, discernment, cleverness, activity, and importance. As a result, he concludes, the primary effect of television is to make the public feel good about feeling bad about politics. Given such an environment, voters can hardly be expected to make rational decisions in choosing their leaders.

These criticisms have merit, but the system may not be quite as bad as the critics may think. For one thing, the pragmatics of business alone is enough to hold some consultants in check. Little is more damaging to one's business than having to testify before a grand jury. Unflattering press coverage of a consultant's negative campaign is enough to deter some potential clients. Also, despite its problems, the campaign process still seems to be rather effective at informing voters. As noted elsewhere, campaign messages are frequently more informative than news coverage of a campaign. Furthermore, voters are remarkably adept at figuring out which candidate best represents them and their values. As Neuman (1986) noted, the paradox is that the system works because the public has learned to bypass the glut of political information available in campaigns; they rely on the opinions of others or look for nonissue cues to identify which candidate will best represent them.

Becoming Critical Observers of the Process

The authors hope this book has helped to explain the role of consultants and the academic community in campaigns. While describing the role of consultants, we have tried to avoid presenting this information as if it were "cookie-cutter" instructions on how to win an election. Such instructions don't exist. Those consultants who offer such advice to their clients soon find themselves with losing clients. There are simply too many variables that must be taken into consideration for any single approach to always work. In some ways, then, we end by agreeing with Plato in his debate with the Sophists. Students of rhetoric will recall that the debate with the Sophists centered on whether teaching should just involve a "how-to" approach to rhetoric (the Sophists' approach) or whether it should involve a more in-depth teaching style that engaged the student into understanding the theory behind the how-to approach. Media consultants are the modern-day Sophists, professionals who advise their client on what to do without necessarily explaining the theory behind their advice. We would agree with Plato, though, that they would give better advice if they at least understood why themselves.

The goal of a book such as this is to enhance the reader's understanding of the campaign process, for only by understanding the process can we become effective observers of it. Critics abound, but critics who have no understanding of campaign processes may not have a firm foundation for their criticisms. Conversely, those who best understand the system—its participants—have little impetus to criticize it. Their economic past and future has come from the system, and they have been successful primarily because they understand it better than most people. If the system changes, they will adjust to those changes; but they will rarely take steps to change that system themselves.

Academic critics provide objective insight into political outcomes, but they often must make those judgments in the absence of confidential internal information. It's simply hard to make an accurate evaluation of an event without all the facts, particularly if some of the participants take efforts to hide some of those facts. Academicians also have the luxury of conducting their analyses after individual political events (elections) are over. Those insights can be helpful to both consultants and other academicians, but their post hoc nature limits their applicability in the observation of current events. Those who are adept at such analysis can translate academic interpretations into current applications, but they may still lack the confidential information that is critical to a decision.

The goal, then, is to reach some type of synthesis in which the individual has the analytical skills of the outside observer and the understanding of the process provided by campaign insiders. Even then, being an objective observer of campaign events can be difficult. At the very least, though, observers should be able to identify those factors that can interfere with their objectivity.

The Sour Grapes Syndrome

Practically anyone can be a critic of political communication. And most are. Our own experience has been that the most vocal critics of political communication are those candidates (or their supporters) who lose. They often blame their loss on the failure of the media to cover the issues they were addressing, the failure of the voters to appreciate the issues that matter, the use of campaign consultants who unfairly used a tax vote against them, or . . . well, you get the idea. Nor is the sour grapes syndrome limited to candidates; blaming the system makes a convenient scapegoat for consultants (to explain why they lost a race they were expected to win), pollsters (to explain why their predictions were wrong), academicians (to explain why the "best" candidate did not win), and nonvoters (to justify their lack of participation).

The catch, of course, is that each of them might be right. Sometimes the media do make choices about issues that influence election outcomes. Voters don't always appreciate the complexity of issues facing the nation or a state. And sometimes a candidate's record is unfairly used against him or her. The problem for the casual voter is to identify which times such criticisms are warranted and which times they are merely the political version of sour grapes. We can't give a cut-and-dried method for making such distinctions, but we can point to some guideposts that might help.

Understanding Strategy

Perhaps the single most important factor that can be learned from a book on this subject is an understanding of campaign strategy. Campaign messages are not tossed onto a blank canvas, but rather are painted with deliberate strokes onto a preexisting political landscape.

Political messages have rhetorical intent. Each message is aimed as some targeted audience and is often done so at the expense of another audience. Becoming an objective observer of the process involves identifying why a particular candidate chose to use a particular message at some particular point in the campaign. Developing the knack of identifying the strategic reasons for a message is a major achievement in understanding the political campaign process.

Understanding the Media

The media is a frequent target for criticism, some of it deserved and some undeserved. Understanding the media, how they function, and their role in modern society helps in identifying those criticisms that are justified. Overall, we live in a highly media-literate society. Most citizens have grown up watching so much television and listening to so much radio that they are artfully attuned to many of the media's techniques and shortcomings. Still, some myths about the impact of modern media exist, and dispelling some of these myths is essential to understanding its role.

Myth no. 1: Modern media have changed politics by diluting the impact of issues by simplifying messages into thirty-second ads. That's only half true. It's true that the media often simplify messages; modern campaigns are often fought with exchanges of messages that are short, simplistic (sometimes overly so), and that overlook the complexities of many issues. The mythical part of the statement, though, is that this effect is a product of the modern media. In fact, such practices have been around for centuries. Patrick Henry's pre–Revolutionary War speech inspired the American colonists to take up arms against the British. But all that most people remembered from Henry's oratorical gem was one line: "Give me liberty, or give me death." It was that simple phrase that served as a rallying cry for the colonists. Similarly, the Texans of 1836 won a war against Mexico behind the rallying cry of "Remember the Alamo." Sound bites, it seems, predate modern media.

Myth no. 2: Modern media have more impact on other people than on ourselves. This myth has been extensively studied by modern scholars under the title of the "Third-Person Effect." Specifically, the third-person effect is a tendency among voters to believe that the media have a greater influence on other people than they do on themselves. It is a vital factor in understanding criticism of the process. Research has consistently shown that critics who call for change in the process do so not because they have been unduly or unfairly influenced by a campaign, but because they believe other voters have succumbed to misleading campaign tactics. The third-person effect, then, is the common impetus behind criticisms of the media, particularly those criticisms that call for restrictions on campaign messages (Salwen, 1998). In other words, fear that others might be influenced by the media is the impetus for censorship campaigns. That create a paradox: for some people, the media's biggest impact may be fear of potential impact.

Identifying One's Own Biases

You can never eliminate your own biases from any analysis. This set of recommendations, for example, is based on the biases of both authors and their experiences at participating in and observing political campaigns. We have omitted other standards that other scholars prefer. Readers, in turn, will develop their own criteria for evaluating campaigns and their messages. Regardless of which specific standards a person uses, though, there should be an attempt to identify what biases are present. Each person can become aware of his or her own biases and look for those biases that may influence his or her observations.

Summary

This chapter has provided an overview of some of the ethical issues involved in political communication. Ethical issues are often philosophical arguments between democratic idealists and political pragmatists. Agreement between the two can sometimes be reached. Philosophically, both sides agree on the repulsive nature of ballot stuffing, dirty tricks, and unnecessary intrusions into people's private lives. Consultants must also contend with the pragmatic impact of ethical questions on their careers. They risk their careers if they ever do anything illegal. They risk their income if they lose a race with advice that leads to charges pertaining to ethics. Ethical questions are still hotly debated on such issues as negative campaigning and the role of consultants in campaigns. Becoming a critical observer of the process involves recognizing the sour grapes syndrome, understanding campaign strategy, understanding the media, and developing the ability to recognize one's own biases.

Ultimate control of political ethics lies with the voters. Acceptable behavior is, at a basic level, defined by the values of the voters and what they find acceptable. The voters can serve as effective monitors, though, only if they have the requisite information to evaluate candidates and their campaigns. Fortunately, they are apparently more adept at making those judgments than many politician would give them credit for being. After all, ethical judgments about public behaviors are complex value decisions.

Republican partisans found the public's acceptance of Bill Clinton's sexual misconduct unthinkable. Democrat partisans could not understand public acceptance of Newt Gingrich's antagonistic approach to legislative issues. But neither partisan side understood the complexity of such issues as well as the public. Gronbeck (2000) argues that public judgment of candidates is based on candidates' motives and actions, their character, and their competence. Each of these factors, in turn, is evaluated by its message source, the audience, the message, and situational expectations. Taken together, these two dimensions create a three-by-four matrix that reflects twelve distinct judgments that individual voters must make before reaching a value-based conclusion about any candidate. Given the complexity of such decisions, it's no wonder that the voters found value judgments about Clinton and Gingrich to be considerably more complex than did the partisans themselves. That doesn't mean, of course, that the voters' judgments are necessarily more "right" than those of the political players, because the voters' judgments can also be clouded by personal biases. Overcoming those biases can be a key element if the public is to be successful at monitoring the ethics of its leaders.

One goal of this book was to make the reader more adept at monitoring political activities by offering two ways of looking at campaigns—an insider's view of those who work in the trenches of campaigns and an outsider's view offered by those who observe and analyze campaigns and their implications. A combination of both views, the authors believe, will make the average citizen a more informed voter. The insider view enables the observer to understand the how and why of some campaign decisions. The outsider view maintains a focus on the ethical and rhetorical implications of campaign activities. If the ideal model of an informed electorate is to be reached, both viewpoints must be appreciated.

QUESTIONS FOR DISCUSSION

1. In the course of researching your opponent's record, you are given a copy of his FBI "rap sheet." It comes from an implacable enemy of your opponent and says he was arrested for theft three decades ago. Clearly, it is genuine. Because your race is for state attorney general, it is clear that the document could help your candidate's campaign. On the other hand, it is illegal to use an FBI criminal record for a political purpose. What do you do with this document to help your campaign? If you make the document public, what is the likely response of your opponent?

2. Down the stretch of the campaign, you become aware that the campaign field director is probably getting a kickback on lawn signs from the printing company. It is possible he is sharing the money with your candidate. Do you undertake a further inquiry to discover the truth? Do you turn the information over to the authorities?

3. To reduce the impact of money on his campaign, your candidate has declared he will take no contributions greater than $100. In the course of the campaign the treasurer reports to you that the candidate gave him some 6,000 checks of $100 each. It is clear the checks are from a well-known special interest in your state and that the candidate intends to accept the contributions. Is acceptance of these contributions right or wrong? What is the downside when your opponent discovers this contribution? As campaign manager, what course of action do you follow?

4. While campaigning in a small county, your campaign receives the endorsement of the local sheriff. On two occasions he has received more votes than there are people registered to vote. It is widely assumed he is stuffing the ballot box and he promises you he will deliver for your candidate "just like in my campaigns." What do you tell him? What is problematic about accepting this sort of endorsement?

REFERENCES

Aberbach, J. (1990). Lobbying for the people. *American Journal, 22,* 161–167.

Abramowitz, A. I. (1978). The impact of a presidential debate on voter rationality. *American Journal of Political Science, 22,* 680–690.

Abramowitz, A. I., & Saunders, K. L. (1998). Ideological realignment in the U.S. electorate. *Journal of Politics, 60,* 634–652.

Abramson, P. R., & Aldrich, J. H. (1982). The decline of electoral participation in America. *American Political Science Review, 76,* 502–521.

Abramson, P., & Claggett, W. (1984). Race-related differences in self-reported and validated turnout. *Journal of Politics, 46,* 719–738.

Abramson, P., & Claggett, W. (1986). Race-related differences in self-reported and validated turnout in 1984. *Journal of Politics, 48,* 412–422.

Abramson, P., & Claggett, W. (1991). Race-related differences in self-reported and validated turnout in the 1988 presidential election. *Journal of Politics, 53,* 186–197.

Abramson, P. R., & Ostrom, C. W. (1991). Macropartisanship: An empirical reassessment. *American Political Science Review, 85,* 181–192.

Adamany, D. (1990). The unaccountability of political money. In M. L. Nugent & J. R. Johannes (Eds.), *Money, elections and democracy* (pp. 95–118). Boulder, CO: Westview Press.

Agranoff, R. (1976). *The management of election campaigns.* Boston: Holbrook Press.

Allport, G. W., & Postman, L. J. (1947). *The psychology of rumor.* New York: Holt, Rinehart and Winston.

Allyn, R. (1999). The good that political consultants do. In D. D. Perlmutter (Ed.), *The Manship School guide to political communication* (pp. 304–310). Baton Rouge: Louisiana State University Press.

Althaus, S. L., & Tewksbury, D. (2000). Patterns of Internet and traditional news media use in a networked community. *Political Communication, 17,* 21–45.

Altschull, J. H. (1995). *Agents of power: The media and public policy.* White Plains, NY: Longman.

American Institute for Political Communication. (1970). *Anatomy of a crucial election.* Washington, DC: American Institute for Political Communication.

Ansolabehere, S., Behr, R., & Iyengar, S. (1993). *The media game: American politics in the television age.* New York: Macmillan.

Ansolabehere, S., Behr, R., & Iyengar, S. (1994). Riding the wave and claiming ownership over issues: The joint effects of advertising and news coverage in campaigns. *Public Opinion Quarterly, 58,* 335–357.

Ansolabehere, S., & Iyengar, S. (1995). Can the press monitor campaign advertising? An experimental study. *Harvard International Journal of Press/Politics, 1,* 72–86.

Ansolabehere, S., & Iyengar, S. (1995). *Going negative: How political advertisements shrink and polarize the electorate.* New York: Free Press.

Archibald, S. J. (1975). A brief history of dirty politics. In R. E. Hiebert, R. F. Jones, J. Lorenz, & E. A. Lotito, *The political image merchants* (pp. 230–236). Washington, DC: Acropolis.

Arnold, M. (2000, April 27). The long history of the attack book. *New York Times,* p. B3.

Arterton, C. (2000). New relationships. *Campaigns & Elections,* 22–23.

Asher, H. (1992). *Polling and the public: What every citizen should know.* Washington, DC: Congressional Quarterly Press.

Associated Press (2000, June 12). Winston County case not first for vote fraud. *Birmingham Post-Herald,* p. D2.

Atkin, C. (1975). Communication and political socialization. *Political Communication Review, 1,* 2–6.

Atkin, C. (1983). Effects of realistic TV violence vs. fictional violence on aggression. *Journalism Quarterly, 60,* 615–621.

Atkin, C., Greenberg, B., Korzenny, F., & McDermott, S. (1979). Selective exposure of televised violence. *Journal of Broadcasting, 23,* 5–14.

Atkin, C., Hocking, J., & McDermott, S. (1979). Home state voter response and secondary media coverage: In S. Kraus (Ed.), *The great debates: Carter vs. Ford, 1976* (pp. 429–436). Bloomington: Indiana University Press.

Atkinson, A. (2000). *Lou Henry Hoover and the rhetoric of place: Building a sense of home and hearth.* Paper presented at the annual meeting of the Eastern Communication Association, Pittsburgh, PA.

Baker, R. K. (1989). *The new fat cats: Members of Congress as political benefactors.* New York: Priority Press.

Balch, G. I. (1974). Multiple indicators in survey research: The concept 'sense of political efficacy.' *Political Methodology, 1,* 1–43.

Baran, S. J. (1999). *Introduction to mass communication: Media literacy and culture.* Mountain View, CA: Mayfield.

Barber, J. D. (1964). *Political leadership in American government.* Boston: Little, Brown.

Barber, J. D. (1972). *The presidential character.* Englewood Cliffs, NJ: Prentice-Hall.

Basil, M. D., & Brown, W. J. (1994). Interpersonal communication in news diffusion: A study of "Magic" Johnson's announcement. *Journalism Quarterly, 71,* 305–320.

Bates, B., & Harmon, M. (1993). Do "instant polls" hit the spot? Phone-in vs. random sampling of public opinion. *Journalism Quarterly, 70,* 369–380.

Beck, P. A., & Jennings, M. K. (1991). Family traditions, political periods, and the development of partisan attitudes. *Journal of Politics, 53,* 742–763.

Becker, L. B., McCombs, M. E., & McLeod, J. M. (1975). The development of political cognitions. In S. H. Chaffee (Ed.), *Political communication: Issues and strategies for research* (pp. 21–63). Beverly Hills, CA: Sage.

Becker, L. B., Sobowale, I. A., Cobbey, R. E., & Eyal, C. H. (1978). Debates' effects on voters' understanding of candidates and issues. In G. F. Bishop, R. G. Meadow, & M. Jackson-Beeck (Eds.), *The presidential debates: Media, electoral, and policy perspectives* (pp. 126–139). New York: Praeger.

Bennet, J. (2000, February 27). The fear of loathing on the campaign trail. *New York Times Magazine,* pp. 52–55.

Bennett, S. (1988). 'Know-Nothings' revisited: The meaning of political ignorance today. *Social Science Quarterly, 69,* 476–490.

Bennett, W. L. (1977). The ritualistic and pragmatic bases of political campaign discourse. *Quarterly Journal of Speech, 63,* 219–238.

Bennett, W. L. (2001). *News: The politics of illusion.* New York: Longman.

Benoit, W. L., Benoit, P. J., & Hanson, G. J. (2000). Political advertising on the Internet. In D. Bystrom, D. B. Carlin, L. L. Kaid, M. Kern, & M. S. McKinney (Eds.), *Communicating politics: Engaging the public in campaign 2000 and beyond* (pp. 11–20). Washington, DC: NCA Summer Conference proceedings.

Benoit, W. L., Blaney, J. R., & Pier, P. M. (2000). Acclaiming, attacking and defending: A functional analysis of U.S. nominating convention keynote speeches. *Political Communication, 17,* 61–84.

Benoit, W. L., Gullifor, P., & Panici, D. A. (1991). President Reagan's defensive discourse on the Iran-contra affair. *Communication Studies, 42,* 272–294.

Benton, M. (1976). The agenda setting function of the mass media at three levels of imformation holding. *Communication Research, 3,* 201–273.

Benze, J. G., & Declercq, E. R. (1985). Content of television political spot ads for female candidates. *Journalism Quarterly, 82,* 278–283, 288.

Benzjian-Avery, A., Calder, B., & Iacobucci, D. (1998, July/August). New media interactive advertising vs. traditional advertising. *Journal of Advertising Research,* pp. 23–32.

Berelson, B. R., Lazarsfeld, P. F., & McPhee, W. N. (1954). *Voting: A study of opinion formation in a presidential campaign.* Chicago: University of Chicago Press.

Berke, R. L. (2000, February 28). Regrets well placed, if questionably timed. *New York Times,* p. A10.

Bernays, E. L. (1947). The engineering of consent. *Annals of the American Academy of Political and Social Science, 250,* 113–120.

Berne, E. (1963). *The structure and dynamics of organizations and groups.* New York: J. B. Lippincott.

Bernstein, A. G. (2000). The effects of message theme, policy explicitness, and candidate gender. *Communication Quarterly, 48,* 159–173.

Bernstein, R., Chadha, A., & Montjoy, R. (2001). Overreporting voting: Why it happens and why it matters. *Public Opinion Quarterly, 65,* 22–44.

Berrigan, J. (1982). The cost effectiveness of grass-roots campaign activities. *Campaigns & Elections, 3(1),* 25–33.

Beville, H. M. (1988). *Audience ratings: Radio, television, cable.* Hillsdale, NJ: Erlbaum

Bineham, J. L. (1988). A historical account of the hypodermic model in mass communication. *Communication Monographs, 55,* 230–246.

Bishop, G. F., Tuchfarber, A. J., & Oldendich, R. W. (1986). Opinion as fictitious issues: The pressure to answer survey questions. *Public Opinion Quarterly, 50,* 240–250.

Bitzer, L. F. (1968). The rhetorical situation. *Philosophy and Rhetoric, 1,* 1–14.

Black, J. (2001). *Battling cyber parody in the political arena: A case study of the rhetorical clash between George W. Bush and gwbush.com.* Paper presented at the annual meeting of the Southern States Communication Association. Lexington, KY.

Blais, A., Nevitte, N., Gidengil, E., & Nadeau, R. (2000). Do people have feelings toward leaders about whom they say they know nothing? *Public Opinion Quarterly, 64,* 452–463.

Bloom, M. (1973). *Public relations and presidential campaigns: A crisis in democracy.* New York: Thomas Crowell.

Blumenthal, S. (1982). *The permanent campaign.* 2nd ed. New York: Touchstone Books.

Blumler, J. G. (1979). The role of theory in uses and gratifications studies. *Communication Research, 6,* 9–36.

Blumler, J. G., & Katz, E. (Eds.). (1974). *The uses of mass communication: Current perspectives on gratification research.* Beverly Hills, CA: Sage.

Blumler, J. G., & McQuail, D. (1969). *Television in politics.* Chicago: University of Chicago Press.

Bonafede, D. (1972). Speechwriters play strategic role in conveying, shaping Nixon's policies. *National Journal, 19,* 311–320.

Bormann, E. (1960). Ghostwriting and the rhetorical critic. *Quarterly Journal of Speech, 46,* 284–288.

Bormann, E. G., Koester, J., & Bennett, J. (1978). Political cartoons and salient rhetorical fantasies: An empirical analysis of the '76 presidential campaign. *Communication Monographs, 45,* 317–329.

Bosdorff, D. M. (1987). Making light of James Watt: A Burkean approach to the form and attitude of political cartoons. *Quarterly Journal of Speech, 73,* 43–59.

Bowers, T. A. (1973). Newspaper political advertising and the agenda-setting function. *Journalism Quarterly, 50,* 552–556.

Box-Steffensmeier, J. M., Jacobson, G. C., & Grant, J. T. (2000). Question wording and the House vote choice: Some experimental evidence. *Public Opinion Quarterly, 64,* 257–270.

Boyle, T. P. (2000). Political web sites: Who will come to visit in 2000? In D. Bystrom, D. B. Carlin, L. L. Kaid, M. Kern, & M. S. McKinney (Eds.), *Communicating politics: Engaging the public in campaign 2000 and beyond* (pp. 22–33). Washington, DC: NCA Summer Conference proceedings.

Braden, S. W. (2001). *The rhetorical use of the benign political scapegoat: Ronald Reagan attacks the federal government.* Paper presented at the annual meeting of the Southern States Communication Association. Lexington, KY.

Bradley, B. (1996). *Time present, time past.* New York: Vintage.

Brigance, W. N. (1956). Ghostwriting: Before Franklin D. Roosevelt and the radio. *Today's Speech,* 10–12.

Brinkman, D. (1968). Do editorial cartoons and editorials change opinions? *Journalism Quarterly, 45,* 724–726.

Brito, R. B. (1999). *Values or facts: The impeachment debate as a struggle to define American morality.* Paper at the National Communication Association Convention. Chicago, IL.

Broder, D. (1999, August 8). Campaign lessons: Candidates quickly learn they need lots of money. *Birmingham News,* p. 3C.

Brosius, H. B., & Bathelt, A. (1994). The utility of exemplars in persuasive communications. *Communication Research, 21,* 48–78.

Brosius, H., & Kepplinger, H. M. (1992). Beyond agenda-setting: The influence of partisanship and television reporting on the electorate's voting intentions. *Journalism Quarterly, 69,* 893–901.

Brown, P., & Levinson, S. C. (1987). *Politeness: Some universal in language usage.* New York: Cambridge University Press.

Browning, G. (1996). *Electronic democracy.* Wilton, CT: Pemberton Press.

Brumas, M. (2000, April 4). Attorney's death tax crusade gets attention. *Birmingham News,* p. 4B.

Bruni, F. (1999, November 1). For Bush, an adjustable speech of tested themes and phrases. *New York Times,* pp. A1, A14.

Bruni, F. (2000, May 8). Bush runs, with a lexicon of his own. *New York Times,* p. A11.

Bruni, F., & Kristof, N. D. (2000, February 28). Bush rues failure to attack bigotry in visit to college. *New York Times,* pp. A1, A10.

Brydon, S. R., & Scott, M. D. (1994). *Between one and many.* Mountain View, CA: Mayfield Publishing.

Buchanan, B. (1991). *Electing a president: The Markle Commission research on campaign '88.* Austin: University of Texas Press.

Burgess, D., Haney, B. Snyder, M., Sullivan, J. L., & Transue, J. E. (2000). Rocking the vote: Using personalized messages to motivate voting among young adults. *Public Opinion Quarterly, 64,* 29–52.

Burke, K. (1973). *The philosophy of literary form* (3rd ed.). Berkeley: University of California Press.

Bush, G. W. (1999). *A charge to keep.* New York: Morrow.

Bush, A., Bush, V., & Harris, S. (1998, March/April). Advertiser perceptions of the Internet as a marketing communications tool. *Journal of Advertising Research,* 17–26.

Bystrom, D. G., & Miller, J. L. (1999). Gendered communication styles and strategies in campaign 1996: The videostyles of women and men candidates. In L. L. Kaid & D. G. Bystrom (Eds.), *The electronic election* (pp. 303–318). Mahwah, NJ: Erlbaum.

Caldeira, G. A., & Patterson, S. C. (1987). Political friendships in the legislature. *Journal of Politics, 49,* 953–975.

Campbell, A. (1966). Interpreting the presidential victory. In M. C. Cummings, Jr. (Ed.), *The national election of 1964.* Washington, DC: Brookings Institution.

Campbell, A., Converse, P. E., Miller, W. E., & Stokes, D. E. (1960). *The American voter.* New York: John Wiley.

Campbell, A., Gurin, G., & Miller, W. E. (1954). *The voter decides.* Evanston, IL: Row, Petersen.

Campbell, A., & Kahn, R. L. (1952). *The people elect a president.* New York: Columbia University Press.

Campbell, K. K., & Jamieson, K. H. (1990). Deeds done in words: Presidential rhetoric and the genres of governance. Chicago: University of Chicago Press.

Canary, D. J., & Spitzberg, B. H. (1993). Loneliness and media gratifications. *Communication Research, 20,* 800–822.

Cantril, A. H., & Cantril, S. D. (1999). *Reading mixed signals: Ambivalence in American public opinion about government.* Baltimore: John Hopkins University Press.

Capella, J. N., & Jamieson, K. H. (1994). Broadcast adwatch effects: A field experiment. *Communication Research, 21,* 342–365.

Capella, J., & Jamieson, K. H. (1997). *Spiral of cynicism: The press and the public good.* New York: Oxford University Press.

Carey, J. W. (1998). The Internet and the end of the national communication system: Uncertain predictions on an uncertain future. *Journalism & Mass Communication Quarterly, 75,* 28–34.

Carl, L. M. (1968). Editorial cartoons fail to reach many readers. *Journalism Quarterly, 45,* 533–535.

Carmines, E. G., & Stimson, J. A. (1989). Issue evolution: Race and the transformation of American politics. Princeton, NJ: Princeton University Press.

Carpenter, R. (1999). *Choosing powerful words.* Boston: Allyn and Bacon.

Cass, D. P. (1962). *How to win votes and influence elections: A nonpartisan guide to effective political work.* Chicago: Public Administration Service.

Cassell, C. A., & Luskin, R. (1988). Simple explanations of turnout decline. *American Political Science Review, 82,* 1321–1330.

Cassidy, M. (2000). Cyber-citizenship: A consideration of the role of the Internet in American politics. In D. Bystrom, D. B. Carlin, L. L. Kaid, M. Kern, & M. S. McKinney (Eds.), *Communicating politics: Engaging the public in campaign 2000 and beyond* (pp. 57–63). Washington, DC: NCA Summer Conference proceedings.

Chaffee, S. H. (1978). Presidential debates: Are they helpful to voters? *Communication Monographs, 45,* 330–346.

Chaffee, S. H., & Kanihan, S. F. (1997). Learning about politics from the mass media. *Political Communication, 14,* 423–430.

Chaffee, S., Ward, S., & Tipton, L. (1970). Mass communication and political socialization. *Journalism Quarterly, 47,* 647–659.

Chaffee, S. H., Zhao, X., & Leshner, G. (1994). Political knowledge and the campaign media of 1992. *Communication Research, 21,* 305–324.

Chandler, K. (2000, June 14). Bennett questions absentees. *Birmingham News,* pp. 1A, 2A.

Chang, M., & Gruner, C. R. (1981). Audience reaction to self-disparaging humor. *Southern Speech Communication Journal, 46,* 419–426.

Checkoway, B. (1993). Interest groups and the bureaucracy. *Journal of Applied Behavioral Science, 17,* 566–582.

Chew, F. (1994). The relationship of information needs to issue relevance and media use. *Journalism Quarterly, 71,* 676–688.

Chong, D. (1993). How people think, reason, and feel about rights and liberties. *American Journal of Political Science, 37,* 867–899.

Chong, D. (1999). Creating common frames of reference on political issues. In D.C. Mutz, P. M. Sniderman, & R. A. Brody (Eds.), *Political persuasion and attitude change* (pp. 195–224). Ann Arbor: University of Michigan Press.

Cloud, Dana L. (1997). *Control and consolation in American culture and politics: Rhetorics of therapy.* Thousand Oaks, CA: Sage.

Coffey, S., & Stipp, H. (1999, March/April). The interactions between computer and television usage. *Journal of Advertising Research,* 61–66.

Cohen, A., & Taylor, E. (2000). *American pharaoh: Richard J. Daley—His battle for Chicago and the nation.* New York: Little, Brown.

Cohen, B. (1963). *The press and foreign policy.* Princeton, NJ: Princeton University Press.

Coleman, K. M., & Davis, C. L. (1976). The structural component of politics and dimensions of regime performance: Their importance for the comparative study of political efficacy. *Comparative Political Studies, 9,* 189–206.

Combs, J. E. (1980). *Dimensions of political drama.* Santa Monica, CA: Goodyear.

Comstock, G. (1989). *The evolution of American television.* Newbury Park, CA: Sage.

Connell, R. W. (1972). Political socialization in the American family: The evidence re-examined. *Public Opinion Quarterly, 36,* 323–333.

Conover, P. J., & Sigelman, L. (1982). Presidential influence and public opinion: The case of the Iran hostage crisis. *Social Science Quarterly, 63,* 249–264.

Conrad, F. G., & Schroder, M. F. (2000). Clarifying question meaning in a household survey. *Public Opinion Quarterly, 64,* 1–28.

Cook, T., & Scioli, F. (1972). Political socialization research in the United States: A review. In D. Nimmo and C. Bonjean (Eds.), *Political attitudes and public opinion.* New York: McKay.

Corcoran, P. E. (1979). *Political language and rhetoric.* Austin: University of Texas.

Cornfield, M. (2000, June). New media, new coverage rules. *Campaigns & Elections,* 55.

Corrado, A. (1997). Party soft money. In A. Corrado, T. E. Mann, D. R. Ortiz, T. Potter, & F. J. Sorauf (Eds.), *Campaign Finance Reform: A sourcebook.* Washington, DC: Brookings Institution.

Costello, W. (1960). *The facts about Nixon.* New York: Viking Press.

Cotter, P. R., Perry, D. K., & Stovall, J. G. (1994). Active and passive indicators of public opinion: Assessing the call-in poll. *Journalism Quarterly, 71,* 169–175.

Couper, M. P. (2000). Web surveys: A review of issues and approaches. *Public Opinion Quarterly, 64,* 464–494.

Couper, M. P., Blair, J., & Triplett, T. (1999). A comparison of mail and e-mail for a survey of employees in federal statistical agencies. *Journal of Official Statistics, 15,* 39–56.

Craig, R. (2000). Expectations and elections: How television defines campaign news. *Critical Studies in Media Communication, 17,* 28–44.

Craig, S. C., Neimi, R. G., & Silver, G. E. (1990). Political efficacy and trust: A report on the NES pilot study items. *Political Behavior, 12,* 289–314.

Crouse, T. (1974). *The boys on the bus.* New York: Ballantine Books.

Cundy, D. T. (1986). Political commercials and candidate image: The effect can be substantial. In L. L. Kaid, D. Nimmo, & K. Sanders (Eds.), *New Perspectives on Political Advertising* (pp. 210–235). Carbondale: Southern Illinois University Press.

Cutbirth, C. W., & Rasmussen, C. (1982). *Political direct mail: The state of the art.* Paper presented at the annual meeting of the Central States Speech Association. Milwaukee, WI.

Dabelko, K. L., & Hernson, P. S. (1997). Women's and men's campaigns for the U.S. House of Representatives. *Political Research Quarterly, 50,* 121–135.

Dallek, M. (2000). *The right moment: Ronald Reagan's first victory and the decisive turning point in American politics.* New York: Free Press.

Dallek, R. (1999). *Ronald Reagan: The politics of symbolism.* Cambridge, MA: Harvard University Press.

Dao, J. (1999, November 15). Old-Timers day meets political fund-raiser at Bradley Garden party. *New York Times,* p. A25.

Daschmann, G. (2000). Vox pop & polls: The impact of poll results and voter statements in the media on the perception of a climate of opinion. *International Journal of Public Opinion, 12,* 160–181.

Davis, R. (1999). *The web of politics: The Internet's impact on the American political system.* New York: Oxford University Press.

Davis, R., & Owen, D. M. (1998). *New media and American politics.* New York: Oxford University Press.

DeFleur, M. H. (1997). *Computer-assisted investigative reporting.* Mahwah, NJ: Erlbaum.

Delli Carpini, M. X. (1989). Age and history: Generations and sociopolitical change. In R. S. Sigel (Ed.), *Political learning in adulthood* (pp. 11–55). Chicago: University of Chicago Press.

Delli Carpini, M. X., & Keeter, S. (1996). *What Americans know about politics and why.* New Haven: Yale University Press.

Delli Carpini, M., Keeter, S., & Webb, S. (1997). The impact of presidential debates. In P. Norris (Ed.), *Politics and the press: The news media and their influences* (pp. 145–164). Boulder, CO: Lynne Rienner.

DeLuca, T. (1995). *The two faces of political apathy.* Philadelphia: Temple University Press.

Denton, R. E. (2000). Dangers of "teledemocracy": How the medium of television undermines American democracy. In R. E. Denton, Jr. (Ed.), *Political communication ethics: An oxymoron* (pp. 91–124). Westport, CT: Praeger.

Denton, R. E., Jr., & Woodward, G. C. (1985). *Political communication in America.* New York: Praeger.

Denzin, N. K., & Lincoln, Y. S. (Eds.). (2000). *The handbook of qualitative research.* Thousand Oaks, CA: Sage.

Deutschmann, P. J., & Danielson, W. A. (1960). Diffusion of knowledge of the major news story. *Journalism Quarterly, 37,* 345–355.

Devitt, E. G., Jr. (1997). Framing politicians: The transformation of candidate arguments in presidential campaign news coverage, 1980, 1988, 1992, and 1996. *American Behavioral Scientist, 40,* 1139–1160.

Devlin, L. P. (1973). The McGovern canvass: A study in interpersonal political campaign communication. *Central States Speech Journal, 24,* 83–90.

Devlin, P. (1986). An analysis of political television commercials, 1952–1984. In L. L. Kaid, D. Nimmo, & K. Sanders (Eds.), *New Perspectives on political advertising* (p. 22). Carbondale: Southern Illinois University Press.

DeVries, W. (1975). Taking the voter's pulse. In R. E. Hiebert, R. F. Jones, J. D. Lorenz, & E. A. Lotito, *The political image merchants* (pp. 62–81). Washington, DC: Acropolis.

DeVries, W., & Tarrance, V. L. (1972). *The ticket-splitter: A new force in American politics.* Grand Rapids, MI: Eerdmans.

Dexter, L. (1969). *How organizations are represented in Washington.* New York: Bobbs-Merrill.

Diamond, E., & Bates, S. (1988). *The spot: The rise of political advertising* (pp. 302–345). Cambridge, MA: MIT Press.

Diamond, G. A., & Cobb, M. D. (1999). The candidate as catastrophe: Latitude theory and the problems of political persuasion. In D. C. Mutz, P. M. Sniderman, & R. A. Brody (Eds.), *Political persuasion and attitude change* (pp. 225–248). Ann Arbor: University of Michigan Press.

Didion, J. (2001). *Political fictions.* New York: Knopf.

Dillman, D. A., Tortora, R. D., Conradt, J., & Bowker, D. (1998). *Influence of plain vs. fancy design on response rates for Web surveys.* Paper presented at the meeting of the American Statistical Association. Dallas, TX.

Dionne, E. J., Jr. (1991). *Why Americans hate politics.* New York: Simon and Schuster.

Dobos, J., & Dimmick, J. (1988). Factor analysis and gratifications construct. *Journal of Broadcasting & Electronic Media, 32,* 335–350.

Domke, D., McCoy, K., & Torres, M. (1998). News media, racial perceptions, and political cognition. *Communication Research, 26,* 570–607.

Dommeyer, C. J., & Moriarty, E. (2000). *Increasing the response rate on e-mail surveys.* Paper presented at the American Association for Public Opinion Research meeting. Portland, OR.

Donahue, G. A., Tichenor, P. J., & Olien, C. M. (1972). Gatekeeping: Mass media systems and information control. In F. G. Kline & P. J. Tichenor (Eds.), *Communication research.* Beverly Hills, CA: Sage.

Doppelt, J. C., & Shearer, E. (1999). *Nonvoters: America's no-shows.* Thousand Oaks, CA: Sage.

Drinkard, J. (2000, February 3). McCain's win nets windfall on Net. *USA Today,* p. 8A.

Drinkard, J. (2000, March 10). Let the fundraising begin—again. *USA Today,* p. 14A.

Drinkard, J., & Pound, E. T. (1999, August 6). GOP donors asked to pay for mailing error; help woman keep job. *USA Today,* p. 4A.

Duffy, M. (1997). High stakes: A fantasy theme analysis of the selling of riverboat gambling in Iowa. *Southern Communication Journal, 62,* 117–132.

Duffy, M., & Gibbs, N. (2001, September 3). How not to rebuild a reputation. *Time,* 34–35.

Duncan, H. D. (1968). *Symbols in society.* New York: Oxford University Press.

Eagly, A. H., Makhijani, M. G., & Klonsky, B. G. (1992). Gender and the evaluation of leaders: A meta-analysis. *Psychological Bulletin, 111,* 3–22.

Easton, D. (1965). *A framework for political analysis.* Englewood Cliffs, NJ: Prentice-Hall.

Edelman, M. (1964). *The symbolic uses of politics.* Urbana: University of Illinois Press.

Egeth, J. (1967). Selective attention. *Psychological Bulletin, 67,* 41–57.

Ehrenhalt, A. (1991). *The United States of ambition: Politicians, power and the pursuit of office.* New York: Random House.

Ehrenhalt, A. (1996). *The lost city: The forgotten virtues of community in America.* New York: Basic Books.

Einhorn, L. J. (1981). The ghosts unmasked: A review of literature on speechwriting. *Communication Quarterly, 30,* 41–47.

Elder, S. (1978). *Interest groups, lobbying, and policymaking.* Washington, DC: Congressional Quarterly Press.

Elliott, W. R., & Sothirajah, J. (1993). Post-debate analysis and media reliance: Influences on candidate image and voting probabilities. *Journalism Quarterly, 70,* 321–335.

Ellul, J. (1965). *Propaganda.* (K. Kellen & J. Lerner, Trans). New York: Knopf. (Original work published 1962)

Erber, R., & Lau, R. R. (1990). Political cynicism revisited: An information-processing reconciliation of policy-based and incumbency-based interpretations of changes in trust in government. *American Journal of Political Science, 34,* 236–253.

Federal Election Commission (1998, November 20). Advisory Opinion #1998–2.

Federal Election Commission (1999, June 10). Advisory Opinion #1999–9.

Federal Election Commission (1999, November 10). Advisory Opinion #1999–17.

Fenno, R. F. (1978). *Home style: House members in their districts.* Boston: Little, Brown.

Ferber, P., & Pugliese, R. (1995). *Communication patterns among state legislators.* Paper presented at the Northeastern Political Science Association, Newark, NJ.

Ferber, P., & Pugliese, R. (1999). *Who you talk to and how you vote: Cue-giving in the New York State Legislature.* Paper presented at the Eastern Communication Association, Charleston, WV.

Ferguson, D. A., & Melkote, S. R. (1997). Leisure time and channel repertoire in a multichannel environment. *Communication Research Reports, 14,* 189–194.

Ferguson, M. A., Hollander, B. A., & Melwani, C. (1989). The "dampening effect" of post-debate commentary: The Bentsen/Quayle debate. Paper at the International Communication Association convention, San Francisco, CA.

Ferguson, Sherry D. (2000). *Researching the public opinion environment: Theories and methods.* Thousand Oaks, CA: Sage.

Files, J. (2000, May 7). For politicians, being funny is a serious business. *New York Times,* p. A24.

Fillippeli, S. (1999, August 29). A buzz about Bush. *Birmingham News,* pp. 1C, 6C.

Finkel, S. E., Guterbock, T. M., & Berg, M. J. (1991). Race-of-interviewer effects in a pre-election poll. *Public Opinion Quarterly, 55,* 313–330.

Fiorina, M. P. (1981). *Retrospective voting in American national elections.* New Haven: Yale University Press.

Fishkin, J. (1995). *The voice of the people: Public opinion and democracy.* New Haven, CT: Yale University Press.

Fleming, E. D. (1959, August). Ghosts in the closet. *Cosmopolitan, 147,* 68–71.

Flemming, G., & Sonner, M. (1999). *Can Internet polling work: Strategies for conducting public opinion research online.* Paper presented at the American Association for Public Opinion Research meeting. St. Petersburg, FL.

Forbes, S. (1999). *A new birth of freedom.* New York: Regnery.

Frankel, M. R., & Frankel, L. R. (1987). Fifty years of survey sampling in the United States. *Public Opinion Quarterly, 51,* S127–S138.

Franklin, C. H. (1992). Measurement and the dynamics of party identification. *American Political Science Review, 77,* 957–973

Frantz, D. (2000, February 21). A beer baron and a powerful publisher put McCain on a political path. *New York Times,* p. A14.

Franzen, J. (1999). Consultants and clients. In D. D. Perlmutter (Ed.), *The Manship School guide to political communication* (pp. 295–302). Baton Rouge: Louisiana State University Press.

Fraser, N., & Gordon, N. (1994). A genealogy of dependency: Tracing a key word of the U.S. welfare state. *Signs, 19,* 309–336.

Friedenberg, R. V. (1997). *Communication consultants in political campaigns: Ballot box warriors.* Westport, CT: Praeger.

Fritz, S., & Morris, D. (1992). *The handbook of campaign spending.* Washington, DC: Congressional Quarterly Press.

Frost, R., & Stauffer, J. (1987). The effects of social class, gender, and personality on physiological responses to filmed violence. *Journal of Communication, 37,* 29–45.

Gallup, G. (1979). Are U.S. teenagers political illiterates? The Gallup Youth survey.

Gamson, W. A. (1996). Media discourse as a framing resource. In A. N. Crigler (Ed.), *The psychology of political communication* (pp. 111–131). Ann Arbor: University of Michigan Press.

Gans, C. (1999, July 19). Footnotes. *NetPulse, 3 (14),* 1.

Gantz, W. (1983). The diffusion of news about the attempted Reagan assassination. *Journal of Communication, 33,* 56–66.

Garlick, R., & Mongeau, P. A. (1992). Majority/minority size and the evaluations of persuasive arguments. *Communication Research Reports, 9,* 45–53.

Garramore, G. M. (1984). Voter responses to negative political ads. *Journalism Quarterly, 61,* 250–259.

Garramore, G. M. (1985). Effects of negative political advertising: The roles of sponsor and rebuttal. *Journal of Broadcasting and Electronic Media, 29,* 147–159.

Garramore, G. M., Atkin, C. K., Pinkleton, B. E., & Cole, R. T. (1990). Effects of negative political advertising on the political process. *Journal of Broadcasting & Electronic Media, 34,* 299–311.

Garrison, B. (1998). *Computer-assisted reporting.* Mahwah, NJ: Erlbaum.

Garver, E. (1994). *Aristotle's rhetoric: An art of character.* Chicago: University of Chicago Press.

Geiger, S. (1993). *Truth in political advertising: The effects of adwatch articles on the evaluation and memory for political candidates.* Paper at the convention of the International Communication Association. Washington, DC.

Gerbner, G., Gross, L., Morgan, M., & Signorielli, N. (1990). Charting the mainstream: Television's contributions to political orientations. In D. A. Graber (Ed.), *Media power in politics.* Washington, DC: Congressional Quarterly Press.

Gerhard, M. E. (1990). A newspaper's 900 telephone poll: Its perceived credibility and accuracy. *Journalism Quarterly, 67,* 508–513.

German, K. M. (1995). Critical theory in public relations inquiry: Future directions for analysis in a public relations context. In W. N. Elwood (Ed.), *Public Relations Inquiry as Rhetorical Criticism* (pp. 279–294). Westport, CT: Praeger.

Gitlin, T. (1980). *The whole world is watching.* Berkeley: University of California Press.

Glass, J., Bengston, V. L., & Dunham, C. C. (1986). Attitude similarity in three generational families: Socialization, status inheritance, or reciprocal influence? *American Sociological Review, 51,* 685–698.

Glenn, R. (2001). *Debating the debates: Assessing the value of televised presidential debates in producing an informed electorate.* Paper presented at the annual meeting of the Southern States Communication Association, Lexington, KY.

Glick, J. A. (1999). Focus groups in political campaigns. In D. D. Perlmutter (Ed.), *The Manship School guide to political communication* (pp. 114–121). Baton Rouge: Louisiana State University Press.

Gold, E. R. (1978). Political apologia: The ritual of self-defense. *Communication Monographs, 45,* 306–316.

Goldzwig, S. R., & Sullivan, P. A. (2000). Electronic democracy, virtual politics, and local communities. In R. E. Denton, Jr. (Ed.), *Political communication ethics* (pp. 51–74). Westport, CT: Praeger.

Goodman, M., & Gring, M. (1999). *The visual byte: Bill Clinton and the polysemic town hall meeting.* Southern Speech Communication Association, St. Louis, MO.

Gore, A. (1993). *Earth in the balance: Ecology and the human spirit.* New York: Plume.

Graber, D. (1971). The press as opinion resource during the 1968 presidential campaign. *Public Opinion Quarterly,* 168–82.

Graber, D. (1972). Personal qualities in presidential images: The contribution of the press. *Midwest Journal of Political Science, 16,* 46–76.

Graber, D. (2001). Adapting political news to the needs of the twenty-first century. In W. L. Bennett & R. Entman (Eds.), *Mediated politics: Communication in the future of democracy* (pp. 433–452). Cambridge, England: Cambridge University Press.

Graber, D. A. (1976). *Verbal behavior and politics.* Urbana: University of Illinois Press.

Graber, D. A. (1987). Framing election news broadcasts: News context and its impact on the 1984 presidential election. *Social Science Quarterly, 68,* 552–568.

Green, D. P., & Palmquist, B. (1994). How stable is party identification? *Political Review, 16,* 437–466.

Greenberg, B. S. (1964). Diffusion of news of the Kennedy assassination. *Public Opinion Quarterly, 28,* 225–232.

Greene County fraud. (1999, June 20). *Birmingham News,* p. 2C.

Greenfield, M. (1999, January 10). A not very good film. *Newsweek,* p. 70.

Greffenius, S. (2001). *The last Jeffersonian: Ronald Reagan and radical democracy.* Boston: American Book Publishers.

Gronbeck, B. E. (1992). Negative narratives in 1988 presidential campaign ads. *Quarterly Journal of Speech, 78,* 333–346.

Gronbeck, B. E. (2000). The ethical performances of candidates in American presidential campaign dramas. In R. E. Denton, Jr. (Ed.), *Political communication ethics: An oxymoron* (pp. 1–22). Westport, CT: Praeger.

Grossman, M. B., & Kumar, M. J. (1981). *Portraying the president: The White House and the news media.* Baltimore: Johns Hopkins University Press.

Gubrium, J. F., & Holstein, J. A., (Eds.). (2001). *Handbook of interview research.* Thousand Oaks, CA: Sage

Gunderson, R. G. (1960). Political phrasemakers in perspective. *Southern Speech Communication Journal, 26,* 22–26.

Gunter, A. C. (1998). The persuasion press inference. *Communication Research, 25,* 486–504.

Gunter, B. (2000). *Media research methods: Measuring audiences, reactions, impact.* Thousand Oaks, CA: Sage.

Gunther, A. (1988). Attitude extremity and trust in the media. *Journalism Quarterly, 65,* 279–287.

Gunther, A., & Lasorsa, D. L. (1986). Issue importance and trust in the mass media. *Journalism Quarterly, 63,* 844–848.

Gunther, A. C., & Christen, T. C. (1999). Effects of news slant and base rate information on perceived public opinion. *Journalism and Mass Communication Quarterly, 76,* 277–292.

Gutgold, N. D. (2000). *Living out loud: How Betty Ford expanded the boundaries of the role of the first lady.* Paper presented at the annual meeting of the Eastern Communication Association, Pittsburgh, PA.

Haas, A. (1979). Male and female spoken language differences: Stereotypes and evidence. *Psychological Bulletin, 86,* 616–626.

Hacker, K. L., Howl, L., Scott, M., & Steiner, R. (1996). Uses of computer-mediated political communication in the 1992 presidential campaign: A content analysis of the Bush, Clinton and Perot computer lists. *Communication Research Reports, 13,* 138–146.

Halbfinger, D. M. (2000, February 1). Money attracts money for rich New Jersey Senate contender. *New York Times,* p. A23.

Hale, J. F. (1994). Yes: Campaign commercials should be regulated. In G. I. Rose (Ed.), *Controversial issues in presidential selection* (pp. 130–137). Albany: State University of New York Press.

Hamilton, B., & Beattie, D. (1999). Modern campaign polling. In D. D. Perlmutter (Ed.), *The Manship School guide to political communication* (pp. 93–106). Baton Rouge: Louisiana State University Press.

Hamm, K. (1991). Patterns of influence among committees, agencies, and interest groups. *Legislative Quarterly, 8,* 379–426.

Hansen, A., Cottle, S., Negrine, R. E., & Newbold, C. (1998). *Mass communication research methods.* Washington Square, NY: New York University Press.

Hart, R. P. (1987). The sound of leadership: Presidential communication in the modern age. Chicago: University of Chicago Press.

Hart, R. P. (1998). *Seducing America: How television charms the modern voter.* Thousand Oaks, CA: Sage.

Hart, R. P. (2000). *Campaign talk: Why campaigns are good for us.* Oxford: Oxford University Press.

Harwood, J. (1998). Viewing age: Lifespan identity and television viewing choice. *Journal of Broadcasting & Electronic Media, 41,* 203–213.

Hastings, C. M. (2000). *A home of her own: Edith Roosevelt's construction of Private White.* Paper presented at the annual meeting of the Eastern Communication Association, Pittsburgh, PA.

Havice, M. J. (1990). Measuring nonresponse and refusals to an electronic telephone survey. *Journalism Quarterly, 67,* 521–530.

Havick, J. (1997). Determinants of national media attention. *Journal of Communication, 47,* 97–111.

Heeter, C. (1988). Gender differences in viewing style. In C. Heeter & B. S. Greenberg (Eds.), *Cableviewing* (pp. 151–166). Norwood, NJ: Ablex.

Heeter, C., & Greenberg, B. S. (1988). *Cableviewing.* Norwood, NJ: Ablex.

Heider, F. (1958). *The psychology of interpersonal relations.* New York: Wiley.

Hellweg, S. A., Pfau, M., & Brydon, S. R. (1992). *Televised presidential debates: Advocacy in America.* New York: Praeger.

Herbst, S. (1993). *Numbered voices: How opinion polling has shaped American politics.* Chicago: University of Chicago Press.

Herbst, S. (1998). *Reading public opinion: How political actors view the democratic process.* Chicago: University of Chicago Press.

Herrnson, P. S. (2000). Hired guns and House races: Campaign professionals in House elections. In J. A. Thurber & C. J. Nelson (Eds.), *Campaign warriors: Political consultants in elections* (pp. 65–90). Washington, DC: Brookings Institution.

Hershey, M. R. (1974). *The making of campaign strategy.* Lexington, MA: D. C. Heath.

Hertog, J. K., Finnegan, J. R., Jr., & Kahn, E. (1994). Media coverage of AIDS, cancer, and sexually transmitted diseases: A test of the public arenas model. *Journalism Quarterly, 71,* 291–304.

Hess, S. (1988). *The presidential campaign.* Washington, DC: Brookings Institution.

Hickson, M. L., & Stacks, D. W. (1992). *NVC: Nonverbal communication studies and applications,* 3rd ed. Dubuque, IA: Brown & Benchmark.

Hill, K. A., & Hughes, J. E. (1998). *Cyberpolitics.* Mahwah, NJ: Rowman & Littlefield.

Hill, K., & Hurley, P. (1984). Nonvoters in voters' clothing: The impact of voting behavior misreporting on voting behavior research. *Social Science Quarterly, 65,* 199–206.

Hinck, E. A., & Hinck, S. S. (1998). *Audience reactions to Clinton and Dole: Some evidence for explaining audience assessments in terms of political strategies.* Paper for the National Communication Association convention. New York, NY.

Hinck, E. A., & Hinck, S. S. (2000). Politeness theory and political debates. In D. Bystrom, D. B. Carlin, L. L. Kaid, M. Kern, & M. S. McKinney, (Eds.), *Communication Politics: Engaging the Public in Campaign 2000 and Beyond* (pp. 124–130). Proceedings of the National Communication Association Summer Conference: Washington, DC.

Hitt, J. (1999, July 25). Campaign cash. *New York Times Magazine,* p. 20.

Hochschild, A. R. (1989). *The second shift: Working parents and the evolution at home.* New York: Viking.

Hofstetter, C. R., Donovan, M. C., Klauber, M. R., Cole, A., Huie, A. J., & Yuasa, T. (1994). Political talk radio: A stereotype reconsidered. *Political Research Quarterly, 47,* 467–479.

Holland, P. (1987). When a woman reads the news. In H. Baehr & G. Dyer (Eds.), *Boxed in: Women in television* (pp. 133–150). New York: Pandora Press.

Holleman, B. (2000). *The forbid/allow asymmetry: On the cognitive mechanisms underlying wording effects in surveys.* Amsterdam: Rodopi.

Hollihan, Thomas A. (2001). *Uncivil wars: Political campaigns in a media age.* Boston: Bedford-St. Martin's.

Holm, T. T. (2000). *The vilification of Kenneth Starr: The rhetorical role of political cartoons in the Clinton-Lewinsky sex scandal.* Paper presented to the Eastern Communication Association Convention, Pittsburgh, PA.

Hosenball, M., Breslau, K., & Jackson, B. (2001, September 3). From bad to worse. *Newsweek, 20*–23.

Hovland, C. I., Lumsdaine, A. A., & Sheffield, F. D. (1949). *Experiments in mass communication.* Princeton: Princeton University Press.

Hu, W. (2000, January 20). Interviewer gets personal with First Lady. *New York Times,* p. C37.

Huang, X., Leong, E., & Stanner, P. (1998, September/October). Comparing the effectiveness of the web site with traditional media. *Journal of Advertising Research,* pp. 44–49.

Huckfeldt, R. R., & Sprague, J. (1995). *Citizens, politics, and social communication: Information and influence in an election campaign.* New York: Cambridge University Press.

Huffington, A. (1999, September 1). Windom case is bellwether for politics. *Birmingham News,* p. 11A.

Hutchins, J. M. (1999). Political media buying. In D. D. Perlmutter (Ed.), *The Manship School guide to political communication* (pp. 122–130). Baton Rouge: Louisiana State University Press.

Impeach this. (2000). *NetPulse, 3(14),* p. 2.

Iorio, S. H., & Huxman, S. S. (1996). Media coverage of political issues and the framing of personal concerns. *Journal of Communication, 46,* 97–115.

Ivins, M., & DuBose, L. (2000). *Shrub: The short but happy political life of George W. Bush.* New York: Random House.

Iyengar, S. (1996). Framing responsibility for political issues. *Annals of the American Academy of Political and Social Science, 456,* 59–70.

Iyengar, S., & Kinder, D. R. (1987). *News that matters.* Chicago: University of Chicago Press.

Jackson, J. S. (1977). Review: The management of election campaigns. *Political Communication Review, 2,* 11–12.

Jacobs, L. R., & Shapiro, R. Y. (1994). Issues, candidate image, and priming: The use of private polls in Kennedy's 1960 presidential campaign. *American Political Science Review, 88,* 527–540.

Jacobs, L. R., & Shapiro, R. Y. (2000). *Politicians don't pander: Political manipulation and the loss of democratic responsiveness.* Chicago: University of Chicago Press.

Jacoby, J., Troutman, T. R., & Whittler, T. E. (1986). Viewer miscomprehension of the 1980 presidential debate: A research note. *Political Psychology, 7,* 297–308.

Jalonick, M. C. (2000, April). Bringing in the bucks on the Web. *Campaigns & Elections,* pp. 48–49.

James, C. (1999, December 19). We're ready for our close-ups now. *New York Times,* p. Y30.

Jamieson, K. (1984). *Packaging the presidency.* New York: Oxford University Press.

Jamieson, K. H. (1988). *Eloquence in an electronic age: The transformation of political speechmaking.* New York: Oxford University Press.

Jamieson, K. H. (1992). *Dirty politics: Deception, distraction and democracy.* New York: Oxford University Press.

Jamieson, K. H. (1996). *Packaging the presidency.* New York: Oxford University Press.

Jamieson, K. H. (2001). *Everything you think you know about politics . . . And why you're wrong.* New York: Basic Books.

Jamieson, K. H., & Birdsell, D. S. (1988). *Presidential debates: The challenge of creating an informed electorate.* New York: Oxford University Press.

Jamieson, K. H., & Campbell, K. K. (1997). *The interplay of influence: News, advertising, politics and the mass media* (4th ed.). Belmont, CA: Wadsworth.

Jeffries, L. W. (1986). *Mass media: Process and effects.* Prospect Heights, IL: Waveland.

Jennings, M. K., & Markus, G. B. (1984). Partisan orientations over the long haul: Results from the three-wave political socialization panel study. *American Political Science Review, 78,* 1000–1018.

Jennings, M. K., & Niemi, R. G. (1968). The transmission of political values from parent to child. *American Political Science Review, 62,* 169–184.

John, K. E. (1989). The polls: A report. *Public Opinion Quarterly, 53,* 590–605.

Johnson, D. W. (2000). The business of political consulting. In J. A. Thurber & C. J. Nelson (Eds.), *Campaign warriors: Political consultants in elections* (pp. 37–52). Washington, DC: Brookings Institution.

Johnson, T. J. (1993). Filling out the racing form: How the media covered the horse race in the 1988 primaries. *Journalism Quarterly, 70,* 300–310.

Johnson-Cartee, K. S., & Copeland, G. A. (1991). *Negative political advertising: Coming of age.* Hillsdale, NJ: Erlbaum.

Jones, C. (1988). *How to speak TV.* Tallahassee, FL: Video Consultants.

Jones, C. A. (2000). Soft money and hard choices: The influence of campaign finance rules on campaign communication strategy. In R. E. Denton, Jr. (Ed.), *Political communication ethics* (pp. 179–202). Westport, CT: Praeger.

Jordan, H. (1982). *Crisis: The last year of the Carter presidency.* New York: Putnam.

Joslyn, R. (1986). Political advertising and the meaning of elections. In L. L. Kaid, D. Nimmo, & K. Sanders (Eds.), *New perspectives on political advertising* (pp. 139–184). Carbondale: Southern Illinois University Press.

Jowett, G. S., & O'Donnell, V. (1986). *Propaganda and persuasion.* Beverly Hills, CA: Sage.

Joy, M. (2001). *Listening in politics.* Paper presented at the annual meeting of the Southern States Communication Association. Lexington, KY.

Judis, J. B. (1999, August 8). Race for presidential cash: No way to run democracy, *Birmingham News,* p. 8C.

Just, M., Crigler, A., & Wallace, L. (1990). Thirty seconds or thirty minutes: What viewers learn from spot advertisements and candidate debates. *Journal of Communication, 40,* 120–133.

Kahn, K. F. (1993). Gender differences in campaign messages: The political advertisements of men and women candidates for U.S. Senate. *Political Research Quarterly, 46,* 481–502.

Kahn, K. F. (1994). Does gender make a difference? An experimental examination of sex stereotypes and press patterns in statewide campaigns. *American Journal of Political Science, 38,* 162–196.

Kaid, L. L. (1996). Technology and political advertising: The application of ethical standards to the 1992 spots. *Communication Research Reports, 13,* 129–137.

Kaid, L. L. (2000). Ethics and political advertising. In R. E. Denton, Jr. (Ed.), *Political communication ethics: An oxymoron* (pp. 147–178). Westport, CT: Praeger.

Kaid, L. L., & Boydston, J. (1987). An experimental study of the effectiveness of negative political advertisements. *Communication Quarterly, 35,* 193–201.

Kaid, L. L., Gobetz, R. H., Garner, J., & Leland, C. M. (1993). Television news and presidential campaigns: The legitimization of television political advertising. *Social Science Quarterly, 74,* 274–285.

Kaid, L. L., Tedesco, J. C., & McKinnon, L. (1993). Presidential ads as nightly news: A content analysis of 1988 and 1992 televised adwatches. *Journal of Broadcasting & Electronic Media, 40,* 279–303.

Kanter, D. L., & Mirvis, P. H. (1989). *The cynical Americans: Living and working in an age of discontent and disillusion.* San Francisco: Jossey-Bass.

Kantrow, B. (1999, August 4). Boastful 1995 ad still posing legal challenge for GOP. *Birmingham News,* p. 5A.

Katosh, J., & Traugott, M. (1981). The consequences of validated and self-reported voting measures. *Public Opinion Quarterly, 45,* 519–535.

Katz, E., & Lazarsfeld, P. F. (1955). *Personal influence: The part played by people in the flow of mass communication.* Glencoe, IL: Free Press.

Keefer, J. D. (1993). The news media's failure to facilitate citizen participation in the congressional policymaking process. *Journalism Quarterly, 70,* 412–424.

Keith, B., Orr, E., Magleby, D., Nelson, C., Wolfinger, R., & Westlye, M. (1988). *The myth of the independent voter.* Berkeley: University of California Press.

Kelley, H. H. (1967). Attribution theory in social psychology. In D. Levine (Ed.), *Nebraska symposium on motivation 15,* (pp. 197–238). Lincoln: University of Nebraska Press.

Kelley, S. (1956). *Professional public relations and political power.* Baltimore, MD: Johns Hopkins University Press.

Kelley, S., Jr. (1983). *Interpreting elections.* Princeton, NJ: Princeton University Press.

Kelley, T. (1999, October 19). Candidate on the stump is surely on the Web. *New York Times.* pp. A1, A15.

Kennedy, K. A., & Benoit, W. L. (1997). The Newt Gingrich book deal controversy: Self-defense rhetoric. *Southern Communication Journal, 62,* 197–216.

Kennedy, M. M. (1980). *Office politics: Seizing power, wielding clout.* New York: Warner

Kenski, H. C. (1996). From agenda-setting to priming and framing. In M. E. Stuckey (Ed.), *The theory and practice of political communication research.* Albany, NY: SUNY Press.

Kern, M. (1989). *30-second politics: Political advertising in the eighties.* New York: Praeger.

Key, V. O., Jr., (1949). *Southern politics.* New York: Vintage.

Key, V. O. (1952). *Politics, parties, and pressure groups.* New York: Thomas Crowell.

Key, V. O., Jr. (1961). *Public opinion and American democracy.* New York: Knopf.

Kinder, D. R., & Sanders, L. M. (1990). Mimicking political debate with survey questions: The case of white opinion on affirmative action for blacks. *Social Cognition, 8,* 73–103.

Kingdon, J. (1973). *Congressmen's voting decisions* (2nd ed.). New York: Harper & Row.

Kingdon, J. W. (1970). Opinion leaders in the electorate. *Public Opinion Quarterly, 34,* 256–261.

Kitchens, J. T., & Powell, L. (1975). Discriminant analysis as an instrument for political analysis. *Southern Speech Communication Journal, 40,* 313–320.

Kitchens, J. T., & Powell, L. (1986). A critical analysis of NCPAC's strategies in key 1980 races: A third party negative campaign. *Southern Speech Communication Journal, 51,* 208–228.

Kitchens, J. T., & Powell, L. (1994). Ticket splitting: Dead or alive? *Campaigns & Elections,* 34–35.

Kitchens, J. T., & Stiteler, B. (1979). Challenge to the 'Rule of Minimum Effect': A case study of the In Man/Out Man strategy. *Southern Speech Communication Journal, 44,* 176–190.

Klapp, O. E. (1964). *Symbolic leaders: Public drama and public men.* New York: Minerva Press.

Klapper, J. (1960). *The effects of mass communication.* New York: Free Press.

Kolodny, R. (2000). Electoral partnerships: Political consultants and political parties. In J. A. Thurber & C. J. Nelson (Eds.), *Campaign warriors: Political consultants in elections* (pp. 110–132). Washington, DC: Brookings Institution.

Kovach, B., & Rosentiel, T. (1999). *Warp speed: America in the age of mixed media.* Washington, DC: Century Foundation.

Kraus, S. (1962). *The great debates.* Bloomington: Indiana University Press.

Kraus, S. (2000). *Televised presidential debates and public policy* (2nd ed.). Hillsdale, NJ: Earlbaum.

Kraus, S., & Davis, D. (1976). *The effects of mass communication on political behavior.* University Park: Pennsylvania State University Press.

Kraus, S., Davis, D., Lang, G. E., & Lang, K. (1976). Critical events analysis. In S. H. Chaffee (Ed.), *Political communication: Issues and strategies for research* (pp. 195–216). Beverly Hills, CA: Sage.

Krosnick, J. A., & Kinder, D. R. (1990). Altering the foundations of support for the president through priming. *American Political Science Review, 84,* 497–512.

Krueger, R. A., & Casey, M. A. (2000). *Focus groups: A practical guide for applied research.* Thousand Oaks, CA: Sage.

Kurtz, H. (1998). *Spin cycle: Inside the Clinton propaganda machine.* New York: Free Press.

Lane, E. (1964). *Lobbying and the Law.* Cambridge: Cambridge University Press.

Lang, K., & Lang, G. E. (1968). *Politics and television.* Chicago: Quadrangle Books.

Larson, C. U. (1995). *Persuasion: Reception and responsibility* (7th ed.). Belmont, CA: Wadsworth.

Larson, S., & Psystrup, P. (2000). The Internet gateway: McCain's new realm of politicking. In D. Bystrom, D. B. Carlin, L. L. Kaid, M. Kern, & M. S. McKinney. (Eds.), *Communicating politics: Engaging the public in campaign 2000 and beyond* (pp. 159–172). Washington, DC: NCA Summer Conference proceedings.

Lash, J. P. (1971). *Eleanor and Franklin.* New York: Signet.

Lau, R. (1982). Negativity in political perceptions. *Political Behavior, 4,* 353–378.

Lau, R. R., Smith, R. A., & Fiske, S. T. (1991). Political beliefs, policy interpretations, and political persuasion. *Journal of Politics, 53,* 644–675.

Lawrence, J. (1999, July 1). Bush breaks fund-raising record. *USA Today,* p. 10A.

Lawrence, J. (2000, October 3). Candidates look to previous debates to sharpen strategies. *USA Today,* p. 14A.

Lazarsfeld, P. F., Berelson, B. R., & Gaudet, H. (1948). *The people's choice.* New York: Columbia University Press.

Lazarsfeld, P. F., Berelson, B., & Gaudet, H. (1968). *The people's choice* (3rd ed.). New York: Columbia University Press.

Lazarsfeld, P. F., & Morton, R. (1960). Mass communication, popular taste and organized social action. In W. Schramm (Ed.), *Mass Communication* (pp. 492–512). Urbana: University of Illinois Press.

Leavitt, P. (2000, January 27). Electionline: Bush TV ads go Spanish for primary in Arizona. *USA Today,* p. 8A.

Leckenby, J. D., & Surlin, S. H. (1976). Incidental social learning and viewer race: "All in the Family" and "Sanford and Son." *Journal of Broadcasting, 20,* 481–494.

Lee, J., & Davie, W. R. (1997). Audience recall of AIDs PSAs among U.S. and international college students. *Journalism & Mass Communication Quarterly, 74,* 7–22.

Lee, R. (2000). Images, issues, and political structure: A framework for judging the ethics of campaign discourse. In R. E. Denton, Jr. (Ed.), *Political communication ethics: An oxymoron* (pp. 23–50). Westport, CT: Praeger.

Leshner, G., & McKean, M. L. (1997). Using TV news for political information during an off-year election: Effects on political knowledge and cynicism. *Journalism and Mass Communication Quarterly, 74,* 69–83.

Levine, J. M., & Murphy, G. (1943). The learning and forgetting of controversial statements. *Journal of Abnormal and Social Psychology, 38,* 507–517.

Levy, C. J. (2000, January 20). Giuliani campaign says it brought in $12 million in '99 donations. *New York Times,* p. C37.

Lewis, C. (Ed.) (1998). *The buying of the Congress.* Washington, DC: Center for Public Integrity.

Lewis, C. (Ed.) (2000). *Our private legislatures: Public service, personal gain.* Washington, DC: Center for Public Integrity.

Lewis, L. K. (1999). Disseminating information and soliciting input during planned organizational change. *Communication Quarterly, 13,* 43–75.

Lippman, W. (1922). *Public opinion.* New York: Macmillan.

Lippmann, W. (1955). *Public opinion.* New York: Free Press.

Littlejohn, S. W. (1996). *Theories of human communication* (5th ed). Belmont, CA: Wadsworth.

Loken, B. (1983). *The effects of direct mail appeals on awareness, readership, and cognitive response content in a community heart health campaign.* Paper presented at the Association for Education in Journalism and Mass Communication. Corvallis, OR.

Lowry, D. T., Bridges, J. A., & Barefield, P. A. (1991). Effects of TV instant analysis and querulous criticism: Following the first Bush-Dukakis debate. *Journalism Quarterly, 67,* 814–825.

Lowy, J. (1999, July 14). Politicians frustrated by critical Web sites. *Birmingham Post-Herald,* p. A2.

Lull, J. (1980). The social uses of television. *Human Communication Research, 6,* 197–209.

Lull, J. (1982). How families select television programs: A mass observational approach. *Journal of Broadcasting, 26,* 801–811.

Magleby, D. B., & Holt, M. (1999). The long shadow of soft money and issue advocacy ads. *Campaign & Elections, 20(4),* 22–27.

Mair, L. (1962). *Primitive government.* New York: Ballantine.

Maltese, J. A. (1994). *Spin control: The White House office of communications and the management of presidential news.* Chapel Hill: University of North Carolina Press.

Mandel, R. B. (1981). *In the running: The new woman candidate.* New York: Ticknor & Fields.

Markus, G. B., & Converse, P. E. (1979). A dynamic simultaneous equation model of electoral change. *American Political Science Review, 73,* 1055–1070.

Martel, M. (1983). *Political campaign debates: Images, strategies, and tactics.* New York: Longman.

Martin, E., DeMaio, T. J., & Campanelli, P. C. (1990). Context effects for census measures of race and Hispanic origin. *Public Opinion Quarterly, 54,* 551–566.

Martin, M. L., Anderson, C. M., & Cos, G. C. (1997). Verbal aggression: A study of the relationship between communication traits and feelings about a verbally aggressive television show. *Communication Research Reports, 14,* 195–202.

Martinelli, K. A., & Chaffee, S. H. (1995). Measuring new-voter learning via three channels of political information. *Journalism and Mass Communication Quarterly, 72,* 18–32.

Matthews, D. R., & Stimson, J. A. (1975). *Yeas and nays: Normal decision-making in the U.S. House.* New York: Wiley.

Mayer, W. G., & Polsby, N. W. (1991). *The divided Demo-crats: Ideological unity, party reform, and presidential elections.* New York: Westview Press.

Mayhew, D. R. (1974). *Congress: The electoral connection.* New Haven, CI: Yale University Press.

McCaid, K. (1989). The Roundtable: Getting results in Washington. *Harvard Business Review, 59,* 114–123.

McCain, J. (1999). *Faith of our fathers.* New York: Random House.

McCarty, J. A., & Shrum, L. J. (2000). The measurement of personal values in survey research: A test of alternative rating procedures. *Public Opinion Quarterly, 64,* 271–298.

McClure, R. D., & Patterson, T. E. (1974). Television news and political advertising. *Communication Research, 1,* 3–31.

McCombs, M. E. (1976). Agenda-setting research: A biblio-graphic essay. *Political Communication Review, 1,* 1–7.

McCombs, M. E. (1992). Explorers and surveyors: Expand-ing strategies for agenda-setting research. *Journalism Quarterly, 69,* 813–824.

McCombs, M., & Shaw, D. L. (1972). The agenda-setting function of the mass media. *Public Opinion Quarterly, 36,* 176–188.

McCombs, M. E., & Shaw, D. L. (1993). The evolution of agenda-setting research: Twenty-five years in the mar-ketplace of ideas. *Public Opinion Quarterly, 36,* 176–185.

McCombs, M., & Stone, G. (Eds.). (1975). *Studies in agenda-setting.* Syracuse, NY: Newhouse Communi-cations Research Center.

McCombs, M., & Weaver, D. (1973). *Voters' need for ori-entation and use of mass media.* Paper for the Inter-national Communication Association, Montreal, Canada.

McCroskey, J. C., Jensen, T., & Todd, C. (1972). The gener-alizability of source credibility scales for public figures. Paper for the Speech Communication Associa-tion. Chicago, IL.

McCroskey, J. D., Richmond, V. P., & Daly, J. A. (1975). The development of a measure of perceived homophily in interpersonal communication. *Human Communication Research, 1,* 322–332.

McFetters, A. (1999, June 21). Keeping beat on campaign trail. *Birmingham News,* p. A6.

McGuire, W. J., & Papageorgis, O. (1961). The relative effi-cacy of various types of prior belief-defense in produc-ing immunity against persuasion. *Journal of Abnormal and Social Psychology, 62,* 327–37.

McLeod, D. M., & Perse, E. M. (1994). Direct and indirect effects of socioeconomic status on public affairs knowledge. *Journalism Quarterly, 71,* 433–442.

McLeod, J. M., Becker, L. B., & Byrnes, J. E. (1973). Another look at the agenda-setting function of the press. *Communication Research, 1,* 131–166.

McLeod, J. M., & Detenber, B. H. (1999). Framing effects of television news coverage of social protest. *Journal of Communication, 49,* 3–23.

McPeek, R. W., & Edwards, J. D. (1975). Expectancy dis-conformation and attitude change. *Journal of Social Psychology, 96,* 193–208.

McPherson, B. (1999, July 24). E-mail provides public, lead-ers with new links. *Pensacola News Journal,* pp. 1C, 3C.

Medhurst, M. J., & DeSousa, M. A. (1981). Political car-toons as rhetorical form: A taxonomy of graphic dis-course. *Communication Monographs, 48,* 197–236.

Medvic, S. K. (2000). Professionalization in congressional campaigns. In J. A. Thurber & C. J. Nelson (Eds.), *Campaign warriors: Political consultants in elec-tions,* (pp. 91–109). Washington, DC: Brookings Institution.

Medvic, S. K. (2001). *Political consultants in U.S. congres-sional elections.* Columbus: Ohio State University Press.

Mendelsohn, H. (1964). Broadcast vs. personal sources of information in emergent public crises: The presiden-tial assassination. *Journal of Broadcasting, 8,* 147–156.

Merton, R. K. (1987). The focussed interview and focus groups: Continuities and discontinuities. *Public Opin-ion Quarterly, 51,* 550–566.

Merton, R. K., Lowenthal, M. F., & Kendall, P. L. (1990). *The focus interview: A manual of problems and proce-dures.* New York: Collier Macmillan.

Miller, A. H., & MacKuen, M. (1979). Informing the elec-torate: A national study. In S. Kraus (Ed.), *The Great Debates: Carter vs. Ford, 1976.* Bloomington: Indiana University Press.

Miller, A. J. (1974). Political issues and trust in government: 1964–1970. *American Political Science Review, 68,* 951–972.

Miller, J. J. (1999). *The campaign theme and an election's controlling frame.* Paper for the Southern Communica-tion Association convention. St. Louis, MO.

Miller, W. E., & Shanks, J. M. (1982). Policy directions and presidential leadership: Alternative interpretations of the 1980 election. *British Journal of Political Science, 12,* 299–356.

Miller, W. E., & Shanks, J. M. (1996). *The new American voter.* Cambridge, MA: Harvard University Press.

Mitchell, A. (1999, December 12). Underdog McCain develops anti-campaign style. *New York Times,* p. Y26.

Mitchell, F. D. (1998). *Harry S. Truman and the news media: Contentious relations, belated respect.* Columbia: University of Missouri Press.

Mitchell, G. (1992). *The campaign of the century: Upton Sinclair's race for governor of California and the birth of media politics.* New York: Random House.

Moore, D. W. (1999, June/July). Daily tracking polls: Too much 'noise' or revealed insights? *Public Perspective,* 27–31.

Morgan, D. L. (1988). *Focus groups as qualitative research.* Newbury Park, CA: Sage.

Morley, D. (1986). *Family television: Cultural power and domestic leisure.* London: Comedia.

Morley, D. (1988). Domestic relations: The framework of family viewing in Great Britain. In J. Lull (Ed.), *World families watch television* (pp. 22–48). Newbury Park, CA: Sage.

Morris, D. (1999). *The new prince.* Los Angeles: Renaissance Books.

Morris, R. (1993). Visual rhetoric in political cartoons: A structuralist approach. *Metaphor and Symbolic Activity, 8,* 195–210.

Morrison, D. E. (1986). *Invisible citizens: British public opinion and the future of broadcasting.* London: John Libbey.

Musso, J., Weare, C., & Hale, M. (2000). Designing Web technologies for local governance reform: Good management or good democracy? *Political Communication, 17,* 1–19.

Mutz, D. C. (1998). *Interpersonal influence: How perceptions of mass collectives affect political attitudes.* Cambridge: Cambridge University Press.

Mutz, D. C., Sniderman, P. M., & Brody, R. A. (1996). *Political persuasion and attitude change.* Ann Arbor: University of Michigan Press.

Myers, F. (1999). Political argumentation and the composite audience: A case study. *Quarterly Journal of Speech, 85,* 55–71.

Myers, R. H. (1999). The inescapability of moral reasons. *Philosophy and Phenomenological Research, 59,* 281–307.

Napolitan, J. (1972). *The election game and how to win it.* New York: Doubleday.

Napolitan, J. (1975). Zeroing in on the voter. In R. E. Hiebert et al. (Eds.), *The political image merchants* (p. 46). Washington, DC: Acropolis Books.

Nathanson, A. I., Perse, E. M., & Ferguson, D. A. (1997). Gender differences in television use: An exploration of the instrumental-expressive dichotomy. *Communication Research Reports, 14,* 176–188.

Neimi, R. G., Craig, S. C., & Mattei, F. (1991). Measuring internal political efficacy in the 1988 National Election Study. *American Political Science Review, 85,* 1407–1413.

Nelson, W. D. (1998). *Who speaks for the President? The White House press secretary from Cleveland to Clinton.* Syracuse, NY: Syracuse University Press.

Neuman, W. R. (1986). *The Paradox of Mass Politics: Knowledge and opinion in the American electorate.* Cambridge, MA: Harvard University Press.

Neuman, W. R., Just, M. R., & Crigler, A. N. (1992). *Common knowledge: News and the construction of political meaning.* Chicago: University of Chicago Press.

Newcombe, N., & Arnkoff, D. B. (1976). Effects of speech style and sex of the speaker on person perception. *Journal of Personality and Social Psychology, 37,* 1293–1303.

Newman, B. I. (1999). *The mass marketing of politics: Democracy in an age of manufactured images.* Thousand Oaks, CA: Sage.

Nicholson, J. (2000, April). Informing, mobilizing. *Campaigns & Elections,* p. 23.

Nimmo, D. (1970). *The political persuaders.* Englewood Cliffs, NJ: Prentice-Hall.

Nimmo, D. (1974). *Popular images of politics.* Englewood Cliffs, NJ: Prentice-Hall.

Nimmo, D., & Savage, R. L. (1976). *Candidates and their images.* Pacific Palisades, CA: Goodyear.

Nixon v. Carver. (1996). U.S. District Court, 518 U.S. 1033, Springfield, MO.

Noble, P., & Kennedy, T. (2000, February 15). Online fundraising continues to skyrocket. *Politics online.* Online update.

Noelle-Neuman, E. (1974). The spiral of silence. *Journal of Communication, 24,* 43–51.

Noonan, P. (1997). *What I saw at the revolution.* New York: Ballantine.

Noonan, P. (1998). *On speaking well.* New York: Regan Books.

Noonan, P. (2000). *The case against Hillary Clinton.* New York: HarperCollins.

Norris, P. (Ed.) (1996). *Women, media, and politics.* New York: Oxford University Press.

Norris, P., Curtice, J., Sanders, D., Scammell, M., & Semetko, H. A. (1999). *On message: Communicating the campaign.* London: Sage.

O'Keefe, G. (1976). The uses-gratifications approach and political communication research. *Political Communication Review, 1,* 8–11.

O'Keefe, G. J., & Sulanowski, B. K. (1995). More than just talk: Uses, gratifications, and the telephone. *Journalism & Mass Communication Quarterly, 72,* 922–933.

O'Keefe, M. T. (1969). The first human heart transplant: A study of diffusion among doctors. *Journalism Quarterly, 46,* 237–242.

O'Leary, B. S. (2000, April). Direct response. *Campaigns & Elections*, p. 24.

Olson, M. (1971). *The logic of collective action.* Cambridge, MA: Harvard University Press.

O'Sullivan, P., & Geiger, S. (1995). Does the watchdog bite? Newspaper ad watch articles and political attack ads. *Journalism and Mass Communication Quarterly, 72,* 771–785.

Orren, K. (1989). Interest group conflict in the federal courts. *American Political Science Review, 70,* 723–741.

Orwell, G. (1949). *The Orwell reader.* New York: Harcourt Brace.

Ostlund, L. E. (1973–74). Interpersonal communication following McGovern's Eagleton decision. *Public Opinion Quarterly, 37,* 601–610.

Owen, D., & Cutbirth, J. (2000). The Internet and the youth vote: Possibilites, challenges, and limitations. In D. Bystom, D. B. Carlin, L. L. Kaid, M. Kern, & M. S. McKinney (Eds.), *Communicating politics: Engaging the public in campaign 2000 and beyond* (pp. 212–222). Washington, DC: NCA Summer Conference proceedings.

Page, B. I., & Brody, R. A. (1972). Policy voting and the electoral process: The Vietnam War issue. *American Political Science Review, 66,* 979–995.

Page, B., & Jones, C. (1979). Reciprocal effects of policy preferences, party loyalties, and the vote. *American Political Science Review, 66,* 979–985.

Paletz, D. L. (2002). *The media in American politics.* New York: Longman.

Parry-Giles, T., & Parry-Giles, S. J. (1996). Political socophilia, presidential campaigning and the intimacy of American politics. *Communication Studies, 47,* 191–205.

Patterson, D. (1999). *Americans are giving up their freedom by not voting.* Birmingham, AL: Policy Exchange Foundation.

Patterson, R. (1999). Bill Bennett and "common culture" politics: Moral and economic fusion in the Reagan presidency. Paper for the Eastern Communication Association, Charleston, WV.

Patterson, S. C. (1959). Patterns of interpersonal relations in a state legislative group: The Wisconsin assembly. *Public Opinion Quarterly, 23,* 101–109.

Patterson, T. (1980). *The mass media election.* New York: Praeger.

Patterson, T. E. (1994). *Out of order.* New York: Knopf.

Patterson, T., & Davis, R. (1985). The media campaign: Struggle for the agenda. In N. Nelson (Ed.), *The elections of 1984.* Washington, DC: Congressional Quarterly Press.

Patterson, T., & McClure, R. (1976). *The unseeing eye.* New York: Putnam.

Paul, I. H. (1956). Impressions of personality: Authoritarianism and the fait accompli effect. *Journal of Abnormal and Social Psychology, 53,* 338–344.

Penner, M., & Penner, S. (1994). Publicizing, politicizing, and neutralizing homelessness: comic strips. *Communication Research, 21,* 766–781.

Perlman, A. M. (1998). *Writing great speeches.* Boston: Allyn & Bacon.

Perlmutter, D. D. (1999). *The Manship School guide to political communication.* Baton Rouge: Louisiana State University Press.

Perlmutter, D. D., & Wu, H. D. (1999). The American political consultant: A profile. In D. D. Perlmutter (Ed.), *The Manship School guide to political communication* (pp. 327–332). Baton Rouge: Louisiana State University Press.

Perloff, R. M. (1998). *Political communication: Politics, press, and the public in America.* Mahwah, NJ: Erlbaum.

Perse, E. M., & Ferguson, D. A. (1993). Gender differences in remote control use. In J. R. Walker & R. V. Bellamy, Jr. (Eds.), *The remote control in the new age of television* (pp. 169–180). Westport, CT: Praeger.

Perse, E. M., Ferguson, D. A., & McLeod, D. M. (1994). Cultivation in the newer media environment. *Communication Research, 21,* 79–104.

Persico, J. E. (1972). The Rockefeller rhetoric: Writing speeches for the 1970 campaign. *Today's Speech, 20,* pp. 57–62.

Pfau, M., & Burgoon, M. (1988). Inoculation in political campaign communication. *Human Communication Research, 15,* 91–111.

Pfau, M., & Loudon, A. (1994). Effectiveness of adwatch formats in deflecting political attack ads. *Journalism and Mass Communication Quarterly, 21,* 324–341.

Pfau, M., Kenski, H. C., Nitz, M., & Sorenson, J. (1990). Efficacy of inoculation strategies in promoting resistance to political attack messages: Application to direct mail. *Communication Monographs, 57,* 25–43.

Pitchell, R. J. (1958). The influence of professional campaign management firms on partisan elections in California. *Western Political Quarterly, 11,* 278–300.

Pohl, F. (1971). *Practical politics.* New York: Ballantine Books.

Polsby, N. W. (1983). *The consequence of party reform.* Oxford: Oxford University Press.

Polsby, N. W., & Wildavsky, A. B. (1968). *Presidential elections. Strategies of American electoral politics.* New York: Charles Scribner's Sons.

Popkin, S. (1991). *The reasoning voter: Communication and persuasion in presidential campaigns.* Chicago: University of Chicago Press.

Potter, W. J., & Ware, W. (1987). An analysis of the contexts of antisocial acts on prime-time television. *Communication Research, 14,* 664–686.

Powell, L. (1974). Strategies in a statewide secondary executive race: A case study. *Georgia Speech Communication Journal, 6,* 18–30.

Powell, L. (1975). The effects of ego-involvement on responses to editorial satire. *Central States Speech Journal, 26,* 34–38.

Powell, L. (1977). Voting intention and the complexity of political images. *Psychological Reports, 40,* 243–246.

Powell, L., & Anderson, R. G. (1984). The impact of TV comedy: A test of the friendship theory. *Journal of Communication Studies, 3,* 13–19.

Powell, L., & Flick, H. (1982). Ticket splitting in Mississippi. Paper for the Southern Speech Communication Association. Hot Springs, AK.

Powell, L., & Kitchens, J. T. (1986). Analyzing campaign strategies: Contingencies, assumptions and techniques. *Southeastern Political Review, 14,* 161–179.

Powell, L., & Kitchens, J. T. (1999). Sex and income as factors associated with exposure to jokes about the Clinton-Lewinsky controversy. *Psychological Reports, 84,* 1047–1050.

Powell, L., & Shelby, A. (1981). A strategy of assumed incumbency: A case study. *Southern peech Communication Journal, 46,* 105–23.

Powell, L., & Shelby, A. N. (1985). Para-political opinion leaders as audience: Communicative goals and media usage. *Communication Research Reports, 2,* 135–140.

Power of polling (1999, November 24). *Louisiana Political Fax Weekly,* p. 2.

Procter, D. E., Aden, R. C., & Japp, P. (1988). Gender/issue interaction in political identity making: Nebraska's woman vs. woman gubernatorial campaign. *Central States Speech Journal, 39,* 190–203.

Procter, D. E., & Schenck-Hamlin, W. J. (1996). Form and variations in negative political advertising. *Communication Research Reports, 13,* 147–156.

Purnick, J. (2000, May 7). Candidates' health has become routine public matter. *New York Times,* p. A24.

Rahn, W. M., Krosnik, J. A., & Breuning, M. (1994). Rationalization and derivations processes in survey studies of political candidate evaluation. *American Journal of Political Science, 32,* 582–600.

Rakow, L. F., & Kranich, K. (1991). Woman as sign in television news. *Journal of Communication, 41,* 20.

Raven, B. H., & Gallo, P. S. (1965). The effects of nominating conventions, elections, and reference group identification upon the perception of political figures. *Human Relations, 18,* 217–229.

Ray, D. (1982). The sources of voting cues in three state legislatures. *Journal of Politics, 44,* 1074–1087.

Reese, M. (1975). Locating the 'switch-split' vote. In R. E. Hiebert, R. F. Jones, J. Lorenz, & E. A. Lotito, *The political image merchants* (pp. 162–164). Washington, DC: Acropolis Books.

Reilly, S. (1999). Outdoor advertising. In D. D. Perlmutter (Ed.), *The Manship School guide to political communication* (pp. 152–155). Baton Rouge: University of Louisiana Press.

Riffe, D., Sneed, D., & Van Ommeren, R. L. (1985). Behind the editorial page cartoon. *Journalism Quarterly, 62,* 378–383.

Riffe, D., & Stovall, J. G. (1989). Diffusion of news of shuttle disaster: What role for emotional response? *Journalism Quarterly, 66,* 551–560.

Ringer, R. J. (1986). *The language of fund-raising direct mail: Differences between letters for national and local constituencies.* Paper presented at the annual meeting of the International Communication Association. Chicago, IL.

Ritter, K. (1968). Ronald Reagan and "The Speech": The rhetoric of public relations politics. *Western Speech, 32,* 50–58.

Roberts, M. S. (1992). Predicting voter behavior via the agenda-setting tradition. *Journalism Quarterly, 69,* 878–892.

Roberts, M. S., & McCombs, M. (1994). Agenda setting and political advertising: Origins of the news agenda. *Political Communication, 11,* 249–262.

Robertson, T. (2001). *Gender matters: The impact of the media and gender in 1998 mixed-gender senatorial and gubernatorial campaigns.* Paper presented at the annual meeting of the Southern States Communication Association. Lexington, KY.

Robinson, M. J., & Sheehan, M. (1983). *Over the wire and on TV: CBS and UPI in campaign '80.* New York: Russell Sage.

Rogers, E. E. (1995). *Diffusion of innovation* (4th ed.). New York: Free Press.

Rogers, E., & Cartano, D. G. (1962). Methods of measuring opinion leadership. *Public Opinion Quarterly, 26,* 435–441.

Romano, L. (2001, September 1). Woman gets one year for stealing Bush tape. *Washington Post,* p. 4A.

Rosenthal, A. (1993). *The third house: Lobbyists and lobbying the states.* Washington, DC: Congressional Quarterly Press.

Rosnow, R. C., & Fine, G. A. (1976). *Rumor and gossip: The social psychology of hearsay.* New York: Elsevier.

Rubin, A. M. (1983). Television uses and gratifications: The interactions of viewing patterns and motivations. *Journal of Broadcasting, 27,* 37–51.

Rubin, A. M. (1984). Ritualized and instrumental television viewing. *Journal of Communication, 34,* 67–77.

Rubin, A. M., & Perse, E. M. (1987). Audience activity and television news gratifications. *Communication Research, 14,* 58–84.

Rubin, A. M., Perse, E. M., & Taylor, D. S. (1988). A methodological examination of cultivation. *Communication Research, 15,* 107–134.

Rubin, A. M., & Rubin, R. B. (1982). Older viewers' TV viewing patterns and motivations. *Communication Research, 9,* 287–313.

Rudd, R. (1986). Issues as image in political campaign commercials. *Western Journal of Speech Communication, 50,* 102–118.

Ruddock, A. (2001). *Understanding audiences: Theory and method.* Thousand Oaks, CA: Sage.

Ryan, J., & Wentworth, W. M. (1999). *Media and society: The production of culture in the mass media.* Boston: Allyn & Bacon.

Sabato, L. (1981). *The rise of political consultants.* New York: Basic Books.

Sabato, L. J. (1991). *Feeding frenzy: How attack journalism has transformed American politics.* New York: Free Press.

Sabato, L. J. (2000). *Feeding frenzy: Attack journalism and American politics.* Lanham, MD: Rowman & Littlefield.

Sabato, L. J., Stencel, M., & Lichter, R. (2000). *Peep show: Media and politics in a age of scandal.* Lanham, MD: Rowman & Littlefield.

Safire, W. (1999, July 12). Remembering the speech that never was given. *Birmingham Post-Herald,* p. A7.

Safire, W. (2000, February 14). New 'vast conspiracy.' *New York Times,* p. A27.

Salisbury, R. (1989). An exchange theory of interest groups. *Legislative Studies Quarterly, 8,* 379–426.

Salmon, C. T., & Neuwirth, K. (1990). Perceptions of opinion "climates" and willingness to discuss the issue of abortion. *Journalism Quarterly, 67,* 567–577.

Salwen, M. B. (1998). Perceptions of media influence and support for censorship: The third-person effect in the 1996 presidential election. *Communication Research, 25,* 259–285.

Schaefer, D. R., & Dillman, D. A. (1998). Development of a standard e-mail methodology: Results of an experiment. *Public Opinion Quarterly, 62,* 378–379.

Schmidt, M. S., & Schmidt, M. J. (1983). *Applications of direct mail in voter turnout activities.* Paper presented at the annual meeting of the International Communication Association. Dallas, TX.

Schotland, R. A. (1992). Proposals for campaign finance reform. *Capital University Law Review, 21,* 429–462.

Schram, M. (1976). *Running for president: A journal of the Carter campaign.* New York: Pocket Books.

Schudson, M. (1978). *Discovering the news: A social history of American newspapers.* New York: Basic Books.

Schultz, D. E., Martin, E., & Brown, W. P. (1988). *Strategic advertising campaigns.* Lincolnwood, IL: NTC Business Books.

Schuman, H., & Presser, S. (1981). *Questions and answers in attitude surveys.* San Diego: Academic Press.

Scott, M. H., & Lyman, S. M. (1968). Accounts. *American Sociological Review, 33,* 46–62.

Sebastian, R. J., Parke, R. D., Berkowitz, L., & West, S. G. (1978). Film violence and verbal aggression: A naturalistic study. *Journal of Communication, 28,* 164–171.

Seelye, K. Q. (1999, November 23). Flashback, courtesy of the G. O. P. *New York Times,* p. A21.

Seib, P. (1994). *Campaigns and conscience: The ethics of political journalism.* Westport, CT: Praeger.

Selby, G. S. (2001). Framing social protest: The Exodus narrative in Martin Luther King's Montgomery bus boycott rhetoric. *Journal of Communication and Religion, 24(1),* 68–93.

Seligman, L. (1961). Political recruitment and party structure: A case study. *American Political Science Review, 55,* 85.

Selnow, G. W. (1998). *Electronic whistle-stops: The impact of the Internet on American politics.* Westport, CT: Praeger.

Selnow, G. W. (2000). Internet ethics. In R. E. Denton, Jr. (Ed.), *Political communication ethics* (pp. 203–240). Westport, CT: Praeger.

Serini, S. A., Powers, A. A., & Johnson, S. (1998). Of horse race and policy issues: A study of gender in coverage of a gubernatorial election by two major metropolitan newspapers. *Journalism & Mass Communication Quarterly, 75,* 194–204.

Sethi, S. (1993). Grassroots lobbying and the corporation. *Journal of Politics, 45,* 8–14.

Seymour-Ure, C. (1974). *The political impact of mass media.* Beverly Hills, CA: Sage.

Shadegg, S. (1972). *The new how to win an election.* New York: Taplinger.

Shadow, M., & Peck, G. (1991, May). Politically speaking. *Campaigns and Elections, 12,* p. 54.

Shaver, K. G. (1983). *An introduction to attribution processes.* Hillsdale, NJ: Erlbaum.

Shaw, D., L., & McCombs, M. (1977). *The emergence of American political issues: The agenda-setting function of the press.* St. Paul, MN: West Publishing.

Shaw, D. L., & McCombs, M. L. (1980). The emergence of American political issues: The agenda-setting function of the press. *Journal of Communication, 32,* 100–127.

Sheehy, G. (1999). *Hillary's choice.* New York: Random House.

Shogan, R. (2001). *Bad news: Where the press goes wrong in the making of the president.* Chicago: Ivan R. Dees.

Sigal, L. (1986). Who: Sources make the news. In R. K. Manoff & M. Schudson (Eds.), *Reading the News* (pp. 9–37). New York: Pantheon.

Sigel, R. S. (1970). *Learning about politics: A reader in political socialization.* New York: Random House.

Sigelman, L. (1982). The nonvoting voter in voting research. *American Journal of Political Science, 26,* 47–56.

Silver, B., Anderson, B., & Abramson, P. (1986). Who over-reports voting? *American Political Science Review, 80,* 613–624.

Silverberg, C. (2000, April). The secret ingredient for successful PAC fundraising: Discipline. *Campaigns & Elections,* pp. 63–64.

Silverman, D. (2001). *Interpreting qualitative data: Methods of analyzing talk, text, and interaction.* Thousand Oaks, CA: Sage.

Simon, J. (1996). Media use and voter turnout in a presidential election. *Newspaper Research Journal, 17,* 25–34.

Simon, R. (1987, March 14). Those Sunday interview shows: They're tougher now, but are they better? *TV Guide, 35 (11),* 4–7.

Skill, T., & Wallace, S. (1990). Family interactions on prime-time television: A descriptive analysis of assertive power interactions. *Journal of Broadcasting & Electronic Media, 34,* 243–262.

Smith, B. A. (1996). Faulty assumptions and undemocratic consequences of campaign finance reform. *Yale Law Journal, 105,* 1049–1091.

Smith, B. A. (1998). Soft money, hard realities: The constitutional prohibition on a soft money ban. *Journal of Legislation, 24,* 179–200.

Smith, G. (1999, June 5). Interview with Larry Powell. Gulf Shores, AL.

Smith, S. E. (1999). *Dancing in the street: Motown and the cultural politics of Detroit.* Cambridge, MA: Harvard University Press.

Smith, T. W. (1995). Little things matter: A sampler of how differences in questionnaire format can affect survey responses. *Proceedings of the American Statistical Association,* 1046–1051.

Stacks, D. W., & Hocking, J. E. (1998). *Communication Research.* New York: Longman.

Staley, S. R. (2001). Ballot-box zoning, transaction cost, and urban growth. *Journal of the American Planning Association, 67,* 13–19.

Stamm, K., & Dube, R. (1994). The relationship of attitudinal components to trust in the media. *Communication Research, 21,* 105–123.

Steakley, J. D. (1983). Iconology of a scandal: Political cartoons and the Eulenburg affair. *Studies in Visual Communication, 9,* 20–48.

Steen, J. (2000, June 25). Maybe you can buy an election, but not with your own money. *Washington Post,* pp. B1, B5.

Steinberg, A. (1976a). *Political campaign management.* Lexington, MA: D.C. Heath.

Steinberg, A. (1976b). *The political campaign handbook.* Lexington, MA: D.C. Heath.

Steinfatt, T. M., Gantz, W., Siebold, D. R., & Miller, L. D. (1973). News diffusion of the Wallace shooting: The apparent lack of interpersonal communication as an artifact of delayed measurement. *Quarterly Journal of Speech, 59,* 401–412.

Stempel, G. H., III, & Hargrove, T. (1996). Mass media audiences in a changing media environment. *Journalism Quarterly, 73,* 549–558.

Sternberg, B. (2000, April). Buying TV time: America's new contract with cable. *Campaigns & Elections,* 71–72.

Stewart, D. W., & Shamdasani, P. N. (1990). *Focus groups: Theory and practice.* Newbury Park, CA: Sage.

Stone, A. E. W. (1999). Stealth campaigning: Winning 'under the radar.' In D. D. Perlmutter, *The Manship School guide to political communication* (pp. 147–151). Baton Rouge: Louisiana State University Press.

Straits, B. C. (1990). The social context of voter turnout. *Public Opinion Quarterly, 54,* 64–73.

Stricker, G. (1964). The operation of cognitive dissonance on pre- and post-election attitudes. *Journal of Social Psychology, 63,* 111–119.

Strother, O. (1999). Television ads. In D. D. Perlmutter (Ed.), *The Manship School guide to political communication* (pp. 186–195). Baton Rouge: Louisiana State University Press.

Strother, R. (1999). Foreword. In D. D. Perlmutter (Ed.), *The Manship School guide to political communication* (pp. viii–xiv). Baton Rouge: Louisiana State University Press.

Suine, K., & Kline, F. G. (1976). Communication, mass political behavior and mass society. In S. Chaffee (Ed.), *Political communication* (pp. 65–84). Beverly Hills, CA: Sage.

Surlin, S. H. (1974). Bigotry on air and in life: The Archie Bunker case. *Public Telecommunication Review, 2,* 34–41.

Surlin, S. H. (1978). *Humor in television entertainment programming: Implications for social relations and social learning.* Paper presented to the Speech Communication Association, Minneapolis, MN.

Swain, W. N. (2001). *If my commercial makes fun of my political opponent, do my race and my gender make a difference?* Paper presented at the annual meeting of the Southern States Communication Association. Lexington, KY.

Swanson, D. L. (1976). Information utility: An alternative perspective in political communication. *Central States Speech Journal, 27,* 95–101.

Swanson, L. L., & Swanson, D. L. (1978). The agenda-setting function of the first Ford-Carter debate. *Communication Monographs, 45,* 347–353.

Tannen, D. (2000, January 20). Bush's sweet talk. *New York Times,* p. A23.

Tate, E. D., & Surlin, S. H. (1976). Agreement with opinionated TV characters across cultures. *Journalism Quarterly, 53,* 199–203, 210.

Taylor, H. (2000). Does Internet research work? Comparing online survey results with telephone survey. *International journal of market research, 42,* 51–63.

Taylor, P. (1990). *See how they run: Electing the president in an age of mediaocracy.* New York: Knopf.

Taylor, P. (1990, June 18–24). In politics, the time for women has arrived. *Washington Post National Weekly,* p. 13.

Taylor, S. E. (1983). Adjustments to threatening events: A theory of cognitive adaptation. *American Psychologist, 38,* 1161–1173.

Taylor. S. B. (1990). *Fob: The incredible story of Fob James, Jr.* Mobile, AL: Greenberry

Tedesco, J. C., McKinnon, L., & Kaid, L. L. (1996). Advertising watchdogs: A content analysis of print and broadcast adwatches from the 1992 presidential campaign. *Harvard International Journal of Press/Politics, 1,* 76–93.

Tedesco, J. C., Miller, J. L., & Spiker, J. A. (1999). Presidential campaigning on the information superhighway: An exploration of content and form. In L. L. Kaid & D. G. Bystrom (Eds.), *The electronic election: Perspectives on the 1996 campaign communication* (pp. 51–63). Mahwah, NJ: Erlbaum.

Teixeira, R. A. (1992). *The disappearing American voter.* Washington, DC: Brookings Institution.

Terhanian, G. (1999). *Understanding online research: Lessons from the Harris Poll Online.* Paper presented at the American Association for Public Opinion Research meeting. St. Petersburg, FL.

Thelan, D. (1996). *Becoming citizens in the age of television: How Americans challenged the media and seized the political initiative during the Iran-Contra debate.* Chicago: University of Chicago Press.

Thomas, R. J. (1999). *How to run for local office: A complete guide for winning a local election.* Westland, MI: R & T Enterprises.

Thurber, J. A., & Nelson, C. J. (Eds.). (2000). *Campaign warriors: Political consultants in elections.* Washington, DC: Brookings Institution.

Todorov, A. (2000). The accessibility and applicability of knowledge: Predicting context effects in national surveys. *Public Opinion Quarterly, 64,* 429–451.

Tomlinson, J. E. (2000). Campaigning in cyberspace: Lessons for political communication in the Net century. In D. Bystrom, D. B. Carlin, L. L. Kaid, M. Kern, & M. S. McKinney (Eds.), *Communicating politics: Engaging the public in campaign 2000 and beyond* (pp. 333–346). Washington, DC: NCA Summer Conference proceedings.

Tourangeau, R., & Rasinski, K. A. (1988). Cognitive processes underlying context effects in attitude measurement. *Psychological Bulletin, 103,* 299–314.

Tourangeau, R., Rips, L. J., & Rasinski, K. (2000). *The psychology of survey response.* New York: Cambridge University Press.

Trenaman, J., & McQuail, D. (1961). *Television and the political image: A study of the impact of television on the 1959 general election.* London: Methuen.

Trent, J. S. (1978). Presidential surfacing: The ritualistic and crucial first act. *Communication Monographs, 45,* 282.

Trent, J. S., & Friedenberg, R. V. (1995). *Political campaign communication: Principles and practices.* 3rd ed. New York: Praeger.

Trent, J. S., & Friedenberg, R. V. (2000). *Political campaign communication: Principles and practices.* 4th ed. Westport, CT: Praeger.

Trent, J. S., & Sabourin, T. (1993). Sex still counts: Women's use of televised advertising during the decade of the '80s. *Journal of Applied Communication Research, 21,* 21–40.

Tuchman, G. (1982). *Making news.* New York: Free Press.

Turner, K. J. (1977). Comic strips: A rhetorical perspective. *Central States Speech Journal, 28,* 24–35.

Turow, J. (1992). *Media systems in society: Understanding industries, strategies and power.* New York: Longman.

Turow, J. (1996). *Media today.* Boston: Houghton Mifflin.

Tyson, G. (1990). *An examination of early voting.* Fort Worth, TX: The Tyson Organization.

Tyson, G. S. (1999). GOTV: Get out the vote. In D. D. Perlmutter (Ed.), *The Manship School guide to political communication* (pp. 131–136). Baton Rouge: Louisiana State University Press

Uslander, E. M., & Weber, R. E. (1979). Reapportionment, gerrymandering and changes in the partisan balance of power in American states. Paper presented at the annual meeting of the American Political Science Association, Chicago.

Van Natta, Jr., D. (2000, February 15). Years ago, a Bush adviser helped draft a push poll against a Texas official. *New York Times,* p. A20.

Vancil, D. L., & Pendell, S. D. (1984). Winning presidential debates. *Western Journal of Speech Communication, 48,* 62–74.

Vertune, J. (2001, September 1). Ex-Bush campaign worker sentenced for forwarding debate video to Gore camp. *Birmingham News,* p. 6A.

Vidmar, N., & Rokeach, M. (1974). Archie Bunker's bigotry: A study in selective perception and exposure. *Journal of Communication, 24,* 36–47.

Viguerie, R. (1975). Direct mail: Campaigning's sleeping giant. In R. E. Hiebert, R. F. Jones, J. Lorenz, & E. A. Lotito (Eds.), *The political image merchants* (pp. 165–167). Washington, DC: Acropolis Books.

Villa, H. E., & Rodgers, R. P. (1999). *Rhetorical clusters of Nazi rhetoric during World War II.* Paper for the Eastern Communication Association, Charleston, WV.

von Drehle, D. (2000, June 25). Awkward oratory as a mark of sincerity. *Washington Post,* pp. A1, A7.

Walker, J. R. (1987). *Exposure to political information during statewide elections: A typology of eligible voters.* Paper presented at the International Communication Association Convention. Montreal, Canada.

Walker, J. R., & Bellamy, R. V. (1991). Gratifications of grazing: An exploratory study of remote control use. *Journalism Quarterly, 68,* 422–431.

Walker, J. R., & Bellamy, R. V. (1993). *The remote control in the new age of television.* Westport, CT: Praeger.

Walker, K. B., & Morley, D. (1991). Attitudes and parental factors as intervening variables in the television violence-aggression relation. *Communication Research Reports, 8,* 41–48.

Wanta, W., & Wu, Y. (1992). Interpersonal communication and the agenda-setting process. *Journalism Quarterly, 69,* 847–855.

Ware, B. L., & Linkugel, W. A. (1973). They spoke in defense of themselves. On the generic criticism of apologia. *Quarterly Journal of Speech, 59,* 273–283.

Warren, D. I. (1972). Mass media and racial crisis: A study of the New Bethel Church incident in Detroit. *Journal of Social Issues, 1,* 111–132.

Weaver, D. (1980). Audience need for orientation and media effects. *Communication Research, 7,* 361–380.

Weaver, D. H., & Wilhoit, G. C. (1980). News media coverage of U.S. senators in four Congresses, 1953–1974. *Journalism Monographs, 67,* 1–34.

Weaver, D. H., Zhu, J., & Willnat, L. (1992). The bridging function of interpersonal communication in agenda setting. *Journalism Quarterly, 69,* 856–867.

Weaver-Lariscy, R. A., Sweeney, B., & Steinfatt, T. (1984). Communication during assassination attempts: Diffusion of information in attacks on President Reagan and the Pope. *Southern Speech Communication Journal, 49,* 258–276.

Webster, J. G. (1998). The audience. *Journal of broadcasting & electronic media, 42,* 190–207.

Webster, J. G., & Lichty, L. W. (1991). *Ratings analysis: Theory and practice.* Hillsdale, NJ: Erlbaum.

Webster, J. G., & Wakshlag, J. J. (1982). The impact of group viewing on patterns of television program choice. *Journal of Broadcasting, 26,* 445–455.

Werrett, W. C. (1933). *Motion pictures and youth: A summary.* New York: Macmillan.

Wertheimer, M. M. (2000). *Barbara Bush's refashioning of the White House.* Paper presented at the annual meeting of the Eastern Communication Association, Pittsburgh, PA.

West, D. M. (1993). *Air wars: Television advertising in election campaigns, 1952–1992.* Washington, DC: Congressional Quarterly Press.

Wheeler, M. E., & Reed, S. K. (1975). Response to before and after Watergate caricatures. *Journalism Quarterly, 52,* 134–136.

Wheeless, L. R., & Schrodt, P. (2001). An examination of cognitive foundations of informational reception apprehension: Political identification, religious affiliation, and family environment. *Communication Research Reports, 18,* 1–10.

Whillock, R. K. (1997). Cyber-politics. *American Behavioral Scientist, 40,* 1208–1225.

Whillock, R. K. (2001). *Federal regulatory oversight in Campaign 2000.* Paper presented at the annual meeting of the Southern States Communication Association, Lexington, KY.

White, B. (2000, June 25). Online innovators showing their stuff in governor's races. *Washington Post,* p. A12.

White, T. H. (1969). *The making of the president 1968.* New York: Atheneum Publishers.

Williamson, J. (1984). *Decoding advertisements: Ideology and meaning in advertising.* New York: Marion Boyars.

Wilson, E. C., & Howard, D. M. (1978). Public perception of media accuracy. *Journalism Quarterly, 55,* 73–76.

Wimmer, R. D., & Dominick, J. R. (1994). *Mass media research.* Belmont, CA: Wadsworth.

Witcover, J. (1999). *No way to pick a president: How money & hired guns have debased American elections.* New York: Farrar, Straus & Giroux.

Wober, J. M., & Gunter, B. (1986). Television audience research at Britain's Independent Broadcasting Authority, 1974–1984. *Journal of Broadcasting and Electronic Media, 30,* 15–31.

Wolfe, A. (1998). *One nation, after all: What middle-class Americans really think about.* New York: Penguin Books.

Woodward, G. C. (1997). *Perspectives on American political media.* Boston: Allyn & Bacon.

Worland, G. (1998). Scandals throughout presidential history. *Washington Post,* p. 4A.

Wyatt, O., Kim, J., & Katz, E. (2000). How feeling free to talk affects ordinary political conversation, purposeful argumentation, and civic participation. *Journalism and Mass Communication Quarterly, 77,* 99–114.

Yanovitzky, I., & Bennett, C. (1999). Media attention, institutional response, and health behavior change. *Communication Research, 26,* 429–453.

Yardley, J. (1999, August 29). Candidates focus on spin, media focus on sensation. *Birmingham News,* pp. 1C, 6C.

Yardley, J. (2000, February 14). Calls to voters at center stage of G. O. P. race. *New York Times,* pp. A1, A16.

Yu, J., & Cooper, H. (1983). A quantitative review of research design effects on response rates to questionnaires. *Journal of Marketing Research, 20,* 36–44.

Zaller, J. (1990). Political awareness, elite opinion leadership, and the mass survey response. *Social Cognition, 8,* 125–153.

Zaller, J. (1992). *The nature and origin of mass opinion.* Cambridge: Cambridge University Press.

Zaller, J. (1996). The myth of massive media impact revived: New support for a discredited idea. In D. C. Mutz, P. M. Sniderman & R. A. Brody (Eds.), *Political persuasion and attitude change* (pp. 17–78). Ann Arbor: University of Michigan Press.

Zaller, J., & Feldman, S. (1992). A simple theory of the survey response: Answering questions versus revealing preferences. *American Journal of Political Science, 36,* 579–616.

Zhang, Y., & Buda, R. (1999). Moderating effects of need for cognition on responses to positively versus negatively framed advertising messages. *Journal of Advertising, 28(2),* 1–15.

Zhu, J. (1992). Issue competition and attention distraction: A zero-sum theory of agenda setting. *Journalism Quarterly, 69,* 825–836.

INDEX